FinTech in Islamic Financial Institutions

"The contents offer a rich, contextual and practical reviews of Fintech in Islamic finance; a useful read for academics and practitioners. Contents are carefully chosen covering a wide range of topics that go deep into integration of Islamic finance with Fintech. Both operational as well as Shariah aspects are discussed broadly, with theoretical and practical implications."
—Rifki Ismal, *Assistant Secretary General, Islamic Financial Services Board (IFSB), Malaysia*

"Not many books on Fintech covers a combination of theory and practices from country- and region-specific examples. The reviews offer directions to effective use of Fintech for sustainable benefits. The topics cover a wide range of behavioral aspects, including adoption of Fintech. Several topics offer interesting and research-worthy ideas of the use of Fintech in Islamic non-banking institutions. These could be meaningful to policymakers and investors."
—Mansur Masih, *Senior Professor, Universiti Kuala Lumpur Business School, Malaysia*

M. Kabir Hassan · Mustafa Raza Rabbani ·
Mamunur Rashid
Editors

FinTech in Islamic Financial Institutions

Scope, Challenges, and Implications in Islamic Finance

Editors
M. Kabir Hassan
University of New Orleans
New Orleans, LA, USA

Mustafa Raza Rabbani
University of Bahrain
Riffa, Bahrain

Mamunur Rashid
Christ Church Business School
Canterbury Christ Church University
Canterbury, Kent, UK

ISBN 978-3-031-14940-5   ISBN 978-3-031-14941-2 (eBook)
https://doi.org/10.1007/978-3-031-14941-2

© The Editor(s) (if applicable) and The Author(s), under exclusive license to Springer Nature Switzerland AG 2022
This work is subject to copyright. All rights are solely and exclusively licensed by the Publisher, whether the whole or part of the material is concerned, specifically the rights of translation, reprinting, reuse of illustrations, recitation, broadcasting, reproduction on microfilms or in any other physical way, and transmission or information storage and retrieval, electronic adaptation, computer software, or by similar or dissimilar methodology now known or hereafter developed.
The use of general descriptive names, registered names, trademarks, service marks, etc. in this publication does not imply, even in the absence of a specific statement, that such names are exempt from the relevant protective laws and regulations and therefore free for general use.
The publisher, the authors, and the editors are safe to assume that the advice and information in this book are believed to be true and accurate at the date of publication. Neither the publisher nor the authors or the editors give a warranty, expressed or implied, with respect to the material contained herein or for any errors or omissions that may have been made. The publisher remains neutral with regard to jurisdictional claims in published maps and institutional affiliations.

This Palgrave Macmillan imprint is published by the registered company Springer Nature Switzerland AG
The registered company address is: Gewerbestrasse 11, 6330 Cham, Switzerland

Foreword

Fintech is a reality; it's useful and the market is growing. Fintech companies have disrupted global financial markets. Since a large part of the Fintech operations is unregulated, industry experts suspect even more disruptions in the coming days. Lack of monitoring poses a threat to the Islamic Fintech industry, as this might clash with the existing multi-layer Shariah supervisory system existing in the Islamic financial system. We have seen the benefits of such supervisory system from the evidence of limited impact of global financial crisis of 2007–2008. Hence, there is a major shift in financial landscape and this book is an attempt in the right direction to bring forward and explore gaps in theoretical as well as empirical views on Fintech and Islamic Fintech. The chapters are relatively shorter, easy to read, and offer a clear view of the matters current to the Fintech universe.

The book covers broader theoretical aspects, emphasizes on supervisory necessities, and reviews potentials of regional collaborations, such as those among GCC, Southeast Asia, and MENA regions. Several chapters are allocated to discuss the theoretical importance of Fintech. The benefits of Fintech are discussed from three dimensions: payment channels, data analytics, and macroeconomic benefits that include financial inclusion, poverty reduction, and financial stability. Major challenges of Islamic Fintech, such as Shariah compliance of the blockchain and bitcoins, lack of talents, and limited collaboration among financial and entrepreneurship sectors are highlighted. Chapters are not too empirical, which will benefit non-expert readers. There are sufficient discussions on relatively emerging concepts. I believe the readers will immensely benefit from the contents.

Ahmet Faruk Aysan, Ph.D.
Professor & Program Coordinator
College of Islamic Studies, Qatar
Foundation
Hamad Bin Khalifa University
Ar-Rayyan, Qatar

Preface

Introduction

Financial institutions serve the society by collecting deposits, providing loans, and offering allied financial services. Primary earnings of these institutions include the difference between interest earned and paid against deposits, loans, and other services. Islamic finance finds this interest synonymous with exploitation and offers an alternative solution based on trade-based financing. The primary objective of this system is to achieve profit and loss sharing between 'partners' in a trade-based financing mechanism. Financial institutions invest heavily in technology to make the customer experience better. Financial technology (Fintech) using mobiles and computers transforms the entire user experience and their level of satisfaction. However, technology requires massive investment at the country-level not only to establish infrastructure but also to create an easy and safe environment for the users to adopt new tools. These investments are rather slow in developing economies where most of the Islamic financial institutions operate.

Fintech poses two challenges for Islamic finance. The first is about multi-level supervision. One of the reasons why Islamic finance is found to be resilient is its multi-layer supervision by internal as well as external supervisors. Aside from the Central Bank, there is a centralized Shariah supervisor board in most countries to look after the macro aspect of Islamic financial activities. Islamic financial institutions are, then, supervised by an internal Shariah Supervisory Board that suggests Shariah compliance of its products and services and approaches of financial activities. Last but not the least, Islamic financial institutions must also comply with regulations by internal and external auditors, and financial reporting standards at home and abroad. Fintech is generally believed to follow a mechanism that bypasses a similar screening process, at least by the central authorities, leading to privacy and transaction without involving middlemen. This has led to a reduction in cost and an increase in convenience. Consequently, Islamic Fintech might face the dilemma: compliance versus convenience.

The second challenge is about adequate Islamic finance instruments to support Fintech. While many Islamic financial institutions are yet to offer a basic technology interface for most of their services, the Islamic financial industry overall faces a 'tech-matching' challenge. There are four major instruments seen among Islamic financial institutions. These are *Murabahah*, *Mudarabah*, *Musharakah*, and Ijarah, among others. More research is needed to ascertain the impact of Fintech companies on profit-and-loss-sharing contracts (*Musharakah* and *Mudarabah*), and how these instruments are matched with fitting Fintech instruments. As the knowledge on these are limited, by Fintech most Islamic financial institutions understand the use of mobile and computer facilities to conduct basic banking facilities, which ensures convenience but does not ensure other common properties of the Fintech mechanism.

This Issue

This edited book aims at covering some of these pressing issues. We cover three major objectives. First, we discuss Fintech, Islamic Fintech, and its underlying challenges. Second, several chapters are committed to finding the potentials of Fintech for Islamic banks and allied institutions that can directly benefit from existing models of Fintech. Third, several chapters consider existing or modified models and discussions that can be applied to Islamic non-banking financial sector.

Hassan, Rabbani, and Rashid introduce the Fintech and Islamic Fintech concepts. They briefly discuss how a widespread 'disruption' could be utilized by the financial institutions. While the chapter recommends several models, concepts, and areas, it also highlights potential challenges that should be resolved to take full advantage of the Fintech revolution.

In Chapter 2, Hassan et al. discuss in detail how Fintech is a disruption and the elements of its disruption. The chapter includes a thorough discussion on peer-to-peer (P2P) lending, crowdfunding, and mobile payment. Alongside discussing the metamorphosis of Fintech, the chapter elaborates on the implications of Fintech in socially valuable activities, particularly for the benefit of the vulnerable during the pandemic.

Islamic Research and Training Institute[1] estimate that global Zakat collection could reach a mammoth $600 billion per year, while only one-tenth of this amount is currently managed by official groups. Chapter 3 discusses a Fintech model based on artificial intelligence for *Zakat*. Zakat is Islamic almsgiving that is mandatory to (financially) eligible Muslims. Zakat needs serious effort to calculate, collect, and distribute at the individual as well as the institutional stage. This chapter shows how a model based on artificial intelligence, blockchain, and machine learning can benefit the process of Zakat collection and distribution among the needy. This process can help transfer billions of dollars from the rich to the poor and immensely contribute to the social cause.

Chapter 4 discusses opportunities that Bahrain can utilize using Fintech. Fintech market in Gulf Cooperation Council (GCC)[2] market is estimated to be around $49 billion (in the year 2020), which is expected to grow at 21% per annum to reach $128 billion by the year 2025. Not only as a growing GCC economy, but Bahrain is also important to the Islamic finance industry as it hosts the Accounting and Auditing Organization for Islamic financial institutions (AAOIFI) that produces Islamic accounting standards. The chapter concludes with discussions on Bahrain being an important jurisdiction for Fintech in GCC.

Chapter 5 continues with an example from important regions with a review of literature on the Middle East and North Africa (MENA) region. The chapter focuses on Fintech initiatives in the United Arab Emirates (UAE) and Bahrain. It demonstrates how these countries can utilize the benefits of Fintech, and transform these countries into important Fintech destinations.

---

[1] https://www.aa.com.tr/en/middle-east/world-zakat-forum-optimizing-funds-to-reduce-poverty/1640107.

[2] https://cdn.salaamgateway.com/reports/pdf/6127a0965afd7898a34f69dadc24b8d17ada0b1b.pdf.

In Chapter 6, Hassan et al. write on the connection between Fintech, industrial revolution 4.0 (IR4.0), and Islamic Fintech. Discussions conclude that an effective blend of awareness and stakeholder support is paramount for successful digital transformation. The chapter recognizes the shortfall of the existing Fintech framework, particularly for the case of Islamic financial institution.

Chapter 7 provides a bibliometric review of the Fintech and Islamic finance literature. The primary objective of this review is to find influential themes, authors, and keywords. The study finds Professor M. K. Hassan as the most influential author in Islamic finance, and Malaysia as the top context of Islamic finance research.

Chapter 8 provides a discussion of Fintech applications and their implications on Islamic banking sector of Pakistan. Using content analysis of the annual reports, the study finds that Islamic banks in Pakistan have been using Fintech since 2006. There has been significant development in terms of payment systems, financial security, and use of machine learning for customer benefits. The forward implications for policymakers are as such effective policy support for the Fintech sector in Pakistan could support economic growth.

Chapter 9 emphasizes on the stakeholder engagement, Islamic Fintech, and COVID-19. The chapter identifies that Fintech has helped the Islamic finance ecosystem to operate efficiently even during the Pandemic, primarily due to the faster and wider acceptance of Fintech globally. While the cost of financial services dropped significantly, Islamic Fintech helped in reducing negative impact on the financial system during COVID-19.

Chapter 10 looks deeper into the implication of Fintech for Islamic financial system, not just for Islamic banks. Abdeljawad, Qamhieh, and Rashid explain the theoretical basis of Fintech in Islamic financial system, its importance for Islamic banking and non-banking financial institutions, growth of the industry, and recent initiatives to integrate Shariah-compliant financial system with Fintech innovation. The chapter also discusses common challenges facing Islamic Fintech.

Chapter 11 discusses the level of Fintech adoption among Islamic Banks from the MENA region. Hassan et al. argue that Fintech benefits the customers immensely from the cost and convenience standpoints. However, overall adoption of Fintech in MENA region is still at an aborning stage.

Chapter 12 addresses an importunate question: how compliant is Fintech in the eyes of the Shariah? The chapter discusses the interplay among Fintech-based financial services, Shariah compliance, and Islamic financial system. Authors have also shed light on the need for and benefits of Fintech-based financial services during the difficult times of COVID-19, and beyond.

Chapter 13 provides details on Islamic views about the two most used Fintech concepts: crowdfunding and peer-to-peer lending. The chapter adds on the Shariah compliance of these instruments while financing relatively smaller but risky Islamic start-ups. Authors argue that, while crowdfunding seems closer to the profit and loss sharing practices, P2P lending needs serious Shariah supervision.

In Chapter 14, Rabbani et al. systematically review cryptocurrency in Islamic and conventional finance literature. They have added discussions on Bitcoin, Ethereum, and Litecoin, and their compliance with Shariah principles. They have broadly concluded that trading in these cryptocurrencies is not compliant in the eyes of Shariah.

Chapter 15 considers the two most highly cited Fintech areas: blockchain and crowdfunding. The authors discuss the current landscape and future potential of these concepts. Chapter 16 extends on the implication of Fintech during the challenging time of COVID-19. Karim et al. discuss how Fintech-based financial instruments could be useful in the post-COVID-19 period. The chapter also adds to the literature on the influence of Fintech on socio-economic development tools and channels available under the broader umbrella of Islamic finance.

Summary and Way Forward

This book forwards three key messages. First, Fintech has become a strong tool to achieve sustainable outcomes in terms of lower cost of financial services, convenience to customers, and lower cost for financial institutions. Second, despite having several benefits, due to limited regulation, abrupt growth of Fintech companies not only disrupted the financial markets but also created a gap between supply and demand of financial services fitting the prerequisites of Fintech universe. Consequently, companies with core technology background will have an upper hand over the companies with limited investment in technology. Also, countries having limited investment in technology will lose technology arbitrage to the countries with a higher amount of investment in technology and conducive regulatory and market environment for Fintech. Third, Islamic

Fintech is growing despite limitations on the fronts of market structure, regulation, and Shariah compliance issues. Islamic Fintech market in the GCC region has reached a $49 billion dollar mark and is expected to grow at a very fast rate2. A strong collaborative effort of the regulators and market participants is expected to develop frameworks to control mushrooming of the Fintech firms, which may jeopardize the stability of the Islamic finance system. Future studies might focus on whether Fintech really addresses the existing problems with Islamic financial system. For instance, studies might consider investigating whether Fintech can resolve the departure of Islamic finance from contracts based on the profit-and-loss-sharing and Qardul Hasan (benevolent loans).

New Orleans, USA M. Kabir Hassan
Riffa, Bahrain Mustafa Raza Rabbani
Canterbury, UK Mamunur Rashid

Contents

Introduction to Islamic Fintech: A Challenge or an Opportunity?   1
Mustafa Raza Rabbani, M. Kabir Hassan, and Mamunur Rashid

Fintech and the Art of Disruption   29
Mustafa Raza Rabbani, M. Kabir Hassan, Mohammad Dulal Miah, and Himani Grewal

A Fintech-Based Zakat Model Using Artificial Intelligence   49
Mustafa Raza Rabbani, M. Kabir Hassan, Shahnawaz Khan, and Aishath Muneeza

Islamic Fintech and Bahrain: An Opportunity for Global Financial Services   65
M. Kabir Hassan, Ammar Jreisat, Mustafa Raza Rabbani, and Somar Al-Mohamed

The Future of Finance and Fintech: Visualizing the Opportunities for Fintech in the MENA Region   89
M. Kabir Hassan, Habeeb Ur Rahiman, Mustafa Raza Rabbani, and Asem Alhomaidi

Fintech Trends: Industry 4.0, Islamic Fintech, and Its Digital Transformation   113
M. Kabir Hassan, Zehra Zulfikar, Mustafa Raza Rabbani, and Mohd. Atif

An Insight into the Fintech and Islamic Finance Literature: A Bibliometric and Visual Analysis 131
M. Kabir Hassan, Abu Bashar, Mustafa Raza Rabbani, and Tonmoy Choudhury

Fintech Innovation and Its Application in Islamic Banking from Pakistan 157
Sitara Karim, Mustafa Raza Rabbani, Abu Bashar, and Ahmed Imran Hunjra

Fintech in the Islamic Banking Sector and Its Impact on the Stakeholders in the Wake of COVID-19 175
M. Kabir Hassan, Rabab Hasan Ebrahim, Mustafa Raza Rabbani, and Hasanul Banna

Fintech and Islamic Financial Institutions: Applications and Challenges 193
Islam Abdeljawad, Shatha Qamhieh Hashem, and Mamunur Rashid

An Assessment of Level of Adoption of Fintech in Islamic Banks in the MENA Region 223
M. Kabir Hassan, Somar Al-Mohamed, Mustafa Raza Rabbani, and Ammar Jreisat

Fintech, Pandemic, and the Islamic Financial System: Innovative Financial Services and Its *Shariah* Compliance 243
M. Kabir Hassan, Mustafa Raza Rabbani, Ammar Jreisat, and Muhammad Mostofa Hossain

An Islamic Finance Perspective of Crowdfunding and Peer-To-Peer (P2P) Lending 263
M. Kabir Hassan, Mustafa Raza Rabbani, Shahnawaz Khan, and Mahmood Asad Moh'd Ali

Islamic Finance and Cryptocurrency: A Systematic Review 279
Mustafa Raza Rabbani, M. Kabir Hassan, Fahmi Ali Hudaefi, and Zakir Hossen Shaikh

Islamic Fintech, Blockchain and Crowdfunding: Current Landscape and Path Forward 307
M. Kabir Hassan, Mustafa Raza Rabbani, Mamunur Rashid, and Irwan Trinugroho

COVID-19 Challenges and the Role of Islamic Fintech   341
Sitara Karim, Mustafa Raza Rabbani, Mamunur Rashid, and Zaheer Anwer

Index   357

NOTES ON CONTRIBUTORS

Abdeljawad Islam is an associate professor in the Banking and Finance department at An-Najah National University, Palestine. He received his Ph.D. in corporate finance from the National University of Malaysia in 2012. His research interests span corporate finance, accounting, and fintech. He has several published papers, books, and conferences in high-ranked journals, series, and proceedings.

Dr. Ali Mahmood Asad Moh'd is currently working as an assistant professor at department of Management and Marketing at University of Bahrain. Dr. Ali has published several research papers in the journals of repute including *Cogent Economics and Finance* and *Journal of Economic Cooperation and Development* etc.

Dr. Al-Mohamed Somar is working as an assistant professor at the American University of the Middle East (AUM), College of Business Administration, Egaila, Kuwait.

Dr. Anwer Zaheer is an associate professor of finance at Sunway University, Malaysia, is equipped with more than 14 years of teaching and industry experience. He has earned Ph.D. degree from the International Centre for Education in Islamic Finance (INCEIF), Malaysia, and an M.B.A. from Quaid-i-Azam University, Pakistan. He has worked in leading Pakistani Universities: University of Management and Technology and The University of Lahore. His teaching includes subjects such as Quantitative Finance, Investments, Macroeconomy, Monetary

Economics, and Islamic Banking. He has published in journals like *Finance Research Letters*, *Journal of Business Research*, *Accounting and Finance*, *Pacific-Basin Finance Journal*, and *International Review of Economics and Finance*.

Dr. Atif Mohd. is an Assistant Professor at the Department of Commerce and Business Studies, Jamia Millia Islamia (JMI), New Delhi (India). Prior to joining JMI in 2016, he also served at the Central University of Himachal Pradesh, Dharamshala, Himachal Pradesh (India) for four years. He has a teaching experience of more than seven years. He earned his Ph.D. from JMI in finance after completing his M.Com. from the same university.

Dr. Banna Hasanul is a Lecturer in Banking and Finance at the Department of Accounting, Finance, and Banking, Business School, Manchester Metropolitan University (MMU), UK. Dr. Banna earned a Ph.D. in Finance and Banking from the University of Malaya with a prestigious Full-Bright scholarship. His research spans banking and finance, financial technology, financial inclusion, digital finance, ESG, managerial ability, and micro-finance. He has published 30+ peer-reviewed articles in high-impact factor journals including *Journal of International Financial Markets, Institutions and Money*, *Annals of Operations Research*, *Finance Research Letters*, *Journal of International Development*, *Annals of Public and Cooperative Economics*, *Journal of Cleaner Production*, *International Journal of Islamic and Middle Eastern Finance and Management*, *Singapore Economic Review*, *Studies in Economics and Finance*, *Journal of Asia Pacific Economy*, among others, 5+ book chapters and 20+ conference papers.

Mr. Bashar Abu is currently pursuing Ph.D. from IMS Unison University, Dehradun. Previously he has completed M.B.A. from Lovely Professional University, Punjab., India.

Dr. Choudhury Tonmoy has joined the King Fahd University of Petroleum and Minerals from Edith Cowan University, Australia, where he was coordinating and lecturing on Risk management in Financial Market and Institutions. In 2021, he has won the prestigious Emerald Literary Award for his works on risk spillover of US states. His research focuses on the multidisciplinary implication of financial management with a strong focus on risk spillover. He has finished his Ph.D. in Banking from Western Sydney University in 2019. He also holds a bachelor's in accounting from Macquarie University, a master's in finance from Australian National University, and an M.Phil. in Management from the University of Wales, UK.

Dr. Ebrahim Rabab Hasan is an Assistant Professor at the Department of Economics and Finance, College of Business Administration. She holds a Ph.D. in Finance from the University of Bradford, UK. Her research interests are in the areas of corporate finance, including dividend policy, capital structure, and cash holdings as well as corporate investments and Financial Technology (Fintech).

Dr. Grewal Himani is working as an Assistant professor at Moradabad Institute of Technology, Moradabad, India. Prior to this she has worked as a lecturer at IMS Unison University, Dehradun.

Professor Dr. Hassan M. Kabir is a Professor of Finance in the Department of Economics and Finance in the University of New Orleans. He currently holds two endowed Chairs—Hibernia Professor of Economics and Finance, and Bank One Professor in Business—in the University of New Orleans. Professor Hassan is the winner of the 2016 Islamic Development Bank (IDB) Prize in Islamic Banking and Finance. Professor Hassan has over 383 papers published/forthcoming in refereed academic journals. Professor Hassan has also been cited as one of the most prolific authors in finance literature in the last fifty years in a paper published in the *Journal of Finance Literature*. His publication record puts him among the top 5.6% of all authors who published in the 26 leading finance journals.

Dr. Hashem Shatha Qamhieh holds a bachelor's degree in architectural engineering, a master's degree in business administration, and a Ph.D. in Economics and Management of Technology. Dr. Shatha has served in different positions and is currently an assistant professor at An-Najah National University in the Finance and Banking department, within the faculty of economics and administrative sciences. Her research focus is on FinTech, financial risk analysis, economic forecasting, and financial network applications.

Hossain Muhammad Mostofa of Bangladeshi Nationality, currently pursuing his Ph.D. from the Academy of Islamic Studies, University of Malaya, Malaysia. He previously has completed his bachelor's degree from the Faculty of Islamic Jurisprudence and Law, University of Al-Azhar, Egypt, awarding a full bright scholarship and the masters from the Faculty of Islamic Revealed Knowledge and Human Sciences, International Islamic University Malaysia (IIUM). Besides, he has obtained a diploma in Media Studies from the International University of Latin America, Cairo, Egypt, and pursued a degree in Islamic Studies under the Bangladesh Madrasha Education Board Dhaka, Bangladesh, and placed 6th position on the merit list and 3rd on talent pool all over the country and achieved another specialized degree of Hadith under the same board. He has authored a book on *Abortion from the Islamic Perspective*, several academic articles, conference papers, and daily newspaper columns in national dailies through the single and joint authorship.

Hudaefi Fahmi Ali is currently a Lecturer at *Fakultas Ekonomi dan Bisnis Islam* (FEBI), *Institut Agama Islam Darussalam* (IAID) Ciamis, Indonesia. He is a former full-time Senior Researcher at the Indonesian Zakat Agency's Center for Strategic Studies (Puskas BAZNAS). He is also a Ph.D. student at the UBD School of Business and Economics, *Universiti Brunei Darussalam*. He earned a Master's degree in Shariah (research in Islamic banking and finance) from the Academy of Islamic Studies, University of Malaya, Malaysia. His academic contributions deal primarily with topical issues in Islamic economics, in particular, Islamic finance and banking as well as Islamic social finance. His contributions include *maqasid al-Shariah* and Islamic banking performance, current issues of zakat administration (e.g. zakat and sustainable development goals/UN SDGs, zakat and COVID-19) as well as local development (e.g. *pesantren* and local economic development. He has used both structured and unstructured data and employed both human intelligence (e.g. inductive, deductive, and abductive reasoning) and artificial intelligence (e.g. machine learning) to answer research questions.

Hunjra Ahmed Imran has over a decade of teaching and research experience at both undergraduate and postgraduate levels. Currently, Ahmed is working in the domain of corporate finance, corporate governance, and sustainability. Ahmed has published in well-reputed journals, i.e. *Finance Research Letters, Technological Forecasting and Social Change, Journal of Environmental Management, Research in International Business and Finance, and Quarterly Review of Economics and Finance*, among others. Ahmed is on Editorial and Referee Board of several ABS and ABDC indexed journals. Ahmed won the 'Outstanding Reviewer Award-2021' by Emerald Literati, Distinguished Reviewer Award-2021 by VIRTUS INTERPRESS and the 'Best University Teacher Award-2020'. Ahmed has already supervised 06 Ph.D.s and over fifty M.S./M.Phil. scholars.

Dr. Jreisat Ammar is an Assistant professor in Finance at the University of Bahrain, and has a Ph.D. in Finance from the University of Western Sydney, Australia. Extensive university teaching experience across finance units at various universities. Research interests in Finance, Banking, Financial Market, and measurement of banking, and financial management. Dr. Jreisat published papers in various Journals to name a few, such as the *Polish Journal of Management Studies*, *Cogent Economics and Finance*, *International Journal of Economics and Business Research*, and the *International Journal of Energy Economics and Policy*. Dr. Jreisat received an Honors-Awards-Grants-Scholarships, San Francisco University, USA, 2016.

Dr. Karim Sitara is serving as an Assistant Professor of Finance and FinTech at ILMA University, Karachi, Pakistan. She is a Ph.D. in Finance and Banking from the School of Economics, Finance, and Banking (SEFB), College of Business, Universiti Utara Malaysia. She has a number of publications in well-known journals. Her research interests include Green Assets, Cryptocurrencies, Financial Economics, Corporate Governance, Sustainability, Energy, Stock Markets, and Financial Markets.

Dr. Khan Shahnawaz received his Ph.D. in Computer Science from the Indian Institute of Technology (Banaras Hindu University), Varanasi, India. His areas of specialization are machine learning, natural language processing, blockchain, and FinTech.

Currently, Dr. Shahnawaz Khan is serving as an assistant professor Faculty of Engineering, Design, and Information and Communications Technology, Bahrain Polytechnic, Bahrain Prior to this he co-founded 2 IT companies and served as a chief technical officer (CTO) and has been associated with IIT (BHU), Saudi Electronic University (SEU), and Galgotias University (GU) as a lecturer, course coordinator, and program coordinator.

Dr. Miah Mohammad Dulal is an Associate Professor and Head of the Department of Economics and Finance at the University of Nizwa, Oman. He has obtained his Master's degree (M.B.A.) in Finance and Ph.D. in Development Economics from Ritsumeikan Asia Pacific University, Japan. Dr. Miah has published several academic books and contributed more than 40 research papers to peer-reviewed international journals. He has attended numerous international conferences as an invited speaker and facilitator in various countries. Dr. Miah's research interest includes institutional economics, corporate finance and governance, Islamic banking and finance, and environmental finance. Currently, he is serving as an editorial member of several journals.

Dr. Muneeza Aishath is an Associate Professor at INCEIF, Malaysia which is known as the global University of Islamic Finance. She has served as the first female Deputy Minister of the Ministry of Islamic Affairs in the Maldives; Deputy Minister of Ministry of Finance and Treasury in the Maldives; Head of Islamic Finance of Capital Market Development Authority of Maldives; member of Islamic Fiqh Academy (National Fatawa Council of Maldives); first chairman of Hajj pilgrimage fund, Maldives Hajj Corporation Limited; chairman of Maldives Center for Islamic Finance Limited which was set by the government of Maldives to strategize the Maldives as the hub of Islamic finance in South Asia; Islamic Finance consultant who developed the first Shariah-compliant Islamic microfinance scheme offered in the Maldives; the Shariah Advisor who structured all the corporate sukuks offered in the Maldives; Shariah Adviser who structured the private sukuk and Islamic treasury instruments for the government of Maldives; and the consultant who drafted the Islamic capital market legal framework for the country.

Dr. Rashid Mamunur is a Senior Assistant Professor of Finance at the School of Business and Economics, Universiti Brunei Darussalam. Prior to joining UBD, Dr. Mamunur taught Finance at the University of Nottingham and East West University (Bangladesh) for over 17 years. Dr. Mamunur publishes widely in Corporate Finance, International Finance and FinTech. Some of his works appeared in *JIFMIM, AAAJ, Pacific-Basin Finance Journal, International Review of Economics and Finance, International Journal of Bank Marketing, Singapore Economics Review, Renewable Energy, Tourism Analysis*. He has led multiple international grants, awarded with school best researcher award, best reviewer award, and edited several special issues for renowned journals. Dr. Mamunur is a Fellow of the Higher Education Academy, United Kingdom. He has been serving as Associated Editor of IMEFM, a ABDC B-ranked Islamic Finance journal, and JECD, a forty-year-old Scopus indexed economic and development journal.

Rahiman Habeeb Ur is currently working as an assistant professor at the college of Business administration, Kingdom University, Bahrain.

Dr. Rabbani Mustafa Raza holds a Ph.D. in Banking and Financial Services from the prestigious Jamia Millia Islamia, University, New Delhi, India. His research areas are Financial Technology (Fintech) and its potential application in Islamic finance and banking industry, Integrating the Halal economy with Islamic finance and exploring the possibilities of Shariah-compliant cryptocurrency. He is serving as an Assistant Professor at the Department of Economics and Finance, University of Bahrain. Prior to this he has been His work has been published in a variety of international journals including *Energy Economics, Research in International Business and Finance (RIBAF), Journal of Islamic and Middle eastern Finance and Management, Economic Research, Journal of Islamic Accounting and Business Research, Heliyon Business and Economics, Environmental Science and Pollution Research* etc.

Shaikh Zakir Hossen is a Lecturer in Commercial Studies Division as a Faculty of Islamic Banking and Finance, under Ministry of Education, Kingdom of Bahrain since 2015. Prior to this, he worked more than 15 years in commercial and academic industry. He has published numerous articles in referred journals and presented many papers in various conferences, both local and abroad exclusively in different areas of Accounting, management, and Islamic Banking and Finance. He has also participated in a variety of seminars, forums, workshops, and international conferences.

Prof. Trinugroho Irwan is a Full Professor of Finance at the Faculty of Economics and Business, Universitas Sebelas Maret (FEB UNS), Indonesia. Currently, he is also the Director of Partnership, Development, and International of UNS and the Chairman of the Center of Fintech and Banking UNS. Irwan was the UNS best lecturer in 2015 and 2018 as well as the finalist of national best lecturer in 2018. Irwan graduated with a Ph.D. degree in banking and finance from the University of Limoges, France. He is also the Vice Chair for Program and International Affairs of the Indonesian Finance Association (IFA). He has done some research projects and consulting to the Indonesia Financial Services Authority (OJK), the Indonesia Deposit Insurance Corporation (IDIC), World Bank, USAID, and Bank Indonesia. Irwan has published a number of papers in reputed journals including *Journal of Financial Stability,*

Economic Modelling, Finance Research Letters, Global Finance Journal, British Accounting Review, Economic Systems, Research in International Business and Finance, Journal of Behavioral and Experimental Finance, Borsa Istanbul Review, International Economics, Economics Bulletin, Emerging Markets Finance and Trade, Singapore Economic Review, International Journal of Emerging Markets, and *Journal of Asia Business Studies.* He also serves as managing editor and associate editor for some reputable journals including the International Review of Economics and Finance (Elsevier). Irwan is also an assessor, peer review team member, and expert for some higher education international accreditation and certification such as ABEST21, FIBAA, and ASEAN University Network-Quality Assurance (AUN-QA).

Zulfikar Zehra is currently working as an Assistant Professor at Shaheed Bhagat Singh College, University of Delhi, Delhi, India. She has obtained a doctorate in Digital Marketing from the Centre for Management Studies (CMS), Jamia Millia Islamia, New Delhi, India. She has also done a research project in Intellectual Property Rights with CropLife International, Washington, DC, USA, during her M.B.A. from Amity University. She has received an Academic Excellence Award from Aligarh Muslim University (AMU), India. She has numerous research publications in various International Journals.

List of Figures

Introduction to Islamic Fintech: A Challenge or an Opportunity?

Fig. 1	Growth of global fintech industry; billion USD (*Source* Statista [updated in March 2022], accessed from https://www.statista.com/outlook/dmo/fintech/worldwide#transaction-value)	4
Fig. 2	Islamic fintech global heatmaps 2021 (*Source* Global Islamic Fintech Report 2021 [Dinar Standard & Elipses, 2021]) *Notes* SEA = Southeast Asia, SSA = Sub-Saharan Africa	6
Fig. 3	Islamic finance core principles (*Source* Author's own compilation)	10
Fig. 4	Challenges faced by the Islamic fintech (*Source* Author's own compilation)	15
Fig. 5	Opportunities for Islamic fintech (*Source* Author's own compilation)	19

Fintech and the Art of Disruption

Fig. 1	Evolution of fintech (*Source* [Arner et al., 2015])	32
Fig. 2	Crowdfunding platform (*Source* Adapted from Rabbani et al. [2021])	36

A Fintech-Based Zakat Model Using Artificial Intelligence

Fig. 1	COVID-19 and global poverty (*Source* www.worldbank.org)	52

Fig. 2 Short-term impact of COVID-19 on poor (*Source* Author's own compilation) 54
Fig. 3 AI-Based Zakat model (*Source* Adapted from [Khan et al., 2021a, b; Rabbani et al., 2021]) 58

Islamic Fintech and Bahrain: An Opportunity for Global Financial Services

Fig. 1 Global Islamic finance assets ($billion) (*Source* DinarStandard, 2021/2022) 70

The Future of Finance and Fintech: Visualizing the Opportunities for Fintech in the MENA Region

Fig. 1 Key participants of Fintech ecosystem (Author's own architecture) 93
Fig. 2 Fintech ecosystem proposed framework (*Source* Developed based on review) 95
Fig. 3 Middle East venture capital investment into Fintech companies (*Source* The Dubai International Financial Centre [DIFC] Fintech Hive and Accenture) 96
Fig. 4 Number of Internet users in a leading country (*Source* International telecommunication Union [ITU]) 98
Fig. 5 Trends of ICT development in MENA region (*Source* ITU World Telecommunication/ICT Indicators database) 98
Fig. 6 Fintech startup creation MENA (*Source* Fintech Focus, KPMG) 103

An Insight into the Fintech and Islamic Finance Literature: A Bibliometric and Visual Analysis

Fig. 1 Scopus research category 136
Fig. 2 Annual scientific publication 136
Fig. 3 Most relevant authors 137
Fig. 4 Source growth 139
Fig. 5 Co-citation analysis of cited Authors 140
Fig. 6 Co-occurrence of author's keywords 143
Fig. 7 Bibliographic coupling of documents 144

Fintech Innovation and Its Application in Islamic Banking from Pakistan

Fig. 1　Evolution of digital banking system (*Source* Adapted from Rahim et al., 2018)　170

Fintech in the Islamic Banking Sector and Its Impact on the Stakeholders in the Wake of COVID-19

Fig. 1　Islamic versus conventional Fintech (*Source* Adapted from DinarStandard (2020)　180
Fig. 2　Islamic Fintech by sector (*Source* Adapted from The Global Islamic Fintech Report, DinarStandard, 2021)　181
Fig. 3　Uses of Islamic Fintech following COVID-19 (*Source* Adapted from Hassan et al., 2020, p. 108)　184

Fintech and Islamic Financial Institutions: Applications and Challenges

Fig. 1　Global consumer Fintech adoption rates for the years 2015, 2017, and 2019 (*Source* EY Global Fintech Adoption Index [2019])　199
Fig. 2　Changes in reasons for using a Fintech challenger for the years 2017 and 2019 (*Source* EY global Fintech Adoption Index [2019])　199
Fig. 3　Top reasons for SMEs to use Fintech globally for the year 2019 (*Source* EY global Fintech Adoption Index [2019])　200
Fig. 4　Subcategories of the Top 100 Fintech Unicorns as of September 2021 (*Source* Researchers calculation based on fintechlabs.com)　201
Fig. 5　The top five Islamic Fintech market sizes within the OIC countries (*Source* Global Islamic Fintech Report [2021])　202
Fig. 6　The Global Islamic Fintech (GIFT) Index (*Source* Global Islamic Fintech Report [2021]; *Note* OIC countries are distinguished using the darker colour)　203

Fintech, Pandemic, and the Islamic Financial System: Innovative Financial Services and Its *Shariah* Compliance

Fig. 1　Fintech-based Islamic Financial Services (*Source* Author's own compilation)　250

Islamic Finance and Cryptocurrency: A Systematic Review

Fig. 1　Bitcoin return in last one year (*Source* https://www.coindesk.com/price/bitcoin) ... 294

Islamic Fintech, Blockchain and Crowdfunding: Current Landscape and Path Forward

Fig. 1　Blockchain application in Islamic finance (*Source* Adapted from Hassan et al. [2020a, 2020b]) ... 310

Fig. 2　No of Fintech Firms in selected OIC countries (*Source* IFN Islamic Fintech) ... 314

Fig. 3　Number of Fintech startups by core technology (*Source* DinarStandard [2018]) ... 315

Fig. 4　Blockchain data structure ... 316

Fig. 5　The overall structure of Blockchain economy and Islamic (*Source* Finance) ... 318

Fig. 6　Smart phone penetration in top 10 countries in the world vs. select OIC countries (September 2018) (*Source* O'Dea [2020]) ... 319

Fig. 7　Future Fintech-based Islamic financial services (*Source* Author's own compilation) ... 325

Fig. 8　Current Islamic trade finance practices (*Source* Author's own architect) ... 326

Fig. 9　Future Blockchain-based Islamic trade finances (*Source* Author's own architect) ... 327

List of Tables

Introduction to Islamic Fintech: A Challenge or an Opportunity?

Table 1	Difference between fintech and traditional banks	8

Fintech and the Art of Disruption

Table 1	Popular investment apps comparison	37
Table 2	Major Cryptocurrencies comparison	38

An Insight into the Fintech and Islamic Finance Literature: A Bibliometric and Visual Analysis

Table 1	Most influential documents	138
Table 2	Most influential journals	138
Table 3	Most important countries	140
Table 4	Top affiliations	141
Table 5	Evolving themes and subthemes in Islamic finance	146

Fintech Innovation and Its Application in Islamic Banking from Pakistan

Table 1	Keywords and theme selection	164
Table 2	Descriptive statistics of variables over the period (2006–2020)	165

Table 3 The impact of selected keywords on profitability (ROA) 167
Table 4 The impact of selected themes on profitability (ROA) 168

An Assessment of Level of Adoption of Fintech in Islamic Banks in the MENA Region

Table 1 Overview of the nine core Fintech technologies 227

An Islamic Finance Perspective of Crowdfunding and Peer-To-Peer (P2P) Lending

Table 1 Types of crowdfunding with description 267
Table 2 Difference between crowdfunding and P2P lending 268

Islamic Finance and Cryptocurrency: A Systematic Review

Table 1 An overview of the literature on Cryptocurrency and sharia compliance 283
Table 2 Analysis of sharia compliance of Cryptocurrency 297

Islamic Fintech, Blockchain and Crowdfunding: Current Landscape and Path Forward

Table 1 Current landscape of Islamic Fintech and future technologies 320

COVID-19 Challenges and the Role of Islamic Fintech

Table 1 Voluntary and compulsory acts of Islamic social finance 350
Table 2 Islamic Fintech and social inclusion elements 351

Introduction to Islamic Fintech: A Challenge or an Opportunity?

Mustafa Raza Rabbani, M. Kabir Hassan, and Mamunur Rashid

1 Introduction

Islamic Finance

Islamic finance differentiates itself from the conventional finance primarily based on its treatment of interest (*Riba*), followed by the equity- and trade-based financing mechanism, avoiding unnecessary risk and uncertainty, and supporting entrepreneurship and mutual solidarity (Saeed et al., 2021). Islamic financial system demotes debt-based financing. The

---

M. R. Rabbani (✉)
Department of Economics and Finance, College of Business administration, University of Bahrain, Sakhir, Bahrain
e-mail: mrabbani@uob.edu.bh

M. K. Hassan
Department of Economics and Finance, University of New Orleans, New Orleans, LA, USA
e-mail: mhassan@uno.edu

M. Rashid
Christ Church Business School, Canterbury Christ Church University, Canterbury, UK
e-mail: mamunur.rashid@canterbury.ac.uk

© The Author(s), under exclusive license to Springer Nature Switzerland AG 2022
M. K. Hassan et al. (eds.), *FinTech in Islamic Financial Institutions*, https://doi.org/10.1007/978-3-031-14941-2_1

system earned much popularity during the global financial crisis of 2007–2008 as its performance stayed stable even when the global conventional banks were collapsing. Islamic finance industry has been growing at a supernormal growth for a very long time. The industry has reached $2.70 trillion value by the year 2020 (IFSB, 2021), which is contributed largely by Islamic banks (around 70%). The growth of Islamic finance industry has slowed down recently due to COVID-19 and geopolitical crises involving systemically important Islamic finance jurisdictions[1] (Yaya et al., 2021). Most significant Islamic finance jurisdictions include Kingdom of Saudi Arabia, Malaysia, United Arab Emirates, Indonesia, and Iran.

Slow growth of Islamic banking in recent years is contributed not only by geopolitical crisis in important Islamic finance jurisdictions but also attributed to the lack of innovation and limited investment in technology when compared to their conventional counterparts (Banna et al., 2021). This trend is changing rapidly as Islamic banks are investing in mobile banking and collaborating with Fintech companies to offer services to survive the competition. Theoretically, Islamic finance broadly stands on three pillars: equity (versus debt), compliance (to Shariah norms), and shared value (Hassan & Rashid, 2018). Fintech operations in Islamic financial institutions might face the challenge of Shariah compliance and might require a different framework than the usual supervision applicable to existing Islamic financial institution.

Fintech and Its Theoretical Basis

Financial Technology also abbreviated as Fintech has emerged as the most disruptive technology in the twenty-first century (Fu & Mishra, 2022; Lv & Xiong, 2022). Even though the global financial crisis of 2007–2008 significantly triggered the rise of Fintech, the need for this drastic change has been fuelled by two factors. First comes declining customer confidence in the traditional financial services, which motivates them to search for alternative solutions. Second involves the rise of technology-based entrepreneurship that intends to develop new concepts, ideas, and applications, mostly for mobile users, that enhances our communication, facilitates our interaction, and transforms our user experience, everywhere financial transaction is involved (Nejad, 2022; Yue et al., 2022).

---

[1] https://www.ifsb.org/press_full.php?id=570&submit=more.

Fintech is defined in several ways. The most usual definition is based on its purpose to make people's life easier by offering financial services using a mobile phone as a channel (Manyika et al., 2016). Since the visualisation of using mobile phones or the internet, Fintech is expected to offer personalized financial services that does not go under the radar of the authorities meant to regulate financial markets and institutions. The peer-to-peer (P2P) transaction framework facilitates need-based lending facilities while checking credit histories, scoring, and eligibility using artificial intelligence and machine learning. Using Fintech, existing banks can modify their existing service and payment framework using mobile applications. For instance, banks offer mobile applications that can be used to apply for credit cards. The process is much faster than manual paper-based applications, which can also reduce the overall cost of issuing a card.

Is Fintech financial entrepreneurship? Fintech companies are often referred to as financial startups. These are generally raw ideas initially, and with gradual refinements, the ideas turn into complete financial solutions offering different financial services. This sort of entrepreneurship is threatening traditional financial institutions, as they are offering various financial services that include lending and borrowing services. Due to a limited legal framework, the Fintech institutions are not yet fully regulated. One simple search on Google Play Store or Apple App Store returns thousands of apps that can manage digital payments. Consequently, the growth of this industry has been branded as a 'financial disruption'.

Financial inclusiveness is highlighted as the most important benefit of Fintech. Due to unique institutional limitation, traditional financial institutions, even microfinance, cannot serve people from all walks of life. Limited access to finance has been the primary barrier to economic growth in most developing and emerging economies (Demirgüç-Kunt et al., 2015). Digital finance makes money transfer easier and less costly (UNSGSA, 2018). Fintech can help reach additional 1.6 billion customers with new financial services, SMEs could get net agricultural financial support, and new social ventures can start with community financial support (Pazarbasioglu et al., 2020; Sahay et al., 2020). This massive support for financial inclusivity is expected to create more jobs, reduce financial inequality, and help countries fulfill millennium development goals (Allen et al., 2016; Klapper et al., 2006) (Fig. 1).

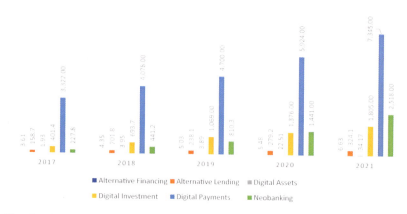

Fig. 1 Growth of global fintech industry; billion USD (*Source* Statista [updated in March 2022], accessed from https://www.statista.com/outlook/dmo/fin tech/worldwide#transaction-value)

Growth of Fintech

The last decade has witnessed a rise of Fintech and allied companies. Statista reports that digital payment is the most important Fintech activity over the years which has reached $7.345 trillion dollars. This segment has been closely followed by neobanking and digital investment. Neobanking is digital banking with no physical existence (on paper) of any lending or deposit activity. Other terms that are commonly used in relation to Fintech include artificial intelligence (or AI in brief), blockchain, cryptocurrency (often referred to as cryptos in brief), digital payments, peer-to-peer (P2P) lending, crowdfunding, InsureTech, and RegTech.

Islamic Fintech market is on the rise. There is a high expectation about Islamic Fintech as it is expected to cover 1.8 billion Muslim population using Fintech services that are 'accessible', adequately 'packaged', and 'transparent' in the eyes of Shariah, consumers, and institutions.[2] Like the conventional Fintech, Islamic Fintech is defined as technological tools easing the distribution of Islamic financial services. Even for the namesake, the commonly used term is Islamic Fintech, general views are of the opinion that the purpose it serves surrounds should give it a

---

[2] https://www.forbes.com/sites/lawrencewintermeyer/2017/12/08/the-future-of-islamic-fintech-is-bright/?sh=4e547b9d65fa.

fitting title—Fintech in Islamic financial institutions—rather than Islamic Fintech.

Going beyond this rhetorical confusion, until the most recent survey by Dinar Standard and Elipses (2021),[3] Islamic Fintech market in the Organization of the Islamic Cooperation Council (OIC) countries stands at US$49 billion by the end of 2020. While the figure is less than 1% of the global Fintech universe, the report has projected a 21% growth rate for the Islamic Fintech by 2025, reaching a value of US$128 billion, whereas the same growth rate for the traditional Fintech is only around 15%. Among a total of 64 countries, two Southeast Asian countries—Malaysia and Indonesia, two Middle Eastern countries—Saudi Arabia and the United Arab Emirates, and one European nation—the United Kingdom, are found to offer the strongest Islamic Fintech ecosystems.

Figure 2 presents the Islamic Fintech heatmaps. Clearly, Asian countries lead Islamic Fintech activities, dominated by Fintech development in Southeast Asia, Middle East, and South and Central Asia. Like the Fintech development in traditional finance shown in Fig. 1, Islamic Fintech development has seen significant growth in digital payment. Other significant segments include alternative finance, wealth management, and fundraising. These activities account for almost 70% of the Fintech development in the selected area. The report (see footnote 3) also publishes that more than 50% of the Fintech-related activities are geared toward raising equity funds in the coming years. This survey provides strong support to Fintech as a strong tool for Islamic SMEs and startups that can raise alternative financing without going to the formal financial markets and institutions. This is another example of 'disruption' in financial markets.

Fintech Entrepreneurship: Benefits and Challenges

Fintech shows enormous potential to change the global economic atmosphere by engaging billions of people through digital financial services and closing the financial exclusion problems created by the traditional financial system. The most common benefit of Fintech is, therefore, financial inclusion that strengthens financial flow. Fintech provides an opportunity for banks and financial institutions to modify existing products and

---

[3] https://cdn.salaamgateway.com/reports/pdf/6127a0965afd7898a34f69dadc24b8d17ada0b1b.pdf.

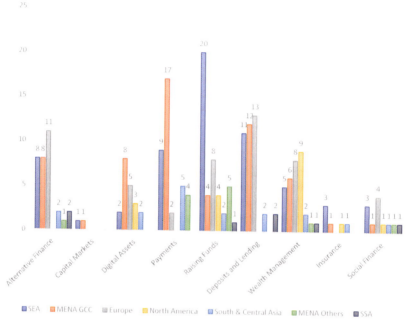

Fig. 2 Islamic fintech global heatmaps 2021 (*Source* Global Islamic Fintech Report 2021 [Dinar Standard & Elipses, 2021]) *Notes* SEA = Southeast Asia, SSA = Sub-Saharan Africa

provide innovative financial services for a better experience at a low cost. However, that modification is expensive and considered as 'disruptive'. Several studies support the view that efficient management of Fintech can benefit Islamic financial institutions by delivering their services to customers previously uncovered by the system (Atif et al., 2021; Hassan et al., 2020; Rabbani et al., 2021a, 2021b).

Since the global financial crisis of 2008, banks and financial institutions across the globe have been facing aggravated financial regulations (Flögel & Beckamp, 2020; Nastiti & Kasri, 2019). Otherwise, these institutions cannot avoid paying huge penalties (Busch, 2021). Although the traditional banks and financial institutions religiously follow these regulations but still the customers have shifted to the digital solutions mainly due to the benefits it brings in terms of innovation, cost, and convenience (Agarwal & Zhang, 2020). Fintech entrepreneurships offer innovative, efficient, and cutting-edge financial services at a very low cost, which comes at sheer benefits to people from remote areas (Anshari et al., 2020; Mosteanu & Faccia, 2021). Fintech has made it possible to streamline the complex traditional financial services into more exciting and accessible to people mainly the millennial and younger generation (Khan et al., 2022; Magnuson, 2018). Accommodating and customizable user experience offered by mobile financial applications help spread the financial services to a wider group of the population. As a result, Fintech companies effectively save ten times more than the traditional financial institutions (Cho & Chen, 2021). At the current stage, Fintech companies are not widely regulated. Young graduates with technological backgrounds are teaming up with people having know-how of the financial sector to develop new ideas that are transferred to valuable Fintech startups.

From these standpoints, the current chapter asks a few basic questions. Do Fintech companies have the capability to outrun the traditional banks and financial institution? What is the level of conformity between the Fintech companies and Islamic finance? Is Fintech a doable business model that supports core Islamic finance principles, such as profit and loss sharing, shared prosperity, and a fair economic system?

Answers are not that straightforward. Banks do business on trust and develop their clientele based on loyalty and customer service for over two centuries. They have developed this 'feeling' that bank is a safe place to keep money and banks do take care of their customers (Andaleeb et al., 2016; Iqbal et al., 2018). This trust is being built over a long period of time backed up by strong customer relationship management (Jreisat et al., 2021).

Banks are comparatively large transnational corporations with massive capital. Fintech startups are dependent on the banks and need to partner with them to win customer trust (Rabbani, 2022). Banks are less risky as compared to Fintech companies as they are more established, and the rates of return are more stable (So, 2021). Banks also have risk management instruments—a lot of these as derivative instruments—to manage financial exposure. Fintech entrepreneurs are overall much riskier than banks. A brief comparison between the banks and the Fintech companies is presented in Table 1.

Given their obvious differences, in brief, banks offer less risky financial transactions, while Fintech offers privacy, cost reduction due to intermediation, and convenience as it is based on technology. In the subsequent sections, we will discuss how Fintech evolved over time with its services and how relevant it is to Islamic finance.

Table 1 Difference between fintech and traditional banks

Points	Fintech	Traditional banks
meaning	Fintech uses computer programs or technology to provide financial solutions to the customers of banks and financial institutions (Rabbani et al., 2020)	Traditional banks are the financial institutions licensed to provide financial services in terms of accepting deposits and advancing loans to individuals and businesses (Li et al., 2017)
Technology	Fintech is tech-based innovation, which is built on the technological innovations like machine learning, artificial intelligence, and quantum computing for making financial services faster, more accurate, and more efficient	Although the traditional banks are slowly and steadily embracing the technology, they are still struggling with the legacy infrastructure. To compete with Fintech firms, there has been a massive change in technology infrastructure among traditional banks
Regulation	Fintech ideas/innovations are not directly regulated yet. Some of the products that came out of the Fintech innovation are facing regulatory restrictions, including 'buy now pay later', cryptocurrency, etc. The regulators are still looking for ways to properly regulate these startups, and it gives them an edge over the traditional banks to work faster and adopt to the needs of the customers	Every country has a union government or central bank to regulate the banks and financial institutions. These regulators make strict regulations to safeguard the interest of the lender and borrowers. Banks are highly regulated financial institutions
Growth potential	There is a clear edge to Fintech in terms of growth potential. The industry is at the growth stage now and there is immense potential to grow further and faster	Banks are growing too. With adoption of right innovations and collaborations, they can grow further. It is easy for a bank to invest in Fintech and find an easier way to get new customers
Risk factors	Fintech startups are considered riskier due to a new and less established nature of business. People still prefer Fintech because it offers flexible, faster, and innovative less expensive financial services	Traditional banks are governed by stricter regulation and that makes them less risky as compared to Fintech

Source Author's own compilation

2 Islamic Finance

Islamic finance has emerged as one of the most important trends of the twenty-first century in the finance world (Abdelsalam & El-Komi, 2016). It has been a key challenge to the conventional financial system (Rabbani et al., 2021a, 2021b). The basic premise of Islamic finance is to establish equality and justice in the society with equal distribution of wealth and fair treatment for everyone. Islamic finance relies on the financial system that adheres to the rules and regulations laid down by the *Shariah*. Shariah laws are prescribed by the guidance from the Holy Qur'an and *Sunnah* (teachings and practices) of the Prophet Muhammad (*Peace be upon him*). These guidelines are often regularized by *Maqasit al Shariah*—the objective of *Shariah*- in literal meaning. Although the Islamic and conventional financial system serves similar clientele, the prohibition of interest rate is the first tangible differentiator between the two. Fixed interest rate has been identified as an economic injustice, as it tends to exploit parties involve in a financial transaction (Yaya et al., 2021). Figure 3 shows a summary of factors that shape the Islamic finance universe.

Prohibitions

a. Non-interest mode of finance: Islamic financial system is a non-interest medium of the financial system. Both lenders and borrowers are not allowed to charge or pre-fix any interest as this is completely non-interest mode of financing method. Interest or *Riba* is strictly prohibited the Islamic law and declared *Haram* (prohibited). *Riba* (interest) is defined as the 'usury', or 'unjust' or 'exploitative' gains made in trade under the *Shariah* law.

b. Prohibition of *Gharar: Gharar* or excessive uncertainty is prohibited under Islamic law. Excessive uncertainty may result in deceit or injustice. Islam also does not permit making extra returns based on extreme uncertainty, which is a regular phenomenon in traditional finance. *Gharar* is defined as any transactions or probable objects whose existence or description is not certain.

c. Prohibited to invest in restricted items: Unlike the conventional financial system, Islamic finance does not allow to trade restrictive items. Trading in certain items, such as alcohol, gambling, pork, entertainment, or any other item declared harmful and illegal by the *Shariah* law, is not permitted in Islamic finance (Hassan et al., 2019).

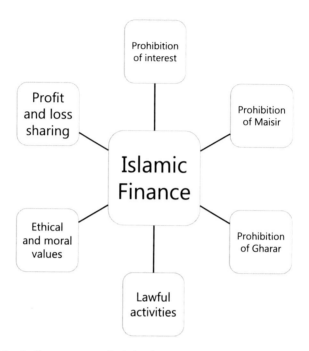

Fig. 3 Islamic finance core principles (*Source* Author's own compilation)

Islamic finance uses a screening mechanism to filter these unlawful activities.

d. Prohibition on speculation and gambling: Speculative transactions like financial derivative and gambling are prohibited under Islamic finance. Derivative for the purpose of hedging is currently discussed in the Islamic finance literature. While speculation is prohibited, Islamic finance promotes profit and loss sharing. Speculation may create wealth by chance without any connection to real productive activity.

Promotion

a. Profit and loss sharing (PLS): Islamic finance believes in shared prosperity. It relies on a trading platform and connects buyers and sellers through real transactions. The parties involved in these transactions will share profit and loss, which average out negative

impact on one of the parties. PLS is possible when financing is done through equity-based instrument, which requires the parties to establish partnerships. Another by-product of the PLS system is that the parties involved are not considered directly as borrowers and lenders; rather they are partners in a partnership business. *Mudarabah* and *Musharakah* are the two popular methods of equity-based PLS methods of financing in Islamic finance. Also, PLS-based financing promotes an asset-backed transaction system.
b. Ethical and moral values: Islam is a complete code of life, which is based on the ethical and moral codes of conduct. Similar codes are also applicable to Islamic finance. Since Islam itself is an ethical system and all the transactions under the Islamic financial system must be governed under the ethical and moral code of conduct laid down by the *Shariah*. The basic moral principle of Islamic finance states that all the transactions under Islamic finance must be aimed at social benefit and holistic development of the society when compared to making individual benefit. Islamic finance promotes sustainable and green transactions through green *Sukuk* and green banking initiatives that target long-term environmental protection. Higher levels of ethical identity of Islamic institutions are also expected by the market participants (Rashid & Hassan, 2014).

3 Point of Convergence Between Fintech and Islamic Finance

Fintech is nothing new. In general terms, Fintech is the integration of technology in the financial industry to offer convenience to customers. Diner's club cards in 1950s and automated teller machines in 1960s have given some clear directions on how technology can shape the financial landscape forever. By 1980s, major stock exchanges and broker-driven trading systems started using the electronic trading platform (Sharma, 2014). Beginning of 2000, we have seen the start of PayPal, making online transfers, and payments completed in seconds. Within the first decade of the new millennium, there are tremendous development in mobile-based payment systems, with Google Pay, Apple Pay, etc. Technopreneurs have worked restlessly to create a new user interface, as such now your smile can make payments using a phone facial recognition system. After mobile payment, the introduction of bitcoins and blockchain is considered another major development in the Fintech universe, which has seen tremendous volatility during the pandemic time (Abdul-Rahim et al., 2022; Talwar et al., 2020).

Ernst and Young (EY) run a Fintech survey,[4] the recent being published in 2019 (EY, 2019), which reports that around 75% of the customers prefer to use Fintech-based services for money transfer and payment. These customers would like to use Fintech for remittance facilities for cross-border transfers. Fintech adoption for money transfer and payment has increased more than threefold during 2015–2019. Another high growth area of adoption is insurance, where mobile-based applications are used to fill in the information to apply for insurance products. The EY survey (EY, 2019) also finds that changes in rates and fees are a primary motivator behind higher rates of Fintech adoption. This helps us rely on the most common definition of Fintech: the delivery of financial services based on technological innovations, specifically using mobile phones and the internet (Banna et al., 2021).

Major Attractions of Fintech

Aside from the most common growth factors, Fintech is commonly cited, even among the non-practitioners and non-users, for mobile payment, blockchain, and cryptocurrencies. Among these, blockchain offers a basic platform that connects computers in a network that can record a series of transactions that cannot be easily altered or removed. It offers several benefits to users. First, the system is secured and private among the users. Second, the blockchain system bypasses the traditional regulatory authorities, including the central banks for a financial transaction, and also does not require a traditional payment service provider, such as a bank or other financial intermediary. Cryptocurrencies can be sued to settle payments or transfer money online, and the records of such transactions and transfers can be securely preserved using blockchain.

While the system comes with privacy and convenience, supervision and regulatory foresight are a major lacking. Banking system is a highly regulated system to keep bankers away from unnecessary risk-taking, so that authorities can safeguard the value of the investors. In Fintech

---

[4] EY Global Fintech Adoption Index (2019).

universe, transactions are unregulated, which may give rise to excessive volatility. There might be a sharp rise in shadow economic activity due to blockchain.

Islamic Finance and Fintech

Islamic finance prohibits interest, uncertainty, and gambling. Islamic financial system places additional restrictions over the usual restriction and monitoring by traditional financial system (Hassan et al., 2019). Alongside usual monitoring by the Central Bank, internal and external auditors, Islamic banks must also pass the screening criteria imposed by Centralised *Shariah* Board and internal *Shariah* Supervisory Board (SSB). Multiple layers of restrictions made a less volatile growth possible for Islamic finance. Customers realize that even during the global financial crisis the Islamic financial institution steps away from a high-risky investment, which establishes the system as a more resilient one compared to the conventional banking system (Yoon et al., 2021).

There has been a significant growth of independent Fintech entrepreneurs (startups) and the ones that integrate their Fintech innovations for a particular Islamic bank. The objective is to offer *Shariah*-compliant financial services with less interference from regulatory bodies. However, some initial compliance to regulatory principles must be met before a Fintech company charter can take place. For instance, the Central Bank of Bahrain issues *Shariah*-compliance certification to crypto trading platforms like Rain, Binance, and CoinMENA to create a level of confidence among Islamic investors. More investment in these Fintech-based innovations is likely to help Islamic finance sector grow.

Islamic finance practices a trade finance mechanism that deals with a peer-to-peer (P2P) platform. Crowdfunding platforms are also used to finance small-scale innovative projects for commercial as well as social causes. Crowdsourcing can have a better fit with Islamic finance as both the systems promote equity-based, profit-sharing, and donation-based financial systems (Yang & Zhang, 2016). 'Buy now pay later' intrinsically supports the trade-based Islamic finance system. This system can be used for raw materials financing, especially in a business-to-business (B2B) platform involving large suppliers and SME buyers.

Fintech has been also instrumental in the rise of Islamic insurance (Takaful) and the bond market (Sukuk). TakaTech and InsureTech enable users to check for updates on various insurance products, compare the market, apply for the chosen product, and update their product, all remotely using their phones. It is expected that the use TakaTech is going to reduce overall insurance processing costs and bring efficiency to Takaful industry (Hasan et al., 2020). InsureTech can use available client data to match its risk profile to offer new products. Artificial intelligence can be employed to do this matching that enhances overall customer experience.

Sukuk industry, both sovereign as well as corporate, is growing fast. The growth has attracted clients from *Shariah*-compliant as well as non-compliant markets. FITCH Rating[5] reports that total *Sukuk* issuance in Q1 2022 grew quarter on quarter by 11.6%. The amount of quarterly issuance is US$64.5 billion. Close to 80% of the *Sukuks* are investment-grade and issuers have a stable outlook. Blockchain technology can benefit the *Sukuk* market farther. Based on blockchain, and profit and loss sharing at the backdrop, Smart Sukuk will be able to finance projects using microfinance and foreign bank in a setup (Chong & Ling, 2021). This arrangement is an efficient alternative to the existing *Sukuk* management system.

4 Challenges

Islamic Fintech is expected to push the Islamic finance sector forward by a bigger margin compared to traditional Islamic financial intermediation. Technology and innovation will make a clear difference. However, the choice of moving into Fintech will come at costs. Figure 4 demonstrates a brief list of factors that may shape the future of Islamic Fintech.

Shariah Non-Compliance

The biggest challenge for an Islamic financial institution whether bank or an Islamic Fintech company is to ensure highest level of compliance with the rules and regulations laid down by the Shariah. Compliance with *Shariah* is an integral component of the survival of Islamic institutions, as these guidelines are observed very closely by the customers and investors before making any financial decision. If it is found that a particular product or an institution has violated the *Shariah* norms, they can

---

[5] https://www.fitchratings.com/research/islamic-finance/global-sukuk-market-outlook-1q22-12-04-2022.

INTRODUCTION TO ISLAMIC FINTECH ... 15

Fig. 4 Challenges faced by the Islamic fintech (*Source* Author's own compilation)

face quarters of criticism which may force them to close their business. According to the Global Islamic Fintech report 2020, more than 76% of the Islamic Fintech startups have already taken the *Shariah*-compliance certification or are planning to obtain it (AMF, 2021). Shariah scholars around the globe are still not clear and have not reached a consensus on whether cryptocurrency is permissible or not (Shahnawaz Khan & Rabbani, 2020). More research is needed to ascertain the level of supervisory control to be optimal in case of Islamic Fintech, given the fact that Fintech under regulation may turn into completely different (possibly unsuccessful) concept. Another challenge lying with respect to *Shariah* non-compliance is the lack of *Shariah* guidelines with respect to the use of digital wallets.

Public Perception of Islamic Finance

This is among the most important challenges faced by the Islamic financial institutions. A growing group of customers believe that Islamic financial products are for Muslims only. They tend to avoid the industry and products altogether as they believe that Muslims are only allowed to use these products. This serious separation is often legitimized on the ground of lack of awareness and extreme rhetorics used by clerics using Arabic in Islamic finance literature. The other group of bank customers are practically unaware of the crucial differences between Islamic and traditional financial systems. These key differences and lack of awareness will have a serious impact on Islamic Fintech adoption. Technology is a taboo among many serious practitioners due to limited knowledge of the convergence between innovation and religion. Serious public awareness campaigns can help reduce these differences and help Islamic Fintech grow further.

Talent Gap

Fintech-based Islamic financial services such as Blockchain and artificial intelligence-based *Zakat*, *Qardh-Al-hasan*, *Mudaraba*, *Murabaha*, *Awqaf*, etc. require a genuine understanding of Islamic principles and technological processes. IFIs must equip themselves with trained personnel, which may require them to have active collaboration with educational institutions to have graduates on the demanding areas of Fintech.

Unfavorable Regulatory Environment

Most Muslim majority countries are lacking in regulatory convergence. There are several cases of Fatwa shopping where dominating Muslim countries tend to impose their rulings on other countries. The standard setters in Islamic finance (AAOIFI, IFSB, etc.) should work together to reduce cross-border and cross-school differences to support cross-border transaction by Islamic Fintech. Islamic countries should also provide tax incentives to help this Fintech grow.

Cyber Security

Sine Fintech relies on a digital technology, the system heavily depends on a mix of online tools like cloud storage, mobile transfer, electronic payment, and cryptocurrency trading. These online facilities face threats from attacks by hackers to steal valuable and personal data and cause millions of dollars of financial as well as non-financial losses. Banks and financial institutions are required to invest in digital security that must be updated on a regular basis. This cost a part of their profit, which may otherwise cost them their reputation. In case of large and reputed banks, even a minor security can cause a bad reputation in the market, resulting in the loss of millions of customers and a drastic fall in stock prices, which is too big a risk for the business to take. Even though Blockchain is found to be secured so far, growing interest in this system will attract unwanted guests (hackers) for which the Fintech companies, mostly startups, are not ready yet.

Competing Against Modern Innovations and Technological Advancement

Thousands of new Fintech concepts are coming out every day. A simple search on Google.com will render millions of links to Fintech concepts and ideas. Most innovative countries are non-Muslim majority countries. Indicatively, this is a sign of competitive loss of Islamic Fintech against its counterparts. Despite having limitations, investment in Fintech in Sub-Saharan Africa, Southeast Asia, and other Asian countries is growing at a tremendous rate (Banna et al., 2021). Islamic countries should come up with an effective policy framework to support techno-entrepreneurship and Fintech-based entrepreneurial activities. Fintech startups are finding it really challenging to keep pace with the stiff competition (Borgogno & Colangelo, 2020). To manage this competition Islamic Fintech is required to ensure Shariah compliance, and investment in Shariah and technological R&D. Cost is one of the major operational risks that Islamic Fintech should consistently research on. Otherwise, Islamic Fintech will lose its competitive edge.

5 OPPORTUNITIES

Muslims account for about half of the world's 1.7 billion unbanked population.[6] Among this (47%), the major portion is Muslim women. Islamic finance caters to the need of 1.8 billion Muslim population globally. A lion share of this population do not use mobile phone, have no or limited access to internet, and have very limited financial literacy (Antara et al., 2016; Ganesan et al., 2020). Islamic finance is present only in 45 countries. Considering these facts, Islamic Fintech can be the right solution to ensure the financial inclusion of the global Muslims. Some early signs of such growth is seen in OIC countries, as Fintech-based financial inclusion strategies are effectively in place in these countries (Karim et al., 2021). COVID-19 pandemic and UN's sustainable development goals have also paved the way for renewed Fintech initiatives for growing Muslim population as many Islamic banks have completely changed their way of offering services using technology and mobile phones (Naeem et al., 2021; Rabbani et al., 2021a, 2021b). Some of the opportunities are listed as follows and Fig. 5.

New Startup

Several government-financed initiatives in Turkey, Malaysia, Bahrain, and Saudi Arabia support and encourage new startup in the Islamic Fintech area. Also, Islamic banking has failed to find a doable framework for SME financing. Therefore, Islamic Fintech can offer alternative financing through digital lending or crowdfunding to start businesses on a smaller scale. Bahrain has started 'Fintech Bay' to support and encourage entrepreneurship initiatives by providing financial assistance (Meero et al., 2021). Islamic banks can collaborate with Fintech companies to offer financial services to entrepreneurs who are previously unbanked (Rabbani et al., 2020).

Financial Inclusion

The rise of Islamic Fintech has seen the adoption of technology in many unknown and unbanked Muslim population. Many *Zakat* institutions

---

[6] https://www.arabnews.com/node/1780506/business-economy.

Fig. 5 Opportunities for Islamic fintech (*Source* Author's own compilation)

have started using Blockchain and artificial intelligence to reach needy and vulnerable Muslim population with charity funds (Khan et al., 2021; Mohammad et al., 2020). Fintech-based financial inclusion is also beneficial to banks globally. Banks have found positive connection between Fintech investment and financial instability and lower return volatility (Banna et al., 2021). Banks can cover more customers at a lower cost, offering tailored services that fit specific needs of the customers. Mobile-based apps, mobile money agents, digital wallets, cross-border payments and remittances using mobile apps, and e-government services supported by Fintech can expand the domain of financial inclusion (Huang et al., 2020; Kang, 2018).

Financial Fraud Detection and Security

Financial fraud is defined as an act of deception for personal or collective gain that comes at the cost of others. It has been a major challenge for regulators and policymakers in the financial sector. The challenges with depositors money, for instance, in a digital financial system is even stiffer. Financial fraud is also connected to bribery and corruption, abuse of market structure, money laundering, terrorist financing, and tax evasion (Nikkel, 2020). Use of Fintech facilities might help regulators keep a record of these transactions and to curb these with prudential actions. Fintech facilities such as RegTech and AML (anti-money laundering) used advanced machine learning and artificial intelligence to detect fraud and identify suspicious transactions in real-time (Ai & Tang, 2011; Kurum, 2020).

Diversity

Some of the pressing problems faced by the modern-day financial institutions include tough regulatory requirements, a threat from cybercrime and stiff competition from Fintech and technology firms (Flögel & Beckamp, 2020; Nguyen, 2020). Fintech can help bring diversity by integrating traditional services with technology-driven digital interfaces and processing systems that can make the user experience better. Blakstad and Allen (2018) point out that organizations with diverse traits and employees with diverse backgrounds bring out-of-the-box ideas that foster innovation. Also, companies with digital diversity 'out-innovate and outperform' others, including in the existing as well as the new entrants to the market.

Partnership and Collaborations

Fintech is essentially a collaboration between Islamic finance, entrepreneurship, education system and regulatory ecosystem. There will be an active partnership between universities and Islamic financial institutions to help them upgrade their technology background, train them in financial know-hows, and update them on new things demanded by the customers. Similar collaborations are possible across the border, Fintech practically opens the border of financial transactions. Hence, as the Fintech entrepreneurship is on the rise, so is the collaboration

(Ntwiga, 2020; Truby, 2020). These collaborations offer multiple benefits to both the Fintech company, financial institutions, and the society at large. For instance, if Fintech can help Islamic banks to establish real profit and loss sharing with the use of technology, the entire Islamic economic landscape will shift. These collaborations will find new ways that can help the IFI's in meeting changing customer needs, opening digital access, brand positioning, and limiting the threats of Fintech by sharing information and tools at the developer stage (Kværnø-Jones, 2021; Romanova & Kudinska, 2016).

6 Conclusion

Fintech products and services are disruptive innovations that leverage financial data and digital technology. There are several areas where Islamic finance can be integrated with Fintech. Existing Fintech innovations are covering digital deposits and payment services, insurance, and basic lending in the Islamic financial system. With the help of advanced modeling, machine learning and artificial intelligence, the range of these services will expand exponentially in the future. Fintech helps in start-up financing, entrepreneurship development, increasing collaboration among institutions and regulatory bodies, helps control corruption and the shadow economy, and helps stabilize financial system. There are several drawbacks too. Fintech is less regulated and open, which is prone to instability and attacks from hackers that may jeopardize the stability of the entire economic system. Islamic Fintech must also be regulated both by external regulators and internal *Shariah* supervisor board. These might make Fintech less cost-efficient and less resilient.

As the benefits of Fintech supplant the drawbacks, there will be an increasing amount of investment in Fintech and Fintech-based inclusion strategies soon. It is important at this stage to have doable business and regulatory models for Islamic Fintech, so that these institutions can help resolve ongoing economic problems in many least developed and emerging countries. Despite its clear advantages over the traditional non-digital form of financial system. Fintech will face stiff competition and harsh realities in terms of unbalanced regulatory assistance. Nonetheless, Fintech is here to dominate. Policymakers should try to accommodate its benefits for the welfare of all.

References

Abdelsalam, O., & El-Komi, M. (2016). Islamic finance: Introduction and implications for future research and practice. *Journal of Economic Behavior & Organization*, *132*(supplement), 1–2. https://doi.org/10.1016/j.jebo.2016.11.004

Abdul-Rahim, R., Khalid, A., Karim, Z. A., & Rashid, M. (2022). Exploring the driving forces of stock-cryptocurrency comovements during COVID-19 pandemic: An analysis using wavelet coherence and seemingly unrelated regression. *Mathematics*, *10*(12), 2116.

Agarwal, S., & Zhang, J. (2020). FinTech, lending and payment innovation: A review. *Asia-Pacific Journal of Financial Studies*, *49*(3), 353–367. https://doi.org/10.1111/ajfs.12294

Ai, L., & Tang, J. (2011). Risk-based approach for designing enterprise-wide AML information system solution. *Journal of Financial Crime*, *18*(3), 268–276. https://doi.org/10.1108/13590791111147488

Allen, F., Demirgüç-Kunt, A., Klapper, L., & Martinez Peria, M. S. (2016). The foundations of financial inclusion: Understanding ownership and use of formal accounts. *Journal of Financial Intermediation*, *27*(C), 1–30.

AMF (2021). *Islamic fintech in the Arab Region : Imperatives , challenges and the way forward Islamic fintech in the Arab Region : Imperatives , challenges and the way forward*. Arab Monetary Fund (no. 173), United Arab Emirates.

Andaleeb, S. S., Rashid, M., & Rahman, Q. A. (2016). A model of customer-centric banking practices for corporate clients in Bangladesh. *International Journal of Bank Marketing*, *34*(4), 458–475.

Anshari, M., Almunawar, M. N., & Masri, M. (2020). Financial technology and disruptive innovation in business: Concept and application. *International Journal of Asian Business and Information Management*, *11*(4), 29–43. https://doi.org/10.4018/IJABIM.2020100103

Antara, P. M., Musa, R., & Hassan, F. (2016). Bridging Islamic financial literacy and halal literacy: The way forward in halal ecosystem. *Procedia Economics and Finance*, *37*, 196–202. https://doi.org/10.1016/s2212-5671(16)30113-7

Atif, M., Hassan, M. K., Rabbani, M. R., & Khan, S. (2021). Islamic finTech: The digital transformation bringing sustainability to Islamic finance. In *COVID-19 and Islamic social finance* (pp. 94–106). Routledge.

Banna, H., Hassan, M. K., & Rashid, M. (2021). Fintech-based financial inclusion and bank risk-taking: Evidence from OIC countries. *Journal of International Financial Markets, Institutions and Money*, *75*, 101447.

Blakstad, S., & Allen, R. (2018). FinTech Revolution: Universal inclusion in the new financial ecosystem. In *FinTech Revolution: Universal inclusion in the new financial ecosystem*. Springer International Publishing. https://doi.org/10.1007/978-3-319-76014-8

Borgogno, O., & Colangelo, G. (2020). Data, innovation and competition in finance: The case of the access to account rule. *European Business Law Review*, *31*(4), 573–609.

Busch, D. (2021). The future of the special duty of care in the financial sector— Perspectives from the Netherlands. *European Business Law Review*, *32*(3), 473–500.

Cho, T.-Y., & Chen, Y.-S. (2021). The impact of financial technology on China's banking industry: An application of the metafrontier cost Malmquist productivity index. *North American Journal of Economics and Finance*, *57*, 101414. https://doi.org/10.1016/j.najef.2021.101414

Chong, F. H., & Ling. (2021). Enhancing trust through digital Islamic finance and blockchain technology. *Qualitative Research in Financial Markets*, *13*(3), 328–341. https://doi.org/10.1108/QRFM-05-2020-0076

Demirgüç-Kunt, A., Klapper, L. F., Singer, D., & Van Oudheusden, P. (2015). The global findex database 2014: Measuring financial inclusion around the world. *World Bank Policy Research Working Paper*, (7255).

Dinar Standard & Elipses. (2021). *Global Islamic Fintech Report 2021*. Accessed from, www.salaamgateway.com.

EY. (2019). *EY Global Fintech Adoption Index 2019*. (EYG no. 002455–19Gbl). Ernst & Young Global Limited. https://www.ey.com/en_gl/ey-global-Fintech-adoption-index

Flögel, F., & Beckamp, M. (2020). Will FinTech make regional banks superfluous for small firm finance? Observations from soft information-based lending in Germany. *Economic Notes*, *49*(2), e12159. https://doi.org/10.1111/ecno.12159

Fu, J., & Mishra, M. (2022). Fintech in the time of COVID-19: Technological adoption during crises. *Journal of Financial Intermediation*, *50*, 100945. https://doi.org/10.1016/j.jfi.2021.100945

Ganesan, Y., Allah Pitchay, A. B., & Mohd Nasser, M. A. (2020). Does intention influence the financial literacy of depositors of Islamic banking? A case of Malaysia. *International Journal of Social Economics*, *47*(5), 675–690. https://doi.org/10.1108/IJSE-01-2019-0011

Hasan, R., Hassan, M. K., & Aliyu, S. (2020). Fintech and Islamic finance: Literature review and research agenda. *International Journal of Islamic Economics and Finance (IJIEF)*, *3*(1), 75–94.

Hassan, M. K., & Rashid, M. (Eds.). (2018). *Management of Islamic finance: Principle, practice, and performance*. Emerald Group Publishing.

Hassan, M. K., Rabbani, M. R., & Ali, M. A. (2020). Challenges for the Islamic finance and banking in post COVID era and the role of Fintech. *Journal of Economic Cooperation and Development*, *41*(3), 93–116. In M. Hargrave. Insurtech (online). Available from, https://www.investopedia.com/terms/i/insurtech.asp. Accessed 9 November 2021.

Hassan, M. K., Rashid, M., Wei, A. S., Adedokun, B. O., & Ramachandran, J. (2019). Islamic business scorecard and the screening of Islamic businesses in a cross-country setting. *Thunderbird International Business Review*, *61*(5), 807–819.

Huang, R. H., Cheung, C. S. W., & Wang, C. M. L. (2020). The risks of mobile payment and regulatory responses: A Hong Kong perspective. *Asian Journal of Law and Society*, *7*(2), 325–343. https://doi.org/10.1017/als.2019.30

IFSB. (2021). *Islamic financial services industry stability report*. Islamic Financial Services Board. IFSB.

Iqbal, M., Nisha, N., & Rashid, M. (2018). Bank selection criteria and satisfaction of retail customers of Islamic banks in Bangladesh. *International Journal of Bank Marketing*, *36*(5), 931–946.

Jreisat, A., Rabbani, M. R., Bashar, A., Ali, M. A. M., & AlAbbas, A. (2021). Is Fintech valuation an art or a science? Exploring the innovative methods for the valuation of Fintech startups. *2021 International Conference on Decision Aid Sciences and Application* (pp. 922–925) (*DASA*). IEEE.

Kang, J. (2018). Mobile payment in Fintech environment: Trends, security challenges, and services. *Human-Centric Computing and Information Sciences*, *8*(1), 1–16. https://doi.org/10.1186/s13673-018-0155-4

Karim, S., Akhtar, M. U., Tashfeen, R., Raza Rabbani, M., Rahman, A. A. A., & AlAbbas, A. (2021). (in press). Sustainable banking regulations pre and during coronavirus outbreak: The moderating role of financial stability. *Economic Research-Ekonomska Istraživanja*, 1–18. https://doi.org/10.1080/1331677X.2021.1993951

Khan, M. S., Rabbani, M. R., Hawaldar, I. T., & Bashar, A. (2022). Determinants of behavioral intentions to use Islamic financial technology: An empirical assessment. *Risks*, *10*(6), 114.

Khan, S., Hassan, M. K., & Rabbani, M. R. (2021). An artificial intelligence-based Islamic FinTech model on Qardh-Al-Hasan for COVID 19 affected SMEs. In *Islamic perspective for sustainable financial system* (pp. 234–249).

Khan, Shahnawaz, & Rabbani, M. R. (2020). (in press) In depth analysis of blockchain, cryptocurrency and sharia compliance. *International Journal of Business Innovation and Research*. https://doi.org/10.1504/ijbir.2020.10033066

Klapper, L., Laeven, L., & Rajan, R. (2006). Entry regulation as a barrier to entrepreneurship. *Journal of Financial Economics*, *82*(3), 591–629.

Kurum, E. (2020). (in press). RegTech solutions and AML compliance: What future for financial crime? *Journal of Financial Crime*. https://doi.org/10.1108/JFC-04-2020-0051

Kværnø-Jones, J. (2021). The significance of boring finTech: Technology imaginaries and value vernaculars in established banks. *Journal of Cultural Economy*, *15*(2), 232–246. https://doi.org/10.1080/17530350.2021.2002174

Li, Y., Spigt, R., & Swinkels, L. (2017). The impact of FinTech start-ups on incumbent retail banks' share prices. *Financial Innovation*, 3(1), 1–16. https://doi.org/10.1186/s40854-017-0076-7

Lv, P., & Xiong, H. (2022). Can FinTech improve corporate investment efficiency? Evidence from China. *Research in International Business and Finance*, 60, 101571. https://doi.org/10.1016/j.ribaf.2021.101571

Magnuson, W. (2018). Regulating fintech. *Vanderbilt Law Review*, 71(4), 1167–1226.

Manyika, J., Lund, S., Singer, M., White, O., & Berry, C. (2016). *Digital finance for all: Powering inclusive growth in emerging economies*. McKinsey Global Institute.

Meero, A., Rahiman, H. U., & Rahman, A. A. A. (2021). The prospects of Bahrain's entrepreneurial ecosystem: An exploratory approach. *Problems and Perspectives in Management*, 18(4), 402–413.

Mohammad, Khan, S., Mustafa., & Yannis. (2020). An artificial intelligence and NLP based Islamic finTech model combining Zakat and Qardh-Al-Hasan for countering the adverse impact of COVID-19 on SMEs and individuals. *International Journal of Economics and Business Administration*, 8(3), 351–364. https://doi.org/10.35808/ijeba/466

Mosteanu, N. R., & Faccia, A. (2021). Fintech frontiers in quantum computing, fractals, and blockchain distributed ledger: Paradigm shifts and open innovation. *Journal of Open Innovation: Technology, Market, and Complexity*, 7(1), 1–19.

Naeem, M. A., Rabbani, M. R., Karim, S., & Billah, S. M. (2021). (in press). Religion vs ethics: Hedge and safe haven properties of sukuk and green bonds for stock markets pre-and during COVID-19. *International Journal of Islamic and Middle Eastern Finance and Management* . https://doi.org/10.1108/IMEFM-06-2021-0252

Nastiti, N. D., & Kasri, R. A. (2019). The role of banking regulation in the development of Islamic banking financing in Indonesia. *International Journal of Islamic and Middle Eastern Finance and Management*, 12(5), 643–662. https://doi.org/10.1108/IMEFM-10-2018-0365

Nejad, M. G. (2022). Research on financial innovations: An interdisciplinary review. *International Journal of Bank Marketing*, 40(3), 578–612. https://doi.org/10.1108/IJBM-07-2021-0305

Nguyen, H. Y. (2020). Fintech in Vietnam and its regulatory approach. In *Perspectives in Law, Business and Innovation* (pp. 115–138). Springer. https://doi.org/10.1007/978-981-15-5819-1_7

Nikkel, B. (2020). Fintech forensics: Criminal investigation and digital evidence in financial technologies. *Forensic Science International: Digital Investigation*, 33, 200908. https://doi.org/10.1016/j.fsidi.2020.200908

Ntwiga, D. B. (2020). Technical efficiency in the Kenyan banking sector: Influence of fintech and banks collaboration. *Journal of Finance and Economics, 8*(1), 13–22.

Pazarbasioglu, C., Mora, A. G., Uttamchandani, M., Natarajan, H., Feyen, E., & Saal, M. (2020). *Digital financial services.* World Bank Group.

Rabbani, M. R., Abdulla, Y., Basahr, A., Khan, S., & Moh'd Ali, M. A. (2020). Embracing of fintech in Islamic finance in the post COVID era. *2020 International Conference on Decision Aid Sciences and Application (DASA)* (pp 1230–1234), IEEE.

Rabbani, M. R., Bashar, A., Nawaz, N., Karim, S., Ali, M. A. M., Khan, A., Rahiman, H., & Alam, S. (2021a). Exploring the role of Islamic fintech in combating the after-shocks of COVID-19: The open social innovation of the Islamic financial system. *Journal of Open Innovation: Technology, Market, and Complexity, 7*(136), 1–19. https://doi.org/10.3390/joitmc7020136

Rabbani, M. R., Ali, M. A. M., Rahiman, H. U., Atif, M., Zulfikar, Z., & Naseem, Y. (2021b). The response of Islamic financial service to the COVID-19 pandemic: The open social innovation of the financial system. *Journal of Open Innovation: Technology, Market, and Complexity, 7*(1), 1–18.

Rabbani, M. R. (2022). Fintech innovations, scope, challenges, and implications in Islamic Finance: A systematic analysis. *International Journal of Computing and Digital Systems, 11*(1), 1–28.

Rashid, M., & Hassan, M. K. (2014). Market values of Islamic banks and ethical identity. *American Journal of Islamic Social Sciences, 31*(2), 43–79.

Romānova, I., & Kudinska, M. (2016). Banking and fintech: A challenge or opportunity? *Contemporary issues in finance: Current challenges from across Europe. Contemporary Studies in Economic and Financial Analysis, 98*, 21–35. Emerald Group Publishing Limited. https://doi.org/10.1108/S1569-375920160000098002

Saeed, S. M., Abdeljawad, I., Hassan, M. K., & Rashid, M. (2021). (in press). Dependency of Islamic bank rates on conventional rates in a dual banking system: A trade-off between religious and economic fundamentals. *International Review of Economics & Finance.* https://doi.org/10.1016/j.iref.2021.09.013

Sahay, M. R., von Allmen, M. U. E., Lahreche, M. A., Khera, P., Ogawa, M. S., Bazarbash, M., & Beaton, M. K. (2020). *The promise of fintech: Financial inclusion in the post COVID-19 era.* International Monetary Fund.

Sharma, S. (2014). The pragmatic review on internet banking and associated services in India. *International Journal of Computing and Corporate Research, 4*(4), ID: 2249054XV4I4072014-20. http://ijccr.com/index.php/-vol-4-issue-4-july-2014

So, M. K. P. (2021). Robo-advising risk profiling through content analysis for sustainable development in the Hong Kong financial market. *Sustainability (Switzerland)*, *13*(3), 1–15. https://doi.org/10.3390/su13031306

Talwar, S., Dhir, A., Khalil, A., Mohan, G., & Islam, A. N. (2020). Point of adoption and beyond: Initial trust and mobile-payment continuation intention. *Journal of Retailing and Consumer Services*, *55*, 102086.

Truby, J. (2020). Fintech and the city: Sandbox 2.0 policy and regulatory reform proposals. *International Review of Law, Computers and Technology*, *34*(3), 277–309. https://doi.org/10.1080/13600869.2018.1546542

UNSGSA. (2018). *Igniting SDG progress through digital financial inclusion*, United Nations Secretary General's Special Advocate for inclusive finance, September 2018, retrieved from, https://sustainabledevelopment.un.org/content/documents/2655SDG_Compendium_Digital_Financial_Inclusion_September_2018.pdf

Yang, D. F., & Zhang, X. L. (2016). Review of the domestic crowdfunding industry development. *Journal of Service Science and Management*, *9*(1), 45–49. https://doi.org/10.4236/jssm.2016.91006

Yaya, R., Saud, I. M., Hassan, M. K., & Rashid, M. (2021). Governance of profit and loss sharing financing in achieving socio-economic justice. *Journal of Islamic Accounting and Business Research*, *12*(6), 814–830.

Yoon, D. E., Choudhury, T., Saha, A. K., & Rashid, M. (2021). Contagion risk: Cases of Islamic and emerging market banks. *International Journal of Islamic and Middle Eastern Finance and Management*, *15*(3), 481–505.

Yue, P., Korkmaz, A. G., Yin, Z., & Zhou, H. (2022). The rise of digital finance: Financial inclusion or debt trap? *Finance Research Letters*, *47*, 102406. https://doi.org/10.1016/j.frl.2021.102604

Fintech and the Art of Disruption

Mustafa Raza Rabbani, M. Kabir Hassan, Mohammad Dulal Miah, and Himani Grewal

1 Introduction

Financial Technology (Fintech) has enormously changed the way businesses were carried out in the financial market landscape (Barberis & Arner, 2016). It is growing rapidly every day as its range of offerings, services, innovations, and number of customers are increasing and

M. R. Rabbani (✉)
Department of Economics and Finance, College of Business administration, University of Bahrain, Sakhir, Bahrain
e-mail: mrabbani@uob.edu.bh

M. K. Hassan
Department of Economics and Finance, University of New Orleans, New Orleans, LA, USA
e-mail: mhassan@uno.edu

M. D. Miah
Department of Economics and Finance, University of Nizwa, Nizwa, Oman
e-mail: dulal@unizwa.edu.om

H. Grewal
Moradabad Institute of Technology, Moradabad, India

© The Author(s), under exclusive license to Springer Nature Switzerland AG 2022
M. K. Hassan et al. (eds.), *FinTech in Islamic Financial Institutions*, https://doi.org/10.1007/978-3-031-14941-2_2

entering to new markets and territories (DinarStandard, 2021). The Fintech disruption has brought us better financial management tools and techniques, more innovative and user-friendly customer experience using mobile payments, crowdfunding, P2P lending, digital banking, regulation technology (Regtech), Insurance technology (Insurtech), and all these benefits come at a relatively cheaper cost (Khan & Rabbani, 2020a; Rabbani, 2022; Rabbani et al., 2020). Fintech companies are proving to be better partners than their competitors to the banks and financial services companies with new and innovative financial services, better and improved products for consumers, and changing the financial services landscape forever. The use of Fintech-based financial services such as digital currency, e.g., bitcoin, intelligent buyer–seller automatically executable smart contract, digital and branchless banking, the implementation of artificial intelligence and natural language procession (NLP)-based services in delivering financial services, use of artificial intelligence and NLP for chatbot and interactive agent that understands the customer sentiments and financial behavior, use of financial technology in the insurance industry, Fintech-based solutions for the new, emerging, and established business that do not have access to traditional financial services in the form of crowdfunding and cryptocurrency, etc. has rendered the traditional financial services obsolete and old-fashioned (Atif et al., 2021; Hassan et al., 2020; Khan & Rabbani, 2020b; Mohammad et al., 2020; Rabbani, et al., 2020).

History of Fintech

Fintech is not something new it is virtually as old as the financial services industry. Arner et al. (2015) describe the history of Fintech in three different phases. Each of these phases experiences a different level of evolution, innovation, and transformation of different kinds in the way consumers interacted and engaged with the financial service providers.

Fintech 1.0 (1866–1967)
This was the first stage of the Fintech evolution which refers to a stage where infrastructure was built to support the globalization of the financial services. Some of these notable innovations in the financial services industry are regarded as the '*transatlantic cable*' (1866) and '*fedwire*' (1918) that facilitated the electronic fund transfer for the first-time using information technology. It might look very basic and elementary for

the current generation, but it was the first step toward a modern and innovative financial service industry that we observe today.

Fintech 2.0 (1967–2008)
Barclays installed its first ATM in 1967 and that marked the start of a more innovative and hassle-free financial services era. This period is also known as the start of analog to the digitization of financial services industry (Leong & Sung, 2018). The next revolution came in the form of the establishment of National Association of Securities Dealers Automated Quotations (NASDAQ), the world's first electronic stock exchange and Society for Worldwide Interbank Financial Telecommunication (SWIFT), a communication system for interstate money transfer.

The Fintech-based innovation continued in the 1980s and saw the rise of mainframe computers and the growth of online banking completely changed the way people used to look at the financial institutions (Ryan & Chan, 2005). The online revolution was a major shift in the way people looked at the financial institutions (Arner et al., 2015).

The 1990s brought the digital banking era where people started to manage their finance in different ways. Moreover, the launch of PayPal in 1998 completely changed the course of handling and making payments worldwide. Resultantly, the internet and information technology found more acceptance among the masses (Jackson, 2004). It looked as if the financial services industry was settled. Amidst the trend that innovations in the industry are peaking up, the global financial crisis of 2008 hit hard the finance world and changed the financial landscape forever by paving the way for the innovation and growth of disruptive technology of the modern era (Rabbani et al., 2021).

Fintech 3.0 (2008–present)
The global financial crisis is regarded as the point of breaking the trust between the banks and its customers as the world suffered an estimated loss of around US$2 trillion due to the failure of bank to safeguard the interest of the customers and other stakeholders (Crotty, 2009). The financial crisis combined with the regulatory changes by the global regulators paved the way for the new financial service providers (Jagtiani & John, 2018). Some of the most innovative and disruptive financial innovations witnessed after 2008 found their acceptance in the society. The launch of Bitcoin and other cryptocurrencies in 2009, Google and Apple pay services, Fintech apps like Stripe and PayTM experienced a widespread

Fig. 1 Evolution of fintech (*Source* [Arner et al., 2015])

popularity. Furthermore, Alibaba created facial recognition technology 'smile to pay'. The evolution of digital-only banks, like N26 and Ila bank, has significantly disrupted in the financial services industry (Pantielieieva et al., 2019).

Definition of Fintech and Financial Disruption

The history of Fintech goes as old as the history of the financial services industry. Since the global financial crisis of 2008, the new breed of Fintech has taken the centerstage which is more disruptive, efficient, and innovative and has almost replaced traditional financial services (Khan et al., 2022). Fintech is clearly a disruptive technology as it is regarded as a threat to banks and financial institutions (Choi et al., 2019). In reality, the financial services industry welcomes Fintech companies as the catalyst of innovation and treats them more like a partner than a competitor. An example of Fintech as disruptive technology could be from Mobile wallets and digital payment apps which facilitate a consumer to transfer money with a click of a button to stock trading apps which makes it possible to do trading by investing in stocks without visiting any stock market or stockbroker. Fintech is a disruptive innovation that has been wholeheartedly embraced by millions of users (Hasan et al., 2020; Saba et al., 2019). While the term 'disruption' carries a little negative inference, the reality is that when it is used in the financial sphere, it has completely different meaning and carries a novel meaning. Today, the demand for Fintech-based financial services is huge and Fintech startups are poised to reshape and redefine the future of the financial services industry (Jagtiani & John, 2018; Pwc, 2017). In fact, the global Fintech market is on a boom and COVID-19 pandemic has further enhanced the customer confidence in

Fintech-based financial services as it is expected to reach US$309.98 billion by 2024 up from US$127.66 billion in 2018 at a cumulative annual growth rate of around 24.8% (Newswire, 2016–2020).

Payment Apps, Lending Platforms, and Investment Apps

Fintech has made it possible to do any kind of financial operation with just a push of a button. It is now possible to pay electricity bills, mobile bills, borrow money from banks, or do crowdsourcing/P2P lending at greater ease and convenience. It is also possible to make an investment without the help of a broker or agent using smart apps. Fintech apps have made all these operations possible and all of these can be done with just a click of a mouse or push of a button (Blakstad & Allen, 2018; Jagtiani & Lemieux, 2018). A solid finance application such as 'Binance' or 'Crypto.com' can handle routine finance tasks such as buying and selling of cryptocurrencies, paying bills, track of spending and investing accounts, etc. (Morgan & Normand, 2021; Siswantoro et al., 2020). It can also be used to trade in stocks, follow your account in real-time, and can help you learn more about the market and build your portfolio of assets. Because of these possibilities and widespread importance, the mobile apps have become quite popular among the consumers (Morgan & Normand, 2021). Some of the popular mobile payment services, lending platforms, and investment apps are reviewed as follows:

Popular Types of Fintech Used By Consumers

Mobile Payment Services

It is also known as the 'mobile money', 'mobile money transfer', and 'mobile wallet'. It generally refers to the payment services regulated and controlled under financial regulation and the operation is performed by the smartphone device (Hossain et al., 2012). It is an alternative to earlier hard cash, check, or credit card. A buyer/consumer can now use his/her smart devices to transfer money to the seller's account. Although it is relatively new and still finding its feet among the rural consumers, it is quite popular among the urban consumers and widely accepted as the preferred medium of payment among the millennial population (Bazley et al., 2017; Kang, 2018). Mobile payment service is regarded as the twenty-first century technology (Alam et al., 2019). The mobile payment use is more popular among the Gen Z and millennial population. In the USA alone, more than 4 million out of 6.5 million new users per year from 2020 to 2025 belong to the millennial and young population (Morgan & Normand, 2021). Some of the popular mobile payment apps are described as follows

Cash App
It is a mobile payment service developed by Square Inc. for making payments to merchants via mobile phone. It is also known as the cash-free and customized debit card that facilitates the financial transactions online without using card. It also allows customers to transfer money from one consumer to another by using the mobile app. There are different versions of cash apps all over the world. 'Benefit Pay' and B-wallet in Bahrain, PayTM in India, and Tele Money in Saudi Arabia have some common characteristics. One of the distinguishing features of the cash app is that it doesn't need the traditional bank account to be linked to the bank. Instead, the customers are identified solely through their email address and phone number.

Apple Pay
It is the mobile digital wallet service available to Apple customers. It is the most widely used mobile payment application across the globe. It has 43.9 million users in 2021. Apple Pay is expected to grow by 14.4 million users per year between 2020 and 2025. The COVID-19 pandemic has certainly proved to be a boom for the contactless mobile payment services. According to the analyst firm 'e-marketer', the mobile payment usage increased by over 29% in 2020 due to the social distancing and other restrictions posed by the government (Naseri, 2021). Like apple pay, there are Samsung pay and google pay which are also quite popular among the users.

Lending Platforms
The lending platforms are the online lending and borrowing platforms where users seeking finance for their venture can upload their information and seek funding from crowdfunding and crowdsourcing. These lending platforms are responsible to match lenders with borrowers to help the individual or businesses in online borrowing/lending (Gutiérrez-Urtiaga & Sáez-Lacave, 2018). It is beneficial to both lenders and borrowers as the app provides the lenders multiple alternative avenues of investment to choose from and it allows the investors to pursue the

borrowers profile and based on the information provided make the investment decision (Bento et al., 2019). Most of the loans are lent through the crowdfunding, which means there are multiple lenders financing a particular borrower (Moysidou & Hausberg, 2020). The borrowers receive the unsecured loan at a competitive rate of interest without support from banks and formal financial institutions in hassle freeway and without much documents and formalities.

As depicted in the figure below, the lending platform also keeps records of the fund raisers. A fund raiser can have and start more than one project. However, the proposed system maintains a record of success or failure and all history of his/her projects and credit scores over the time. Interested investors or lenders can access this information to be sure about his/her history and reputation. This process aims to tackle the issue of borrower's reputation and generates confidence about the borrowers and their credit scores. Some of the popular lending platforms are described as follows.

Lending Tree

Lending tree was founded in 1996 in Charlotte, North Carolina, USA. The lending tree does not charge any service fee from the borrowers or the lenders for the services of matching lenders with the borrowers. It is an online lending platform headquartered in the USA. It allows the borrower to register on the platform and seek funding from multiple sources. It allows borrowers to meet with the potential multiple lenders and find the loans at suitable terms and conditions.

Better

Better was founded in 2014 with the objective of redefining the whole mortgage process. It started in partnership with 'Avex funding'—a California-based mortgage company. In 2015, it acquired the originator and partner 'Avex funding'. Now, Better mortgage corporation provides home loans, real estate services, insurance policies, and settlement services. Better is also rated A+ with the better business bureau and the app has received BBB accreditation. Better works very much like the other lending platforms with the only difference being that it does not charge the lending fee, so the closing cost with the Better is cheaper than the other mortgage companies. Since better does not charge any interest or commission from the borrower as they sell their loans to the end users.

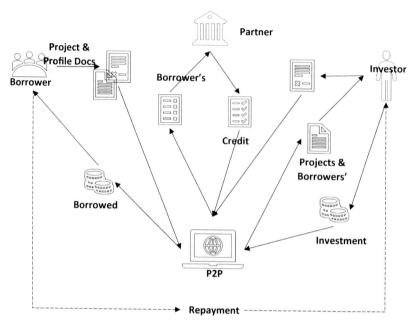

Fig. 2 Crowdfunding platform (*Source* Adapted from Rabbani et al. [2021])

The better uses technology to match borrowers with the investors who are interested in buying the loan from the borrowers. This process allows the borrower to find the loans at the cheapest rate possible and it brings a unique financial solution by getting compensated through the RSUs.

Besides these two, there are other lending platforms operating in the market which directly interact with lenders and borrowers. Most popular among them are, perform, Upstart, Prosper, Funding Circle Payoff, etc.

Investment Apps
Investment apps allow investors to buy and sell securities online. They are generally simple to use and designed in such a way that is more engaging for the less qualified person. The investment apps are not only easy to use but also provide free financial advice to the users in addition to providing some additional financial services. These apps require a very small initial investment and provide various alternative avenues of investment to the users. There are many investment apps available like e-trade, Sofi, Fidelity

Table 1 Popular investment apps comparison

Points	Sofi	Robinhood	E*Trade
Fess	0% on trading and 1.25% on Cryptocurrency	It requires 0% fees for trading	It requires 0% for trading, 0.30% for automated accounts and 0.35% to 1.25% for managed accounts
Investment types	The investors can create investment account for Stocks, Cryptocurrencies, and ETFs	Provides options for investing in ETFs, stocks, Cryptocurrencies, and ADR	Provides options for investing in ETFs, stocks, Cryptocurrencies, bonds, mutual funds, Certificate of deposit, and futures
Minimum balance required	$0	$0	$0 (US$500 for core portfolio)

Go, Robinhood, Acorns, Ellevest, etc. Most popular among them are described and compared below (Table 1).

It can be observed from the above table that almost all the investment apps are having same characteristics and provide competitive services. The investors can buy and sell securities without paying any fees. There is no minimum account balance to maintain, and it provides various investment accounts based on the investors' need.

2 Cryptocurrency

In 2008, a Japanese named 'Satoshi Nakamoto' (it is believed that Satoshi Nakamoto is his pseudo name) published a paper titled 'Bitcoin: Peer to Peer Electronic Cash System', which revolutionized the whole finance and outlined the creation of a new currency called 'Bitcoin' (Ballis & Drakos, 2020; Guhan et al., 2018). It is believed that the global financial crisis has facilitated the innovation of cryptocurrency to cater to the need for an alternative currency (Ahmed et al., 2020). Cryptocurrency is considered the most sensational financial innovations of the twenty-first century (Gómez & Demmler, 2018). It has created a lot of buzz in the global financial market and has become a phenomenon in recent years (Abubakar et al., 2019). A Cryptocurrency or 'Crypto' is a digital currency that can be used to buy and sell goods and services, but unlike traditional currency, cryptocurrency uses an online ledger secured by the technology called

Table 2 Major Cryptocurrencies comparison

	Bitcoin (BTC)	Litecoin (LTC)	Ethereum (ETH)
Market capitalization	The market capitalization of Bitcoin is US$596.86 billion (as on June 6, 2022)	The market capitalization of Litecoin is US$4.52 billion (as on June 6, 2022)	The market cap is US$224.65 Billion (as on June 6, 2022)
Current market price	Launched in 2008 and is currently selling at US$32,600 (as on 06/06/2022)	Launched on October 7 2011, and is currently selling at US$64.80 (as on 06/06/2022)	Launched on 30 July 2015 and is currently selling at US$1876 as on 06/06/2022
Data source	crypto.com	crypto.com	crypto.com

Cryptography. There are more than 6000 cryptocurrencies trading in the market currently with the total capitalization reaching up to 1000 Billion USD in May 2021 (Benedetti & Kostovetsky, 2021). Some of the more popular Cryptocurrencies are reviewed as follows (Table 2).

3 Benefits and Risks to Consumers

The rampaging COVID-19 has forced people to maintain social distancing and closure of business and production facilities. Such measures have boosted digital cash transfer and mobile payment Fintech platforms. Hence, it can be perceived that the benefits of Fintech have never been so evident that emerged during the time of COVID-19 (Alawi et al., 2022; Khan et al., 2022). It has provided multiple benefits to the consumers in terms of giving many alternative choices, access to world-class financial services with compliance and increased security at lower cost, higher speed, convenience, and with more transparency. The use of new technology like Blockchain has revolutionized the finance world in terms of delivering process efficiency, enhancing user experience, reducing cost, and reducing risk in the business (Jreisat et al., 2021; Rabbani et al., 2021). Fintech comes with all these benefits to the customers but not without risks. In this section, we highlight the benefits and risks of Fintech to consumers.

Benefits

Low Cost
Fintech has enabled the integration of multiple technology and process like linking multiple bank accounts and cards in a single interface. This process empowers Fintech to deliver efficient service at the lowest possible cost (Banna et al., 2021). Unlike traditional financial institutions, Fintech startups and solution providers do not charge superfluous fees (Jagtiani & John, 2018). Using Fintech like BFC (Bahrain Financing Company) app, customers can transfer money across the globe without worrying about heavy conversion fees (Selim, 2020).

Improved Compliance and Security
Due to its unique positioning as a disruptive technological innovation and disruptor, Fintech easily traverses the local regulatory requirement and legal hurdles. Fintech startups put more emphasis on maintaining a seamless compliance department to ensure that the transactions are vetted properly. It uses next-generation IT systems that helps them identify glitches and rectify them on real-time basis unlike the traditional financial institutions that have no such system.

High Speed and Convenience
Technological advancements such as Fintech have made transactions and processes much faster and efficient. Traditional customers' needs to wait the whole day standing in the bank queue to complete a transaction. Certain transactions were allowed to be performed within a stipulated time. Fintech has completely removed such restrictions as transactions can be performed at any time and from anywhere.

Stimulus Payments to Consumers
As the world is fighting the negative effects brought about by the COVID-19 pandemic, poverty worldwide increased manifold due to the lockdown restrictions and loss of job. The situation became grave and governments and civil societies had to come up to help the poor and affected. In this situation, financial technology became the lifeline in distributing the stimulus and aid packages. By teaming with established financial institutions and governmental agencies, Fintech startups have played a key role in saving millions of lives by offering aids.

Direct Cash Payments
During the pandemic, few things worked marvelously for the vulnerable and affected, one of them is the hard cash. Several organizations across the globe used Fintech-based applications to transfer cash and incentives directly to customers electronic wallets. There were many programs like 'Project 100' in the USA, to provide 100 million USD directly to customer's account. Other such initiatives include, 'Spot me' initiative by the popular Fintech provider 'Chime' to direct access to the stimulus packages.

Helping Small and Medium Enterprises (SMEs)
The lockdown and social distancing measures imposed during the pandemic brought tough time for the SMEs. The use of Fintech apps peaked during recent months as restaurants and other SMEs survived due to the use of Fintech and mobile payment apps. For example, in Bahrain, the government launched 'Benefit Pay' a mobile payment app for contactless payment during the pandemic. Restaurants and supermarkets offer contactless and cashless delivery during the pandemic and Fintech played a pivotal role in reaching out to the customers.

Financing Became More Obtainable
Fintech-enabled solutions, like crowdfunding and P2P lending, have revolutionized the finance industry with easy and hassle-free financing opportunities (Rabbani et al., 2021). The traditional financing methods make it difficult for the startups and less established organizations, which usually cannot provide documents required by the mainstream financial institutions, to obtain funding. Fintech, like crowdfunding and P2P lending, has made it easy and convenience for SMEs to avail loan facilities.

4 REGULATION

Fintech has taken the whole finance industry by storm as many established financial institutions are still not able to make changes to the existing setup to embrace this disruption. Since it is growing at a rapid rate, the potential threats of fraud, theft, money laundering, and cybersecurity are on the rise (Hendershott et al., 2021). These risks have proved to be great challenges for policymakers and regulators as well (Fenwick & Vermeulen, 2020; Ivanova, 2019). There are many views with regards to regulating Fintech. The view suggests that these startups tend to bring a huge risk;

so they should be heavily regulated to protect the customers from any potential fraud or security lapse (Arner et al., 2019; Ribisel, 2018). Other View suggests that since these startups are based on innovation, heavy regulation can hamper their innovative behavior. The regulators must be soft in regulating Fintech as opposed to the traditional banks (Razak et al., 2021).

The regulatory bodies can adopt one or more of the following approaches in regulating Fintech.

a. Case by case restraint: In this case, the regulators allow Fintech-based financial services to hit the financial market with extensive oversight. Based on the need to regulate the product the regulating bodies bring the regulation to protect against any potential mishappening (Söylemez, 2019).

b. Structured Experimental Approach: Under this approach, the Fintech products and financial services are tested under the specified control mechanism. It enables the Fintech firms to test the products and services with minimum regulatory requirements.

c. Single Window: It allows Fintech products and services to enter the market under a simplified framework.

d. Hands off: Under this framework, the Fintech products go to the market without any regulatory requirements, and it is intervened later by the regulatory authority.

Besides these regulatory frameworks, the regulators can use different regulatory tools to regulate a Fintech. Commonly used tools are described as follows.

a. Wait and See: Fintech-based innovations are allowed to be launched in the market without any restrictions and their performances are monitored over the time to see if they fit into the environmental and social requirements. If they present any risk, then strict rules are brought in to control them.

b. Test and learn: The products are tested in a live environment to see their reaction and bring appropriate regulation with involvement from regulators.

c. Waiver/exemption: Exemption is granted for certain types of innovations which are good for the environment and bring positive changes into the society.
d. Regulatory sandbox: A virtual regulatory environment where the innovations are tested in a virtual time-bound manner. It is appropriate for the markets with great supervisory capability with more active and non-licensed players.

5 Conclusion

The chapter takes a comprehensive look at the disruption called Fintech. It started with a thorough discussion on the history of Fintech. Then Fintech is defined in the modern context. Then the chapter provides an overview of the payment apps, lending platforms, and investment Apps. Lending platforms like P2P lending and crowdfunding are defined and described. The chapter provides a discussion on cryptocurrency. It is concluded that the cryptocurrency can be regarded as the most disruptive innovation of the twenty-first century.

Fintech has come as a blessing for many customers and entrepreneurs. There is no denying that it all started way before the ongoing pandemic, but it proved to be a blessing for the Fintech startups. The disruptive technology has brought positive changes in the society in terms of delivering valuable stimulus and financial aid to the vulnerable and affectioned by the pandemic.

The findings of the study suggests that the Fintech disruption has been a blessing in disguise for the overall growth and development of the finance community. The Fintech disruption has brought many benefits for the society including enhancing efficiency and transparency in financial transactions by bringing better financial management tools, mobile payments, P2P lending, and some fast-forwarding solutions like Regtech and Insurtech.

References

Abubakar, M., Hassan, M. K., & Haruna, M. A. (2019). Cryptocurrency tide and Islamic finance development: Any issue? In *International Finance Review*. https://doi.org/10.1108/S1569-376720190000020019

Ahmed, S., Grobys, K., & Sapkota, N. (2020). Profitability of technical trading rules among cryptocurrencies with privacy function. *Finance Research Letters*, 35. https://doi.org/10.1016/j.frl.2020.101495

Alam, N., Gupta, L., & Zameni, A. (2019). *Fintech and Islamic finance: Digitalization, development and disruption*. Digitalization, Development and Disruption. Springer International Publishing. https://doi.org/10.1007/978-3-030-24666-2

Alawi, S. M., Karim, S., Meero, A. A., Rabbani, M. R., & Naeem, M. A. (2022). Information transmission in regional energy stock markets. *Environmental Science and Pollution Research*, 1–13.

Arner, D. W, Gibson, E., & Barberis, J. (2019). FinTech and its regulation in Hong Kong. In *states, international organizations and strategic partnerships* (pp. 431–453). Edward Elgar Publishing Ltd. https://www.scopus.com/inward/record.uri?eid=2-s2.0-85088021481&partnerID=40&md5=0395daa7b586ec5e98346f9d74bab3ac

Arner, D. W., Barberis, J., & Buckley, R. P. (2015). The evolution of fintech: A new post-crisis paradigm? *Georgetown Journal of International Law*, 47, 1271.

Atif, M., Hassan, M. K., Rabbani, M. R., & Khan, S. (2021). (in press). Islamic fintech: The digital transformation bringing sustainability in Islamic finance. In *COVID-19 and Islamic Social Finance*.

Ballis, A., & Drakos, K. (2020). Testing for herding in the cryptocurrency market. *Finance Research Letters*, 33. https://doi.org/10.1016/j.frl.2019.06.008

Banna, H., Kabir Hassan, M., & Rashid, M. (2021). Fintech-based financial inclusion and bank risk-taking: Evidence from OIC Countries. *Journal of International Financial Markets, Institutions and Money*, 75(October), 1–20. https://doi.org/10.1016/j.intfin.2021.101447

Barberis, J., & Arner, D. W. (2016). Fintech in China: From shadow banking to P2P lending. In *New Economic Windows* (pp. 69–96). Springer-Verlag Italia s.r.l. https://doi.org/10.1007/978-3-319-42448-4_5

Bazley, J., Rayner, C. S., & Power, A. P. (2017). Zoona mobile money: Investing for impact (cases A and B). *Emerald Emerging Markets Case Studies*, 7(2), 1–27. https://doi.org/10.1108/EEMCS-06-2016-0122

Benedetti, H., & Kostovetsky, L. (2021). Digital tulips? Returns to investors in initial coin offerings. *Journal of Corporate Finance*, 66(101786).

Bento, N., Gianfrate, G., & Thoni, M. H. (2019). Crowdfunding for sustainability ventures. *Journal of Cleaner Production*, 237. https://doi.org/10.1016/j.jclepro.2019.117751

Blakstad, S., & Allen, R. (2018). *Fintech revolution: Universal inclusion in the new financial ecosystem*. Universal Inclusion in the New Financial Ecosystem. Springer International Publishing. https://doi.org/10.1007/978-3-319-76014-8

Choi, H., Jung, Y., & Choi, Y. (2019). Understanding of the fintech phenomenon in the beholder's eyes in South Korea. *Asia Pacific Journal of Information Systems*, 29(1), 117–143. https://doi.org/10.14329/apjis.2019.29.1.117

Crotty, J. (2009). Structural causes of the global financial crisis: A critical assessment of the 'new financial architecture.' *Cambridge Journal of Economics*, 33(4), 563–580.

DinarStandard. (2021). Islamic fintech report 2018: Current landscape & path forward. In *Dubai Islamic Economy Development Centre*. https://www.dinarstandard.com/wp-content/uploads/2018/12/Islamic-Fintech-Report-2018.pdf

Fenwick, M., & Vermeulen, E. P. M. (2020). Fintech, overcoming friction and new models of financial regulation. In *Perspectives in Law, Business and Innovation* (pp. 205–225). Springer. https://doi.org/10.1007/978-981-15-5819-1_11

Gómez, G. L., & Demmler, M. (2018). Social currencies and cryptocurrencies: Characteristics, risks and comparative analysis. *CIRIEC-Espana Revista De Economia Publica, Social y Cooperativa*, 93, 265–291. https://doi.org/10.7203/CIRIEC-E.93.10978

Guhan, S., Arumugham, S., Janakiraman, S., Adem, S., Halaburda, H., Rikken, O., Janssen, M., Kwee, Z., Elkatawneh, H. H., Science, O., Outlook, I., Vs, C., Database, D., Lemieux, V. L., Markets, C., Cases, U., Macilamani, S., Specialist, G. B., Al-megren, S., ... Yousefi, Z. (2018). Secure provenance using an authenticated data structure approach. *Computers and Security*. https://doi.org/10.1109/BigDataCongress.2017.85

Gutiérrez-Urtiaga, M., & Sáez-Lacave, M.-I. (2018). The promise of reward crowdfunding. *Corporate Governance: An International Review*, 26(5), 355–373. https://doi.org/10.1111/corg.12252

Hasan, R., Hassan, M. K., & Aliyu, S. (2020). Fintech and Islamic finance: Literature review and research agenda. *International Journal of Islamic Economics and Finance (IJIEF)*, 1(2), 75–94. https://doi.org/10.18196/ijief.2122

Hassan, M. K., Rabbani, M. R., & Ali, M. A. (2020). Challenges for the Islamic finance and banking in post COVID era and the role of fintech. *Journal of Economic Cooperation and Development*, 43(3), 93–116.

Hendershott, T., Zhang, X., Leon Zhao, J., & Zheng, Z. (2021). Fintech as a game changer: Overview of research frontiers. *Information Systems Research*, 32(1), 1–17. https://doi.org/10.1287/isre.2021.0997

Irum S., Rehana K., & Imran S. C. (2019). Fintech and Islamic finance-challenges and opportunities. *Review of Economics and Development Studies*, 5(4), 581–590. https://doi.org/10.26710/reads.v5i4.887

Ivanova, P. (2019). Cross-border regulation and fintech: Are transnational cooperation agreements the right way to go? *Uniform Law Review*, 24(2), 367–395. https://doi.org/10.1093/ulr/unz021
Jackson, E. M. (2004). *The PayPal wars: Battles with eBay, the media, the mafia, and the rest of planet earth*. World Ahead Publishing.
Jagtiani, J., & Lemieux, C. (2018). Do fintech lenders penetrate areas that are underserved by traditional banks? *Journal of Economics and Business, 100*, 43–54. https://doi.org/10.1016/j.jeconbus.2018.03.001
Jagtiani, J., & John, K. (2018). Fintech: The impact on consumers and regulatory responses. *Journal of Economics and Business, 100*(November 2018), 1–6. https://doi.org/10.1016/j.jeconbus.2018.11.002
Jreisat, A., Rabbani, M. R., Bashar, A., Ali, M. A. M., & AlAbbas, A. (2021). Is fintech valuation an art of science? Exploring the innovative methods for the valuation of fintech startups. *2021 International Conference on Decision Aid Sciences and Application (DASA)*, (pp. 922–925). IEEE.
Kang, J. (2018). Mobile payment in fintech environment: Trends, security challenges, and services. *Human-Centric Computing and Information Sciences, 8*(1). https://doi.org/10.1186/s13673-018-0155-4
Khan, S., & Rabbani, M. R. (2020a). In depth analysis of blockchain, cryptocurrency and sharia compliance. *International Journal of Business Innovation and Research, 1*(1), 1. https://doi.org/10.1504/ijbir.2020.10033066
Khan, S., & Rabbani, M. R. (2020b). Chatbot as Islamic Finance Expert (CaIFE) When finance meets artificial intelligence. *Proceedings of the 2020b 4th International Symposium on Computer Science and Intelligent Control*, 1–5.
Khan, M. S., Rabbani, M. R., Hawaldar, I. T., & Bashar, A. (2022). Determinants of behavioral intentions to use Islamic financial technology: An empirical assessment. *Risks, 10*(6), 114.
Leong, K., & Sung, A. (2018). Fintech (Financial Technology): What is it and how to use technologies to create business value in fintech way? *International Journal of Innovation, Management and Technology, 9*(2), 74–78.
Mohammad, K. S., Mustafa, & Yannis. (2020). An artificial intelligence and NLP based Islamic fintech model combining Zakat and Qardh-Al-Hasan for countering the adverse impact of COVID 19 on SMEs and individuals. *International Journal of Economics and Business Administration, VIII*(Issue 2), 351–364. https://doi.org/10.35808/ijeba/466
Morgan, J. P., & Normand, J. (2021). *Perspectives digital transformation and the rise of fintech*, (Issue February).
Moysidou, K., & Hausberg, J. P. (2020). In crowdfunding we trust: A trust-building model in lending crowdfunding. *Journal of Small Business Management, 58*(3), 511–543. https://doi.org/10.1080/00472778.2019.1661682

Naseri, R. N. N. (2021). What is a population in online shopping research? A perspective from Malaysia. *Turkish Journal of Computer and Mathematics Education (TURCOMAT), 12*(4), 654–658.

Newswire, P. R. (2016). Global fintech investment market 2016–2020. Lon-Reportbuyer.

Pantielieieva, N., Krynytsia, S., Khutorna, M., & Potapenko, L. (2019). Fintech, transformation of financial intermediation and financial stability. In *2018 International Scientific-Practical Conference on Problems of Infocommunications Science and Technology, PIC S and T 2018* (pp. 553–559). https://doi.org/10.1109/INFOCOMMST.2018.8632068

Pwc. (2017). Fintech's growing influence on financial services. In *Global Fintech Report*.

Rabbani, M. R., Abdulla, Y., Basahr, A., Khan, S., & Ali, M. A. M. (2020a). Embracing of fintech in Islamic finance in the post COVID era. *2020 International Conference on Decision Aid Sciences and Application (DASA)* (pp. 1230–1234). IEEE.

Rabbani, M. R., Abdulla, Y., Basahr, A., & Khan Moh'd Ali, M. A., S. (2020b). Embracing of fintech in Islamic finance in the post COVID era. *International Conference on Decision Aid Sciences and Application (DASA), 2020*, 1230–1234.

Rabbani, M. R. (2022a). (in press). COVID-19 and its impact on supply chain financing and the role of Islamic fintech: Evidence from GCC Countries. *International Journal of Agile Systems and Management (IJASM)*

Rabbani, M. R. (2022b). Fintech innovations, scope, challenges, and implications in Islamic Finance: A systematic analysis. *International Journal of Computing and Digital Systems, 11*(1), 1–28.

Rabbani, M. R., Bashar, A., Nawaz, N., Karim, S., Ali, M. A. M., Khan, A., Rahiman, H., & Alam, S. (2021). Exploring the role of Islamic fintech in combating the after-shocks of COVID-19: The open social innovation of the Islamic financial system. *Journal of Open Innovation: Technology, Market, and Complexity, 7*, 136.

Razak, M. I. A., Dali, N. A. M., Dhillon, G., & Manaf, A. W. A. (2021). Fintech in Malaysia: An appraisal to the need of shariah-compliant regulation. *Pertanika Journal of Social Sciences and Humanities, 28*(4), 3223–3233. https://doi.org/10.47836/PJSSH.28.4.40

Ribisel, L. (2018). *Fintech regulation: How do regulators react to technology in financial services? A comparative study*. Jusletter IT.

Ryan, S., & Chan, S. (2005). The evolution of online banking. *IABE-2005 Annual Conference, 87*.

Selim, M. (2020). The effects of eliminating Riba in foreign currency transactions by introducing global fintech network. *International Journal of Islamic and*

Middle Eastern Finance and Management, 14(3), 506–523. https://doi.org/10.1108/IMEFM-01-2020-0035

Shafayat Hossain, M., Kabir, A. M., Mazumder, P., Aziz, A., Hassan, M., & Zunaid Baten, M. (2012). Long distance appliance control using mobile short messaging service and internet in parallel. *2012 International Conference on Informatics, Electronics and Vision, ICIEV 2012.* https://doi.org/10.1109/ICIEV.2012.6317360

Siswantoro, D., Handika, R., & Mita, A. F. (2020). The requirements of cryptocurrency for money, an Islamic view. *Heliyon, 6*(1). https://doi.org/10.1016/j.heliyon.2020.e03235

Söylemez, Y. (2019). Fintech ecosystem and banking: The case of Turkey. *In Handbook of Research on Strategic Fit and Design in Business Ecosystems.* https://doi.org/10.4018/978-1-7998-1125-1.ch014

A Fintech-Based Zakat Model Using Artificial Intelligence

Mustafa Raza Rabbani, M. Kabir Hassan,
Shahnawaz Khan, and Aishath Muneeza

1 Introduction

The COVID-19, the largest health crisis in the modern times, is turning into a global economic and financial crisis. The pandemic could cause a loss of about 10% of the global Gross Domestic Products (GDP),

---

M. R. Rabbani (✉)
Department of Economics and Finance, College of Business Administration, University of Bahrain, Sakhir, Bahrain
e-mail: mrabbani@uob.edu.bh

M. K. Hassan
Department of Economics and Finance, University of New, Orleans, New Orleans, LA, USA
e-mail: mhassan@uno.edu

S. Khan
Engineering, Design, and Information & Communications Technology, Bahrain Polytechnic, Isa Town, Bahrain
e-mail: shahnawaz.rs.cse@itbhu.ac.in

A. Muneeza
International Centre for Education in Islamic Finance, Kuala Lumpur, Malaysia
e-mail: muneeza@inceif.org

© The Author(s), under exclusive license to Springer Nature Switzerland AG 2022
M. K. Hassan et al. (eds.), *FinTech in Islamic Financial Institutions*, https://doi.org/10.1007/978-3-031-14941-2_3

leading to a closure of millions of businesses and rendering more than 200 million people unemployed (Le et al., 2021). Economists are speculating that this pandemic-born financial crisis could be more devastating than the great depression of the 1930s (Abakah et al., 2021). It has already created enormous human suffering. As of January 24, 2022, 8 P.M. GMT, more than 351 million people have already got the direct infection and around 5,600,000 people have lost their lives due to this novel coronavirus (Panakaje et al., 2022).

There is a need to identify the immediate concerns and work on it to minimize the damage to the society (Fu & Mishra, 2022). A varied and comprehensive set of policy interventions from various sections of the society, including government, entrepreneurs, general public, and policymakers are required to meet this colossal challenge. The government and other participants should immediately try and develop a comprehensive health support system and the finance community must assess and respond to the social and economic impact this virus is going to bring to the society. It has also ignited actions from the institutions and people eager to help (Hashmi et al., 2021). The present study proposes a solution based on Islamic finance to tackle the social and economic problem created by the virus. Islamic finance offers a wide range of financial services well-suited to each stage of pandemic COVID-19. One such important Islamic Financial Service Zakat can be the potential warrior in fight against the economic consequences of COVID-19 (Khan et al., 2021b).

The objectives of this chapter are to evaluate the economic impact of COVID-19 on poor and economically insecure by shedding light into various stages of COVID-19 pandemic where Zakat can be utilized and proposing an Artificial Intelligence (AI) and Natural Language Processing (NLP)-based Islamic Fintech model for helping poor and economically insecure section of society affected by the COVID-19.

This chapter is divided into five sections. Followed by this introduction, section two discusses poverty and COVID-19 while section three focuses on the impact of COVID-19 on poor and vulnerable sections of the society. Section four analyzes *Maqasid Al-Sharia* (objectives of Islamic law) and economic potential of *Zakat* in helping poor during pandemic. Section five discusses the details of the proposed Fintech model for Zakat using AI followed by the conclusion.

2 POVERTY AND COVID-19

Poverty creates social disharmony (Moser, 1998). In simplest of the word, the poverty can be defined as the state of being poor with no financial resources and being dependent on others to satisfy their needs (Brady & Bostic, 2015). The United Nations sees poverty as the state of deprivation reflected in terms of low consumption level, low health condition and lack of housing facility, and lack of access to the education and learning (Anser et al., 2020). Thus, poverty is not only about lack of accessibility to food, cloth, and shelter but also about lack of access to credit facilities (Hassan & Khan, 2007).

Understanding poverty is significant from the point of view of the current pandemic as it revolves around the 'income'. Most of the analysis of poverty revolves around the numerical parameters of having resources or not having resources (Hassan & Saleem, 2017). But there is a need to go beyond the simple measure of money and study the poverty from the other factors than the absence of money (Bashir, 2018; Haque & Yamao, 2011).

The COVID-19 pandemic is unique in another sense that, in the modern era there is no other example of such as the mass transmission of disease (Killeen & Kiware, 2020). Despite the fact that technological innovation has been on the rise in the last 100 years and still the world is not able to control or eliminate it as it happened in other health emergency like EBOLA and SARS (Bin-Nashwan et al., 2020). It is a fact that the continuous spread of the deadly COVID-19 and slow progress of the vaccination will push many people into the state of starvation, besides the increase in corruption, crime, and related criminal activities will get a push (Hassan et al., 2020, 2021).

In addition to its immediate effect on health and lives, coronavirus continues to take its toll on everyone especially on the economically poor and vulnerable section of the society due to the state-imposed lockdown and restrictions to control the spread of virus (Rabbani et al., 2021a; 2021b). Mehler et al. from the world bank analyze the data related to the economic impact of COVID-19 and he concludes that the current pandemic is likely to cause the increase in global poverty first time since 1988 and it is expected to go further up. It is expected to take 49 million people into extreme poverty and 23 million of these figures are expected to be from Sub-Sahara Africa region and 16 million from Asia. The global report on food crises reveals that due to COVID-19 it is expected that an additional 130 million people could be added to the starvation by the end of 2020. We already have about 135 million people who are at the crisis level of food security and starvation in 2019 (Food Crisis Report, 2020). It is hard for the poor to follow the government's restriction measures of social quarantine, lockdown, and isolation. Immediate strategies to minimize the economic impact of the pandemic on poor and vulnerable should be introduced (Panakaje et al., 2022; Rabbani, 2022).

As it can be also seen from Fig. 1 the share of the world population living on $ 1.9 per day will increase to 8.6% in 2020 from 8.2% in 2019 or in other words it will jump from 632 to 665 million people. The COVID-19-related reason for global poverty and its impact on poor is massive as it is expected that it will increase the global poverty by 0.7%. The other way to understand above figure from the World Bank is that the COVID-19 and its associated reasons will push 49 million people into the extreme poverty. All these estimations and projections are having high degree of uncertainty as so far the most affected countries due to COVID-19 are the advanced and relatively developed countries where there is very less number of absolute poverty (Abdullah & Rabbani, 2021; Habeeb et al., 2021).

Fig. 1 COVID-19 and global poverty (*Source* www.worldbank.org)

3 Impact of COVID-19 on Poor and Vulnerable Section of the Society

The economic shock of the COVID-19 can affect the poor and already vulnerable section of the society in a massive way (Jreisat et al., 2021b). It can affect their well-being and welfare through the following channels.

Impact on Wage Income

- The wage income of the daily wage earners and laborers has been a massive hit due to the lockdown and stoppage in production activities (Habeeb et al., 2021).
- The direct income has also been affected adversely due to the illness and taking care of the sick family member or relatives (Sharma et al., 2020).
- The direct effect on labor and salaried class has also been because of the loss of employment due to lay off, decline in quantity of work, etc. (Aday & Aday, 2020).
- The indirect effect on labor income has been due to the decrease in aggregate demand disruptions in the channels of distribution resulting into the closure of factories or due to restriction of mobility, etc (Rabbani, 2022).

Impact on Consumption

- There has been a direct impact on consumption due to an increase in healthcare expenditure and on already credit-strained households (Adekoya & Oliyide, 2021; Rehman et al., 2021).
- Disruption in the channels of disruption resulting into the increase in prices of the certain necessary commodities such as, medicines and food items has impacted the consumption adversely (Bresser-Pereira, 2020).

Disruption in Services

- Disruption in travel and transportation, closure of hotels, and due to quarantine have adversely affected the tourism and hospitality industry (Ozili, 2020).

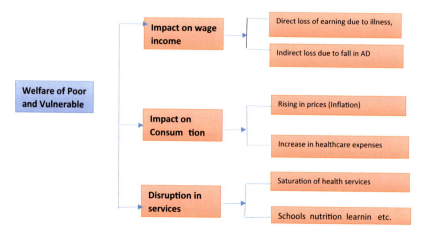

Fig. 2 Short-term impact of COVID-19 on poor (*Source* Author's own compilation)

- Due to the focus on COVID-19 by the health officials, it has resulted into the increase in non-communicable and other disease (Sharif et al., 2020).
- Suspension of classes in schools and universities posing challenge for the administration for student retention and for the students the problem of learning and nutrition (Khan et al., 2021a, b).

The above channels are reflected in Fig. 2.

4 Maqasid Al-Sharia and the Economic Potential of Zakat in Helping the Poor During Pandemic

As the world economists respond to the COVID-19 and economic shock created by the novel coronavirus. There is a need to engage a varied and wide-ranging set of participants to address this massive challenge. The virus has created a massive human, financial, and emotional sufferings (Panakaje et al., 2022; Rabbani et al., 2021). Islamic finance can be one of the most important stakeholder in response to the COVID-19 pandemic through a broad range of ethical and moral financial services directly directed toward helping the poor and vulnerable (Naeem et al., 2021; Rabbani et al., 2021). Islamic view of poverty alleviation is based on the Islamic principle of social justice, financial inclusion, reduction in inequality of income, and belief in Almighty Allah (Naeem et al., 2021). Islamic finance defines the poverty as a situation where a person is not able to fulfill any of his following five obligations (Adewale & Haron, 2017; Yap, 2011): religious duties; physical self; intellect or knowledge; offspring; and wealth.

Islamic finance has some unique financial instruments, such as *Zakat*, *Qardh-Al-Hasan*, *Awqaf*, etc. which can act as the emergency support programs by the various governments and NGOs to help the COVID affected people (Rabbani et al., 2021). This section discusses Zakat as the poverty alleviation and emergency support Islamic financial service to help the COVID-19 affected poor and vulnerable section of society. The present chapter also proposes an AI and NLP-based Islamic Fintech model for Zakat to be used during and post-COVID to overcome the adverse economic effect of it (Rabbani, 2022; Rabbani et al., 2020). The proposed model will not only help in overcoming the adversities of COVID-19 but also help in achieving the broader objective of financial inclusion, social justice, and social welfare.

Zakat is one of the five basic pillars and only compulsory financial obligation in Islam. It is the only economic and financial obligation on all well-off Muslims. It is very unique financial instrument in Islamic finance as it transfers wealth from rich to poor. As Zakat is one of the five pillar, and there are serious consequences for non-payment and denial of payment of Zakat, anyone denying the payment of Zakat ceases to be the Muslim (Mohammad et al., 2020; Rabbani et al., 2021). Zakat is mentioned 82 times in Holy Qura'an and importance of it can be understood from the fact that out of which it has been mentioned more than 30 times along with Salah (The second pillar). It can be explained as per the Holy Qur'an as-

Explanation from Verses of Holy Qura'an: The compulsory and obligatory donation from the well-off Muslims to the poor Muslims. It is treated as the religious obligation to tax. In Islam the origin meaning of Zakat is taken as to purify, to pure or to increase. Islam treats social wellbeing of the poor and deprived at the front and included Zakat as the part of the faith. (Ahmad & Mahmood, 2009; Noor et al., 2011)

There are various opinions regarding the *Nisab* of the Zakat as which articles should be included for Zakat calculation. *Nisab* means to be eligible to pay Zakat the one's wealth must be over the prescribed threshold. Zakat for *Zakatable* assets, as established by the Holy Prophet Muhammad (Peace be upon him) must be calculated based on the 2.5% of the total monetary value of the assets (Al-Bukhari, 2004).

COVID-19 has its impact on every community and Muslim community is not an exception. It might have affected Muslim community more because of close-nit nature of Muslim families. Also size of Muslim family is comparatively larger (Hassan et al., 2020). There is devastating financial impact on the Muslims as there is widespread job loss, bereavements, and millions are pushed to misery. As put in by the Raza Khan (1908) in his famous book 'The essentials of the Islamic faith', In the midst of any crisis or trauma, Muslims must turn to their faith for inspiration, guidance, hope, and recovery. One key concept we are reminded here by the doctors and health personnel during this trauma is the sacrifice. As explained by Girard and Hassan (2008) in their work on 'faith-based investing', that the sacrifice and patience is the DNA of Islam.

Zakat is essentially the wealth tax on Muslims is also a sacrifice of the wealth. The 2.5% of the assets that have been owned over a year is to pay the poor and needy. It isn't a charity rather it is the duty of the Muslims to purify the rest of their wealth (Hassan & Khan, 2007). Zakat has played a pivotal role in fight against the COVID in Pakistan, UK, Bahrain and Saudi Arabia, through different private and governmental organizations (Mohammad et al., 2020).

As the community is approaching a long war against this pandemic and this is just a beginning. Instant cash transfer nature of Zakat makes it one of the most solid and reliable Islamic financial services to help poor and needy during and after effects of COVID (Mahmuddin et al., 2020). The world bank has estimated that the global annual Zakat fund is estimated to reach 600 billion dollars this year and this could prove to be a great boost to the global economy in time of this crisis. This compulsory donation from the Muslims which represent the one fourth of the world population could save millions of people from this humanitarian catastrophe (Ali et al., 2020; Rachman & Nur Salam, 2018). Islamic banks and financial institutions has already adopted the financial disruption called Fintech (Bashar & Rabbani, 2021; Jreisat et al., 2021a) and it has resulted into positive effect on their profit and overall performance in terms of achieving the objective. The proposed AI-based Fintech model can help the governments around the world and NGOs in war against the COVID. It will prove to be a stepping stone in this fight by providing a reliable, transparent, inclusive, and efficient financial model (Hassan et al., 2020; Mohammad et al., 2020).

5 AI Based Islamic Fintech Model for Zakat

Islamic Fintech is identified as one of the important tool to achieve the Islamic finance objective of social justice and financial inclusion (Khan et al., 2022). The proposed Fintech model uses AI and NLP to auto verify the documents and from the borrowers as well as receivers to disperse the amount of Zakat. The proposed AI-based Fintech model is depicted in Fig. 3.

The Fintech platform requires each user of the platform to register by creating a login ID. The platform uses e-KYC to verify the identity of the users in real time using AI. Once the user is registered, he/she can be registered as the lender (Donor of *Zakat*) or the borrower (recipient of *Zakat*). The recipient can login and provide its details by giving the proof of need and the amount it requires each period to fulfill its need. The recipient can be an individual, Small and Medium Enterprises (SME), or anyone in need of funds suffered by the financial crisis or the pandemic. It is to be noted that the entity registering itself as the recipient must provide the valid proof of the need to qualify as a recipient of Zakat. Zakat cannot be given to everyone as there are certain sharia requirements, which must be fulfilled by an entity. The platform classifies such users as the 'recipient of Zakat'. The platform also uses Blockchain technology to provide security to the donor and to verify how many times the amount has been transferred to the recipient. Blockchain is the technology used in case of Cryptocurrency (Karim et al., 2022; Rabbani et al., 2021a, 2021b).

The other type of user is known as the lender (donor of Zakat). It is important to note that the donor must provide proof of Halal source of income. Zakat can be given only from the Halal source of income. The system uses machine learning, digital image processing, and AI to verify the documents provided by each user.

6 Conclusion

Zakat is the compulsory donation from the rich and able Muslims which must be given to the poor and needy within a year. This immediate benefit nature of Zakat is well suited to tackle an economic crisis such as the one caused by COVID-19. The present study offers a solution to the social

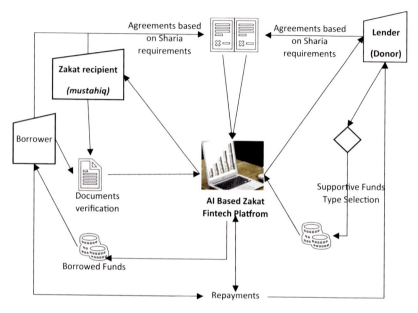

Fig. 3 AI-Based Zakat model (*Source* Adapted from [Khan et al., 2021a, b; Rabbani et al., 2021])

and economic problem created by the virus. Islamic finance offers a wide range of financial services well-suited to each stage of pandemic COVID-19. An important Islamic Financial Service *Zakat* can be the potential warrior in the fight against the economic consequences of COVID-19. Islam advocates the system of wealth distribution with a view to create a society where there is no accumulation of wealth and concentration of economic power, no amassing, and no profiteering; a civilization where there is no one dying for food nor multi-millionaires; a society where justice prevails in all aspects of life, be it social, political, or economic; an economic system which works on the model of poverty alleviation, equal distribution of wealth and social justice. Zakat being the third pillar of Islam after *Tawheed (Oneness of Allah)* and *Salah (prayer)*, it is the first pillar in the Islamic economic system. It is the first and most important tool for eradicating poverty, helping poor, and bringing the economic justice to the Muslim society. Zakat is the most important tool for combating poverty and equitable distribution of wealth and removing social and economic evils from the Islamic society. The proposed AI-based Fintech model can help the governments around the world and NGOs in war against the COVID. It will prove to be a stepping stone in this fight by providing a reliable, transparent, inclusive, and efficient financial model.

REFERENCES

Al Bukhari, A. M. B. I. B. I. (2004). *Sahih al-Bukhari*. Dar Ibn Haitham.

Abakah, E. J. A., Caporale, G. M., & Gil-Alana, L. A. (2021). Economic policy uncertainty: Persistence and cross-country linkages. *Research in International Business and Finance, 58*. https://doi.org/10.1016/j.ribaf.2021.101442

Abdullah, Y., & Rabbani, M. R. (2021). COVID-19 and GCC Islamic market indices. *2021 International Conference on Sustainable Islamic Business and Finance (SIBF)*.

Aday, S., & Aday, M. S. (2020). Impact of COVID-19 on the food supply chain. *Food Quality and Safety, 4*(4), 167–180.

Adekoya, O. B., & Oliyide, J. A. (2021). How COVID-19 drives connectedness among commodity and financial markets: Evidence from TVP-VAR and causality-in-quantiles techniques. *Resources Policy, 70*(October), 101898. https://doi.org/10.1016/j.resourpol.2020.101898

Adewale, A. A., & Haron, R. (2017). Democracy and socio-economic inclusion in Nigeria: Reducing the mutual exclusivity through Islamic microfinance. *Al-Shajarah, Special Issue: Islamic Banking and Finance*, 1–26. https://www.scopus.com/inward/record.uri?eid=2-s2.0-85039920816&partnerID=40&md5=553b03232305d53ab41ff6e29b79d83b

Ahmad, M. U., & Mahmood, A. (2009). Zakat fund-concept and perspective. *International Journal of Monetary Economics and Finance, 2*(3–4), 197–205. https://doi.org/10.1504/IJMEF.2009.029058

Ali, M. M., Bashar, A., Rabbani, M. R., & Abdullah, Y. (2020). Transforming business decision making with Internet of Things (IoT) and Machine Learning (ML). *2020 International Conference on Decision Aid Sciences and Application (DASA), Sakheer, Bahrain* (pp. 674–679). https://doi.org/10.1109/DASA51403.2020.9317174

Anser, M. K., Yousaf, Z., Zaman, K., Nassani, A. A., Alotaibi, S. M., Jambari, H., Khan, A., & Kabbani, A. (2020). Determination of resource curse hypothesis in mediation of financial development and clean energy sources: Go-for-green resource policies. *Resources Policy, 66*. https://doi.org/10.1016/j.resourpol.2020.101640

Bashar, A., & Rabbani, M. R. (2021). Exploring the role of web personalization in consumer green purchasing behavior: A conceptual framework. *2021 Third*

International Sustainability and Resilience Conference: Climate Change, 23–28.

Bashir, A.-H. (2018). Reducing poverty and income inequalities: Current approaches and Islamic perspective. *Journal of King Abdulaziz University, Islamic Economics, 31*(1), 93–104. https://doi.org/10.4197/Islec.31-1.5

Bin-Nashwan, S. A., Al-Daihani, M., Abdul-Jabbar, H., & Al-Ttaffi, L. H. A. (2020). Social solidarity amid the COVID-19 outbreak: Fundraising campaigns and donors' attitudes. *International Journal of Sociology and Social Policy*. https://doi.org/10.1108/IJSSP-05-2020-0173

Brady, D., & Bostic, A. (2015). Paradoxes of social policy: Welfare transfers, relative poverty, and redistribution preferences. *American Sociological Review*. https://doi.org/10.1177/0003122415573049

Bresser-Pereira, L. C. (2020). Financing COVID-19, inflation and fiscal constraint. *Brazilian Journal of Political Economy, 40*(4), 604–621. https://doi.org/10.1590/0101-31572020-3193

Fu, J., & Mishra, M. (2022). Fintech in the time of COVID–19: Technological adoption during crises. *Journal of Financial Intermediation, 50*. https://doi.org/10.1016/j.jfi.2021.100945

Girard, E. C., & Hassan, M. K. (2008). Is there a cost to faith-based investing: Evidence from FTSE Islamic indices. *The Journal of Investing, 17*(4), 112–121.

Habeeb, S., Rabbai, M. R., Ahmad, N., Ali, M. A. M., & Bashar, A. (2021). Post COVID-19 challenges for the sustainable entrepreneurship. *2021 International Conference on Sustainable Islamic Business and Finance (SIBF)*.

Haque, M. S., & Yamao, M. (2011). Prospects and challenges of Islamic microfinance programmes: A case study in Bangladesh. *International Journal of Economic Policy in Emerging Economies, 4*(1), 95–111. https://doi.org/10.1504/IJEPEE.2011.038875

Hashmi, S. M., Chang, B. H., & Rong, L. (2021). Asymmetric effect of COVID-19 pandemic on E7 stock indices: Evidence from quantile-on-quantile regression approach. *Research in International Business and Finance, 58*. https://doi.org/10.1016/j.ribaf.2021.101485

Hassan, A., & Saleem, S. (2017). An Islamic microfinance business model in Bangladesh: Its role in alleviation of poverty and socio-economic well-being of women. *Humanomics, 33*(1), 15–37. https://doi.org/10.1108/H-08-2016-0066

Hassan, M. K., Rabbani, M. R., & Ali, M. A. (2020). Challenges for the Islamic finance and banking in post COVID era and the role of fintech. *Journal of Economic Cooperation and Development, 43*(3), 93–116.

Hassan, M. K., Rabbani, M. R., & Abdullah, Y. (2021). Socioeconomic impact of COVID-19 in MENA region and the role of Islamic finance. *International Journal of Islamic Economics and Finance (IJIEF), 4*(1), 51–78.

Jreisat, A., Rabbani, M. R., Bashar, A., Ali, M. A. M., & AlAbbas, A. (2021a). Is fintech valuation an art of science? Exploring the innovative methods for the valuation of fintech startups. *2021 International Conference on Decision Aid Sciences and Application (DASA)* (pp. 922–925). IEEE.

Jreisat, A., Rabbani, M. R., Hatamleh, Z. M., & Grewal, H. (2021b). COVID-19: A closer look at the MENA banking sector. *2021 International Conference on Decision Aid Sciences and Application (DASA)*.

Kabir Hassan, M., & Masrur Khan, J. (2007). Zakat, external debt and poverty reduction strategy in Bangladesh. *Journal of Economic Cooperation*.

Karim, S., Rabbani, M. R., & Bawazir, H. (2022). Applications of blockchain technology in the finance and banking industry beyond digital currencies. In *Blockchain Technology and Computational Excellence for Society 5.0* (pp. 216–238). IGI Global.

Khan, S., Hassan, M. K., & Rabbani, M. R. (2021a). An AI-based Islamic fintech model on qardh-al-hasan for COVID-19 affected SMEs. In *Islamic Perspective For Sustainable Financial System*.

Khan, S., Al-Dmour, A., Bali, V., Rabbani, M. R., & Thirunavukkarasu, K. (2021b). Cloud computing based futuristic educational model for virtual learning. *Journal of Statistics and Management Systems, 24*(2), 357–385.

Khan, M. S., Rabbani, M. R., Hawaldar, I. T., & Bashar, A. (2022). Determinants of behavioral intentions to use Islamic financial technology: An empirical Assessment. *Risks, 10*(6), 114.

Killeen, G. F., & Kiware, S. S. (2020). Why lockdown? Why national unity? Why global solidarity? Simplified arithmetic tools for decision-makers, health professionals, journalists and the general public to explore containment options for the 2019 novel coronavirus. *Infectious Disease Modelling, 5*, 442–458. https://doi.org/10.1016/j.idm.2020.06.006

Le, T.-H., Le, A. T., & Le, H.-C. (2021). The historic oil price fluctuation during the COVID-19 pandemic: What are the causes? *Research in International Business and Finance, 58*. https://doi.org/10.1016/j.ribaf.2021.101489

Mahmuddin, R., Rafi, I., Aqbar, K., & Iskandar, A. (2020). Hukum Menyegerakan Penyerahan Zakat Harta dan Zakat Fitrah di Saat pandemi COVID-19. *Bustanul Fuqaha: Jurnal Bidang Hukum Islam, 1*(2), 125–136.

Mohammad, Khan, S., Mustafa, & Yannis. (2020). An AI and NLP based Islamic fintech model combining Zakat and Qardh-Al-Hasan for countering the adverse impact of COVID-19 on SMEs and individuals. *International Journal of Economics and Business Administration, VIII*(Issue 2), 351–364. https://doi.org/10.35808/ijeba/466

Moser, C. O. N. (1998). The asset vulnerability framework: Reassessing urban poverty reduction strategies. *World Development*. https://doi.org/10.1016/S0305-750X(97)10015-8

Naeem, M. A., Rabbani, M. R., Karim, S., & Billah, S. M. (2021). Religion vs ethics: Hedge and safe haven properties of Sukuk and green bonds for stock markets pre-and during COVID-19. *International Journal of Islamic and Middle Eastern Finance and Management*.

Noor, R. M., Nik Mohd Rashid, N. M. N., & Mastuki, N. (2011). *Zakat and tax reporting: Disclosures practices of Shariah compliance companies* (pp. 877–882). https://doi.org/10.1109/CHUSER.2011.6163862

Ozili, P. (2020). COVID-19 in Africa: Socio-economic impact, policy response and opportunities. *International Journal of Sociology and Social Policy, 99617*. https://doi.org/10.1108/IJSSP-05-2020-0171

Panakaje, N., Rahiman, H. U., Rabbani, M. R., Kulal, A., Pandavarakallu, M. T., & Irfana, S. (2022). COVID-19 and its impact on educational environment in India. *Environmental Science and Pollution Research*, 1–17.

Rabbani, M. R., Abdulla, Y., Basahr, A., Khan, S., & Moh'd Ali, M. A. (2020). Embracing of fintech in Islamic finance in the post COVID era. *2020 International Conference on Decision Aid Sciences and Application (DASA)*, 1230–1234.

Rabbani, M. R., Khan, S., Hassan, M. K., & Ali, M. (2021). 7 AI and Natural language processing (NLP) based FinTech model of Zakat for poverty alleviation and sustainable development for Muslims in India. In *COVID-19 and Islamic Social Finance: 104*.

Rabbani, M. R. (2022a). (in press). COVID-19 and its impact on supply chain financing and the role of Islamic fintech: Evidence from GCC countries. *International Journal of Agile Systems and Management (IJASM)*.

Rabbani, M. R., Khan, S., & Atif, M. (2022b). (in press). Machine learning based P2P lending Islamic fintech model for Small and Medium Enterprises (SMEs) in Bahrain. *International Journal of Business Innovation and Research*.

Rabbani, M. R, Bashar, A., Nawaz, N., Karim, S., Ali, M. A. M., Rahiman, H. U., & Alam, M. S. (2021a). Exploring the role of islamic fintech in combating the aftershocks of COVID-19: The open social innovation of the islamic financial system. *Journal of Open Innovation: Technology, Market, and Complexity, 7*(2). https://doi.org/10.3390/joitmc7020136

Rabbani, M. R., Sarea, A., Khan, S., & Abdullah, Y. (2021b). Ethical concerns in AI (AI): The role of regtech and Islamic finance. *The International Conference On Global Economic Revolutions*, 381–390.

Rabbani, M. R. (2022). Fintech innovations, scope, challenges, and implications in Islamic Finance: A systematic analysis. *International Journal of Computing and Digital Systems, 11*(1), 1–28.

Rachman, M. A., & Nur Salam, A. (2018). The reinforcement of zakat management through financial technology systems. *International Journal of Zakat, 3*(1), 57–69. https://doi.org/10.37706/ijaz.v3i1.68

Raza Khan, I. A. (1908). *The essentials of the Islamic faith.* The importance of the highest respect for Allah Ta'ala and the Prophet (saw).

Raza Rabbani, M., Mohd, A., Ali, M., Rahiman, H. U., Atif, M., Zulfikar, Z., & Naseem, Y. (2021). The response of Islamic financial service to the COVID-19 pandemic: The open social innovation of the financial system. *Journal of Open Innovation: Technology, Market, and Complexity,* 7(1), 85. https://doi.org/10.3390/joitmc7010085

Rehman, A., Ishaque, A., Malik, S., Rehman, S. U., Hussain, A., Khan, M., Zeeshan, M., & Afridi, F. E. A. (2021). Exploring asymmetric nexus between tourism, economic growth and CO_2 emissions in the context of Pakistan. *International Journal of Energy Economics and Policy,* 11(3), 338–345. https://doi.org/10.32479/ijeep.10929

Sharif, A., Aloui, C., & Yarovaya, L. (2020). COVID-19 pandemic, oil prices, stock market, geopolitical risk and policy uncertainty nexus in the US economy: Fresh evidence from the wavelet-based approach. *International Review of Financial Analysis,* 70(April), 101496. https://doi.org/10.1016/j.irfa.2020.101496

Sharma, A., Adhikary, A., & Borah, S. B. (2020). COVID-19's impact on supply chain decisions: Strategic insights from NASDAQ 100 firms using twitter data. *Journal of Business Research,* 117, 443–449.

Yap, K. B. (2011). Islamic banking: The convergence of religion, economic self-interest and marketing. In *Handbook of Islamic Marketing* (pp. 226–247). Edward Elgar Publishing Ltd. https://www.scopus.com/inward/record.uri?eid=2-s2.0-84882023163&partnerID=40&md5=d2754c22a5a6bde6d4a2054e8379d575

Islamic Fintech and Bahrain: An Opportunity for Global Financial Services

*M. Kabir Hassan, Ammar Jreisat,
Mustafa Raza Rabbani, and Somar Al-Mohamed*

1 Introduction

Islamic financial sector is currently one of the fastest-growing segments of the global financial sector (Chong & Liu, 2009; Lawal & Ajayi, 2019). It plays an increasingly critical role when it comes to the global social

M. K. Hassan
Department of Economics and Finance, University of New, Orleans, New Orleans, LA 70148, USA
e-mail: mhassan@uno.edu

A. Jreisat (✉) · M. R. Rabbani
Department of Economics and Finance, College of Business Administration, University of Bahrain, Zallaq, Kingdom of Bahrain
e-mail: abarham@uob.edu.bh

M. R. Rabbani
e-mail: mrabbani@uob.edu.bh

S. Al-Mohamed
Department of Finance, College of Business Administration, American University of the Middle East, Eqaila, Kuwait
e-mail: somar.al-mohamad@aum.edu.kw

financing needs (Azwirman et al., 2019). This is because it serves a core population of approximately 1.8 billion Muslims worldwide as well as provides ethical finance to an enlarged worldwide audience. In addition to fostering a nascent Islamic Fintech ecosystem, global Fintech advancements are also influencing Islamic finance (Islamic Development Bank Group, 2020).

Technology has been an imperative component of the global financial services industry for a long time, probably since the dawn of the twenty-first century. It is widely agreed that Automated Teller Machines (ATMs), mainframe computer networks, and digital stock exchanges were among the early financial technology innovations. The "Fintech" revolution, however, has raised a great deal of concern about the impact of new technologies on the financial services industry, because of new technological enablers being introduced into the sector (Hassan et al., 2020; Rabbani et al., 2021a, 2021b). Due to this disruption, financial services are reshaping their business models, their operational models, and their customer experiences in an exciting way that will be able to serve the global consumer market and serve evolving business needs. Considering these emerging global Fintech trends, Islamic finance has a great deal of opportunity (Hassan et al., 2021).

As part of the evaluation process, we begin by defining Fintech and assessing its trajectory and development. As a result of this disruption of the financial sector, we are seeing the creation of a variety of new business models, operational models, and customer experiences. As defined by Dinar Standard, an advisory firm based in the United States, Fintech is described as being technologies that are driven by the Fourth Industrial Revolution and are enhancing and/or disrupting current financial services, operations, business models, and customer engagement (DinarStandard, 2021).

In the recent past, advanced technologies such as artificial intelligence, robotics, blockchain, and others have slowly made their way into the finance world (Khan & Rabbani, 2020; Khan et al., 2022). The Islamic banking sector has not been left out of these revolutions. In the Gulf Cooperation Council as well as around the world, Bahrain is considered a major hub for Islamic finance and banking. Bahrain possesses the highest concentration of Islamic banks in the world. An important objective of this study is to discover the impact of Fintech on the future of Islamic finance in Bahrain (Jreisat et al., 2021; Rabbani et al., 2022).

Bahrain is the world's foremost center for Islamic finance. Over the past few years, Islamic finance has experienced explosive growth. According to Thomson Reuters' 2018 report, the industry has grown by 11%, but not at its full potential (IFSB, 2020). There were many reasons as to why Islamic finance failed to grow at an unimaginable rate. A major reason could be that Islamic financial institutions have not been able to convince the community that they are truly Islamic and follow all the rules prescribed by the Quran, the Sunnah, and the Shariah. The Islamic community has not been convinced that interest-based financial systems are haram, just as drinking alcohol or eating pork are. In contrast, Muslims are not allowed to eat pork or to drink alcohol, yet they are willing to give and accept *riba/interest* (Farooq & El-Ghattis, 2018). Muslims are yet to be convinced about Sharia and the services offered by Sharia-based groups as they do not have faith in the Islamic financial system. Furthermore, Islamic financial institutions may not be able to create products and services that meet the demands of the potential consumer market. The conventional mode of financing has become increasingly difficult to complete, as it is a very complex system, and people are so accustomed to it (Jusni et al., 2019).

This chapter explores the Fintech fundamentals and helps the Islamic finance industry make sense of this wave of change as it is happening. In the Islamic finance industry, Fintech has no longer been confined to a fantasy or a fad. With this technology, the entire financial sector (both conventional and Islamic) will be on a level playing field. Hopefully, this will contribute to the development of the Islamic financial industry. Those who focus on innovation and transparency will be able to gain future market dominance. With modern technology, business models can be developed with Sharia-compliant goods that scale well and can be marketed successfully. A Fintech-driven change in society could have enormous social benefits, so it should be viewed as an opportunity instead of a threat. The economy and society can both benefit from the change. Currently, there are only a few platforms in the Islamic world offering financial services. When the Islamic Fintech market is compared to the global market, it is indeed very small (compared to conventional Fintech). On the other hand, the beginnings of this industry have proven to be reliable and accepted in recent years. Islamic crowdfunding blockchain, which is the primary element of Islamic finance, is already used on several platforms. Several countries, including Brunei Darussalam, Bahrain, Malaysia, and the United Arab Emirates, regulate Fintech to help financial institutions and startups collaborate in developing innovative business models. Collaboration between regulators and industry will play a vital role in paving the road for the adoption of Fintech worldwide in key areas such as regulatory implications of technological advancements and financial products and services development.

The chapter consists of the following sections: the second section focuses on Islamic Fintech's global gaps and opportunities. Bahrain's central bank has recently implemented new regulations, which are discussed in the third section. The fourth section discusses emerging technologies in Bahrain. In the fifth section, we explain the gaps and opportunities in Bahrain's Islamic Fintech market. Finally, the study draws important conclusions about how the Islamic financial system in the Kingdom of Bahrain can be further developed, based on open innovation, social inclusion, and embracing the new technology.

2 Gaps and Opportunities in Global Islamic Fintech

In the last few years, Islamic finance technology has grown significantly still the primary focus has been on peer-to-peer lending, creating a gap in the availability of Islamic finance for consumers and businesses (Khan et al., 2022). As identified by this study, there are many gaps in the Islamic Fintech ecosystem. Below are a few of those gaps (Banna et al., 2021; Rabbani et al., 2021a, 2021b).

a. Artificial intelligence and its role in wealth management: Artificial intelligence refers to the ability of a machine to perform the same tasks as a human, such that computers can be exploited to fuel human intelligence. There is a need for Islamic Fintech to be more automated and more readily accessible, which is the most important gap identified. To succeed, Islamic Fintech needs to become more automated by introducing innovative models and extending the range of equity investments. A Fintech company based in the United States, called Mint provides automated financial statement analysis for its users (DinarStandard, 2021).
b. Blockchain: There is still room for growth for Islamic trade finance as the market is still relatively small. It is crucial that smart contracts

and blockchain are utilized since they will not only provide independent verification but also documentation, and they can be used to streamline business processes, as well as payments and remittances. The blockchain can be used by Islamic banks to develop new and innovative products, generate more revenue, and reduce transaction costs (Hassan et al., 2020, 2022; Karim et al., 2022).

c. Analytical and big data applications in Islamic banking: The most asset of financial institutions is data in today's data-driven world. Financial technology has simplified the banking process. With the introduction of big data and the solution of complex financial problems, it has reshaped the financial landscape. With the use of big data, applications in Islamic finance such as takaful, re-takaful, sukuk, ijarah, and equity investments are becoming more relevant. In the case of proper implementation of data analytics, the information can be used to improve, enhance, and grow the banking sector of the country, contributing more effectively to the growth of the nation. The customer interacts with the bank every time he or she makes a purchase, every time they call, every time they make an enquiry, every time they shop, every time an ATM card is used, every time an app is used, and so on means a huge amount of data that can open many new avenues for banks and increase the bank's growth (Bashar et al., 2021; Sun et al., 2020).

Islamic finance continued to grow quite steadily (Fig. 1), and its assets grew rapidly after the financial crisis. Based on Dinar Standard, 2021/2022, it's predicted that Islamic finance assets will amount to $3472 billion by 2024. With the COVID-19 pandemic, Islamic financial system has another chance to appear as a serious competitor to the conventional financial system with its social financial services (Hassan et al., 2020, 2021; Rabbani et al., 2021a). As the open social innovation of the financial system post-COVID-19, Islamic finance has a crucial role to play (Abdullah & Rabbani, 2021; Dharani et al., 2022; Habeeb et al., 2021; Panakaje et al., 2022; Rabbani, 2022a, 2022b).

3 New Regulations by Bahrain's Central Bank

Even though Bahrain is a small country, its growing economy offers opportunities to invest within a conducive business environment designed to help your firm succeed. With strengths in the finance, technology,

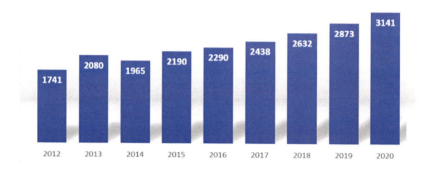

Fig. 1 Global Islamic finance assets ($ billion) (*Source* DinarStandard, 2021/2022)

manufacturing, and logistics sectors, Bahrain's economy is the most diversified in the Gulf Cooperation Council (GCC) region. Businesses of all sizes can thrive under our pro-innovation business policies and laws.

It is imperative that Bahrain and the rest of the Middle East have clear legal and regulatory frameworks for the financial sector which has continued to undergo changes and reforms over the past year. International best practices indicate that regulators have continued to seek to liberalize and modernize legislation to facilitate business opportunities for investors. An analysis is provided here of some of the significant legal and regulatory developments in Bahrain's Fintech industry. In November 2018, introducing open banking regulations in Bahrain was the first step in establishing open banking in the Middle East, by implementing rules governing the provision of account information services and payment initiating services. Obtaining the explicit consent of consumers, open banking allows for the sharing of consumers' private information, in a standardized and secure manner, between organizations. Third-party providers of financial services can gain access to information efficiently and economically with the help of application programming interfaces, which enables the development of innovative Fintech solutions (Karim et al., 2021; Meero et al., 2021).

Bahrain implemented the United Nations Model Law on Electronic Transferable Records as national law in January 2019. The electronic transferable records that have been enacted thus far are essentially electronic copies of paper documents and instruments, such as bills of lading, bills of exchange, checks, promissory notes, and warehouse receipts. Bahrain also updated its Electronic Communications and Transactions Law, allowing greater use of electronic communications in business, among other things. "Electronic documents can be accessed by their holders to request the delivery of a specific product and to request payment".

The Central Bank of Bahrain, under its regulatory framework, provides services in cryptocurrency trading, dealing, investment advisory, and portfolio management for crypto assets on behalf of principals, agents, custodians, or as a cryptocurrency exchange located in Bahrain or abroad. A "global crypto-asset service license," which is a license that allows individuals or corporations domiciled in another country to operate within Bahrain, is available to individuals or corporations domiciled or incorporated abroad (Meero et al., 2021).

As well, the CBB published a directive in March 2019 about "Digital Financial Advice" (also known as "Robo-Advice"), which is using technology to provide financial advice. A comprehensive governance and control framework is necessary for digital financial advice because it relies primarily on algorithms and assumptions. CBB, the Information & eGovernment Authority, and Benefit together launched eKYC, the first electronic data exchange initiative in the Middle East. Using a state-of-the-art online platform and database, the financial institution will be able to authenticate and verify the client's identity, information, and financial standing before providing financial services to him or her. Also, it facilitates the launch of products and services offered by Fintech companies via internet applications and the development of these products (DinarStandard, 2021; "Leveraging Islam. Fintech to Improv. Financ. Incl.," 2020).

Insurance aggregators (i.e., brokers operating online platforms) will be affected by new CBB regulations beginning August 19, 2019. Internet-based applications or mobile applications. Comparing and purchasing insurance policies through a platform or app that allows users to access several insurance companies that offers them the option of finding and selecting insurance quotes from several insurance companies. Laws No. 30 of 2018 governing personal data protection and Law No. 31 of 2018 governing competition went into effect on January 18, 2019 and August 1, 2019, respectively. According to the PDPL, individuals are granted several rights regarding the collection, processing, and storing of their personal data. Organizations are now required to manage personal data in new ways. To wit, ensuring fair handling of personal data, the informed consent of individuals, and direct access to their rights (DinarStandard, 2021; Kukreja et al., 2021).

CBB has partnered with Bank ABC and Ila Bank, BENEFIT, Bahrain Islamic Bank (BisB), and the National Bank of Bahrain (NBB) to create FinHub 973, Bahrain's first digital Fintech lab. Through the program, financial institutions and Fintech startups can collaborate to create a collaborative ecosystem in the Fintech sector. The success of Bahrain's Fintech sector is due in part to the collaborative efforts of the people who are participating in the creation of an ecosystem which includes new rules and regulations which fit into this framework. In the years to come, the Fintech industry is expected to continue growing at a rapid rate as it grows (Abbasi et al., 2021; Chinnasamy et al., 2021; Narayan, 2020).

4 Emerging Technologies in the Kingdom of Bahrain

Bahrain is taking steps to enhance digital transformation. Economic development in Bahrain follows the pillars of sustainability, fairness, and competitiveness. Also, the Digital Government Strategy 2022 emphasizes the use of emerging technologies to transform government services. In this area, the Kingdom has established itself as a regional leader thanks to its adoption of a range of emerging technologies. The government has taken on a regulatory role to empower technology companies and foster their growth. This has resulted in the growth of the economy, the creation of jobs, and the progress of humanity for the Kingdom, thereby improving the quality of life of its citizens.

Forms of Emerging Technologies in Bahrain

The Bahraini telecom industry became the first in the Gulf to liberalize in 2011, resulting in a massive economic shift. It has one of the best ICT infrastructures in the region, thanks to its well-established ICT infrastructure. The UN eGovernment Development Index describes the Kingdom as the number one country in the Arab world for ICT Development Index (IDI) and the fourth at the world level for Telecommunication Infrastructure Index (TII). Bahrain is ranked fourth in the global category of internet penetration, according to the World Economic Forum Global Competitiveness Report (Causevic, 2018; Meero et al., 2021).

The Kingdom uses artificial intelligence to enhance government services. Thus, public sector procedures, including judicial procedures, have been streamlined, supporting business continuity. In addition, there are two international conferences in Bahrain related to artificial intelligence and the judiciary. Moreover, the education sector was able to manage smoothly thanks to the cloud-based remote educational gateway, EDUNET, which were able to educate during the beginning of the COVID-19 era. iGA (Information & eGovernment Authority) developed BeAware Bahrain, an app developed in-house to prevent the spread of the virus. Despite its rapid launch, it has been vital in limiting its spread (Mohamed et al., 2021; Rabbani et al., 2020).

Developing Bahrain's Tech Ecosystem

Bahrain's economic growth is driven by advances in artificial intelligence, biotechnology, materials science, and robotics. It is Bahrain's intention to foster innovation by creating a conducive ecosystem. It encourages developers, designers, and deployers of new technologies to comply with international standards and to adopt values consistent with the Kingdom. Government Action Plan and Vision 2030 of the Kingdom will both be facilitated by emerging technologies. Central Bank of Bahrain (CBB), Economic Development Board (EDB), and other government agencies continue to adopt new technologies and innovations (Daud et al., 2021; Hassan et al., 2021).

Technology in the Financial Sector (Fintech)

Bahrain maintains one of the most stable financial services sectors in this region and values innovation in a stable regulatory environment. As part of Bahrain's Fintech regulatory sandbox, the Central Bank of Bahrain (CBB) launched a program in 2017 that allows companies to test out their solutions under supervision for up to one year. It's the region's first initiative of its kind and has the potential of creating opportunities for Fintech firms to grow and flourish. For an application to be considered for deployment after the sandbox period ends, solutions must demonstrate innovation, a benefit for the customer, technical testing, and an intention to deploy in Bahrain. Since the sandbox's inception, several

Fintech companies have emerged, the first of which is *Tarabut* Gateway, which works with financial institutions in the region. Further, the initiative will further enhance Bahrain's position as a leader for financial services across the GCC. This is because it provides a safe, partially deregulated business environment. Additionally, CBB facilitates business innovation. This unit ensures Bahrain's financial services are properly regulated and implemented (Information & eGovernment Authority, 2021). Bahrain has established itself as a leading financial technology center within the MENA region, and Fintech companies in Bahrain have been leveraging the dominance of this regional hub for their success.

Accelerator for Startups
It has taken significant steps to develop Bahrain's economy to attract foreign direct investments into Bahrain and set the direction for the development of the Fintech industry in Bahrain. Flat6Labs is an accelerator based in Bahrain founded by Tamkeen with the aim of accelerating and launching both local and international startup companies. Through the accelerator, mentorship, business development, and capital opportunities are offered to companies.

Open Banking
Bahrain's position as a leader in Fintech has been further enhanced by the implementation of the Open Banking initiative in June of this year. In a move that is replicating the UK, Bahraini and other global financial centers have become the first Middle Eastern country to implement Open Banking. In Bahrain, a new system has been launched based on the Open Banking platform of the Fintech Tarabut Gateway, which has been adopted by the National Bank of Bahrain (NBB).

In the Era of IoT (Internet of Things)
The first IoT connectivity standard of the GCC was devised by Bahrain and supported the use of the Narrowband Internet of Things (NB-IoT) within the international telecommunications system (IMS). A few countries from the Middle East have been selected to take part in ITU's harmonization project for the narrowband IoT spectrum. Government entities have been provided frequency bands by the Information & eGovernment Authority (iGA) in support of smart cities, the Internet of Things, and the Machine-to-Machine (M2M) communication goals of Vision 2030 (Information & eGovernment Authority, 2021).

Cellular networks, technologies, and platforms are key components of Bahrain's IoT and M2M networks. To support increased Internet speeds and connectivity with 5G, the fiber networks and wireless were reorganized. Internet of Things is used by many Bahraini companies and government entities to support Bahrain's economic development. NSSA (National Space Science Agency) was established in Bahrain by the end of 2018. Through events, NSSA is promoting science and technology related to satellite manufacturing, monitoring satellites, tracking satellites, and creating imagery in Bahrain. A satellite will be launched by Bahrain in the third quarter of 2021. A satellite will use artificial intelligence technologies and their application in remote sensing as part of the Internet of Things (monitoring of factories' gas emissions).

"Lift," the new online portal from APM Terminals Bahrain, allows customers to check delivery status, track shipments, and collect shipping information. Through the technology, customers can view real-time cargo status in a box feature, allowing management of Terminal processes in all their aspects. The Marasi integrated electronic portal provides a single point of access and also offers a variety of port services.

Further, IoT is employed to automate its irrigation usage, increasing efficiency, as well as the Electricity and Water Authority to automate distribution, which includes data collection, analytics, and execution. Batelco and Bahrain's Economic Development Board (EDB) recently launched "Brinc Centre," with the aim of supporting IoT and free enterprise in the Gulf. International Airport of Bahrain has adopted the latest unified communications, video clouds, and IoT solutions from Bahrain Airport Company (BAC). These new systems result in more efficient, safer, and more comfortable airport operations, as well as a more pleasant passenger experience. Real-time connectivity for large volumes of data is provided by these advanced systems (Information & eGovernment Authority, 2021).

Technology Based on Blockchains
Several industry leaders have adopted blockchain technology with major benefits, including increased efficiency, improved traceability, and enhanced transparency, among other things, speedier transactions, and lower costs. Kingdom-wide blockchain strategy has been developed by the Economic Development Board in partnership with the Information & eGovernment Authority (iGA) to set up the general direction and support adoption by the public and private sectors. Among

the blockchain applications found in Bahrain's public sector are first, to achieve Bahrain's Economic Vision 2030, the General Directorate of Traffic (GDT) has established the Blockchain Vehicle Registration project. Using modern technologies, Bahrain promotes the development of services and promotes the private sector. Vehicle registrars now have access to more accurate and up-to-date information about each vehicle than ever before, while reducing costs associated with basic vehicle data maintenance. Secondly, blockchain technology, adopted by the University of Bahrain (UOB), is used to award the first certificates in the region. UOB academic certificates can now be verified using blockchain technology worldwide, providing enhanced security. As a result, employers and universities can easily share digital certificates that cannot be falsified. Lastly, APM Terminals, which operates KBSPs, collaborates with several stakeholders on blockchain adoption. As soon as KBSP has configured its systems, a blockchain map will include Bahrain (Information & eGovernment Authority, 2021).

Analytical Techniques
Government data is utilized by entities, organizations, and governing bodies to make informed decisions, conduct research, and develop new solutions. Bahrain's Open Data Portal provides public sector data that may be reused, analyzed, and shared without restrictions while adhering to all rules regarding personal data protection.

The use of big data in Bahrain has enabled many projects, such as the national census, to be implemented. This provides an analysis of large amounts of data, reducing administrative costs, time, and effort. Consumer Price Index reports provide real-time indicators of inflation in the Kingdom by collecting data from a variety of sources. Bahraini government records are a valuable source of information about foreign visitors, Bahraini tourists, and hotel occupancy. National Space Science Agency (NSSA) will collect data on the environment, agriculture, climate, and other topics using the country's first satellite. The Kingdom can better analyze big data by utilizing this approach.

Suggest a Data Set
In assisting the Kingdom to create an infrastructure and economy that is fit for the twenty-first century, the Information & eGovernment Authority will produce large amounts of data, especially in the medical and educational fields. Through the Bahrain Open Data Platform, all stakeholders

have access to large official data sets. A variety of official data from government agencies can be accessed using the Open Data Platform. The information is available in a variety of graphical representations and raw data formats. The Telecommunications Regulatory Authority (TRA) facilitates the dissemination of data by allowing you to fill out an appropriate form or by allowing you to submit a proposal through the TRA website.

Cloud Computing
Bahrain is an early leader in e-Government. The country implemented a government-wide digitalization initiative in the GCC region. Cloud computing has reduced operational costs and increased productivity for the government, and improved public services. As part of Bahrain's policy to adopt cloud technologies, a clear roadmap and guidance are provided. Cloud Computing solutions should be considered as an integral part of government IT planning and implementation processes. AWS was appointed as the kingdom's official cloud infrastructure provider in 2017. Since adopting Cloud First, Bahrain has achieved several milestones. The iGA, for example, has transferred 1357 IT operations to Amazon cloud computing servers; transferred more than 14,500 government emails to Azure cloud computing; and certified 550 government and semi-government employees for use of Amazon cloud computing.

Innovation Center at the University of Bahrain
At the University of Bahrain, the Cloud Innovation Center will provide students with a range of cloud-based technologies and opportunity to work with other public sector organizations to solve urgent challenges and engage in new ideas with the use of Amazon's innovation process and expertise. Participants work together, identify what lessons they learned, and publish what they learned to come up with solutions to complex problems.

Pay with an eWallet
Several innovative electronic payment solutions can be utilized in Bahrain to conduct payments securely, quickly, and conveniently at the point of initiating a transaction, in line with Vision 2030 goals. In Bahrain, some of the most popular eWallets are b-Wallet and AFS. Other popular options include StcPay by SMBC, Benefit Pay by BHA, and MaxWallet by Credimax. Bahrain has chosen to make electronic wallets which is the National Portal accepts this payment method as an official method of payment.

Know Your Customer (KYC) Electronically
A key initiative for the Bahraini Central Bank (CBB) aims to transform the financial services sector into a paperless one, by moving to the electronic Know Your Customer (eKYC) initiated by the Kingdom's financial institutions as part of their initiatives. The move will also involve the launch of a national platform for digital identity and a platform for electronic KYC in 2019. It is under the supervision of the Central Bank of Bahrain (CBB) and in collaboration with the IGA that Benefit operates the country's first automated KYC platform, which is targeted at commercial banks, financial service providers, and money exchange networks. Many banks and financial institutions realize that with the use of a national digital identity database, they can verify the identity of their customers, authenticate their information, and share the information digitally prior to delivering products or services. The government is among the entities that can access customer data, such as iGA. In addition to its platform, Benefit has created an Application Programming Interface (API) that integrates with financial institutions' core systems and digital channels. Fintech companies can verify customers' identities using Open Banking in Bahrain through their mobile and online apps.

Machine Learning, or Artificial Intelligence (AI)
The Bahrain government has improved the government's service delivery and has strengthened Bahrain's e-Government achievements through the application of modern technology such as Artificial Intelligence (AI). Training programs are also available in Bahrain. The Bahrain Polytechnic Artificial Intelligence Academy is a joint venture between Tamkeen and the Bermuda Polytechnic and Microsoft Corporation. It encourages creativity and innovation among students. Bahrain's first academy of its kind aims to train and qualify students and teachers in Bahraini universities and schools.

First Deputy Chairman of the Supreme Council for Youth and Sports, Shaikh Khalid bin Hamad Al Khalifa initiated a tournament to spur innovation among students in artificial intelligence as part of his efforts to encourage innovation. This competition provides students with the opportunity to showcase their ideas in the business world. The World Economic Forum's Center for the Fourth Industrial Revolution will pilot a new set of guidelines for government procurement of AI in Bahrain in 2019. To help governments use artificial intelligence responsibly and sustainably, we developed guidelines in collaboration with the Economic Development Board and the International Governance Assembly.

Introducing Robotics
Several of Bahrain's initiatives have been launched to demonstrate its commitment to adopting robotics to enhance customer service delivery in the kingdom. Fintech leaders in Bahrain are a great example of this initiative. Fatema is the first digital employee to be developed by Bahrain's Arab Banking Corporation. Dana has been appointed as Bahrain Islamic Bank's first virtual employee. The World Robotics Olympiad in Bahrain was a notable 2018) held in Bahrain. Participants from government and private primary, secondary, and intermediate schools presented their robotics designs and construction ideas. As The 2015 VEX robotics competition organized by Bahrain was part of its participation in the world VEX robotics championship, and there were several national qualifying events for Middle School, High School, and Elementary School students. Youths have been trained in how to install and program robots as part of the training program funded by the Ministry of Labour and Social Development. A major goal of the program is to inspire the next generation of scientists and technology leaders to pursue careers in science and technology. Additionally, Robotic Process Automation has been implemented within the Ministry of Finance to increase productivity, reduce human error, decrease costs, and improve efficiency (Russell et al., 2015; Wisskirchen et al., 2017).

Oil & Gas 4th Industrial Revolution
As a result of the advent of the Fourth Industrial Revolution, Oil and Gas 4.0, including artificial intelligence and the Internet of Things, will transform downstream, midstream, and upstream activities. Industry 4.0 is a Smart Oil Economy initiative that seeks to transform manufacturing into a Smart Oil Economy and Industry 4.0 initiative to improve the efficiency and productivity of the Kingdom's Oil & Gas Sector as well as creating greater value.

Smart Cities
The progress that is being made in the Kingdom in terms of ICT has a significant impact on the enhancement of sustainability, economic stability, and the well-being of the citizens. Bahrain is, therefore, preparing to become one of the next smart cities—areas built with the

latest in economic and social technologies for improving the health of its citizens without destroying the environment.

a. Smart traffic lights, which combine Sensors and artificial intelligence in traditional traffic lights, are one of several smart city initiatives the Telecommunications Regulatory Authority (TRA) has adopted.
b. Solar energy is being promoted by the Electricity and Water Authority and affordable loans are available for the installation of a complete solar energy system (Bell et al., 2017).
c. The 3rd Smart Cities Symposium, held by the University of Bahrain in 2020, was designed to raise awareness of the forum which will provide insight into the prospects of Smart Cities and be a place where ideas can be shared.

Fourth Industrial Revolution Education
Curriculum development and education outcomes are significantly impacted by the Fourth Industrial Revolution. As part of efforts to cultivate a knowledge-based, diversified, and sustainable economy, Bahrain aims to ensure that all its citizens have access to a comprehensive and fair education. This goal has been achieved by developing the Economic Vision 2030 (Bandara et al., 2019; Eleftheriadis & Myklebust, 2018).

5 Gaps and Opportunities in Bahrain Islamic Fintech

Islamic Finance Development Indicator—2021 (IFDI) ranks Bahrain as the fourth-placed country in the world for Islamic finance and second in the MENA region. It is worth noting that the Bahrain Islamic Bank put into place the first set of Islamic banking regulations in 1978. During this time, Bahrain has been dedicated to promoting Sharia compliance in Islamic banks including principles, rules, and norms. This makes them suitable for both mainstream Islamic finance and individuals developing Sharia-compliant products (Banna et al., 2021; IFSB & Secretariat, 2017). Bahrain's history has consistently been a leading center for Islamic finance development because it attaches great importance to innovation and customer service. The largest concentration of Islamic financial institutions in the region is in Bahrain, which is responsible for almost all aspects of Islamic finance and Islamic products. ICD's Islamic Finance

Development Report 2021 places us second in the MENA region and fourth globally for Islamic finance development.

A Leading Knowledge Hub

The number of wholesale Islamic banks in Bahrain is 11, the highest concentration in the entire Middle East. There are six retail Islamic banks in Bahrain. As a highly connected ecosystem, we offer expertise in most areas of Islamic finance, including investment management, Sukuk issuance, insurance, and reinsurance.

An Expanding Takaful Industry

There are currently six Takaful companies and two Retakaful companies in Bahrain, which makes it an ideal jurisdiction for this industry. The Central Bank of Bahrain has also implemented a Takaful model which assists in assessing whether a company is a solvent.

Regional Leader in Islamic Finance

Bahrain is currently one of the largest Islamic finance and banking markets in the region, with USD 32.6 billion in Islamic bank assets, according to the results from the second quarter of 2021.

Promoting Innovation in Government

Bahrain's central bank is continuously developing new initiatives and policy tools for improving Bahrain's position as a leading Islamic finance country, including a new model for new issuance of Takaful insurance products and Sharia-compliant investments such as the Wakalah.

Setting up a Successful Platform

Over the past few years, there has been an unprecedented growth of Fintech companies around the world, especially in the Middle East, which combines finance and technology. This ongoing digital transformation is at the very core of Bahrain's overall strategy, which aims to foster new opportunities for innovation for both Fintech companies and global financial institutions, opening new avenues of growth. Bahrain Fintech

Bay is the leading Fintech hub for MENA, offering coworking spaces, innovation labs, advisory services, and collaboration platforms.

Future-Oriented Governmental Policy

In Bahrain, the development of a Fintech ecosystem has been fueled by unprecedented regulatory reforms in the region and established the basis for new business models in sectors such as crowdfunding, insurtech, robo-advice, and crypto-assets. Among the Central Bank of Bahrain's key objectives is to reform policies to boost activity and funding in the financial sector, as well as to ensure quality and competitiveness.

Legal Sandbox

Fintech companies and digitally oriented financial institutions use regulatory sandboxes to test new products and services before they are launched on the main market. Bahrain introduced regulatory sandboxes in 2016. Several Fintech companies have been nurtured by the Fintech sandbox since its inception.

Crowdfunding Initiatives

To facilitate the rollout of Sharia-compliant equity-based and debt-based activities in Bahrain, the Central Bank of Bahrain will introduce regulations to regulate crowdfunding activities.

Establishing a Local Test Market of Exceptional Quality

It's one of the most connected economies in the Middle East, and its young, digitally savvy population makes Bahrain an ideal place to launch and fund financial technology startups and scale-ups, which can then expand their products into regional markets and even internationally.

6 CONCLUSION

Even though Islamic Fintech is growing at an unprecedented rate, it is unfair at this point to compare the development of this industry with that of conventional Fintech companies. With the advent of Fintech in recent times, Islamic finance has undoubtedly had the opportunity of catching up with their conventional counterparts. In the world of finance, Fintech has changed everything, and it is anticipated that the integration of AI and blockchain technology will completely change the face of Islamic banking. During the past few years, there has been a technological revolution occurring in the financial sector, better known as Fintech. There are countless emerging technologies that have slowly made their way into the world in recent years such as artificial intelligence, robotics, blockchain technology, and others. There is no doubt that the Islamic banking sector is not exempt from the influence of these innovations. In terms of Islamic finance and banking, Bahrain is considered one of the major hubs, both in the Gulf Cooperation Council and globally. In fact, Bahrain has the highest concentration of Islamic banks in the world. The goal of this study is to determine to what extent Fintech will have an impact on the future of Islamic finance in Bahrain. The Bahraini telecom industry became the first in the Gulf to liberalize in 2011, resulting in a massive economic shift. It has one of the best ICT infrastructures in the region, thanks to its well-established ICT infrastructure. As a result of the United Nations eGovernment Development Index, the Kingdom is ranked fourth in the world for ICT Development Index (IDI), and first in the Arab world for Telecommunication Infrastructure Index (TII), by the United Nations. In terms of internet penetration, Bahrain ranks fourth globally in the Global Competitiveness Report by the World Economic Forum.

REFERENCES

Abbasi, K., Alam, A., Du, M. A., & Huynh, T. L. D. (2021). FinTech, SME efficiency and national culture: Evidence from OECD countries. *Technological Forecasting and Social Change, 163.* https://doi.org/10.1016/j.techfore.2020.120454

Abdullah, Y., & Rabbani, M. R. (2021). COVID-19 and GCC Islamic market Indices. *2021 International Conference on Sustainable Islamic Business and Finance (SIBF).*

Azwirman, Zulhelmy, & Suryadi, A. (2019). Analysis of islamicity performance index on sharia banks in Indonesia. *International Journal of Innovation, Creativity and Change, 10*(3), 25–36. https://www.scopus.com/inward/record.uri?eid=2-s2.0-85079659014&partnerID=40&md5=658920a211e7e9f268dc5370f6783f36

Bandara, O. K. K., Tharaka, V. K., & Wickramarachchi, A. P. R. (2019). Industry 4.0 maturity assessment of the Banking Sector of Sri Lanka. *Proceedings – IEEE International Research Conference on Smart Computing and Systems Engineering, SCSE 2019,* 190–195. https://doi.org/10.23919/SCSE.2019.8842818

Banna, H., Kabir Hassan, M., & Rashid, M. (2021). Fintech-based financial inclusion and bank risk-taking: Evidence from OIC countries. *Journal of International Financial Markets, Institutions and Money, 75*(October), 1–20. https://doi.org/10.1016/j.intfin.2021.101447

Bashar, A., Rabbani, M., Khan, S., & Ali, M. A. M. (2021). Data driven finance: A bibliometric review and scientific mapping. *International Conference on Data Analytics for Business and Industry (ICDABI), 2021,* 161–166.

Bell, W. P., Wild, P., Foster, J., & Hewson, M. (2017). Revitalising the wind power induced merit order effect to reduce wholesale and retail electricity prices in Australia. *Energy Economics, 67,* 224–241. https://doi.org/10.1016/j.eneco.2017.08.003

Causevic, E. (2018). The relationship between the performance of Islamic and conventional banks. In *Lecture notes in networks and systems* (Vol. 28, pp. 256–264). Springer. https://doi.org/10.1007/978-3-319-71321-2_23

Chinnasamy, G., Madbouly, A., & Reyad, S. (2021). Fintech: A pathway for MENA region. In *Studies in computational intelligence* (Vol. 935, pp. 135–151). Springer Science and Business Media Deutschland GmbH. https://doi.org/10.1007/978-3-030-62796-6_7

Chong, B. S., & Liu, M. H. (2009). Islamic banking: Interest-free or interest-based? *Pacific Basin Finance Journal, 17*(1), 125–144. https://doi.org/10.1016/j.pacfin.2007.12.003

Daud, S. N. M., Ahmad, A. H., Khalid, A., & Azman-Saini, W. N. W. (2021). Fintech and financial stability: Threat or opportunity? *Finance Research Letters, November,* 102667. https://doi.org/10.1016/j.frl.2021.102667

Dharani, M., Hassan, M. K., Rabbani, M. R., & Huq, T. (2022). Does the Covid-19 pandemic affect faith-based investments? Evidence from global sectoral indices. *Research in International Business and Finance, 59*, 101537.
DinarStandard. (2021). Islamic fintech report 2018: Current landscape & path forward. In *Dubai Islamic Economy Development Centre.* https://www.dinars tandard.com/wp-content/uploads/2018/12/Islamic-Fintech-Report-2018. pdf
Eleftheriadis, R. J., & Myklebust, O. (2018). Industry 4.0 and cyber physical systems in a Norwegian industrial context. *Lecture Notes in Electrical Engineering, 451,* 491–499. https://doi.org/10.1007/978-981-10-5768-7_52
Farooq, M. O., & El-Ghattis, N. (2018). In Search of the Sharī'ah. *Arab Law Quarterly, 32*(4), 315–354. https://doi.org/10.1163/15730255-12322051
Habeeb, S., Rabbai, M. R., Ahmad, N., Ali, M. A. M., & Bashar, A. (2021). Post COVID-19 challenges for the sustainable entrepreneurship. *2021 International Conference on Sustainable Islamic Business and Finance (SIBF).*
Hassan, M. K., Rabbani, M. R., & Abdullah, Y. (2021). Socioeconomic Impact of COVID-19 in MENA region and the Role of Islamic Finance. *International Journal of Islamic Economics and Finance (IJIEF), 4*(1), 51–78.
Hassan, M. K., Rabbani, M. R., Brodmann, J., Bashar, A., & Grewal, H. (2022). Bibliometric and Scientometric analysis on CSR practices in the banking sector. *Review of Financial Economics.*
Hassan, M. K., Rabbani, M. R., & Ali, M. A. (2020). Challenges for the Islamic Finance and banking in post COVID era and the role of Fintech. *Journal of Economic Cooperation and Development, 43*(3), 93–116.
IFSB. (2020). Stability report 2020. In *Islamic Financial Services Board.*
IFSB, T., & R. D. of the Secretariat. (2017). *Islamic financial service industry stability report 2017.*
Islamic Development Bank Group. (2020). *the Covid-19 Crisis and Islamic Finance* (Issue September). https://irti.org/product/the-covid-19-crisis-and-islamic-finance/
Jreisat, A., Rabbani, M. R., Bashar, A., Ali, M. A. M., & AlAbbas, A. (2021). Is Fintech valuation an art of science? Exploring the innovative methods for the valuation of Fintech startups. *2021 International Conference on Decision Aid Sciences and Application (DASA)* (pp. 922–925). IEEE.
Jusni, J., Possumah, B. T., Aswan, A., & Syamsuddin, A. R. (2019). Financing profitability optimization: Case study on sharia business unit of regional development banks in Indonesia. *Banks and Bank Systems, 14*(1), 1–10. https://doi.org/10.21511/bbs.14(1).2019.01
Karim, S., Naeem, M. A., Meero, A. A. et al. (2021). Examining the role of gender diversity on ownership structure-sustainable performance nexus: fresh evidence from emerging markets. *Environmental Science and Pollution Research.* https://doi.org/10.1007/s11356-021-17459-6

Karim, S., Rabbani, M. R., & Bawazir, H. (2022). Applications of Blockchain Technology in the Finance and Banking Industry Beyond Digital Currencies. In *Blockchain Technology and Computational Excellence for Society 5.0* (pp. 216–238). IGI Global.

Khan, S., & Rabbani, M. R. (2020). Artificial Intelligence and NLP based Chatbot as Islamic Banking and Finance Expert. *2020 International Conference on Computational Linguistics and Natural Language Processing (CLNLP 2020), Seoul, South Korea on July, 20–22*.

Khan, M. S., Rabbani, M. R., Hawaldar, I. T., & Bashar, A. (2022). Determinants of behavioral intentions to use Islamic financial technology: An empirical assessment. *Risks, 10*(6), 114.

Kukreja, G., Gupta, R., & Gupta, A. (2021). Fintech in oman: Present and future scenario. In *Studies in computational intelligence* (Vol. 954, pp. 173–183). Springer Science and Business Media Deutschland GmbH. https://doi.org/10.1007/978-3-030-72080-3_10

Lawal, I. M., & Ajayi, J. M. A. (2019). The role of Islamic social finance towards alleviating the humanitarian crisis in North-East Nigeria. *Jurnal Perspektif Pembiayaan Dan Pembangunan Daerah, 6*(5), 545–558. https://doi.org/10.22437/ppd.v6i5.6508

Leveraging Islamic Fintech to Improve Financial Inclusion. (2020). In *Leveraging Islamic Fintech to improve financial inclusion.* https://doi.org/10.1596/34520

Meero, A., Rahiman, H. U., & Rahman, A. A. A. (2021). The prospects of Bahrain's entrepreneurial ecosystem: An exploratory approach. *Problems and Perspectives in Management, 18*(4), 402.

Mohamed, H. Y., Hamdan, A., Karolak, M., Razzaque, A., & Alareeni, B. (2021). FinTech in Bahrain: The Role of FinTech in Empowering Women. In A. B., H. A., & E. I. (Eds.), *International Conference on Business and Technology, ICBT 2020: Vol. 194 LNNS* (pp. 757–766). Springer Science and Business Media Deutschland GmbH. https://doi.org/10.1007/978-3-030-69221-6_57

Narayan, S. W. (2020). Does fintech matter for Indonesia's economic growth? *Buletin Ekonomi Moneter Dan Perbankan, 22*(4), 437–456. https://doi.org/10.21098/bemp.v22i4.1237

Panakaje, N., Rahiman, H. U., Rabbani, M. R. et al. (2022). COVID-19 and its impact on educational environment in India. *Environmental Science and Pollution Research, 29*, 27788–27804. https://doi.org/10.1007/s11356-021-15306-2

Rabbani, M.R. (2022a). COVID-19 and its impact on supply chain financing and the role of Islamic Fintech: Evidence from GCC countries. *International Journal of Agile Systems and Management (IJASM)*, in press.

Rabbani, M. R. (2022b). Fintech innovations, scope, challenges, and implications in Islamic Finance: A systematic analysis. *International Journal of Computing and Digital Systems, 11*(1), 1–28.

Rabbani, M. R., Bashar, A., Nawaz, N., Karim, S., Ali, M. A. M., Khan, A., Rahiman, H., & Alam, S. (2021a). Exploring the role of Islamic Fintech in combating the after-shocks of COVID-19: The open social innovation of the Islamic financial system. *Journal of Open Innovation: Technology, Market, and Complexity, 7*, 136.

Rabbani, Mustafa Raza, Sarea, A., Khan, S., & Abdullah, Y. (2021b). Ethical Concerns in Artificial Intelligence (AI): The role of RegTech and Islamic finance. *The International Conference On Global Economic Revolutions* (pp. 381–390).

Rabbani, M.R., Khan, S., & Atif, M. (2022). Machine Learning based P2P Lending Islamic FinTech Model for Small and Medium Enterprises (SMEs) in Bahrain. *International Journal of Business Innovation and Research*, in press.

Rabbani, Mustafa Raza, Abdullah, Y., Bashar, A., Khan, S., & Ali, M. A. M. (2020). Embracing of Fintech in Islamic Finance in the post COVID era. *2020 International Conference on Decision Aid Sciences and Application (DASA), Sakheer, Bahrain, 2020*, 1230–1234. https://doi.org/10.1109/DASA51403.2020.9317196

Russell, S., Hauert, S., Altman, R., & Veloso, M. (2015). Robotics: Ethics of artificial intelligence. *Nature*. https://doi.org/10.1038/521415a

Standard, D. (2021). *Global Islamic fintech report*.

Sun, H., Rabbani, M. R., Sial, M. S., Yu, S., Filipe, J. A., & Cherian, J. (2020). Identifying big data's opportunities, challenges, and implications in finance. *Mathematics, 8*(10). https://doi.org/10.3390/math8101738

Wisskirchen, G., Thibault, B., Bormann, B. U., Muntz, A., Niehaus, G., Soler, G. J., & Von Brauchitsch, B. (2017). Artificial Intelligence and Robotics and Their Impact on the Workplace. *IBA Global Employment Institute*.

The Future of Finance and Fintech: Visualizing the Opportunities for Fintech in the MENA Region

M. Kabir Hassan, Habeeb Ur Rahiman, Mustafa Raza Rabbani, and Asem Alhomaidi

1 Introduction

A mature and developed Fintech ecosystem is essential to fostering the type of technological innovation required to make commercial markets and systems further effective and enhance the overall client experience (KPMG, 2020). Moreover, provided the extent of financial technology, a brilliant Fintech ecosystem can invigorate the wider regional economy

---

M. K. Hassan
Department of Economics and Finance, University of New, Orleans, New Orleans, LA 70148, USA
e-mail: mhassan@uno.edu

H. U. Rahiman (✉)
College of Business Administration, Kingdom University, Riffa, Kingdom of Bahrain
e-mail: h.rahiman@ku.edu.bh

M. R. Rabbani
Department of Economics and Finance, College of Business Administration, University of Bahrain, Zallaq, Kingdom of Bahrain
e-mail: mrabbani@uob.edu.bh

© The Author(s), under exclusive license to Springer Nature Switzerland AG 2022
M. K. Hassan et al. (eds.), *FinTech in Islamic Financial Institutions*, https://doi.org/10.1007/978-3-031-14941-2_5

by enticing capable, motivated individuals and grow into a locus of innovative thinking and commercial activity. Fintech ecosystems facilitate development opportunities for several sectors, comprising advanced payment systems, big data analytics, and algorithmic-based asset management system. The Middle East and North Africa (MENA) regions are one of the world's most divergent regions (Atif et al., 2022), covering three continents and 21 countries, with a populace of close to 600 million. This region is known to be diverse in its political, economic, and cultural aspects and comprises the six Arab states that are participants of the Gulf Coordination Council (GCC) (Rabbani, 2022a, 2022b). This multiplicity is manifested in the enormously different junctures of progression of the Fintech industries across the region. As per the major reports, Dubai, Abu Dhabi, Bahrain, and Riyadh have been labeled MENA's leading Fintech ecosystems (Hassan et al., 2021a, 2021b; Rabbani et al., 2021). Startup Genome a research institution explored heaps of countries around the globe based on considerations comprising funding, exits, ability, or talent, and focus as well as ecosystem players comprising policymakers and founders (Startup Genome, 2020).

During 2020, the Fintech sector has the significant distinctions between financial services and technology businesses. The basic difference between these two kinds of Fintech is that the corporations delivering financial services be likely to be the ones introducing the bigger amounts of funding. Some of these firms are also engendering comparatively high profits given their phase of advancement but at the same time experiencing comparatively high annual deficits. We examine little disparity in terms of stakeholder returns to date between the segments. The Paytech vertical, which comprises both types of Fintech, does stand up out from the other verticals in periods of shareholder gains which might be associated with the profitable exits carrying place away in this business line (Dharani et al., 2022; Jreisat et al., 2021; Karim et al., 2022).

Currently, Fintech ecosystems are still in progress in the GCC and MENA and confront impediments to development. For example, GCC administrations have been boosting financial e-services and digitized

---

A. Alhomaidi
Department of Finance, King Saud University, Riyadh,
Kingdom of Saudi Arabia
e-mail: aalhomaidi@ksu.edu.ksa

financial connections. However, several of these projects have been delayed, and few private-sector firms with digital capability have joined the effort. Therefore, this study is intended to understand the level of eco-system existing in GCC and explore elements required to develop Fintech ecosystems in GCC.

The Fintech literature has grown exponentially in recent years. It started only after the global financial crisis of 2008 and has been on the rise since then (Lee & Shin, 2018; Rabbani et al., 2020, 2021; Thakor, 2020), identifying the banks' prospects (Abu Daqar et al., 2020), identifying the trend (Das, 2019), and investigating the expansion of a startup (Goldstein et al., 2019). Study on officials' reaction to innovations in Fintech is yet evolving, with academics suggesting the testimony of financial institutions and banks fostering innovative tech-based, digital, or implementing supportive methodologies such as collaboration (Al Nawayseh, 2020; Liu et al., 2020; Rupeika-Apoga & Thalassinos, 2020; Zavolokina et al., 2016). However, the sensible procedure directing banks' measures continues unclear.

Banks today are facing enormous challenges from various small payment gateway service providers (Hassan et al., 2021a, 2021b). The underlying technologies such as Artificial intelligence, Quantum computing, Blockchain, etc. used by the Fintech startups bring risk and resistance to changes to the traditional financial institutions such as banks (Asmarani & Wijaya, 2020; Muthukannan et al., 2020; Shin & Choi, 2019; Sugiarti et al., 2019). Over 20% of the total conventional financial institution in the world gaining will be dropped to the entry of Fintech during 2020 (Goo & Heo, 2020; Hasan et al., 2020; Langley & Leyshon, 2021; Muthukannan et al., 2020). One of the key points associated with this modification however due to advanced solutions and facilities linked with incubators and various new Fintech-based institutions (Gazel & Schwienbacher, 2020; Liu et al., 2020; Zhang-Zhang et al., 2020). The institutions like banks and technology companies such as communication industry and mobile technology corporations are crafting a new ecosystem of business services (Cheng & Qu, 2020; Legowo et al., 2021; Ntwiga, 2020; Sheng, 2021; Wang et al., 2021). Thus, conventional banks which are believed as the leading institutions have prospects in the Fintech ecosystem, but nonetheless have challenges in supporting their philosophy and methods with that of others in the ecosystem (Alam et al., 2021; Moh'd Ali et al., 2020; Sun et al., 2020). In this respect, call out for an investigation into modern and evolving ecosystems as innovative know-hows and services do not inevitably align with most current banking standards and practices (Baber, 2020; Buchak et al., 2018; Mazza Basya & Utami Silfia Ayu, 2020; Phan et al., 2020). Thus, examining the Fintech programs of present institutions offers vital insights into the nature and structure of the forthcoming financial eco-systems (Basole & Patel, 2018; Muthukannan et al., 2020; Vovchenko et al., 2019).

To theoretically reinforce the growing method and actions of existing financial institutions within the current setup, we derive within the ideas of identifying and reacting. Sensing includes firms' capabilities to obtain sufficient expertise quickly and the associated adjustments that they control within the organization (Sviridov & Nekrasova, 2020). Reactions are firms' capabilities and readiness to take action toward technology-supported change (Buckley et al., 2019; Carbó Valverde et al., 2020; Soloviev, 2018). Organizations with the capabilities to know risks or prospects, but do not have the capabilities or readiness to take measures driven by the outcomes resulting from their identifying capabilities are at a threat of taking advantage of prospects and still fail (Buckley et al., 2019; Carbó Valverde et al., 2020; Diemers et al., 2015; Hendrikse et al., 2020; Sugeng et al., 2020). Also, organizations with the skills and inclination to act involve proper expertise before accepting results. Knowing-and-replying capabilities have been explored comprehensively in the ground of management; for example, in executive science (Wójcik, 2021) and advertising and promotion. Zhukov et al. (2019) described the capabilities to feel managerial difficulties as a prerequisite for decision-associated actions toward changing to modifications. Still et al. (2016) further emphasized that detecting is an intellectual method of rapidly monitoring and evolving meaning when confronted with a quickly changing atmosphere (Jiao et al., 2021; Wójcik, 2021; Zarrouk et al., 2021; Ziyaad & Mohamad, 2016) (Fig. 1).

2 Participants of Fintech Ecosystem

Banks and Financial institutions, venture capital funds, and non-public equity firms might promote deep substance and market proficiency to the ecosystem (Galazova & Magomaeva, 2019; Langley & Leyshon, 2021; Söylemez, 2019). Also, several of these monetary institutions can invigorate their own invention by creating alliances with Fintech startups (Lee & Shin, 2018; Omarini, 2018; Pooley, 2020; Valero et al., 2020).

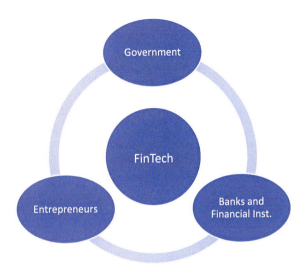

Fig. 1 Key participants of Fintech ecosystem (Author's own architecture)

3 Fintech Ecosystem Design

Marketing Environment

Fintech ecosystems ought to generate an inclusive cost advantage for operating in a country or territory if they are to succeed. This act will facilitate affordable infrastructures such as land and real estate, apparatus, technology, and services (Lynch, 2013; Shmuratko & Sheludko, 2019; Sudarto & Inggriantara, 2020). An Additional element is the degree of incorporation and collaboration among the participants. Technology hubs, where financiers and entrepreneurs have related business goals and are cohesive, make it simpler for the ecosystem to grow. These groups stimulate the accessibility of various expertise such as banking analysts, IT designers and developers, and other managerial workforce (Beausoleil-Morrison et al., 2001; Decae, 1984; Yadav et al., 2011).

Governance Support

In GCC, administrations can change many facets of the ecosystem, including reducing regulation attached to business such as registration formalities, copyright, initial public offering (IPO) obligations, etc. and maintaining taxes and levies lower (Arli et al., 2021; Arner et al., 2020; Nurfadilah & Samidi, 2021; Yang, 2017). However, the scope of the government's interest can differ (Abdullah & Rabbani, 2021). In comparatively strong Fintech ecosystems such as in certain developed countries like China, United Kingdom, and United States, the private sector overshadows the service provider landscape.

Financial Accessibility

Accessibility to financial source to Fintech ecosystem is possible in various sources (Demir et al., 2020; Navaretti et al., 2018; Senyo & Osabutey, 2020). Mainly Rulings Authorities may support the building of the Fintech hubs, by offering seed funds, interest-free loans, and grants, or even via establishment of supportive infrastructure (Anshari et al., 2020; Pambudianti et al., 2020; Suryono et al., 2021). This can be accomplished with financial institution like banks in a confederation (Karim et al., 2021; Rabbani et al., 2022). The government may additionally facilitate primary monetary support to venture capital or private equity funds, financial institutions, and different incubators to promote financing in small businesses (Allen et al., 2020; Fauzia, 2020; Philippon, 2019; Zarrouk et al., 2021).

Venture capital funds and private equities are conventional shareholders in Fintech startups (Borgogno & Colangelo, 2020; Najib et al., 2021; Ozili, 2020). Capitals' contribution will usually rise as these small business versions gain impetus and reach essential mass.

Financial Know-How

Comprehensive monetary know-how is essential to structure the proprietorship of a Fintech ecosystem (Khan et al., 2022). Advice-giving facilities to entrepreneurs from the initial phases of idea cohort over commercialization, and finally deliver legal and governing counseling to guarantee devotion to resident law and levy guidelines is an essential element of Fintech ecosystem (Rasiwala & Kohli, 2020). These specialists can also be involved in promoting economic or governing measures to reduce the formation and procurement of startups. In addition, by fostering decreased commercial laws and policies like registration and intellectual property rights, these specialists help entrepreneurs and monetary services companies and improve the attraction of the overall ecosystem (Jamaruddin & Markom, 2020; Mazza Basya & Utami Silfia Ayu, 2020; Prayitno & Setyowati, 2020) (Fig. 2).

Currently in the Middle East, only 1% of the global Fintech investment is reflected and represented. The Fintech sector throughout the Middle East is expanding at a compounded annual growth rate (CAGR) of 30%. It is estimated that by 2022 (Fig. 3), 465 Fintech firms in the Middle East will bring in over $2 billion in venture capital funding, equated to the 30 Fintechs that amassed approximately $80 million in 2017. A Lot of the capital spending in the province has surged to some of the more dynamic sectors of Fintech. Startups concentrated on payments and transfers, online lending, digital banking, blockchain, RegTech, crowdfunding, and

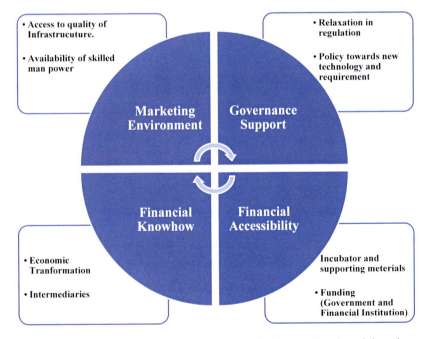

Fig. 2 Fintech ecosystem proposed framework (*Source* Developed based on review)

cryptocurrency companies are promising and most frequently surrounded by the territory. It means most of the financing continues to focus on the payments space and approximately 85% of Fintech companies in the MENA province manage the transfer of funds, payments, and remittances division. Justifiably, most of the investing in the region has surged to the payments area, as the province stays a source for payments-associated activity. Most of the Gulf regions particularly UAE and Saudi Arabia is a powerful force in remittances due to a vast number of its expatriate inhabitants, which signifies the majority of the country's total population. In 2017, expatriate transfer of funds from the UAE equaled $44.5 billion, three-quarters of which was remitted via money exchange firms and one-quarter delivered through banks. The significant saturation of mobile appliances and internet connectivity has partly led to this movement in the territory. In the Middle East, mobile penetration surpassed 100% in 2017, at the same time as smartphone penetration reached 60%. During 2019, Bahrain, the UAE, and Qatar are among the highly penetrated marketplaces in the globe. Saudi Arabia and Kuwait joined them during 2019 in launching 5G networks.

The 2020 World Economic Forum's Global Competitiveness Report is devoted to explain the main concern for revival and recovery and contemplating the developing blocks of a change in the direction of

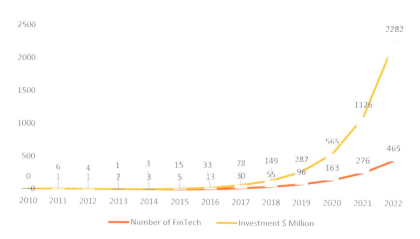

Fig. 3 Middle East venture capital investment into Fintech companies (*Source* The Dubai International Financial Centre [DIFC] Fintech Hive and Accenture)

new economic systems that merge "productivity", "people", and "planet" targets. As per the report, the ITU world telecommunication estimates that at the end of 2019, a bit additional than 51% of the worldwide population, or 4 billion individuals, are using the Cyberspace or internet. For example, in the United States, e-commerce has soared by 24% in one single year from July 2019 to July 2020, which means it has subsequently risen by an average of 10% per year from 2010 to 2019. Universally, the total number of courses related to e-learning has grown sharply, as around 1.2 billion children are out of educational institutions due to COVID-19 regulations. Working at home, online entertainment through OTT (Over the top) platforms, and other, telemedicine, videoconferencing has all remained on the rise ever since the beginning of the pandemic.

According to the World Economic Forum's 2020 Global Competitiveness Report (Startup Genome, 2020) (Fig. 4), out of 140 countries, Bahrain ranked 38th for the adoption of information and communication technologies (ICT). This is one of the vital factors for countries looking for adoption of Fintech. Mobile-cellular telephone and mobile-broadband subscriptions are the other key factors revealed in this report, and state 158% 10th position and 147% 5th position, respectively. Similarly, among the user of internet, the country stands for 98% of the population which is 3rd position.

4 Emerging Role of MENA in Investment Fund

Numerous investment funds have arisen over the years that compete for a crucial role in the worldwide Fintech investing ecosystem (Fig. 5). Based on our various observations, nearly six investments have taken place in Bahrain and the UAE ever since late 2017 concentrated on relationships with other projects or direct investment in pioneering firms. Entirely, these funds have grown approximately $1.5 billion in investment. As a later development, numerous of these Fintech-related funds started to swing from concentrating on external prospects to relaying more of their capital to promising prospects within the region. In several instances, these resources associate with the strategic projects set by administrators in Bahrain and the UAE. These programs seek out to attract world-class ability to the province, additionally diversifying the economies within every nation, and placing the province as a participant in the international venture investing ecosystem.

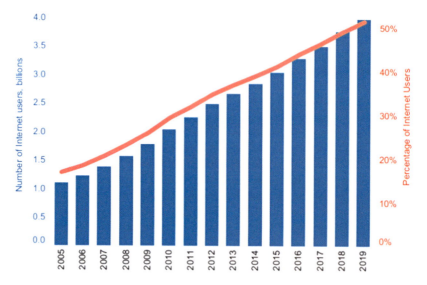

Fig. 4 Number of Internet users in a leading country (*Source* International telecommunication Union [ITU])

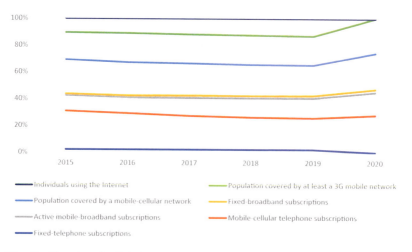

Fig. 5 Trends of ICT development in MENA region (*Source* ITU World Telecommunication/ICT Indicators database)

Frontier markets remain strong in terms of growth capability. While short-term winds exist, we believe the long-term version of frontier markets continues undamaged. The structural prospect is like developing markets 30 years ago, excepting that the growth curve is expected to be faster due to the availability of technology. For shareholders, frontier markets recommend local diversity across the Middle Eastern and African regions. We have seen frontier markets push eccentric changes to boost macro development. The resource category continues in its initial phases of growth compared to greater developing markets, with smaller overseas investor proprietorship and under-researched marketplace coverage. The current motivation for coverage to frontier markets is certain to contribute to a locally different asset class with alluring demographics and improved understanding of goods all catalyzed by the implementation of technology in methods industry earlier have not witnessed.

Compared to another region in MENA, UAE has a highly sophisticated ecosystem, with numerous public and private programs encouraging invention. These comprise the Dubai International Financial Centre, which administers a $100 million Fintech deposit and the county's initial Fintech accelerator, Fintech Hive; and similarly, Global market in Abu Dhabi, which established its RegLab (regulatory laboratory) explicitly to support new businesses crack their governing issues. In other nations, central banks are doing measures to promote digitization and innovation. Lebanon just permitted electronic sign, which is likely to enhance virtual banking, operations, and trade. Lebanon has one of the highly active digital ecosystems in the province. This development is due to Banque du Liban's 2013 guarantee of more than $600 million to pledge up to 75% of all commercial banks' funds in regional startups.

The proportion of digital products offered is yet extremely tiny linked to Western countries, but the vogue is shifting, Fintechs are currently further recognized than always before, and I think banks are far beyond wide open to discovering alliances. Current examples of this comprise Kuwait's Ahli United, which introduced a rent-payment mobile application; Beirut-based start-up FOO, which offers digital solutions for local banks and telecom service providers; and even global companies like US-based Fintech Ripple, which engaged cross-border payment contracts with three MENA banks namely, Kuwait Finance House, National Commercial Bank, and National Bank of Kuwait. Several organizations are pressing more, capitalizing clearly on grassroots visionaries. The previous year, Arab Bank was the earliest investor in the region to establish its own $30 million Fintech venture capital finance, and telecom service suppliers Alfa and Touch launched a $48 million Beirut-based finance to invest in data and communication know-hows. Support from conventional investors such as these delivers Fintechs with faith, grip, and the capability to size quicker. Financial organizations and larger firms, for their role, gain from the suppleness, quickness, and technological skills of young businesspersons. They are instantaneously competent to extend consumers a facility that would have transferred more time and money to build internally.

5 Fintech Investment in MENA Region

The United Arab Emirates is prominent in the approach when it comes to applying Fintechs to promote and build smart cities. Following is the list of forecasts for the finance and banking industry in the MENA region.

Investment in Fintech

Clifford Chance has identified the UAE as the MENA prominent financial technology marketplace, forecasting that it will rise to $2.5 billion by 2022. The rise in Fintech ventures clearly focuses on the growing need for tech-empowered and customer centrical banking. Consequently, the digital drive that was inflicted on businesses by COVID-19 suggests we can anticipate seeing several digital banks remain to come to life cycle as financial organizations make the switch from conventional to online.

Comparably, we too go to see those substantial adjustments in customer expenditure patterns because COVID-19 is affecting requirements for digital banking. Corresponding to the National Economic Register stated by Emirate's news report organization WAM, UAE's e-commerce region released the maximum quantity of permits—196—in May 2020, while the initial five months of 2020 witnessed a 300% increase in customer need for e-commerce facilities. It is expected that customers will remain to choose online spending and that will remain to raise the need for digital payments in 2021 and beyond.

Relationship Banking

The shift away from client-centric banking remained so steady that we hardly observed it. There was a moment while having a special connection with the regional branch common place (Jakšič & Marinč, 2019; Kotarba, 2016; Li et al., 2017). Digital expertise altered this, aiming at accessibility, growing rivalry, and creating the mobile consumer experience as the crucial differentiator (Srivastava, 2020). Whilst these innovations have helped clients in several ways, in some cases, it has positioned the importance away from the consumer-centrical model which then well-defined banking (Musabegović et al., 2019).

The rise of pandemic became this gradually evident and underlined that there is nevertheless a demand for relationship banking, especially for susceptible and non-digital consumers. The disaster squeezed several people's business strengths and offered rise to many queries on the financial assistance offered to customers. Additionally, clients availing from banking facilities throughout this period that usually necessary face-to-face communication, such as mortgages, we're currently going all through this process digitally. COVID-19 has stressed the various demands of clients varying on their condition and shows the significance of focusing on bespoke and custom-made services reliant on clients' individual demands and desires. The study has observed a revert to relationship banking in 2021 as the main concern but is now blended with the accessibility and advantages presented by digital banking. It is a complicated balance out but using the appropriate technology will be crucial for banks to pact with consumers in the proper way, matching their expectations.

Increase in Cloud Banking

Cloud banking has stood on the cliff over current years, the recognized technology threat has avoided this from being fulfilled in any substantial manner. Though, now the company's threat to not execute cloud technology has overhauled this technology threat. Considering the current pandemic and client requirements make banks adopt procedures and policies quickly in reaction to altering control and client needs, which relic, on-premises methods were not constructed for. As the catastrophe remains to grow, banks are steering screens on just how to continue. This has highlighted the necessity to get a structure that permits banks to turn swiftly and efficiently. Cloud technology is vital to banks playing and remaining in this new era. Whilst this change was forever predictable, changes in 2020 have rendered this a non-negotiable, and therefore, we will see the extensive implementation of cloud banking in 2021.

Embedded Finance

Though the market will not see great expertise and non-banking performers joining the banking business in any substantial way in 2021, we are able to anticipate these participants to take cautious, strategic movements in the direction of creating a significant, long-lasting existence. Large technology and banks believe in a different way and move about at various times, which poses questions to both players. Government is additionally a lingering concern for large technology firms. There are essential measures to take over to steer these problems which non-banking companies will remain to meet through 2021.

6 FINTECH STARTUPS DISTRIBUTION AMONG MENA COUNTRIES

Amongst the MENA nations, the Fintech market prospects, products, and services in seven Arabian nations, with certain instances indicating the development of their ecosystems. The UAE, Egypt, Jordan, Lebanon, Morocco, Kuwait, and Saudi Arabia. The choice of those nations is ascribed to the statistic that those nations' deposit accounts for nearly 92% of the total quantity of startups in 12 Arab Nations in MENA. In particular, UAE only accommodates 30 Fintech startups, followed by Egypt (17), together of Jordan and Lebanon (15), Morocco (8), and equally Kuwait and Saudi Arabia (6) each.

Fintech is gained better prominence after 2020 with the payments segment previously displaying indications of merging, particularly in the GCC province (Fig. 6). Crowdfunding and loaning platforms are established to remain to develop particularly programs with a concentration on geographies. For example, Eureeca, one of the equity crowdfunding platforms, is one of MENA's openings Fintech startups that ran worldwide. For 2020, startups from the second wave segments, involving payments, wealth management, insurance, and blockchain, have raised to fame.

The overall observation in various research and reports reveals two different approaches, one part of the observation reveals banks' adoption of Fintech considering various intermediaries' interference in payment bypassing traditional banking system. This development could create a major challenge to traditional banking operators like commercial and investment banks. Middle East can be considered as an important example to notice changes taking place in the region. The Fintech ecosystem in the

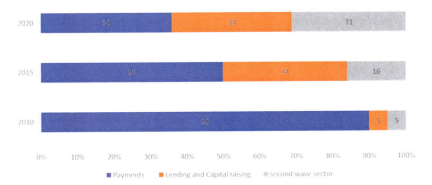

Fig. 6 Fintech startup creation MENA (*Source* Fintech Focus, KPMG)

Middle East is considered by a convinced level of flaw and contrast: The ecosystem is embryonic quickly once it originates to organizing advanced explanations, yet it is stressed to entice supplementary funding that will increase its footmark and influence. Banks are eager to participate with Fintechs in a wide variety of experimental schemes; however, they are hesitant to incorporate Fintechs into their approach, as they prefer to follow a "wait and see" attitude. Customer behavior around the Middle East, mainly in KSA, is exemplified by a readiness to embrace advanced solutions proposed by banks; in specific, when it occurs to peer-to-peer cash transfers, bank account aggregation, and computerized investing advice. Though banks are not leveraging the extensive suite of Fintech features to deliver clients' requirements and needs to improve the regular banking journey and knowledge.

7 Conclusion

The present study has observed an increase in Fintech-related movement in various parts of the MENA region especially in Bahrain and the UAE. It can be noticed that regulators and policymakers encourage by extracting to expand their economies and financial scope beyond their traditional framework. The Gulf region is currently considered to be the most effective region by adopting all the advanced and innovative technologies. The world has witnessed Dubai as one of the most prominent places for the most recent technologically experienced country. One of the key outcomes of the MENA region is establishing a welcoming permissible and regulatory atmosphere for Fintech startups and matured development proposals through progress-thinking programs. An essential part of this approach is establishing a facilitating environment adept of inviting and encouraging foreign firms contained by their corresponding countries. The information transfer likely to result from this will push the advancement of a lively, regional Fintech ecosystem. Most noticeably, counties like Bahrain and the UAE are initially on in their attempts to build into *the* Fintech hub in the area. Most of the counties in the MENA region are adopting and considering the outcome of Fintech and putting their efforts in effectively establishing a bright Fintech ecosystem.

REFERENCES

Abdullah, Y., & Rabbani, M. R. (2021). COVID-19 and GCC Islamic market Indices. *2021 International Conference on Sustainable Islamic Business and Finance (SIBF)*.

Abu Daqar, M. A. M., Arqawi, S., & Karsh, S. A. (2020). Fintech in the eyes of Millennials and Generation Z (the financial behavior and Fintech perception). *Banks and Bank Systems*. https://doi.org/10.21511/bbs.15(3).2020.03

Al Nawayseh, M. K. (2020). Fintech in COVID-19 and beyond: What factors are affecting customers' choice of fintech applications? *Journal of Open Innovation: Technology, Market, and Complexity*. https://doi.org/10.3390/joitmc 6040153

Alam, M., Rabbani, M. R., Tausif, M. R., & Abey, J. (2021). Banks' performance and economic growth in India: A panel cointegration analysis. *Economies*, *9*(1), 38.

Allen, F., Gu, X., & Jagtiani, J. (2020). *A survey of Fintech research and policy discussion a survey of fintech research and policy discussion**. Federal Reserve Bank of Phildadelphia.

Anshari, M., Almunawar, M. N., & Masri, M. (2020). Financial technology and disruptive innovation in business: Concept and application. *International Journal of Asian Business and Information Management*. https://doi.org/10. 4018/IJABIM.2020100103

Arli, D., van Esch, P., Bakpayev, M., & Laurence, A. (2021). Do consumers really trust cryptocurrencies? *Marketing Intelligence and Planning*. https:// doi.org/10.1108/MIP-01-2020-0036

Arner, D. W., Buckley, R. P., Zetzsche, D. A., & Veidt, R. (2020). Sustainability, FinTech and Financial Inclusion. *European Business Organization Law Review*. https://doi.org/10.1007/s40804-020-00183-y

Asmarani, S. C., & Wijaya, C. (2020). Effects of fintech on stock return: Evidence from retail banks listed in Indonesia stock exchange. *Journal of Asian Finance, Economics and Business.* https://doi.org/10.13106/jafeb.2020.vol7.no7.095

Atif, M., Rabbani, M. R., Bawazir, H., Hawaldar, I. T., Chebab, D., Karim, S., & AlAbbas, A. (2022). Oil price changes and stock returns: Fresh evidence from oil exporting and oil importing countries. *Cogent Economics & Finance, 10*(1), 2018163.

Baber, H. (2020). FinTech, crowdfunding and customer retention in Islamic Banks. *Vision.* https://doi.org/10.1177/0972262919869765

Basole, R. C., & Patel, S. S. (2018). Transformation through unbundling: Visualizing the global FinTech ecosystem. *Service Science.* https://doi.org/10.1287/serv.2018.0210

Beausoleil-Morrison, I., Clarke, J. A., Denev, J., Macdonald, I. A., Melikov, A. K., & Stankov, P. (2001). Further developments in the conflation of CFD and buildings simulation. *Second National IBPSA-USA Conference.*

Borgogno, O., & Colangelo, G. (2020). The data sharing paradox: BigTechs in finance. *European Competition Journal.* https://doi.org/10.1080/17441056.2020.1812285

Buchak, G., Matvos, G., Piskorski, T., & Seru, A. (2018). Fintech, regulatory arbitrage, and the rise of shadow banks. *Journal of Financial Economics.* https://doi.org/10.1016/j.jfineco.2018.03.011

Buckley, R. P., Arner, D. W., Veidt, R., & Zetzsche, D. A. (2019). Building FinTech Ecosystems: Regulatory Sandboxes, Innovation Hubs and Beyond. *SSRN Electronic Journal.* https://doi.org/10.2139/ssrn.3455872

Carbó Valverde, S., Rodríguez Fernández, F., & Cuadros Solas, J. (2020). Taxonomy of the Spanish FinTech ecosystem and the drivers of FinTechs' performance. *Estabilidad Financiera.*

Cheng, M., & Qu, Y. (2020). Does bank FinTech reduce credit risk? Evidence from China. *Pacific Basin Finance Journal.* https://doi.org/10.1016/j.pacfin.2020.101398

Das, S. R. (2019). The future of fintech. *Financial Management.* https://doi.org/10.1111/fima.12297

Decae A.E. (1984). A coryonthe origin of spiders and the primitive function of spidersilk. *Journal of Arachnology.*

Demir, A., Pesqué-Cela, V., Altunbas, Y., & Murinde, V. (2020). Fintech, financial inclusion and income inequality: A quantile regression approach. *European Journal of Finance.* https://doi.org/10.1080/1351847X.2020.1772335

Dharani, M., Hassan, M. K., Rabbani, M. R., & Huq, T. (2022). Does the Covid-19 pandemic affect faith-based investments? Evidence from global sectoral indices. *Research in International Business and Finance, 59*, 101537.

Diemers, D., Lamaa, A., Salamat, J., & Steffens, T. (2015). *Developing a FinTech ecosystem in the GCC.* Strategy&.

Fauzia, I. Y. (2020). Enhancing the literacy of Shariah financial technology for generation X, Y and Z in Indonesia. *Jurnal Minds: Manajemen Ide Dan Inspirasi.* https://doi.org/10.24252/minds.v7i2.15871

Galazova, S. S., & Magomaeva, L. R. (2019). The transformation of traditional banking activity in digital. *International Journal of Economics and Business Administration.* https://doi.org/10.35808/ijeba/369

Gazel, M., & Schwienbacher, A. (2020). Entrepreneurial fintech clusters. *Small Business Economics.* https://doi.org/10.1007/s11187-020-00331-1

Goldstein, I., Jiang, W., & Karolyi, G. A. (2019). To FinTech and beyond. *Review of Financial Studies.* https://doi.org/10.1093/rfs/hhz025

Goo, J. J., & Heo, J. Y. (2020). The impact of the regulatory sandbox on the fintech industry, with a discussion on the relation between regulatory sandboxes and open innovation. *Journal of Open Innovation: Technology, Market, and Complexity.* https://doi.org/10.3390/JOITMC6020043

Hasan, R., Hassan, M. K., & Aliyu, S. (2020). Fintech and Islamic finance: Literature review and research agenda. *International Journal of Islamic Economics and Finance (IJIEF), 1*(2), 75–94. https://doi.org/10.18196/ijief.2122

Hassan, M. K., Rabbani, M., & Daouia, C. (2021a). Integrating Islamic finance and Halal industry: Current landscape and future forward. *International Journal of Islamic Marketing and Branding, 6*(1), 60–78.

Hassan, M. K., Rabbani, M. R., & Abdullah, Y. (2021b). Socioeconomic impact of COVID-19 in MENA region and the role of Islamic finance. *International Journal of Islamic Economics and Finance (IJIEF), 4*(1), 51–78.

Hendrikse, R., van Meeteren, M., & Bassens, D. (2020). Strategic coupling between finance, technology and the state: Cultivating a Fintech ecosystem for incumbent finance. *Environment and Planning A.* https://doi.org/10.1177/0308518X19887967

Jakšič, M., & Marinč, M. (2019). Relationship banking and information technology: The role of artificial intelligence and FinTech. *Risk Management.* https://doi.org/10.1057/s41283-018-0039-y

Jamaruddin, W. N., & Markom, R. (2020). The Application of Fintech in the operation of Islamic banking. *Syariah and Law in Facing COVID-19: The Way Forward.*

Jiao, Z., Shahid, M. S., Mirza, N., & Tan, Z. (2021). Should the fourth industrial revolution be widespread or confined geographically? A country-level analysis of fintech economies. *Technological Forecasting and Social Change.* https://doi.org/10.1016/j.techfore.2020.120442

Jreisat, A., Rabbani, M. R., Bashar, A., Ali, M. A. M., & AlAbbas, A. (2021). Is Fintech valuation an art of science? Exploring the innovative methods for the valuation of fintech startups. *2021 International Conference on Decision Aid Sciences and Application (DASA)*, (pp. 922–925). IEEE.

Karim, S., Akhtar, M. U., Tashfeen, R., Raza Rabbani, M., Rahman, A. A. A., & AlAbbas, A. (2021). Sustainable banking regulations pre and during coronavirus outbreak: The moderating role of financial stability. *Economic Research-Ekonomska Istraživanja*, 35, 1–18.

Karim, S., Rabbani, M. R., & Bawazir, H. (2022). Applications of blockchain technology in the finance and banking industry beyond digital currencies. In *Blockchain Technology and Computational Excellence for Society 5.0* (pp. 216–238). IGI Global.

Khan, M. S., Rabbani, M. R., Hawaldar, I. T., & Bashar, A. (2022). Determinants of behavioral intentions to use Islamic financial technology: An empirical assessment. *Risks*, 10(6), 114.

Kotarba, M. (2016). New factors inducing changes in the retail banking customer relationship management (CRM) and their exploration by the FinTech industry. *Foundations of Management*. https://doi.org/10.1515/fman-2016-0006

KPMG. (2020). *Fintech focus* (Issue July).

Langley, P., & Leyshon, A. (2021). The platform political economy of FinTech: Reintermediation, consolidation and capitalisation. *New Political Economy*. https://doi.org/10.1080/13563467.2020.1766432

Lee, I., & Shin, Y. J. (2018). Fintech: Ecosystem, business models, investment decisions, and challenges. *Business Horizons*. https://doi.org/10.1016/j.bushor.2017.09.003

Legowo, M. B., Subanidja, S., & Sorongan, F. A. (2021). Fintech and bank: Past, present, and future. *Jurnal Teknik Komputer*. https://doi.org/10.31294/jtk.v7i1.9726

Li, Y., Spigt, R., & Swinkels, L. (2017). The impact of FinTech start-ups on incumbent retail banks' share prices. *Financial Innovation*. https://doi.org/10.1186/s40854-017-0076-7

Liu, J., Li, X., & Wang, S. (2020). What have we learnt from 10 years of Fintech research? A scientometric analysis. *Technological Forecasting and Social Change*. https://doi.org/10.1016/j.techfore.2020.120022

Lynch, T. (2013). Writing up qualitative research: Methodology. *English Language Teaching Center*. https://doi.org/10.1007/s13398-014-0173-7.2

Mazza Basya, M., & Utami Silfia Ayu, B. (2020). Analisis SWOT dengan Model Importance Performance Analysis (IPA) Pada Layanan Fintech Bank Syariah di Indonesia. *El-Qist: Journal of Islamic Economics and Business (JIEB)*. https://doi.org/10.15642/elqist.2020.10.2.179-191

Moh'd Ali, M. A., Basahr, A., Rabbani, M. R., & Abdulla, Y. (2020). Transforming business decision making with Internet of Things (IoT) and Machine

Learning (ML). *2020 International Conference on Decision Aid Sciences and Application (DASA)* (pp. 674–679).

Musabegović, I., Özer, M., Đuković, S., & Jovanović, S. (2019). Influence of financial technology (Fintech) on financial industry. *Ekonomika Poljoprivrede.* https://doi.org/10.5937/ekopolj1904003m

Muthukannan, P., Tan, B., Gozman, D., & Johnson, L. (2020). The emergence of a Fintech ecosystem: A case study of the Vizag Fintech Valley in India. *Information and Management.* https://doi.org/10.1016/j.im.2020.103385

Najib, M., Ermawati, W. J., Fahma, F., Endri, E., & Suhartanto, D. (2021). Fintech in the small food business and its relation with open innovation. *Journal of Open Innovation: Technology, Market, and Complexity.* https://doi.org/10.3390/joitmc7010088

Navaretti, G. B. mname, Calzolari, G. mname, Mansilla-Fernandez, J. M. mname, & Pozzolo, A. F. mname. (2018). Fintech and banking. Friends or foes? *SSRN Electronic Journal.* https://doi.org/10.2139/ssrn.3099337

Ntwiga, D. B. (2020). Technical efficiency in the Kenyan banking sector: Influence of Fintech and banks collaboration. *Journal of Finance and Economics.*

Nurfadilah, D., & Samidi, S. (2021). How the COVID-19 crisis is affecting customers' intention to use Islamic fintech services: Evidence from Indonesia. *Journal of Islamic Monetary Economics and Finance.* https://doi.org/10.21098/jimf.v7i0.1318

Omarini, A. E. (2018). Fintech and the future of the payment landscape: The mobile wallet ecosystem – A challenge for retail banks? *International Journal of Financial Research.* https://doi.org/10.5430/ijfr.v9n4p97

Ozili, P. K. (2020). Financial Inclusion and Fintech during COVID-19 crisis: Policy solutions. *SSRN Electronic Journal.* https://doi.org/10.2139/ssrn.3585662

Pambudianti, F. F. R., Purwanto, B., & Maulana, T. N. A. (2020). The implementation of fintech: Efficiency of MSMEs loans distribution and users' financial inclusion index. *Jurnal Keuangan Dan Perbankan.* https://doi.org/10.26905/jkdp.v24i1.3218

Phan, D. H. B., Narayan, P. K., Rahman, R. E., & Hutabarat, A. R. (2020). Do financial technology firms influence bank performance? *Pacific Basin Finance Journal.* https://doi.org/10.1016/j.pacfin.2019.101210

Philippon, T. (2019). The FinTech opportunity. *The Disruptive Impact of FinTech on Retirement Systems.* https://doi.org/10.1093/oso/9780198845553.003.0011

Pooley, H. (2020). Why banks are missing an opportunity to capture the lucrative small and medium enterprise market. *Journal of Payments Strategy and Systems, 13*(4), 337–351.

Prayitno, G., & Setyowati, R. (2020). The existence of Sharia supervisory board in Sharia Fintech: Legal basis and problematic in Indonesia. *Syariah: Jurnal Hukum Dan Pemikiran.* https://doi.org/10.18592/sjhp.v20i2.4060

Rabbani, M.R;, Kayani, U., Bawazir, H., & Hawaldar, I. T. (2022). A commentary on emerging market banking sector spill over Covid vs GFC pattern analysis. *Heliyon, e09074.*

Rabbani, M.R. (2022a). COVID-19 and its impact on supply chain financing and the role of Islamic Fintech: Evidence from GCC countries. *International Journal of Agile Systems and Management (IJASM)* (in press).

Rabbani, M. R. (2022b). Fintech innovations, scope, challenges, and implications in Islamic Finance: A systematic analysis. *International Journal of Computing and Digital Systems, 11*(1), 1–28.

Rabbani, M. R., Bashar, A., Nawaz, N., Karim, S., Ali, M. A. M., Khan, A., Rahiman, H., & Alam, S. (2021). Exploring the role of Islamic Fintech in combating the after-shocks of COVID-19: The open social innovation of the Islamic financial system. *Journal of Open Innovation: Technology, Market, and Complexity, 7,* 136.

Rabbani, Mustafa Raza, Khan, S., & Thalassinos, E. I. (2020). FinTech, blockchain and Islamic finance: An extensive literature review. *International Journal of Economics and Business Administration, 8*(2), 65–86. https://doi.org/10.35808/ijeba/444

Rasiwala, F. S., & Kohli, B. (2020). Artificial intelligence in FinTech. *International Journal of Business Intelligence Research.* https://doi.org/10.4018/ijbir.20210101.oa3

Rupeika-Apoga, R., & Thalassinos, E. I. (2020). Ideas for a regulatory definition of FinTech. *International Journal of Economics and Business Administration.* https://doi.org/10.35808/ijeba/448

Senyo, P. K., & Osabutey, E. L. C. (2020). Unearthing antecedents to financial inclusion through FinTech innovations. *Technovation, 98.* https://doi.org/10.1016/j.technovation.2020.102155

Sheng, T. (2021). The effect of Fintech on banks' credit provision to SMEs: Evidence from China. *Finance Research Letters.* https://doi.org/10.1016/j.frl.2020.101558

Shin, Y. J., & Choi, Y. (2019). Feasibility of the fintech industry as an innovation platform for sustainable economic growth in Korea. *Sustainability (switzerland).* https://doi.org/10.3390/su11195351

Shmuratko, Y. A., & Sheludko, S. A. (2019). Financial technologies' impact on the development of banking. *Financial and Credit Activity: Problems of Theory and Practice.* https://doi.org/10.18371/fcaptp.v4i31.190792

Soloviev, V. (2018). Fintech ecosystem in Russia. *Proceedings of 2018 11th International Conference 'Management of Large-Scale System Development', MLSD 2018.* https://doi.org/10.1109/MLSD.2018.8551808

Söylemez, Y. (2019). Fintech ecosystem and banking: The case of Turkey. *Handbook of Research on Strategic Fit and Design in Business Ecosystems.* https://doi.org/10.4018/978-1-7998-1125-1.ch014

Srivastava, K. (2020). Unfolding FinTech: A paradigm shift in Indian banking. *Paideuma Journal, 13*(4), 129–136.

Startup Genome. (2020). *The Global Startup Ecosystem Report 2020 (GSER 2020).*

Still, K., Huhtala, T., & Saraniemi, S. (2016). FinTech as Business and Innovation Ecosystems. *Proceedings of ISPIM Conferences.*

Sudarto, N., & Inggriantara, A. (2020). Business strategy for PT Finansindo Mikro facing competition in microfinance business. *International Journal of Research in Engineering, Science and Management.* https://doi.org/10.47607/ijresm.2020.386

Sugeng, S., Tobing, C. I., & Fajarwati, R. (2020). Indonesian Fintech: Business ecosystem and regulation. *Diponegoro Law Review.* https://doi.org/10.14710/dilrev.5.2.2020.277-295

Sugiarti, E. N., Diana, N., & Mawardi, M. C. (2019). Peran Fintech Dalam Meningkatkan Literasi Keuangan Pada Usaha Mikro Kecil Menengah Di Malang. *E-Jra.*

Sun, H., Rabbani, M. R., Ahmad, N., Sial, M. S., Cheng, G., Zia-Ud-Din, M., & Fu, Q. (2020). CSR, co-creation and green consumer loyalty: Are green banking initiatives important? A moderated mediation approach from an emerging economy. *Sustainability, 12*(24), 10688.

Suryono, R. R., Budi, I., & Purwandari, B. (2021). Detection of Fintech P2P lending issues in Indonesia. *Heliyon.* https://doi.org/10.1016/j.heliyon.2021.e06782

Sviridov, O., & Nekrasova, I. (2020). Development trends of the Fintech ecosystem in Russian economy. *Vestnik Volgogradskogo Gosudarstvennogo Universiteta. Ekonomika.* https://doi.org/10.15688/ek.jvolsu.2019.4.19

Thakor, A. V. (2020). Fintech and banking: What do we know? *Journal of Financial Intermediation.* https://doi.org/10.1016/j.jfi.2019.100833

Valero, S., Climent, F., & Esteban, R. (2020). Future banking scenarios. Evolution of digitalisation in Spanish banking. *Journal of Business Accounting and Finance Perspectives.* https://doi.org/10.35995/jbafp2020013

Vovchenko, N. G., Galazova, S. S., Sopchenko, A. A., & Dzhu, O. S. (2019). Fintech ecosystem as an instrument of sustainable development provision. *International Journal of Economics and Business Administration, 7,* 147–155. https://doi.org/10.35808/ijeba/379

Wang, R., Liu, J., & Luo, H. (2021). Fintech development and bank risk taking in China. *European Journal of Finance.* https://doi.org/10.1080/1351847X.2020.1805782

Wójcik, D. (2021). Financial geography I: Exploring FinTech – Maps and concepts. *Progress in Human Geography*, 45(3), 566–576. https://doi.org/10.1177/0309132520952865

Yadav, A., Subedi, D., Lundeberg, M. A., & Bunting, C. F. (2011). Problem-based learning: Influence on students' learning in an electrical engineering course. *Journal of Engineering Education*, 100(2), 253–280.

Yang, H. (2017). The UK's Fintech industry support policies and its implications. *SSRN Electronic Journal*. https://doi.org/10.2139/ssrn.2919191

Zarrouk, H., Ghak, T. El, & Bakhouche, A. (2021). Exploring economic and technological determinants of fintech startups' success and growth in the United Arab Emirates. *Journal of Open Innovation: Technology, Market, and Complexity*. https://doi.org/10.3390/joitmc7010050

Zavolokina, L., Dolata, M., & Schwabe, G. (2016). The FinTech phenomenon: Antecedents of financial innovation perceived by the popular press. *Financial Innovation*. https://doi.org/10.1186/s40854-016-0036-7

Zhang-Zhang, Y., Rohlfer, S., & Rajasekera, J. (2020). An eco-systematic view of cross-sector fintech: The case of Alibaba and Tencent. *Sustainability (switzerland)*. https://doi.org/10.3390/su12218907

Zhukov, S., Kopytin, I., & Maslennikov, A. (2019). Fintech ecosystem the largest private cryptosystems. *Mezhdunarodnye Protsessy*. https://doi.org/10.17994/IT.2019.17.1.56.2

Ziyaad, M., & Mohamad, S. (2016). Financial Innovation and riding the fintech Wave The fintech Ecosystem. 2, *Ciawm*.

Fintech Trends: Industry 4.0, Islamic Fintech, and Its Digital Transformation

M. Kabir Hassan, Zehra Zulfikar, Mustafa Raza Rabbani, and Mohd. Atif

1 INTRODUCTION

The technological advent in finance and banking started in 1945 when cheques were introduced as a new medium of paying money. In 1958, the Bank of America came up with the concept of credit card. Afterward in 1967, Automatic Teller Machines (ATMs) were developed, followed by the arrival of a debit card as a financial transaction instrument (Agarwal & Chua, 2020; Li et al., 2020). Subsequently in the mid-1990s, Internet banking came into existence because of the progression of the Internet. Almost after a decade, in the 2000s, crowdfunding and mobile payment

---

M. K. Hassan
Department of Economics and Finance, University of New, Orleans, New Orleans, LA 70148, USA
e-mail: mhassan@uno.edu

Z. Zulfikar (✉)
Department of Business Process Management, Delhi Skill and Entrepreneurship University, New Delhi, India
e-mail: zehra.zulfikar@sbs.du.ac.in

© The Author(s), under exclusive license to Springer Nature Switzerland AG 2022
M. K. Hassan et al. (eds.), *FinTech in Islamic Financial Institutions*,
https://Doi.org/10.1007/978-3-031-14941-2_6

started because of Fintech development. In 2009, Bitcoins were introduced by Satoshi Nakamoto as a digital currency (Ashta & Biot-Paquerot, 2018; Holmes & King, 2019; Zavolokina et al., 2016).

According to Stewart and Jürjens (2018) Fintech is defined "as the use of platforms of technology and mobile devices to access transaction notifications, bank account and credit, as well as debit alerts via push notifications through short message service, application or another way of getting notifications" (Stewart & Jürjens, 2018). Whereas Islamic Fintech, is explained as "Fintech with Shariah principles and Islamic values" (Goud et al., 2021; Khan et al., 2022; Shaikh, 2021).

In the last two decades, the volatile advancement in the field of artificial intelligence, machine learning, and big data handling techniques has been witnessed in the banking sector too resulting in the increase in the productivity and profitability (Hassan et al., 2020; Rabbani et al., 2020, 2021a). The practice of applying the models of Artificial Intelligence on the data collected, warehoused, and administered by banks have attained the generic nomenclature as Fintech and BigTech (Frost, 2020). This data has an ever-increasing size, complexity, and variability which requires the use of computer assisted statistical software to deal with it in a way that it helps in developing business strategies for the future. The five ways in which Fintech can propose improvements in business models for the banks are using the digital platforms, including prospective customer sections, having better accuracy in the selection of customers, minimizing operational costs, and business process optimization (Hill, 2018; Vershinina et al., 2018).

In the present time, the requirements of the banks' customers have changed because a major section of the consumers consists of young and middle-aged people who are very well versed with technology and do not like to physically visit the banks for their investment and saving

---

M. R. Rabbani
Department of Economics and Finance, College of Business Administration, University of Bahrain, Zallaq, Kingdom of Bahrain
e-mail: mrabbani@uob.edu.bh

Mohd. Atif
Department of Commerce and Business Studies, Jamia Millia Islamia, New Delhi 110025, India
e-mail: matif1@jmi.ac.in

needs (Karim et al., 2021a; Rabbani et al., 2021b). Traditional bank models are incapable of catering to their needs and choices. Industry 4.0 aids in satisfying ever-changing customer needs and increasing the output by introducing innovative banking products and automating routine and specialized processes (Nugroho Soebandrija, 2019).

The development of any financial system must be done on the basis of sustainability (Karim et al., 2021a). Sustainability of any system is explained as "the situation of creating a system where it meets the demand of the current generation without compromising the future generation or providing an ability to the future generation to meet its own needs" (Rabbani et al., 2021c). The notion of "sustainable development" was introduced in 1960s, which was based on following ethical and moral values. Conserving and preserving environment from the detrimental effects of the growing industrial development is the primary goal of the sustainability theory (Memili et al., 2018; Merello et al., 2022; Wüstenhagen, 2003). The standards and procedures for practicing sustainability are laid down by United Nations' 2015 agenda of Sustainable Development Goals (SDGs) (Atif et al., 2021). Protocols in line with United Nations' SDGs can assist in bringing sustainability to Finance sector too. The concept of Fintech is based on principles of sustainability provided that the regulators make sure that financial integrity, consumer data security, and financial inclusion are properly handled (Jreisat et al., 2021; Rabbani, 2022a, 2022b).

Although the regulation in Fintech is becoming far more active in Fintech space due to the inherent risk possessed in terms of product innovation and potential disruption it brings to the overall functioning of the global financial system (Banna et al., 2021; Clements, 2021). There is an absence of any widely acknowledged one regulatory organization that can act as an umbrella body for all the Islamic financial institutions especially for the newest and state-of-the-art division known as the Islamic Fintech (Hassan et al., 2021; Naeem et al., 2021).

Much expected, as alike to the availability of traditional financial services regulation, guidelines of Islamic financial institutions, including Islamic Fintech's, are dealt through the formal channels only (Nguyen et al., 2021; Valerio, 2020). Islamic finance and its innovations must go through the strict Shariah norms. As such, the major regulators involved in the development of code of practice and the lawful facilitative structure for Islamic Fintech are seen where there is significant activity already taking place. Few of the major regulators are Bank Negara Malaysia and

Securities Commission (Malaysia), Central Bank of Saudi Arabia (SAMA) Financial Services Authority (Indonesia) and, policymakers in Western countries for instance, Financial Conduct Authority in the UK, who allows Islamic Fintech's to function within their conventional regulatory framework. However, at the international level, Bahrain-based AAOIFI (the Accounting and Auditing Organization for Islamic Financial Institutions) is actively defining Sharia standards for certain segments of Islamic Fintech activities, e.g., crowdfunding, cryptocurrency voluntarily (Brika, 2022; Hassan et al., 2020; Muryanto et al., 2021). According to reports generated from the industry by performing a global survey on Islamic Fintech's, among the 100 survey respondents approximately 56% of the Islamic Fintech's expect to gather equity funding in 2021 with an estimated round size of USD 5 million. This shows a persistent trust in the growing Islamic financial services worldwide. The respondents of the survey also illustrated the major obstacles in its success path, namely, Lack of Capital, Finding Talent, and Consumer Education. Also, the survey results show that Payments, Deposits & Lending, and Raising Funds are the top growth segments in 2021 (Dinar Standard, 2021).

The remaining chapter proceeds as follows. In section two we provide an extensive review of literature related to the overall Fintech industry, Industry 4.0, Islamic Fintech, and digital transformation. Section three provides the discussion part of the chapter and finally in section four we conclude.

2 Review of Literature

In this section we provide the extensive review of literature related to the overall Fintech industry, Industry 4.0, Islamic Fintech, and digital transformation. The literature review is divided into four sections covering the developments in Fintech, Industry 4.0, Islamic Fintech, and its digital transformation.

Fintech

In the present, the working definition of the Financial Stability Board (FSB) for Fintech is "technologically activated financial innovation, which could result in new business models, applications, processes or products with an associated material effect on financial markets and institutions and in the provision of financial services" is most widely used in the available literature. Therefore, it can be said that the term Fintech refers to a wide range of software which brings innovation that can be applied in existing banks and new entrants or which are in the process of being restructured (Duran & Griffin, 2021; Omarini, 2020; Wu & Yuan, 2021). According to some researchers it is said that Fintech is not only restricted to information technology in finance, but it can also be used in explaining start-ups, new generations, technologies, companies, products, chance, digitalization, and threats (Pawłowska & Staniszewska, 2021; Schueffel, 2016).

Financial technology abbreviated as Fintech also means as financial services provided with the help of technology with an objective to produce innovative financial and banking products and to provide a hassle-free experience to the users and customers (Hassan et al., 2020; Khan & Rabbani, 2020; Rabbani et al., 2021d).

Fintech is also defined as "The fusion of Information Technology and Finance for providing the financial services at an affordable cost with a seamless user-friendly experience" (Hassan et al., 2020). Fintech includes all financial services ranging from crowdfunding, mobile payments, robot advisory services, digital currency like Cryptocurrency/Bitcoin, Blockchain technology, etc. (Rabbani et al., 2021a, 2021b, 2021c, 2021d).

Industry 4.0

The term "Industry 4.0" refers to the idea of penetration of technology in all areas of society like communication, production, finance, transportation, and services (Bandara et al., 2019; Nugroho Soebandrija, 2019). These developments are a result of digital integration between devices and processes that can exchange and process massive amount of data. Automation, which means the accessibility of such machines that can perform highly complex tasks, also plays a vital role in it. Technologies like Artificial Intelligence, Internet of Things, Biometrics, Data Analytics, Blockchain, etc., have enabled organizations in building customized products and delivering personalized services along with the help of Internet and smart electronic devices (Eleftheriadis & Myklebust, 2018; Riyanto et al., 2019). The ten major pillars of Industry 4.0 are Internet of

Things, Big data, System integration, Cloud computing, Additive manufacturing, Augmented reality, Simulation, Robotics, Artificial Intelligence, and Cyber Security (Riyanto et al., 2019).

Apparently, it may seem that human labor and insights are substituted by Industry 4.0; however, on the contrary, human intervention is required in the decision-making process and they play a vital part in the installation, maintenance, and upgradation of the entire process (Naeem et al., 2021; Rabbani et al., 2021d). Thus, it can be said that Industry 4.0 works in synchronization with the human resource system. Generally, there has been a suspicion that the physical–digital integration can leave negative effects on the society and the environment due to its nature of being overly complex to monitor and administer. However, effective framework, multi-stakeholders' approach, and open dialogs can help in fighting out its consequences (Bandara et al., 2019). The very nature of Industry 4.0, i.e., automation, big data analysis, and transparency makes it to be an apt supporter of Fintech's and especially Islamic Fintech's (Sun et al., 2020).

Islamic Fintech

Islamic financial technology means providing sharia-obedient financial services to the customers of Islamic banks and Islamic financial institutions with the help of financial technology. Islamic Fintech emphasizes on providing the financial services, products, and investments by fulfilling the requirements of sharia at a reasonable cost with advanced technology (Hassan et al., 2021; Rabbani et al., 2021c).

Islamic Fintech is comprehensive, transparent, ethical, and favorable to all the stakeholders and follows the principles of sharia as compared to the traditional financial institutions (Rabbani, 2022a, 2022b). In the forthcoming period it is expected that different governments take steps toward adopting this concept. Islamic financial institutions need to make strategic moves and make their portfolio Fintech attractive by including financial services based on artificial intelligence, blockchain and data analytics. Crowdfunding, P2P lending, digital payments, digital authentication, and sharia-compliant cryptocurrencies are some of the significant areas in the development of Islamic Fintech. Likewise, novel and innovative solutions could be proposed by Fintech developers for the prevailing issues by using the dynamics of cloud computing, big data analytics, cryptocurrency, etc. (Rabbani et al., 2022).

"Fintech promises to reshape the Islamic financial landscape by improving processes' efficiencies, cost-effectiveness, increased distribution, Sharīah compliance and financial inclusion" (Razak et al., 2021). Islamic Finance services providers are currently in a process of fully or partially embracing Fintech. Some of the torch bearers in this arena are Saudi Arabia, the UAE, Malaysia, Bahrain, Brunei, Indonesia, Oman, and others (Soloviev, 2018; Söylemez, 2019).

Islamic financial institutions have happily accepted Fintech as a way of an innovative technique to provide financial services with open arms, as it gives the flexibility of operations based on the principles of sharia. It is evident that Fintech supports the concept of sustainable development and therefore, Islamic countries are enthusiastically adopting it. A recent initiative is taken by Fintech Bay in Bahrain where it has recently launched "Global Islamic and Sustainable Fintech Center" (GIFSC) in association with its local, regional, and international collaborators (Meero et al., 2021). Islamic countries like Malaysia, Saudi Arabia, Bahrain, and Iran have introduced regulatory "sandboxes" for making alterations in their regulatory framework in order to supplement and support modernization required in Islamic finance. The idea behind creating such institutions and amendments in policies is to introduce, adopt, and merge Fintech with Islamic finance in order to bring sustainability and innovation in the system (Karim et al., 2021b; Meero et al., 2021). Generally, such institutions also aim to identify and meet the unrecognized demands of the prospective Islamic financial service users so that continuous development and long-lasting growth could be achieved.

Even though there is a high growth in the number of countries which are involved in Islamic Fintech activity, or are well-equipped to facilitate such activity, no specific ranking criteria existed to compare such countries in the Islamic Fintech space until Global Islamic Fintech Report, 2021 presented the first Global Islamic Fintech (GIFT) Index. This Index shows the countries that are most prepared for the growth of Islamic Fintech Market and Ecosystem in their dominions (Elipses, 2019; Hasan et al., 2020; "Leveraging Islam. Fintech to Improv. Financ. Incl.," 2020). An aggregate of 32 indicators across 5 different categories for each country was used by the index. The five categories were namely, Regulation; Capital; Infrastructure; Talent; and Islamic Fintech Market & Ecosystem. The index included 64 OIC (Organization of Islamic Cooperation) and non-OIC countries which were included on the basis of their current Islamic Fintech market activities like the existence of Islamic finance capital (an indicator of development in Islamic Fintech), and their preference to the global Fintech ecosystem (e.g., China, Japan). Among 64 countries, 9 out of the Top 10 (90%) countries are a member of OIC, Muslim majority countries; except UK, which has a flourishing Islamic Fintech ecosystem because of various factors like active Islamic Fintech Muslim population, the existence of several Islamic Fintech's; developed regulatory system; a growing Fintech sector; availability of experts from developed Islamic Fintech. Whereas 8 out of top 20 countries are non-OIC member countries including the USA, Canada, etc. (DinarStandard, 2021; IFSB, 2020).

3 Discussion

Digital Fintech research basically starts with analyzing Fintech comprising financial instruments and machines (Gün, 2019). Fintech consists of six business models mainly, lending, wealth management, insurance services, crowdfunding, payment, and capital markets. Innovative and creative technological ideas resulting in growth of Fintech are somehow dependent on the use of artificial intelligence, big data, and machine learning (Baber, 2020; Daud et al., 2022; Suryanto et al., 2020). The impact of using data may be complex or multidimensional but the industry is required to have proper surveillance on its protection. It is to be understood that not only technology requires being in safe hands but also the data. Anonymity and confidentiality of consumers' personal data, data leaks, and data access restrictions must be assured by Fintech. Proper policies should be framed regarding personal data protection. Consumers must be educated about internet usage and its threats. Also, technology integration can be used by Fintech to sustain the quality of software and avoid fraudulent practices (Acar & Çitak, 2019).

It is evident from the Fintech trends that more the growth in financial technology services more will be the competition in industry. The side effects of online loan services like moral hazard, information asymmetry, and loan defaults are widely observed. The problems of money laundering arising from the prevalence of Bitcoins are another area of concern for the Fintech's (Hassan et al., 2020; Khan & Rabbani, 2020). Principles of consumer protection and risk management are the two main factors that should be taken care by promoters and regulators in the finance and banking industry to encourage innovation and technology usage (Hernández et al., 2019; Yuniarti & Rasyid, 2020).

Payment model is somehow also affected by the innovation in the Fintech sector as it is a part of Fintech business models. Various advancements in payment methods including electronic wallets, payment gateways, and electronic money have taken place (Kang, 2018; Moon & Kim, 2017). It has become possible because there is a huge level of distinction between payment designs in the sense of transaction settlement methods and e-commerce developers who develop different payment techniques according to the requirements of the clients (Andria et al., 2021). Due to the presence of different methods of payment, adoption research is widely undertaken by the researchers (Daragmeh et al., 2021). Irrespective of using a multidimensional network with the same shared infrastructure, mobile payment system strives to provide value by assisting in speedy transactions along with resolving the customers' problems and creating satisfaction. Biometrics are found to be useful according to some studies concerning benefits received, individual security issues, and trust in electronic payments for e-commerce. One of the drawbacks of online payments availability of a huge number of online currencies making it difficult for the regulators to control and authenticate the transactions (Daragmeh et al., 2021; Khiewngamdee & Yan, 2019; Natarajan, 2021). P2P lending is such a financial service that gathers both lenders and borrowers at one unified podium. Studies have determined the reason behind what makes it difficult for investors to invest in P2P lending, which is called as information asymmetry. Investment decision in P2P lending is also affected by moral hazard which tends out be a huge problem. Finally, to ascertain the benefit of P2P lending, policies and regulations are to be examined continually. Consequently, P2P lending is developing day-by-day as people are becoming more aware (Rabbani et al., 2022).

The Global Islamic Fintech Report presented the data collected from the industry as global investigation of Islamic Fintech's. Approximately 100 survey respondents were included in the study out of which 56% of Islamic Fintech's are expected to raise equity funding in 2021 with an average amount of USD 5 million (DinarStandard, 2019). This depicts that the Fintech is continuously growing and spreading its reach and operations. The study also performed exploratory research on finding the obstacles in the growth of Fintech's. Some of the major obstacles explored are Lack of Capital, low consumer literacy, and Talent acquisition. On the other hand, the study revealed the fastest growing areas in the industry are Payments, Raising Funds, and Deposits & Lending (Daud et al., 2021).

"Tayyab" is an example of an Islamic bank which acts as a perfect example of digitalization of Islamic Fintech's. It provides all the services which a traditional bank offers but on the digital platform. The services include online account opening, delivery of cards electronically, electronic payments, electronic *Sadaqah and Zakat* services, *Salah* and *Adhan* timetable, *Tasbih, Qibla direction, maps* to locate mosques, halal restaurants, etc., are provided through their banking application. Tayyab ensures that its customers perform all the financial and religious responsibilities and operations strictly in compliance with *Shariah* laws and keeping themselves away from interest and *Riba*. It has also obtained a certification from Shariah Review Bureau.

Another notable research undertaken in the area of digitalization of Islamic Fintech is the establishment of "IslamicFintech4SD Gearbox" model. It has been developed to establish an association between various financial and non-financial institutions like multinational companies, start-ups, P2P lending, and crowdfunding organizations (Deng et al., 2019; Goud et al., 2021; Vergara & Agudo, 2021). This model ensures that the association is made strictly in accordance with the Shariah laws. The model guides Islamic Fintech's to work on the principles of sustainable development, for which it has proposed a five-step framework. The five steps include easy online account opening along with e-KYC and Digital ID creation, digital payment system, customized Islamic financial services offered with the help of Artificial Intelligence and Blockchain technology, providing government services following the previous steps in order to achieve financial inclusion and lastly, the Shariah compliance (Atif et al., 2021).

4 Conclusion

It was after the global financial crisis (2008), the development of e-finance and mobile upgradation for the finance sector took place which created an urge to develop Fintech. The advancement in technology comprised a combination of social networking services, artificial intelligence, e-finance innovation, internet technology, social media, and huge analytic data. This evolution in the finance sector forced conventional financial institutions including banks, to upgrade their systems in a more precise manner. Eventually, it created an opportunity for start-ups to enter the financial service sector. The increasingly widespread use of Fintech enables the automation of banking transactions, and customers can make payments using mobile phones and tablets (mobile banking). Therefore, bank employees need to play more of a consultant role rather than conducting transactions directly. Fintech should be considered as an integral part of business rather than claiming to be disturbing. It should help the economy to change and grow. Government should consider Fintech as a way of developing the finance industry and therefore, assist people in using digital methods of payment and electronic money. This would help people to make payment from anywhere and anytime which makes it easier and reasonable.

Industry 4.0 is complementing the growth of the Fintech industry. The concept of Industry 4.0 can be summarized as an integration of the influencing power of the web, advanced devices, and technological advancement like processing of huge algorithms through advanced analytics, artificial intelligence, etc. It has encouraged firms and big companies to give more emphasis on customer needs and to produce those goods and services which are required and liked by customers. It is essential to use the state-of-the-art computer vision techniques, such as deep learning, to identify tools, components, and actions by visual control systems. Industry 4.0 is proving to be a boon for Islamic Fintech's as well because it is bringing automation and synchronization in financial service products and their regulatory framework of Shariah laws.

Greater focus on well-individualized services enables Fintech and BigTech companies to provide efficient services with new technologies, including those based on artificial intelligence. Artificial Intelligence algorithms play an increasing role in determining customer scoring, identifying bank frauds, or segmenting customers. The increasingly widespread use of Fintech technology enables the automation of banking transactions, and customers can make payments using mobile phones and tablets (mobile banking). Therefore, bank employees need to play more a consultant role rather than conducting transactions directly.

Islamic Fintech's are becoming popular day-by-day not only in OIC countries but also in non-OIC countries especially in the UK where a growth of around 10% is expected to be seen by the next year followed by Singapore, Hongkong, USA, Australia, Switzerland, Canada, Bangladesh, and Luxemburg. Regulators and promoters of Islamic Fintech's need to focus on issues like consumer technology awareness and literacy, management of risk, creation of an apex regulatory institution, cyber security, and availability of sustainable standards, procedures, rules and regulations, and impact of COVID-19 on the sector.

The Accounting and Auditing Organization for Islamic Financial Institutions (AAOIFI) has established standards for Islamic Fintech's. At present, twenty-one Islamic countries have adopted these standards. These standards and protocols are developed according to Islamic laws, values, and ethics. It is highly expected that other countries would also take notice of these standards and the regulators would include them in their setups as well. Fintech inevitably poses a challenge to traditional banking because of its dynamism and accuracy in targeting customers. Therefore, Islamic financial institutions should also adopt Fintech practices in their operations.

References

Acar, O., & Çitak, Y. E. (2019). Fintech integration process suggestion for banks. In S. S. (Ed.), *3rd world conference on technology, innovation and entrepreneurship, WOCTINE 2019* (Vol. 158, pp. 971–978). Elsevier B.V. https://doi.org/10.1016/j.procs.2019.09.138

Agarwal, S., & Chua, Y. H. (2020). Fintech and household finance: A review of the empirical literature. *China Finance Review International, 10*(4), 361–376. https://doi.org/10.1108/CFRI-03-2020-0024

Andria, F., Ananda, D. R., Rahmi, A., & Bon, A. T. (2021). Fintech payment application in improving customer services. *11th Annual International Conference on Industrial Engineering and Operations Management, IEOM 2021* (pp. 4114–4124). https://www.scopus.com/inward/record.uri?eid=2-s2.0-85114235320&partnerID=40&md5=df5ec27584689df8d8512e98837f722d

Ashta, A., & Biot-Paquerot, G. (2018). Fintech evolution: Strategic value management issues in a fast changing industry. *Strategic Change, 27*(4), 301–311. https://doi.org/10.1002/jsc.2203

Atif, M., Hassan, M. K., Rabbani, M. R., & Khan, S. (2021). Islamic FinTech: The digital transformation bringing sustainability to Islamic finance. In *COVID-19 and Islamic Social Finance* (pp. 91–103). Routledge.

Baber, H. (2020). Fintech, crowdfunding and customer retention in Islamic Banks. *Vision.* https://doi.org/10.1177/0972262919869765

Bandara, O. K. K., Tharaka, V. K., & Wickramarachchi, A. P. R. (2019). Industry 4.0 maturity assessment of the Banking Sector of Sri Lanka. *Proceedings – IEEE International Research Conference on Smart Computing and Systems Engineering, SCSE 2019* (pp. 190–195). https://doi.org/10.23919/SCSE.2019.8842818

Banna, H., Kabir Hassan, M., & Rashid, M. (2021). Fintech-based financial inclusion and bank risk-taking: Evidence from OIC countries. *Journal of International Financial Markets, Institutions and Money*, 75(October), 1–20. https://doi.org/10.1016/j.intfin.2021.101447

Brika, S. K. M. (2022). A bibliometric analysis of fintech trends and digital finance. *Frontiers in Environmental Science*, 9. https://doi.org/10.3389/fenvs.2021.796495

Clements, R. (2021). Regulating Fintech in Canada and the United States: Comparison, challenges and opportunities. In *The Routledge Handbook of Fintech* (pp. 416–454). Taylor and Francis. https://www.scopus.com/inward/record.uri?eid=2-s2.0-85108371949&partnerID=40&md5=adc63ed466136df46518dd86d0a6b02f

Daragmeh, A., Lentner, C., & Sági, J. (2021). Fintech payments in the era of COVID-19: Factors influencing behavioral intentions of "Generation X" in Hungary to use mobile payment. *Journal of Behavioral and Experimental Finance*, 32. https://doi.org/10.1016/j.jbef.2021.100574

Daud, S. N. M., Ahmad, A. H., Khalid, A., & Azman-Saini, W. N. W. (2022). Fintech and financial stability: Threat or opportunity? *Finance Research Letters*. https://doi.org/10.1016/j.frl.2021.102667

Daud, Siti Nurazira Mohd, Ahmad, A. H., Khalid, A., & Azman-Saini, W. N. W. (2021). Fintech and financial stability: Threat or opportunity? *Finance Research Letters*, November, 102667. https://doi.org/10.1016/j.frl.2021.102667

Deng, X., Huang, Z., & Cheng, X. (2019). Fintech and sustainable development: Evidence from China based on P2P data. *Sustainability (Switzerland)*, 11(22). https://doi.org/10.3390/su11226434

DinarStandard. (2019). State of the Global Islamic Economy Report 2019/20. In *Dubai International Financial Centre*.

DinarStandard. (2021). Islamic Fintech Report 2018: Current Landscape & Path Forward. In *Dubai Islamic Economy Development Centre*. https://www.dinarstandard.com/wp-content/uploads/2018/12/Islamic-Fintech-Report-2018.pdf

Duran, R. E., & Griffin, P. (2021). Smart contracts: Will Fintech be the catalyst for the next global financial crisis? *Journal of Financial Regulation and Compliance*, 29(1), 104–122. https://doi.org/10.1108/JFRC-09-2018-0122

Eleftheriadis, R. J., & Myklebust, O. (2018). Industry 4.0 and cyber physical systems in a Norwegian industrial context. *Lecture Notes in Electrical Engineering*, 451, 491–499. https://doi.org/10.1007/978-981-10-5768-7_52

Elipses. (2019). *The global islamic Fintech report* (Issue December). https://ceif.iba.edu.pk/pdf/IslamicFintechReport19.pdf

Frost, J. (2020). The economic forces driving Fintech adoption across countries. In *The technological revolution in financial services: How banks, fintechs, and customers win together* (pp. 70–89). University of Toronto Press. https://www.scopus.com/inward/record.uri?eid=2-s2.0-85091541206&partnerID=40&md5=572c6a0e4c66288730b7bea66a78f43f

Goud, B., Uddin, T. A., & Fianto, B. A. (2021). Islamic Fintech and ESG goals: Key considerations for fulfilling maqasid principles. In *Islamic Fintech* (pp. 16–35). Taylor and Francis. https://doi.org/10.4324/9781003014614-2

Gün, M. (2019). The path to Fintech development research on islamic finance in Turkey. In *Impact of Financial Technology (Fintech) on Islamic Finance and financial stability* (pp. 65–96). IGI Global. https://doi.org/10.4018/978-1-7998-0039-2.ch005

Hasan, R., Hassan, M. K., & Aliyu, S. (2020). Fintech and Islamic Finance: Literature review and research agenda. *International Journal of Islamic Economics and Finance (IJIEF)*, *1*(2), 75–94. https://doi.org/10.18196/ijief.2122

Hassan, M. K., Rabbani, M., & Daouia, C. (2021). Integrating Islamic finance and Halal industry: Current landscape and future forward. *International Journal of Islamic Marketing and Branding*, *6*(1), 60–78.

Hassan, M. K., Rabbani, M. R., & Ali, M. A. (2020). Challenges for the Islamic Finance and banking in post COVID era and the role of Fintech. *Journal of Economic Cooperation and Development*, *43*(3), 93–116.

Hernández, E., Öztürk, M., Sittón, I., & Rodríguez, S. (2019, June). Data Protection on Fintech Platforms. In *International Conference on Practical Applications of Agents and Multi-Agent Systems* (pp. 223–233). Springer.

Hill, J. (2018). *Fintech and the remaking of financial institutions*. Elsevier. https://doi.org/10.1016/C2016-0-03863-9

Holmes, C., & King, R. (2019). The evolution of business-to-business Fintech: What the future holds. *Journal of Payments Strategy and Systems*, *13*(3), 217–225. https://www.scopus.com/inward/record.uri?eid=2-s2.0-85073917956&partnerID=40&md5=991f7027dc3d7b51c2cdafcdb178d7ac

IFSB. (2020). Stability report 2020. In *Islamic Financial Services Board*.

Jreisat, A., Bashar, A., Alshaikh, A., Rabbani, M. R., & Moh'd Ali, M. A. (2021, December). Is Fintech valuation an art or a science? Exploring the Innovative methods for the valuation of Fintech startups. In *2021 International Conference on Decision Aid Sciences and Application (DASA)* (pp. 922–925). IEEE.

Kang, J. (2018). Mobile payment in Fintech environment: Trends, security challenges, and services. *Human-Centric Computing and Information Sciences*, *8*(1). https://doi.org/10.1186/s13673-018-0155-4

Karim, S., Akhtar, M. U., Tashfeen, R., Raza Rabbani, M., Rahman, A. A. A., & AlAbbas, A. (2021a). Sustainable banking regulations pre and during coronavirus outbreak: The moderating role of financial stability. *Economic Research-Ekonomska Istraživanja*, 1–18.

Karim, S., Naeem, M. A., Meero, A. A., & Rabbani, M. R. (2021b). Examining the role of gender diversity on ownership structure-sustainable performance nexus: Fresh evidence from emerging markets. *Environmental Science and Pollution Research*, 1–16.

Khan, S., & Rabbani, M. R. (2020). In depth analysis of blockchain, cryptocurrency and Sharia compliance. *International Journal of Business Innovation and Research*, 1(1), 1. https://doi.org/10.1504/ijbir.2020.10033066

Khan, M. S., Rabbani, M. R., Hawaldar, I. T., & Bashar, A. (2022). Determinants of behavioral intentions to use Islamic financial technology: An empirical assessment. *Risks*, 10(6), 114.

Khiewngamdee, C., & Yan, H.-D. (2019). The role of Fintech e-payment on APEC economic development. In H. X. (Ed.), *2nd International Conference on Physics, Mathematics and Statistics, ICPMS 2019* (Vol. 1324, Issue 1). Institute of Physics Publishing. https://doi.org/10.1088/1742-6596/1324/1/012099

Leveraging Islamic Fintech to Improve Financial Inclusion. (2020). *Leveraging Islamic Fintech to Improve Financial Inclusion.* https://doi.org/10.1596/34520

Li, J., Li, J., Zhu, X., Yao, Y., & Casu, B. (2020). Risk spillovers between Fintech and traditional financial institutions: Evidence from the U.S. *International Review of Financial Analysis*, 71. https://doi.org/10.1016/j.irfa.2020.101544

Meero, A., Rahiman, H. U., & Rahman, A. A. A. (2021). The prospects of Bahrain's entrepreneurial ecosystem: An exploratory approach. *Problems and Perspectives in Management*, 18(4), 402.

Memili, E., Fang, H. "Chevy," Koc, B., Yildirim-Öktem, Ö., & Sonmez, S. (2018). Sustainability practices of family firms: The interplay between family ownership and long-term orientation. *Journal of Sustainable Tourism*, 26(1), 9–28.

Merello, P., Barberá, A., & la Poza, E. D. (2022). Is the sustainability profile of Fintech companies a key driver of their value? *Technological Forecasting and Social Change*, 174. https://doi.org/10.1016/j.techfore.2021.121290

Moon, W. Y., & Kim, S. D. (2017). A Payment Mediation Platform for heterogeneous Fintech schemes. In X. B. (Ed.), *2016 IEEE Advanced Information Management, Communicates, Electronic and Automation Control Conference, IMCEC 2016* (pp. 511–516). Institute of Electrical and Electronics Engineers Inc. https://doi.org/10.1109/IMCEC.2016.7867264

Muryanto, Y. T., Kharisma, D. B., & Ciptorukmi Nugraheni, A. S. (2021). Prospects and challenges of Islamic Fintech in Indonesia: A legal viewpoint.

International Journal of Law and Management. https://doi.org/10.1108/IJLMA-07-2021-0162

Naeem, M. A., Rabbani, M. R., Karim, S., & Billah, S. M. (2021). Religion vs ethics: hedge and safe haven properties of Sukuk and green bonds for stock markets pre-and during COVID-19. *International Journal of Islamic and Middle Eastern Finance and Management.*

Natarajan, H. (2021). Fintech's impact on payments—Part 2. *Journal of Payments Strategy and Systems,* 15(1), 4–6. https://www.scopus.com/inward/record.uri?eid=2-s2.0-85108177551&partnerID=40&md5=e0ba716ecbceff49f518f24e9fc4baff

Nguyen, L., Tran, S., & Ho, T. (2021). Fintech credit, bank regulations and bank performance: A cross-country analysis. *Asia-Pacific Journal of Business Administration.* https://doi.org/10.1108/APJBA-05-2021-0196

Nugroho Soebandrija, K. E. (2019). Dynamic capability and disruptive innovation within perspectives of industry 4.0, research result and innovation on people's prosperity. *IOP Conference Series: Materials Science and Engineering,* 508(1). https://doi.org/10.1088/1757-899X/508/1/012101

Omarini, A. (2020). Fintech: A new hedge for a financial re-intermediation. Strategy and risk perspectives. *Frontiers in Artificial Intelligence,* 3. https://doi.org/10.3389/frai.2020.00063

Pawłowska, M., & Staniszewska, A. (2021). Impact of Fintech on the level of competition in the EU banking sector. In *Financial and economic systems: Transformations and new challenges* (pp. 537–560). World Scientific Publishing Co. https://doi.org/10.1142/9781786349507_0019

Rabbani, M. R. (2022a). COVID-19 and its impact on supply chain financing and the role of Islamic Fintech: Evidence from GCC countries. *International Journal of Agile Systems and Management (IJASM),* in press.

Rabbani, M. R. (2022b). Fintech innovations, scope, challenges, and implications in Islamic Finance: A systematic analysis. *International Journal of Computing and Digital Systems, Forthcoming.*

Rabbani, M. R., Abdulla, Y., Basahr, A., Khan, S., & Moh'd Ali, M. A. (2020). Embracing of Fintech in Islamic Finance in the post COVID era. *International Conference on Decision Aid Sciences and Application (DASA), 2020,* 1230–1234.

Rabbani, M. R., Jreisat, A., AlAbbas, A., Bashar, A., & Ali, M. A. M. (2021a). Whether Cryptocurrency is a threat or a revolution? An ESG perspective. *2021a International Conference on Sustainable Islamic Business and Finance (SIBF).*

Rabbani, M. R., Bashar, A., Nawaz, N., Karim, S., Ali, M. A. M., Khan, A., Rahiman, H., & Alam, S. (2021b). Exploring the role of Islamic Fintech in combating the after-shocks of COVID-19: The open social innovation of the

Islamic financial system. *Journal of Open Innovation: Technology, Market, and Complexity*, 7, 136.

Rabbani, M. R., Sarea, A., Khan, S., & Abdullah, Y. (2021c). Ethical Concerns in Artificial Intelligence (AI): The Role of RegTech and Islamic Finance. *The International Conference On Global Economic Revolutions*, 381–390.

Rabbani, M. R., Asad Mohd. Ali, M., Rahiman, H. U., Atif, M., Zulfikar, Z., & Naseem, Y. (2021d). The response of Islamic financial service to the COVID-19 pandemic: The open social innovation of the financial system. *Journal of Open Innovation: Technology, Market, and Complexity*, 7(1). https://doi.org/10.3390/joitmc7010085

Rabbani, M. R., Khan, S., & Atif, M. (2022). Machine Learning based P2P Lending Islamic Fintech Model for Small and Medium Enterprises (SMEs) in Bahrain. *International Journal of Business Innovation and Research*, in press.

Razak, M. I. A., Dali, N. A. M., Dhillon, G., & Manaf, A. W. A. (2021). Fintech in Malaysia: An appraisal to the need of shariah-compliant regulation. *Pertanika Journal of Social Sciences and Humanities*, 28(4), 3223–3233. https://doi.org/10.47836/PJSSH.28.4.40

Riyanto, A., Primiana, I., Yunizar, & Azis, Y. (2019). Digital branch: Banking innovation in Indonesia to face 4.0 industry challenges. *IOP Conference Series: Materials Science and Engineering*, 662(7). https://doi.org/10.1088/1757-899X/662/7/072002

Schueffel, P. (2016). Taming the beast: A scientific definition of Fintech. *Journal of Innovation Management*, 4(4), 32–54. https://doi.org/10.24840/2183-0606_004.004_0004

Shaikh, S. A. (2021). Using Fintech in scaling up Islamic microfinance. *Journal of Islamic Accounting and Business Research*, 12(2), 186–203. https://doi.org/10.1108/JIABR-10-2019-0198

Soloviev, V. I. (2018). Fintech ecosystem and landscape in Russia. *Journal of Reviews on Global Economics*, 7(Special Issue), 377–390. https://doi.org/10.6000/1929-7092.2018.07.32

Söylemez, Y. (2019). Fintech ecosystem and banking: The case of Turkey. In *Handbook of Research on Strategic Fit and Design in Business Ecosystems*. https://doi.org/10.4018/978-1-7998-1125-1.ch014

Standard, D. (2021). *Global Islamic Fintech report*.

Stewart, H., & Jürjens, J. (2018). Data security and consumer trust in Fintech innovation in Germany. *Information and Computer Security*, 26(1), 109–128. https://doi.org/10.1108/ICS-06-2017-0039

Sun, H., Rabbani, M. R., Sial, M. S., Yu, S., Filipe, J. A., & Cherian, J. (2020). Identifying big data's opportunities, challenges, and implications in finance. *Mathematics*, 8(10). https://doi.org/10.3390/math8101738

Suryanto, S., Rusdin, R., & Dai, R. M. (2020). Fintech as a catalyst for growth of micro, small and medium enterprises in Indonesia. *Academy of Strategic*

Management Journal, *19*(5), 1–12. https://www.scopus.com/inward/rec ord.uri?eid=2-s2.0-85098198612&partnerID=40&md5=f5654b0c876dfa9 7b72de067425659cd

Valerio, L. (2020). *Fintech regulation: Exploring new challenges of the Capital markets Union*. Exploring New Challenges of the Capital Markets Union. Springer International Publishing. https://doi.org/10.1007/978-3-030-423 47-6

Vergara, C. C., & Agudo, L. F. (2021). Fintech and sustainability: Do they affect each other? *Sustainability (Switzerland)*, *13*(13). https://doi.org/10.3390/ su13137012

Vershinina, A. A., Zhdanova, O. A., Pashkovskaya, M. V, & Nazarova, E. V. (2018). Fintech Accelerators: Infrastructural institutions within the Fintech ecosystem. *International Journal of Mechanical Engineering and Technology*, *9*(1198–1205), 1198–1205. https://www.scopus.com/inward/record.uri? eid=2-s2.0-85059282925&partnerID=40&md5=784c691eda1885c116ba7 6817e3afb9c

Wu, G., & Yuan, H. (2021). The impact of Fintech on the profitability of state-owned commercial banks in China. *2021 4th International Symposium on Big Data and Applied Statistics, ISBDAS 2021*, *1955*(1). https://doi.org/ 10.1088/1742-6596/1955/1/012007

Wüstenhagen, R. (2003). Sustainability and competitiveness in the renewable energy sector: The case of Vestas wind systems. *Greener Management International*, *44*, 105–115. https://www.scopus.com/inward/record.uri?eid=2- s2.0-10244239257&partnerID=40&md5=dbacc79348549a4282b435cae20 84d8f

Yuniarti, S., & Rasyid, A. (2020). Consumer Protection in Lending Fintech Transaction in Indonesia: Opportunities and Challenges. In V. S., M. M.B., L. C.-H., G. T.L., Mujiarto, & S. A. (Eds.), *2nd International Conference on Computer, Science, Engineering, and Technology, ICComSET 2019* (Vol. 1477, Issue 5). Institute of Physics Publishing. https://doi.org/10.1088/ 1742-6596/1477/5/052016

Zavolokina, L., Dolata, M., & Schwabe, G. (2016). Fintech – What's in a name? *2016 International Conference on Information Systems, ICIS 2016*. https://www.scopus.com/inward/record.uri?eid=2-s2.0-850113 13931&partnerID=40&md5=151a0787ac5465c74ac6853ad3cf9027

An Insight into the Fintech and Islamic Finance Literature: A Bibliometric and Visual Analysis

M. Kabir Hassan, Abu Bashar, Mustafa Raza Rabbani, and Tonmoy Choudhury

1 INTRODUCTION

The finance industry has achieved unprecedented growth during the last two decades mainly due to the emergence of technological innovation

M. K. Hassan
University of New, Orleans, New Orleans, LA 70148, USA
e-mail: mhassan@uno.edu

A. Bashar (✉)
School of Management, IMS Unison University, Dehradun 248009, India
e-mail: abu.bashar03@iuu.ac

M. R. Rabbani
Department Economics and Finance, College of Business Administration, University of Bahrain, Zallaq, Kingdom of Bahrain
e-mail: mrabbani@uob.edu.bh

T. Choudhury
Department of Accounting & Finance, KFUPM Business School, King Fahd University of Petroleum and Minerals, Dhahran, Kingdom of Saudi Arabia
e-mail: tonmoy.choudhury@kfupm.edu.sa

© The Author(s), under exclusive license to Springer Nature Switzerland AG 2022
M. K. Hassan et al. (eds.), *FinTech in Islamic Financial Institutions*,
https://doi.org/10.1007/978-3-031-14941-2_7

(Rangkuti et al., 2020; Wang et al., 2021). Growth of performance in the finance industry can be attributed to increased communication, faster back-office processing, and efficient client interface (Pwc, 2017). Gradually the industry has seen a shift from traditional financial services to digitisation, product innovation and new innovative business models among the financial services firms (Abdullah & Rabbani, 2021; Rabbani et al., 2021b). New and innovative financial services include Fintech-based financial services with the use of disruptive technologies such as Internet of things (Moh'd Ali et al., 2020), artificial intelligence (Sun et al., 2020), blockchain (Khan & Rabbani, 2020; Rabbani et al., 2021a), Regtech (Rabbani et al., 2021c), robotic automation (Mehrotra & Menon, 2021), machine learning (Hassan et al., 2020a, 2020b, 2020c, 2021) and quantum computing (Habeeb et al., 2021; Rabbani et al., 2021d; Rabbani et al., 2022a, 2022b). The Fintech-based financial services include, crowdfunding, P2P lending, Robo-advisors, Insuretech and Regtech, etc. (Rabbani, 2022; Sun et al., 2020). The traditional development model of the finance industry has completely changed with the advent of this disruption in the finance sphere (Jreisat et al., 2021; Bureshaid et al., 2021). In view of this, the research in finance and banking industry has taken a new shift to examine the influence of technology on the finance and banking industry (Rabbani et al., 2022a, 2022b; Khan et al., 2022).

Moreover, scholars have done studies on Fintech adoption (Bureshaid et al., 2021), Fintech during the time of COVID-19 and challenges for Fintech in the post-COVID era (Banna et al., 2021; Hassan et al., 2020a, 2020b, 2020c; Yan et al., 2021), Fintech-enabled financial inclusion and the role of Fintech in removal of poverty and income distribution (Demir et al., 2020; Kandpal & Mehrotra, 2019; Wibowo & Aumeboonsuke, 2020), role of Regtech in Fintech governance (Arner et al., 2017; Chirulli, 2021; Pantielieieva et al., 2020), the impact of Fintech on the performance of banks and financial institutions (Banna et al., 2021; Bashayreh & Wadi, 2021; Fadhul & Hamdan, 2020). Additionally, the research in the Fintech area peaked during the last few years as Fintech found its space in the finance world due to the repercussions of the global financial crisis and ongoing global pandemic (Rabbani, 2022).

Fintech has played a key role in transforming business decision-making and providing choices to customers as well as financial institutions (Abu Bashar & Rabbani, 2021). It has fostered the development of the finance industry with its innovative financial services resulting in improved financial services at reduced cost and increased transparency (Gimpel et al., 2018; Lee & Shin, 2018). Trading and investment with the use of artificial intelligence, blockchain and big data can result in improved efficiency, increased speed, promoting liquidity and enhancing efficiency and stability of the financial market (Li & Xu, 2021). Regulators can analyse, warn, prevent and can estimate the risk associated with innovation and disruption more efficiently (Arner et al., 2017). Additionally, with the use of big data analytics, it is possible to save huge costs by reducing staff duplication. Finally, it has resulted in a massive transformation in the lives of the poor and vulnerable during the COVID-19 pandemic as Fintech became the only option to reach them due to social distancing and lockdown measures and additionally, it resulted in the huge financial inclusion (Hassan et al., 2022; Khan et al., 2022).

To reconnoitre the boundaries and research pattern in the Islamic finance and Fintech domain that has completely transformed the lives of the multitudes, the present chapter analysed the current research pattern in the Islamic finance and Fintech domain. Most of the research papers retrieved were published post-2015 (Scopus database). The present chapter explores the most prolific authors, most cited documents, most influential institutions, most contributing countries, etc. to the Islamic finance and Fintech literature. Moreover, the chapter investigated the emerging research topics in the area, and acknowledged the challenges and future development trends.

Bibliometrics has been one of the most widely used techniques in the academic literature for quantitative and statistical analysis of the academic literature. It uses advanced computer programs such as VOSViewer, R-Studio and biblioshiny, etc., thereby improving the presentation of the results and improving the experience of the readers. It has been adopted widely by academic scholars in different fields of study such as finance, banking, human resource and marketing (Janková, 2021; Khan et al., 2020; Zheng & Kouwenberg, 2019; Zhang et al., 2019).

The contribution of the chapter is summarised as follows. It summarises the basic features of Islamic finance and Fintech application, annual production, types of publication, current research trend and future research direction using co-occurrence analysis. Second, it explores the most prolific authors, most influential countries, document, organisation and affiliation and collaboration research network of journals, authors, and affiliations, etc. Third, with the current trends, the study provides future research directions in the Islamic finance and Fintech area and possible development directions.

The remaining chapter is organised as follows. In the next section, we provide the research methodology used for the chapter and the data extraction method. Section three presents the results obtained using VOSviwer and R-studio. Section four provides the future research direction and finally in section five we conclude.

2 Methodology

This review study used bibliometric analysis tools to assess and visualise the trends and substances of Fintech and Islamic finance literature. According to (Alshater et al., 2021a, 2021b; Campbell et al., 2009) bibliometric tools can be used by scholars to evaluate the effectiveness of a journal or an individual researcher (Bashar et al., 2021). Citations and co-citations analysis can be applied to evaluate the intellectual structure of the state of the subject and information regarding evolution of themes and subthemes can be retrieved (Han et al., 2021).

Scopus database is used for data collection, it is one of the most comprehensive abstract and citation databases and is widely used for bibliometric studies (Costa et al., 2017; Khan et al., 2020). A combination of boolean search strings containing keywords such as Fintech, financial technology, Islamic finance, big data, artificial intelligence, blockchain, bitcoin, recommenders, chatbots, automated services with OR and logical operators is applied to abstract, title and keywords on the Scopus search engine interface. This search query returned 4678 documents between 2001 and 2021. The extracted data is then examined carefully by researchers to assure that it is having a central idea of financial technology, cleaning of data is done using exclusion criteria like it must be written in English language, it should be journal articles, review articles and book chapters. This step excludes all irrelevant literature from the dataset, remaining only 2248 kinds of literature which are arranged properly to be used in further analysis. The excluded documents included filtering all the documents one by one based on the title and abstract and unrelated studies were excluded. For descriptive and bibliometric analysis Biblioshiny interface of R application is used, while VOSviewer is used for network visualisation. Similar methods were used by (Khan et al., 2020; Xue et al., 2020).

3 Data Analysis and Visualisation

The data accessed from Scopus database consists of 2248 kinds of literature that have been published by 726 sources (Journals, books, etc.) with average citations of 7.6 documents. The assessment of the dataset reveals that 3404 authors are engaged in publishing this literature. Figure 1 shows the subject category in the Scopus database. The category Economics, Econometrics and Finance contains 654 articles which amount to 26% of the total literature. The next major subject category is Business, Management and Accounting that have published 19% of the current dataset (19%). There are other subject categories like engineering, computer science and multidisciplinary which have been published about Fintech in Islamic finance. Most of these studies published in engineering and computer science journals are addressing the technological components of Fintech and its possible application in the Islamic finance and banking industry.

The publication trend in Fintech research is illustrated in Fig. 2. It can be observed that the research trend in Islamic Fintech and Islamic finance have grown over the years. The research in the subject has encountered exponential growth from the year 2010 onwards. This trend reveals the fact that Fintech has been an integral part of Islamic finance and has investigated its varieties of applications to gain efficiency and provide an excellent customer experience.

Most Influential Author

Figure 3 presents the most influential authors with the maximum number of publications. The top author is Hassan MK with 62 publications in Islamic finance and Fintech. Saiti B is the second top author in this list having 34 scientific literatures. Third ranked author is Oseni UA and has published 26 articles. The fourth rank is the same as the first ranked author i.e. Kabir Hassan M with 21 publications. Kabir Hassan is the most prolific author in Islamic finance and Fintech and contributed significantly to the advancement of the subject.

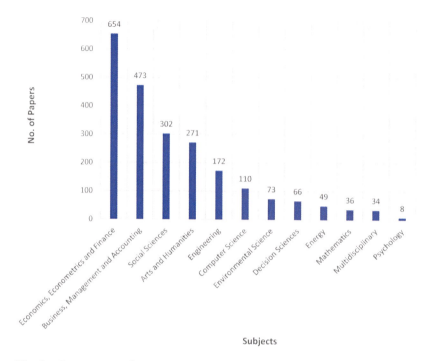

Fig. 1 Scopus research category

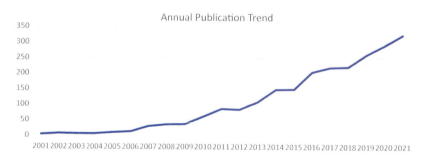

Fig. 2 Annual scientific publication

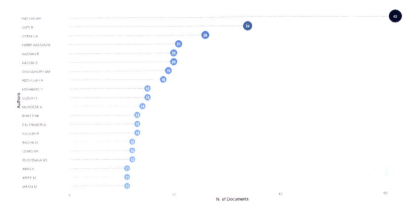

Fig. 3 Most relevant authors

Most Important Documents

Top 10 most influential documents are presented in Table 1. The top-ranked document is "Shaping Halal into a Brand" written by Wilson Jaj in the year 2010 and attracted 313 citations. The second document in this list is "How 'Islamic' is Islamic banking?" authored by Khan F and has been cited by 277 since 2010. The third document written by Hayat R., has been cited 173 times since it was published in 2011. The other documents in the list have also significantly contributed to the development of academic literature on the overall growth of Islamic Finance and Fintech. The documents on the theme of Islamic mutual funds (Causse, 2012; Oseni et al., 2012), Islamic stock markets (Ghlamallah et al., 2021) and Islamic stock pricing (Naifar & Mseddi, 2013) had substantially contributed in Islamic finance research.

Influential Journals

Table 2 reports the sources with maximum publication on the subject. The sources are ranked based on their h-index, while g-index and m-index is also included for better understanding of the impact of these journals on Islamic finance. The top journal is "ARAB LAW QUARTERLY", having an h-index of 7, attracted 137 citations and published 25 papers since 2007. This journal is publishing articles related to the laws of Arab nations, Islamic banking and shariah-compliant financing which are in the

Table 1 Most influential documents

Author	Year	Tittle	Total citations	TC per Year
Wilson JAJ	2010	Shaping Halal into a Brand	313	24
Khan F	2010	How "Islamic" is Islamic banking?	277	21
Hayat R	2011	Risk and return characteristics of Islamic equity funds	173	14
El-Gama MA	2006	Islamic finance	167	10
Ho CSF	2014	Understanding Islamic finance	155	17
Jawadi F	2014	Conventional and Islamic stock price performance: An empirical investigation	130	14
Rosyl SA	2003	Performance of Islamic and mainstream banks in Malaysia	114	6

Note TC, Total Citations

Table 2 Most influential journals

Sources	h_index	g_index	m_index	TC	NP	PY_start
Arab Law Quarterly	7	10	0.44	137	25	2007
Al-Shajarah	4	4	0.50	48	21	2015
Applied Economics	4	9	0.40	117	9	2013
Advanced Science Letters	3	5	0.38	36	8	2015
Academy of Accounting and Financial Studies Journal	4	6	0.80	75	6	2018
Applied Economics Letters	2	3	0.25	14	4	2015
Academy of Strategic Management Journal	2	2	0.29	7	3	2016
Accounting Research Journal	2	3	0.18	49	3	2012
Afro-Asian Journal Of Finance and Accounting	2	3	0.20	18	3	2013
Accounting and Finance	2	2	0.33	28	2	2017

preferable scope of the journal. The second most contributing journal is "AL-SHAJARAH", it has contributed 21 research articles, having an h-index of 4 and cited 48 times since 2015. This journal is the Journal of the International Institute of Islamic Thought and Civilization engaged aggressively in publishing quality literature on Islamic finance.

The growth of the sources publishing on Islamic finance and Fintech is shown in Fig. 4 Majority of these journals started publishing from 2005

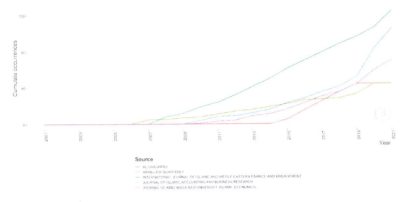

Fig. 4 Source growth

onwards, these journals have published substantial literature on Islamic finance and achieved growth at an increasing rate. International Journal of Islamic and Middle Eastern Finance AND Management has witnessed growth the most. However, it started contributing to the research growth of Islamic finance and Fintech from 2007 onwards and gained tremendous attraction from scholars. The other important sources growing at a fast pace in the space of publishing literature on Islamic finance and Fintech are Arab Law Quarterly, Al-Sharjah and Journal of King Abdulaziz University, Islamic Finance. These findings are consistent with the findings of the most influential sources discussed in the previous section.

Country and Affiliations

The contribution of the countries and affiliations are important to understand the intellectual contribution to the growth of Islamic finance and Fintech. Countries are ranked based on the number of articles it has published, total citations, average article citation, single country paper, multiple country paper and presented in Table 3. Malaysia is the top country, contributing 397 articles and its articles are cited 3212 times. The majority of the literature is written alone by Malaysian scholars (341), and only 56 articles are published with international collaborations. This journal has only 8 average article citations which is far lower than the other important countries publishing on Islamic finance and Fintech. The United Kingdom and the USA are placed in second and third rank with

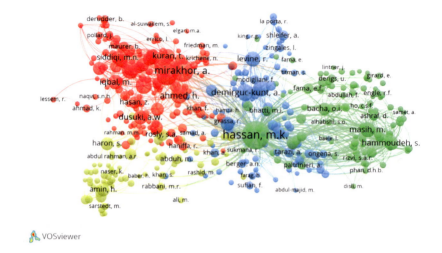

Fig. 5 Co-citation analysis of cited Authors

Table 3 Most important countries

Country	Articles	TC	AAC	SCP	MCP
Malaysia	397	3212	8	341	56
United Kingdom	107	2024	19	78	29
USA	105	1769	17	69	36
Australia	50	751	15	32	18
France	24	530	22	15	9
Saudi Arabia	71	517	7	53	18
Tunisia	40	440	11	34	6
Turkey	54	293	5	32	22
Pakistan	71	239	3	39	32
Indonesia	92	221	2	81	11
Bahrain	32	206	6	21	11

Note TC, Total Citations; AAC, Average Article Citations; SCP, Single Country Production; MCP, Multiple Country Production

107 and 105 articles, respectively. These countries have attracted a significant number of citations on the literature they have published, and they have also achieved substantial average article citation scores.

Table 4 Top affiliations

Affiliations	Articles
International Islamic University Malaysia	179
Universiti Kebangsaan Malaysia	82
University Of Malaya	82
Universiti Utara Malaysia	68
University of New Orleans	62
Universiti Teknologi Mara	57
International Islamic University	48
Universiti Sains Islam Malaysia	43
Universiti Sains Malaysia	41
Universitas Airlangga	33

In continuation to the findings of the important countries, top affiliations are presented in Table 4. The top 4 affiliations in the list are International Islamic University Malaysia (179 articles), Universiti Kebangsaan Malaysia (82 articles), University of Malaya (82 articles) and Universiti Utara Malaysia (68 articles) are from Malaysia. The University of New Orleans (62 articles) of the United States has also contributed substantially to the development of research in Islamic finance and Fintech.

Co-Citation Analysis

Co-citation analysis is a semantic similarity examination of literature, it determines the frequency of two documents cited together by other documents (Alshater et al., 2021a, 2021b). VOSviewer application is used to analyse the co-citations of authors. The science mapping of co-citation of cited authors is presented in Fig. 5. Minimum citations of an author are kept at 30 for better visualisation, 443 authors meet the minimum criteria and included in the visualisation network. The network thus obtained consists of 4 clusters which are represented by different coloured clusters. The largest cluster is red coloured and contains 158 authors, the second largest cluster is represented by green colour and made up of 107 authors. The blue-coloured cluster consists of 104 authors and the smallest cluster in the network contains 74 authors and represented by yellow colours.

The first cluster is combining the authors researching and publishing on core Islamic financial topics and includes a range of subtopics of

Islamic finance like Islamic asset pricing (Al Mamun et al., 2021), risk sharing finance (Shafique et al., 2013), risk sharing index (Doumpos et al., 2017), Islam and economic performance (Kuran, 2018), Islamic financial contracts (Rabbani et al., 2022a; Lajis, 2019), ethical issues in decision-making (Khan et al., 2021a, 2021b, 2021c), Islamic financial product development (Warsame, 2015). Green cluster is combining the literature related to shariah compliance and regulations, the scholars have investigated various aspects and perspectives of Islamic finance. Few of the important topics in this cluster are dividend pay-out and shariah compliance (Bugshan et al., 2021), determinant of fees in Islamic finance (Al Mamun et al., 2021), shariah-compliant equity investment (Yildirima & Ilhanb, 2018), Islamic equities (Walkshäusl & Lobe, 2012), Islamic commodities (Dewandaru et al., 2017), shariah-compliant mutual fund (Wilson, 2012) and Islamic stock markets (Ashraf et al., 2020).

The blue-coloured cluster has combined the literature on the application of technology in Islamic finance. The major topics in this cluster are the adoption of artificial intelligence (Elrefai et al., 2021), blockchain technologies (Khan et al., 2021a, 2021b, 2021c), chatbots (Kopalle et al., 2021), automatic response mechanism (Elrefai et al., 2021), online financial advisor (Saadna et al., 2022) and other important application of disruptive technologies in Islamic finance. The last and smallest cluster (yellow) of this network has accommodated literature on marketing and consumer behaviour towards Islamic finance.

4 Keyword Co-Occurrence Analysis

It refers to the common presence of keywords in the dataset, the visualisation network is based on the frequency of the most occurring keywords which are similar to each other and refer to a particular subject (Khan et al., 2021a). VOSviewer is used to create the network of co-occurrence of the author's keywords. A minimum number of occurrences of a keyword is kept at 5, 238 keywords met the criteria out of 4366 keywords. The obtained network is based on four clusters (Fig. 6), the first cluster is represented by red colour and contains 81 items, the green-coloured cluster is made of 78 keywords, cluster represented by blue keywords consists of 43 keywords, the smallest cluster contains 35 keywords and is represented by yellow colour.

AN INSIGHT INTO THE FINTECH ... 143

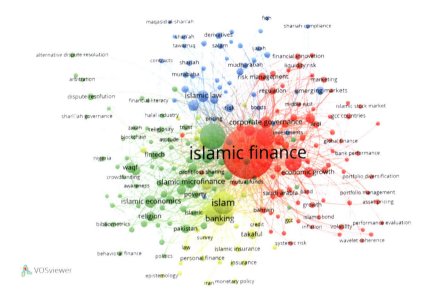

Fig. 6 Co-occurrence of author's keywords

The keyword occurrence network shows that Islamic finance is the most important keyword that has occurred the maximum number of times (size of the node denotes the strength of the frequency of occurrence). The second important keyword is Islamic banking, which is one of the core and common keywords of the subject. These keywords are clustered according to their nearness and similarity with other keywords. The major keywords which have occurred in the above network are "Islamic economics", "Islamic Microfinance", "Corporate Governance", "sukuk", "Islamic Financial Institutions", "Waqf", "Shariah", "Takaful", "Fintech", "Risk Management", "Corporate Social Responsibility", "Sharia Compliance", "Portfolio Diversification", "Asset Pricing", "Crowdfunding", "Economic Growth", "religion", "Islam", etc. These topics are highly interrelated and depict the state of research in Islamic finance and Fintech.

Bibliographic Coupling of Documents

Bibliographic coupling is a comprehensive tool for visualising the intellectual structure of the scientific literature, two documents are said to be bibliographically coupled if they cite a third document in common in their references (Costa et al., 2017). Bibliographic coupling network is created using VOSviewer application and presented in Fig. 7. For creating a bibliographic network, the minimum number of citations of a document is kept at 20, 236 documents met the minimum criteria of inclusion and hence included in the analysis.

The network map shows the growth of Islamic finance literature over the period. Before 2008 the research in Islamic finance was focussed on its fundamentals and its growth, from 2012 onwards the scholars focussed more on customer-centric research i.e. customer's attitudes and perceptions towards Islamic finance (Ahmed et al., 2020; Amin et al., 2014), while the research focus shifted more towards reporting (Alhabshi et al., 2018; Laila et al., 2021; Ryder & Turksen, 2009), value-based Islamic banking and its reporting (Algabry et al., 2020), evaluation of Maqāsid ul-Shari'āh's in financial reporting standards for Islamic financial institutions (Mukhlisin, 2021). The performance of Islamic banks is investigated by scholars to understand the difference between conventional and Islamic finance, the role of the shariah committee in the overall performance of the Islamic financial institutions (Khalil & Boulila Taktak, 2020), the

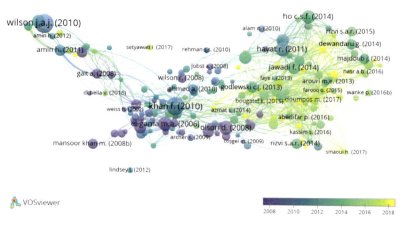

Fig. 7 Bibliographic coupling of documents

objectives and metrics for gauging the performance of banks (Almansour, 2019; Doumpos et al., 2017; Mohd Noor et al., 2019). The efficiency of Islamic banking firms is studied to understand the determinants of technical efficiency of the Islamic banks, the role of regulations on bank efficiency, the role of oil prices on the performance (ElMassah et al., 2019; Khan et al., 2021b; Kuanova et al., 2021) and adoption of Fintech such as artificial intelligence, blockchain technologies and machine learning algorithms (Abu Basha et al., 2021; Hafssa & Oumaima, 2020; Hassan et al., 2020a, 2020b, 2020c; Rabbani et al., 2020) from 2015 onwards.

5 Future Expansion

The bibliometric analysis and scientific mapping help us in indicating several future research directions for the further development of Islamic finance literature. The themes and subthemes which have evolved over the period are presented in Table 5.

Most of the existing literature is qualitative in nature, there is a need for empirical studies that can help in better understanding and generalisation of the concepts of Islamic finance. There is a need for examination of the differences and similarities of shariah frameworks and regulations. Research can be extended to evaluate the cross-cultural analysis of Islamic finance; most of the existing studies are either conducted for a country or a specific geographical area. The role of sustainable finance in the overall performance shall be investigated. Moreover, the behavioural aspects of finance shall be empirically investigated using developed consumer behaviour theories and its applications in Islamic finance. The adoption of technologies has disrupted Islamic finance, the technologies can be evaluated from various applicability and its overall impact on the customer experience, reporting and performance of Islamic financial institutions.

6 Conclusion

The chapter contributes to the understanding of Islamic finance and Fintech literature with the use of bibliometric analysis using 2248 documents obtained from the Scopus databases between 2001 and 2021. First, Fintech is an ongoing financial innovation that has attracted a lot of buzz in the financial market and second, Islamic finance has proved its worth as the fastest growing financial system and emerged as the main contender to the conventional finance world post the global financial crisis

Table 5 Evolving themes and subthemes in Islamic finance

Research Themes	Sub Themes	Citations
The fundamentals of Islamic Finance	Growth of Islamic Finance	Doumpos et al. (2017)
	Shariah Regulations	Kuanova et al. (2021)
	Shariah Regulatory Framework	Aziz et al. (2021)
	Islamic Risk Sharing Models	Hassan et al. (2020a, 2020b, 2020c)
	Islamic Financial product pricing	Khan et al. (2021a, 2021b, 2021c)
	Sustainable Islamic Finance	Khan (2019)
Customer Centric Approach	Attitude and perception towards Islamic finance	Masvood (2019)
	Behavioural finance	Kumari and Sar (2017)
	Religion and Islamic financial behaviour	Laila et al. (2021)
	Marketing theories and financial behaviour	Calzadilla et al. (2021)
	Cross-cultural customer behaviour towards finance	Alzadjal et al. (2021)
Reporting of Islamic Finance	Accounting of Islamic finance	Laila et al. (2021)
	Local accounting standards and Islamic accounting standards	Hassan et al. (2019)
Islamic institutions performance	Determinants of efficiency	Alshater et al. (2020)
	Role of shariah committee	Juhro et al. (2020)
	Islamic reporting and performance	Laila et al. (2021)
	Role of regulations	Biancone and Radwan (2018)
Adoption of Fintech	AI in Finance	Königstorfer and Thalmann (2020)
	Blockchain	Aziz et al. (2021)
	Bitcoin	Rabbani et al. (2020)
	Machine learning	Rabbani et al. (2020)

of 2008. From various aspects, the chapter analysed the publications in the Islamic finance and Fintech area using data visualisation tools such as, VOSViewer, R-studio and biblioshiny.

The development of literature in Fintech and its application in the Islamic finance literature, Fintech is a growing field and benefits from the innovations in the fields, such as, big data, machine learning, contributing country to the literature, followed by the United Kingdom, USA and Australia. The most contributing institution emerged as the International Islamic University, Malaysia. As far as the most prolific author contributing to the field of Islamic finance literature, Prof. M. Kabir Hassan from the University of New Orleans, USA has contributed the maximum number of research articles and deservingly also received the maximum citations.

The chapter also performed the keyword co-citation analysis of the cited author, keyword co-occurrence analysis and bibliographic coupling of the documents. The results of the analysis indicated 4 clusters (see Fig. 5) which are represented by different coloured clusters. The largest cluster is red coloured and contains 158 authors, the second largest cluster is represented by green colour and is made up of 107 authors. The keyword occurrence network shows that Islamic finance is the most important keyword that has occurred the maximum number of times. Bibliographic coupling network is created using VOSviewer application and presented in Fig. 7. For creating a bibliographic network, the minimum number of citations of a document is kept at 20, 236 documents met the minimum criteria of inclusion and hence included in the analysis.

The findings of the study play a key role in the further growth of the academic literature on Fintech and its application in Islamic finance by encouraging future researchers and academicians. However, the content used in the chapter is limited to the keyword Fintech and Islamic finance and the use of Scopus database only, the use of more diverse keywords is expected to give a more enriched result.

REFERENCES

Abu Basha, S., Elgammal, M. M., & Abuzayed, B. M. (2021). Online peer-to-peer lending: A review of the literature. *Electronic Commerce Research and Applications, 48*. https://doi.org/10.1016/j.elerap.2021.101069

Abdullah, Y., & Rabbani, M. R. (2021). COVID-19 and GCC Islamic market Indices. *2021 International Conference on Sustainable Islamic Business and Finance (SIBF)*.

Ahmed, T., Kabir, S., & Aziz, A. (2020). Exploring the prospects for Islamic home finance in the UK: Evidence from the industry practitioners' perspective. *International Journal of Business and Society, 21*(1), 353–368.

Al Mamun, M. A., Hassan, M. K., Kalam Azad, M. A., & Rashid, M. (2021). A hybrid review of Islamic pricing literature. *Singapore Economic Review*, 1–33. https://doi.org/10.1142/S0217590821420029

Algabry, L., Alhabshi, S. M., Soualhi, Y., & Alaeddin, O. (2020). Conceptual framework of internal Sharīʿah audit effectiveness factors in Islamic banks. *ISRA International Journal of Islamic Finance*, 12(2), 171–193. https://doi.org/10.1108/IJIF-09-2018-0097

Alhabshi, S. M., Agil, S. K. S., & Ahmed, M. U. (2018). Financial reporting dimensions of intangibles in the context of islamic finance. *Al-Shajarah, Special Issue: ISLAMIC BANKING AND FINANCE*, 375–396. https://www.scopus.com/inward/record.uri?eid=2-s2.0-85060052419&partnerID=40&md5=cabc65a437a28f35f42169b2f4d588a9

Almansour, A. (2019). Muslim investors and the capital market: The role of religious scholars. *Pacific Basin Finance Journal*, 58. https://doi.org/10.1016/j.pacfin.2019.101211

Alshater, M. M., Hassan, M. K., Khan, A., & Saba, I. (2020). Influential and intellectual structure of Islamic finance: A bibliometric review. *International Journal of Islamic and Middle Eastern Finance and Management*. https://doi.org/10.1108/IMEFM-08-2020-0419

Alshater, M. M., Hassan, M. K., Rashid, M., & Hasan, R. (2021a). A bibliometric review of the Waqf literature. *Eurasian Economic Review*. https://doi.org/10.1007/s40822-021-00183-4

Alshater, M. M., Saad, R. A. J., Abd. Wahab, N., & Saba, I. (2021b). What do we know about zakat literature? A bibliometric review. *Journal of Islamic Accounting and Business Research*, 12(4), 544–563. https://doi.org/10.1108/JIABR-07-2020-0208

Alzadjal, M. A. J., Abu-Hussin, M. F., Md Husin, M., & Mohd Hussin, M. Y. (2021). Moderating the role of religiosity on potential customer intention to deal with Islamic banks in Oman. *Journal of Islamic Marketing*. https://doi.org/10.1108/JIMA-05-2020-0150

Amin, H., Amin, H., Rahim, A., Rahman, A., & Abdul Razak, D. (2014). Consumer acceptance of Islamic home financing. *International Journal of Housing Markets and Analysis*, 7(3), 307–332. https://doi.org/10.1108/IJHMA-12-2012-0063

Arner, D. W., Barberis, J., & Buckley, R. P. (2017). FinTech, regTech, and the reconceptualization of financial regulation. *Northwestern Journal of International Law and Business*, 37(3), 373–415. https://www.scopus.com/inward/record.uri?eid=2-s2.0-85029366261&partnerID=40&md5=8d52c44c1d5a6142c39beb3f914927c5

Ashraf, D., Rizwan, M. S., & Azmat, S. (2020). Not one but three decisions in sukuk issuance: Understanding the role of ownership and governance. *Pacific Basin Finance Journal*. https://doi.org/10.1016/j.pacfin.2020.101423

Aziz, M. R. A., Khalid, N. S. B., Firdaus, M. H. B. A., Yatim, A. F. B. M., Navamohan, F. A. B. M. A., & Omar, M. N. W. B. (2021). A review on literatures of Islamic financial institutions and market between 2010–2020. *Library Philosophy and Practice, 2021,* 1–35.

Banna, H., Kabir Hassan, M., & Rashid, M. (2021). Fintech-based financial inclusion and bank risk-taking: Evidence from OIC countries. *Journal of International Financial Markets, Institutions and Money, 75*(October), 1–20. https://doi.org/10.1016/j.intfin.2021.101447

Bashar, A., & Rabbani, M. R. (2021). Exploring the role of web personalization in consumer green purchasing behavior: A conceptual framework. *Third International Sustainability and Resilience Conference: Climate Change, 2021,* 23–28.

Bashar, A., Rabbani, M., Khan, S., & Ali, M. A. M. (2021). Data driven finance: A bibliometric review and scientific mapping. *International Conference on Data Analytics for Business and Industry (ICDABI), 2021,* 161–166.

Bashayreh, A., & Wadi, R. M. A. (2021). The Effect of Fintech on Banks' Performance: Jordan Case. In A. B., H. A., & E. I. (Eds.), *International Conference on Business and Technology, ICBT 2020: Vol. 194 LNNS* (pp. 812–821). Springer Science and Business Media Deutschland GmbH. https://doi.org/10.1007/978-3-030-69221-6_62

Biancone, P. P., & Radwan, M. (2018). Sharia-compliant financing for public utility infrastructure. *Utilities Policy, 52,* 88–94. https://doi.org/10.1016/j.jup.2018.03.006

Bugshan, A., Alnori, F., & Bakry, W. (2021). Shariah compliance and corporate cash holdings. *Research in International Business and Finance, 56.* https://doi.org/10.1016/j.ribaf.2021.101383

Bureshaid, N., Lu, K., & Sarea, A. (2021). Adoption of fintech services in the banking industry. In *Studies in Computational Intelligence* (Vol. 954, pp. 125–138). Springer Science and Business Media Deutschland GmbH. https://doi.org/10.1007/978-3-030-72080-3_7

Calzadilla, J. F., Bordonado-Bermejo, M. J., & González-Rodrigo, E. (2021). A systematic review of ordinary people, behavioural financial biases. *Economic Research-Ekonomska Istrazivanja, 34*(1), 2767–2789. https://doi.org/10.1080/1331677X.2020.1839526

Campbell, D., Picard-Aitken, M., Côté, G., Macaluso, B., Robitaille, J.-P., Bastien, N., Laframboise, M.-C., Lebeau, L.-M., Mirabel, P., Larivière, V., & Archambault, É. (2009). Bibliometrics as a performance measurement tool for research evaluation: The case of research funded by the national cancer institute of Canada. *12th International Conference on Scientometrics and Informetrics, ISSI 2009* (pp. 301–312).

Causse, G. (2012). Islamic finance: An alternative finance or an antidote to the crisis of capitalism? In J. F. & J. F. (Eds.), *International Symposia in Economic*

Theory and Econometrics (Vol. 22, pp. 173–196). https://doi.org/10.1108/S1571-0386(2012)0000022014

Chirulli, P. (2021). FinTech, RegTech and SupTech: Institutional challenges to the supervisory architecture of the financial markets. In *Routledge Handbook of Financial Technology and Law* (pp. 447–464). Taylor and Francis. https://doi.org/10.4324/9780429325670-24

Costa, D. F., de Melo Carvalho, F., de Melo Moreira, B. C., & do Prado, J. W. (2017). Bibliometric analysis on the association between behavioral finance and decision making with cognitive biases such as overconfidence, anchoring effect and confirmation bias. *Scientometrics, 111*(3), 1775–1799. https://doi.org/10.1007/s11192-017-2371-5

Demir, A., Pesqué-Cela, V., Altunbas, Y., & Murinde, V. (2020). Fintech, financial inclusion and income inequality: A quantile regression approach. *European Journal of Finance.* https://doi.org/10.1080/1351847X.2020.1772335

Dewandaru, G., Masih, R., Bacha, O. I., & Masih, A. M. M. (2017). The role of Islamic asset classes in the diversified portfolios: Mean variance spanning test. *Emerging Markets Review, 30*, 66–95. https://doi.org/10.1016/j.ememar.2016.09.002

Doumpos, M., Hasan, I., & Pasiouras, F. (2017). Bank overall financial strength: Islamic versus conventional banks. *Economic Modelling, 64*, 513–523. https://doi.org/10.1016/j.econmod.2017.03.026

ElMassah, S., AlSayed, O., & Bacheer, S. M. (2019). Liquidity in the UAE Islamic banks. *Journal of Islamic Accounting and Business Research, 10*(5), 679–694. https://doi.org/10.1108/JIABR-02-2017-0018

Elrefai, A. T., Elgazzar, M. H., & Khodeir, A. N. (2021). Using artificial intelligence in enhancing banking services. In P. R. (Ed.), *11th IEEE Annual Computing and Communication Workshop and Conference, CCWC 2021* (pp. 980–986). Institute of Electrical and Electronics Engineers Inc. https://doi.org/10.1109/CCWC51732.2021.9375993

Fadhul, S., & Hamdan, A. (2020). The role of "fintech" on banking performance. In D. N. A. (Ed.), *15th European Conference on Innovation and Entrepreneurship, ECIE 2020* (Vols. 2020-September, pp. 911–914). Academic Conferences and Publishing International Limited. https://doi.org/10.34190/EIE.20.230

Ghlamallah, E., Alexakis, C., Dowling, M., & Piepenbrink, A. (2021). The topics of Islamic economics and finance research. *International Review of Economics and Finance, 75*, 145–160. https://doi.org/10.1016/j.iref.2021.04.006

Gimpel, H., Rau, D., & Röglinger, M. (2018). Understanding FinTech start-ups – A taxonomy of consumer-oriented service offerings. *Electronic Markets, 28*(3), 245–264. https://doi.org/10.1007/s12525-017-0275-0

Habeeb, S., Rabbai, M. R., Ahmad, N., Ali, M. A. M., & Bashar, A. (2021). Post COVID-19 challenges for the sustainable entrepreneurship. *2021 International Conference on Sustainable Islamic Business and Finance (SIBF).*

Hafssa, Y., & Oumaima, B. (2020). Blockchain and smart sukuk: New determinant of development of the sukuk market. *2020 IEEE International Conference on Technology Management, Operations and Decisions, ICTMOD 2020.* https://doi.org/10.1109/ICTMOD49425.2020.9380613

Han, R., Lam, H. K. S., Zhan, Y., Wang, Y., Dwivedi, Y. K., & Tan, K. H. (2021). Artificial intelligence in business-to-business marketing: A bibliometric analysis of current research status, development and future directions. *Industrial Management and Data Systems, 121*(12), 2467–2497. https://doi.org/10.1108/IMDS-05-2021-0300

Hassan, M. K., Aliyu, S., Huda, M., & Rashid, M. (2019). A survey on Islamic Finance and accounting standards. *Borsa Istanbul Review, 19,* S1–S13. https://doi.org/10.1016/j.bir.2019.07.006

Hassan, M. K., Aliyu, S., Saiti, B., & Abdul Halim, Z. (2020a). A review of Islamic stock market, growth and real-estate finance literature. *International Journal of Emerging Markets, 16*(7), 1259–1290. https://doi.org/10.1108/IJOEM-11-2019-1001

Hassan, M. K., Rabbani, M. R., & Ali, M. A. (2020b). Challenges for the Islamic Finance and banking in post COVID era and the role of Fintech. *Journal of Economic Cooperation and Development, 43*(3), 93–116.

Hassan, M. K., Karim, M. S., & Muneeza, A. (2020c). A conventional and Sharī'ah analysis of bitcoin. *Arab Law Quarterly, 35*(1–2), 155–189. https://doi.org/10.1163/15730255-BJA10033

Hassan, M. K., Rabbani, M. R., Brodmann, J., Bashar, A., & Grewal, H. (2022). Bibliometric and Scientometric analysis on CSR practices in the banking sector. *Review of Financial Economics.*

Janková, Z. (2021). A bibliometric analysis of artificial intelligence technique in financial market. *Scientific Papers of the University of Pardubice, Series D: Faculty of Economics and Administration, 29*(3). https://doi.org/10.46585/sp29031268

Jreisat, A., Rabbani, M. R., Bashar, A., Ali, M. A. M., & AlAbbas, A. (2021). Is Fintech Valuation an Art of Science? Exploring the Innovative Methods for the Valuation of Fintech Startups. *2021 International Conference on Decision Aid Sciences and Application (DASA),* (pp. 922–925). IEEE.

Juhro, S. M., Narayan, P. K., Iyke, B. N., & Trisnanto, B. (2020). Is there a role for Islamic finance and R&D in endogenous growth models in the case of Indonesia? *Pacific Basin Finance Journal, 62.* https://doi.org/10.1016/j.pacfin.2020.101297

Kandpal, V., & Mehrotra, R. (2019). Financial inclusion: The role of fintech and digital financial services in India. *Indian Journal of Economics and Business,*

18(1), 95–104. https://www.scopus.com/inward/record.uri?eid=2-s2.0-850 78895210&partnerID=40&md5=9e64c01e4a9fa4ca88ba1291b319ad9d

Khalil, A., & Boulila Taktak, N. (2020). The impact of the Shariah Board's characteristics on the financial soundness of Islamic banks. *Journal of Islamic Accounting and Business Research*. https://doi.org/10.1108/JIABR-08-2018-0127

Khan, T. (2019). Reforming Islamic finance for achieving sustainable development goals. *Journal of King Abdulaziz University, Islamic Economics*, 32(1), 3–21. https://doi.org/10.4197/Islec.32-1.1

Khan, S., & Rabbani, M. R. (2020). In depth analysis of blockchain, cryptocurrency and Sharia compliance. *International Journal of Business Innovation and Research*, 1(1), 1. https://doi.org/10.1504/ijbir.2020.10033066

Khan, A., Hassan, M. K., Paltrinieri, A., Dreassi, A., & Bahoo, S. (2020). A bibliometric review of takaful literature. *International Review of Economics and Finance*, 69, 389–405. https://doi.org/10.1016/j.iref.2020.05.013

Khan, A., Goodell, J. W., Hassan, M. K., & Paltrinieri, A. (2021a). A bibliometric review of finance bibliometric papers. *Finance Research Letters*. https://doi.org/10.1016/j.frl.2021.102520

Khan, A, Hassan, M. K., Paltrinieri, A., & Bahoo, S. (2021b). Trade, financial openness and dual banking economies: Evidence from GCC Region. *Journal of Multinational Financial Management*, 62.

Khan, D., Jung, L. T., & Hashmani, M. A. (2021c). Systematic literature review of challenges in blockchain scalability. *Applied Sciences (Switzerland)*, 11(20). https://doi.org/10.3390/app11209372

Khan, M. S., Rabbani, M. R., Hawaldar, I. T., & Bashar, A. (2022). Determinants of behavioral intentions to use Islamic financial technology: An empirical assessment. *Risks*, 10(6), 114.

Königstorfer, F., & Thalmann, S. (2020). Applications of Artificial Intelligence in commercial banks – A research agenda for behavioral finance. *Journal of Behavioral and Experimental Finance*, 27. https://doi.org/10.1016/j.jbef.2020.100352

Kopalle, P. K., Gangwar, M., Kaplan, A., Ramachandran, D., Reinartz, W., & Rindfleisch, A. (2021). Examining artificial intelligence (AI) technologies in marketing via a global lens: Current trends and future research opportunities. *International Journal of Research in Marketing*. https://doi.org/10.1016/j.ijresmar.2021.11.002

Kuanova, L. A., Sagiyeva, R., & Shirazi, N. S. (2021). Islamic social finance: A literature review and future research directions. *Journal of Islamic Accounting and Business Research*, 12(5), 707–728. https://doi.org/10.1108/JIABR-11-2020-0356

Kumari, N., & Sar, A. K. (2017). Recent developments and review in behavioral finance. *International Journal of Applied Business and Economic Research*,

15(26), 235–250. https://www.scopus.com/inward/record.uri?eid=2-s2.0-85041176949&partnerID=40&md5=ec96401dcf86ec4a87f543c861e2ccd7

Kuran, T. (2018). Islam and economic performance: Historical and contemporary links. *Journal of Economic Literature*, 56, 1292–1359. https://doi.org/10.1257/jel.20171243

Laila, N., Salleh, M. C. M., Rusydiana, A. S., & Sukmaningrum, P. S. (2021). A survey on Islamic economics and finance literatures indexed by scopus Q1 via thematic analysis approach. *Review of International Geographical Education Online*, 11(4), 453–468. https://doi.org/10.33403/rigeo.800661

Lajis, S. M. (2019). Fintech and risk-sharing: A catalyst for islamic finance. In *Islamic Finance, Risk-Sharing and Macroeconomic Stability* (pp. 237–254). Palgrave Macmillan. https://doi.org/10.1007/978-3-030-05225-6_12

Lee, I., & Shin, Y. J. (2018). Fintech: Ecosystem, business models, investment decisions, and challenges. *Business Horizons*, 61(1), 35–46. https://doi.org/10.1016/j.bushor.2017.09.003

Li, B., & Xu, Z. (2021). Insights into financial technology (FinTech): A bibliometric and visual study. *Financial Innovation*, 7(1), 1–28.

Masvood, Y. (2019). A critical evaluation of articles related to islamic banking. *International Journal of Recent Technology and Engineering*, 8(2), 302–306. https://doi.org/10.35940/ijrte.B1057.0782S419

Mehrotra, A., & Menon, S. (2021). Second round of FinTech – Trends and challenges. *2nd International Conference on Computation, Automation and Knowledge Management, ICCAKM 2021*, 243–248. https://doi.org/10.1109/ICCAKM50778.2021.9357759

Moh'd Ali, M. A., Basahr, A., Rabbani, M. R., & Abdulla, Y. (2020). Transforming Business Decision Making with Internet of Things (IoT) and Machine Learning (ML). *2020 International Conference on Decision Aid Sciences and Application (DASA)*, 674–679.

Mohd Noor, N. S., Mohd. Shafiai, M. H., & Ismail, A. G. (2019). The derivation of Shariah risk in Islamic finance: a theoretical approach. *Journal of Islamic Accounting and Business Research*, 10(5), 663–678. https://doi.org/10.1108/JIABR-08-2017-0112

Mukhlisin, M. (2021). Level of Maqāsid ul-Sharī'āh's in financial reporting standards for Islamic financial institutions. *Journal of Islamic Accounting and Business Research*, 12(1), 60–77. https://doi.org/10.1108/JIABR-03-2020-0090

Naifar, N., & Mseddi, S. (2013). Sukuk spreads determinants and pricing model methodology. *Afro-Asian Journal of Finance and Accounting*, 3(3), 241–257. https://doi.org/10.1504/AAJFA.2013.054425

Oseni, U. A., AbiaKadouf, H., Ansari, A. H., & Olayemi, A. A. M. (2012). The value proposition of Islamic financial intermediation: Some current legal and regulatory challenges. *Australian Journal of Basic and Applied Sciences*,

6(11), 239–245. https://www.scopus.com/inward/record.uri?eid=2-s2.0-84871787907&partnerID=40&md5=a7c804dd1483f2a7f7ac4b23465f62a6
Pantielieieva, N., Khutorna, M., Lytvynenko, O., & Potapenko, L. (2020). FinTech, RegTech and traditional financial intermediation: Trends and threats for financial stability. In *Lecture notes on data engineering and communications technologies* (Vol. 42, pp. 1–21). Springer. https://doi.org/10.1007/978-3-030-35649-1_1

Pwc. (2017). FinTech's growing influence on Financial Services. In *Global Fintech Report*.

Rabbani, M. R. (2022). Fintech innovations, scope, challenges, and implications in Islamic Finance: A systematic analysis. *International Journal of Computing and Digital Systems, 11*(1), 1–28.

Rabbani, M. R., Khan, S., & Thalassinos, E. I. (2020). FinTech, blockchain and Islamic finance: An extensive literature review. *International Journal of Economics and Business Administration, 8*(2), 65–86. https://doi.org/10.35808/ijeba/444

Rabbani, M. R., Jreisat, A., AlAbbas, A., Bashar, A., & Ali, M. A. M. (2021a). Whether Cryptocurrency is a threat or a revolution? An ESG perspective. *2021a International Conference on Sustainable Islamic Business and Finance (SIBF)*.

Rabbani, M. R., Sarea, A., Khan, S., & Abdullah, Y. (2021b). Ethical Concerns in Artificial Intelligence (AI): The role of RegTech and Islamic finance. *The International Conference On Global Economic Revolutions* (pp. 381–390).

Rabbani, M. R., Bashar, A., Nawaz, N., Karim, S., Ali, M. A. M., Rahiman, H. U., & Alam, M. S. (2021c). Exploring the role of islamic fintech in combating the aftershocks of COVID-19: The open social innovation of the islamic financial system. *Journal of Open Innovation: Technology, Market, and Complexity, 7*(2), 136.

Rabbani, M. R., Bashar, A., Atif, M., Jreisat, A., Zulfikar, Z., & Naseem, Y. (2021d). Text mining and visual analytics in research: Exploring the innovative tools. In *2021 International Conference on Decision Aid Sciences and Application (DASA)* (pp. 1087–1091). IEEE. University of Bahrain.

Rabbani, M. R., Bawazir, H., Khan, S., Karim, S., & Chebab, D. (2022a). Smart contract-based Islamic Fintech model for Mudaraba financing. *International Journal of Business Innovation and Research*, in press.

Rabbani, M. R., Kayani, U., Bawazir, H. S., & Hawaldar, I. T. (2022b). A commentary on emerging markets banking sector spillovers: Covid-19 vs GFC pattern analysis. *Heliyon, 8*(3), e09074.

Rangkuti, R. P., Amrullah, M., Januar, H., Rahman, A., Kaunang, C., Shihab, M. R., & Ranti, B. (2020). Fintech Growth Impact on Government Banking Business Model: Case Study of Bank XYZ. *8th International Conference on*

Information and Communication Technology, ICoICT 2020. https://doi.org/10.1109/ICoICT49345.2020.9166227

Ryder, N., & Turksen, U. (2009). Islamophobia or an important weapon An analysis of the US financial war on terrorism. *Journal of Banking Regulation, 10*(4), 307–320. https://doi.org/10.1057/jbr.2009.10

Saadna, Y., Boudhir, A. A., & Ben Ahmed, M. (2022). An Analysis of ResNet50 Model and RMSprop Optimizer for Education Platform Using an Intelligent Chatbot System. In B. A. M., T. H.L., M. T., S. P., & B. A. (Eds.), *4th International Conference on Networking, Intelligent Systems and Security, NISS 2021* (Vol. 237, pp. 577–590). Springer Science and Business Media Deutschland GmbH. https://doi.org/10.1007/978-981-16-3637-0_41

Shafique, O., Hussain, N., & Taimoor Hassan, M. (2013). Differences in the risk management practices of Islamic versus conventional financial institutions in Pakistan: An empirical study. *Journal of Risk Finance, 14*(2), 179–196. https://doi.org/10.1108/15265941311301206

Sun, H., Rabbani, M. R., Sial, M. S., Yu, S., Filipe, J. A., & Cherian, J. (2020). Identifying big data's opportunities, challenges, and implications in finance. *Mathematics, 8*(10). https://doi.org/10.3390/math8101738

Walkshäusl, C., & Lobe, S. (2012). Islamic investing. *Review of Financial Economics, 21*(2), 53–62. https://doi.org/10.1016/j.rfe.2012.03.002

Wang, X., Sadiq, R., Khan, T. M., & Wang, R. (2021). Industry 4.0 and intellectual capital in the age of FinTech. *Technological Forecasting and Social Change, 166.* https://doi.org/10.1016/j.techfore.2021.120598

Warsame, M. (2015). The role of Islamic finance in enhancing the economic prospects of Kenyan Muslims: An empirical study on Kenyan Islamic banking sector. *International Journal of Applied Business and Economic Research, 13*(9), 6885–6911. https://www.scopus.com/inward/record.uri?eid=2-s2.0-84963563157&partnerID=40&md5=203b2750ebbe50ad21e20f0368f8f4c7

Wibowo, M., & Aumeboonsuke, V. (2020). Bank financial capability on MSME lending amid economic change and the growth of Fintech companies in Indonesia. *Thailand and the World Economy, 38*(2), 63–87. https://www.scopus.com/inward/record.uri?eid=2-s2.0-85093892679&partnerID=40&md5=08e26ded5cf2137950ec09d465ea4627

Wilson, R. (2012). Legal, regulatory and governance issues in Islamic finance. In *Legal, Regulatory and Governance Issues in Islamic Finance.* Edinburgh University Press.

Xue, W., Li, H., Ali, R., & Ur Rehman, R. (2020). Knowledge mapping of corporate financial performance research: A visual analysis using cite space and ucinet. *Sustainability (Switzerland), 12*(9). https://doi.org/10.3390/SU12093554

Yan, C., Siddik, A. B., Akter, N., & Dong, Q. (2021). Factors influencing the adoption intention of using mobile financial service during the COVID-19 pandemic: The role of FinTech. *Environmental Science and Pollution Research.* https://doi.org/10.1007/s11356-021-17437-y

Yildirima, R., & Ilhanb, B. (2018). Shari'ah screening methodology - New Shari'ah compliant approach. *Journal of Islamic Economics, Banking and Finance, 14*(1), 168–191. https://doi.org/10.12816/0051173

Zhang, D., Zhang, Z., & Managi, S. (2019). A bibliometric analysis on green finance: Current status, development, and future directions. *Finance Research Letters, 29*, 425–430. https://doi.org/10.1016/j.frl.2019.02.003

Zheng, C., & Kouwenberg, R. (2019). A bibliometric review of global research on corporate governance and board attributes. *Sustainability (Switzerland), 11*(12). https://doi.org/10.3390/su10023428

Fintech Innovation and Its Application in Islamic Banking from Pakistan

Sitara Karim, Mustafa Raza Rabbani, Abu Bashar, and Ahmed Imran Hunjra

1 INTRODUCTION

The current dynamic environment with multiple advancements and innovations has sparked the need to adopt and adapt to the present challenges to sustain businesses. Financial technology, one of the fast-emerging

---

S. Karim
Nottingham University Business School, University of Nottingham Malaysia Campus, Semenyih, Malaysia

M. R. Rabbani
Department Economics and Finance, College of Business Administration, University of Bahrain, Bahrain, Kingdom of Bahrain
e-mail: mrabbani@uob.edu.bh

A. Bashar (✉)
School of Management, IMS Unison University, Dehradun, India
e-mail: abu.bashar03@iuu.ac

A. I. Hunjra
Department of Business Administration, Ghazi University, Dera Ghazi Khan, Pakistan

© The Author(s), under exclusive license to Springer Nature Switzerland AG 2022
M. K. Hassan et al. (eds.), *FinTech in Islamic Financial Institutions*, https://doi.org/10.1007/978-3-031-14941-2_8

paradigms of the present businesses has evolved as a significant benchmark to set a business distinctive and competitive (Khan et al., 2022; Rabbani et al., 2022). The applications of Fintech innovations are evident in multiple businesses and organizational processes to be successful in the global environment. The history reveals three significant eras of the Industrial Revolution (IR). The first industrial revolution (IR 1.0) has occupied the usage of water and power machines to enhance the production. The second industrial revolution (IR 2.0) shifted to electric power for increasing production capacity. The third industrial revolution (IR 3.0) is the period of advanced electronic devices and information technology to automate the production and increase the power plants' capacities manifold (Ali et al., 2019). The fourth industrial revolution (IR 4.0) is the current era, which is marked with digital advancements through the usage of internet and information technology (Rahim et al., 2018). Due to abrupt innovation, the digital is changing at a rapid rate where organizations failing to adopt these technologies may suffer financial losses in the long run.

The present global environment demands the adoption of technological innovations as it is impossible to live without internet, handheld mobile, and tablet devices. The financial industry, without exception, has been undergoing rapid technological innovations to facilitate its customers and to provide financial services without disruption (Rabbani et al., 2021a). Since, the financial sector is occupied with several regulatory and financial constraints blocking its way to completely adopt technological innovations, but an increasing trend in the usage of financial technologies is commendable (Rabbani, 2022). Moreover, due to its fast pace, the Fintech adoption is creating disruption for some of the financial and banking industry areas (Hassan et al., 2020a). In the same vein, Islamic finance and banking industry is also facing an increase in cost, implementation bottlenecks, limited awareness by employees, and greater pressures faced due to competition from the conventional banks (Abdullah & Rabbani, 2021).

The investment in the Fintech-based operations reveals growth of Fintech at extremely sharp pace where the year 2017 tracked the highest financing in Fintech of $16 billion as compared to 2016 where the investment was about $13 billion (CB Insights, 2018). Correspondingly, in 2018, Fintech-based venture capital funding was dominant in Asia with the investment of approximately $23 billion for 563 contracts. The United States, second to Asia, has invested around $12 billion, with 569 agreements, and Europe revealed approximately $4 billion investment in 363 contracts (Insights CB, 2019). With these magnificent investments in Fintech all around the globe, the adoption of Fintech innovation in the Islamic banking industry is still emerging (Rabbani et al., 2021b). In the GCC region, Bahrain is striving to be the leader in Fintech innovations through its continuous efforts and developments (Ali et al., 2019). Malaysia, among other Islamic countries, is also taking an active participation in adopting digital parameters in their banks (Karim et al., 2020a). Malaysia has also integrated its Islamic finance industry with the *Halal* economy to create a comprehensive '*halal ecosystem*' (Hassan et al., 2021a, 2021b). Pakistan is also among those countries that are still evolving in the adoption of Fintech innovations in the Islamic banking sector. The conventional banks in Pakistan have shown remarkable developments and growth in the application of Fintech innovations, but the concept of Fintech innovations in its ripened form is still nonexistent in the Islamic banks of Pakistan (Saba et al., 2019).

Pakistan is an emerging economy, according to the statistics of the World Bank (2019). The banking sector in Pakistan is regulated by the State Bank of Pakistan (SBP). Banks in Pakistan are divided into five main categories: public sector commercial banks, specialized banks, local private banks, Islamic banks, and foreign banks. The current study considers only Islamic banks to investigate the application of Fintech innovations in banking industry.

As a regulatory body for Islamic Financial Institutions (IFIs), the *Shariah* regulatory body is Accounting and Auditing Organization for Islamic Financial Institutions (AAOIFI) that provides guidelines for compliance and adoption of several types of financial innovations. Being a regulatory body, AAOIFI needs to monitor the compliance of Islamic financial institutions with the rules and policies offered by the organization (Selim & Hassan, 2019). The Pakistani Islamic banks have found Shari'a Compliance Board (SCB) under the constitution of 2000.

To fulfill the research objective of the present chapter, the content analysis approach of keywords selection and thematic method through the annual reports of Islamic banks in Pakistan were used to extract the information on the adoption of Fintech solutions in the Islamic banks of Pakistan. The period covered for the content analysis was from 2006 to 2020 to highlight the level of Fintech applications in the Islamic banking industry of Pakistan. The extracted information revealed five significant Fintech applications namely, digital wallets, biometrics, smart contracts, distributed ledger, and machine learning adopted by the Islamic banks in Pakistan. Further analysis using the system Generalized Method of Moments (S-GMM) revealed that digital wallets, biometrics, and smart contracts have been fully adopted by the Islamic banks in Pakistan whereas distributed ledger and machine learning are still evolving.

The findings of the study have provided substantial implications for the academicians and practitioners of the current competitive environment where academicians can extend this work in different emerging and developed economies. And for policymakers, the study has drawn significant takeaways to facilitate banks with sufficient funding to completely apply the Fintech innovations and enhance the overall performance of banks. In this way, banks can provide a user-friendly experience to the customers without disruptions by implementing Fintech innovations in their banks.

The rest of the chapter is arranged in the following manner. Section two presents the literature review of earlier studies. Section three gives methodology used for the study. Section four provides results of content analysis along with discussion. Finally, the chapter concludes in section five with research implications and recommendations.

2 Literature Review

Application of Fintech Innovations in the Islamic Banking Industry

In present era, the need to adapt to the changing global environments has been surmounted significantly. Digital literacy is one of the key mechanisms which cover Fintech innovations and Fintech solutions to provide ease to the customers' experiences. Fintech has changed the lifestyles, working preferences, and modes of communication across the world. With the recent technological advancements, financial technologies are assisting human beings to reduce human errors and accelerate the performance in different ways (Hassan et al., 2021a, 2021b). As mentioned earlier, the history shows gradual evolution of technology over four industrial revolutions (Rahim et al., 2018). Figure 1 presents the pictorial form of evolution of digital banking system over the last two decades and it is evident that commencing with internet banking and customer relationship management (CRM), Fintech innovations have broaden its scope in the 2021 in the form of branchless banking and cloud interaction.

In particular, the three main categories where financial sector can benefit from technological innovations are conversational (face-to-face) banking termed as front office; secondly there is a middle office where the application of Fintech is based on fraud detection and risk management practices such as cyber-security, mobile hacks, and other malpractices (Bashar et al., 2021, Bashar & Rabbani, 2021). Additionally, there is a back office in the financial industry which underwrites the risks associated with financial activity (Hassan et al., 2021a, 2021b). This report concludes that major applications of Fintech solutions in the financial sector are related to front and middle offices providing recommendations to the industry on how they can adopt Fintech-enabled approaches to overcome the challenges associated with risk exposures and financial crisis.

The major takeaways for Islamic financial industry from this report are the ways how Fintech can be implemented in all the Islamic banking operations. From the point of view of Islamic Shari'a, Islamic financial industry can also adopt Fintech innovations that are used to protect the industry as well as the customers from the fraudulent practices, cyber-security issues, default risk, liquidity risk, credit risk, etc. Additionally, there are several other technologies that need to be adopted by the Islamic financial industry to enhance its growth and provide user-friendly mechanisms for its customers. Deloitte and the European Financial Management Association conducted a survey which revealed that Fintech innovations in Islamic financial system are still in their infancy (Deloitte, 2017). This gap can be covered by the Islamic finance sector by taking some significant steps in developing strategic plans, integrating technology with the business operations, creating more awareness among the public, and recruiting the individuals who are experts in artificial intelligence and financial technology.

Prior literature also highlights that Fintech innovations will have a huge influence on the future growth and prospects of Islamic financial industry with the relevant adoption of different technologies to provide efficiency to the whole banking mechanism (Rabbani et al., 2020). It is argued that Islamic financial industry, having significant implications for Muslims and religious ethnicity, cannot deny the importance of adoption of Fintech innovations into its processes and operations. In addition to the application of Fintech solutions in the general finance industry, it has very specific application in the Islamic financial services industry ranging from interactive Chatbots (Khan & Rabbani, 2020a, 2020b), Fintech model on *Zakat*, *Qardh-Al-Hasan* and *Awqaf to* help the COVID-19 affected

SMEs and individuals (Dharani et al., 2022; Rabbani et al., 2021a), smart Islamic banking, and use of RegTech technology for Shari'a compliance of the Islamic financial institutions.

Islamic Finance and Adoption of Fintech Solutions

Scholars of Islamic finance have recently grabbed their attention toward Fintech innovations. It is important to note that research on Islamic finance and adoption of Fintech innovations in the Islamic banking industry has not reached a consensus. These studies discussed some of the technologies and ignored others. In other words, the scope of the earlier studies has remained limited to specific themes of Fintech innovations (Lutfi & Ismail, 2016; Ng et al., 2015; Torabi, 2017; Wahjono & Marina, 2017). Given the fact that adoption of Fintech innovations on Islamic banking industry is still juvenile, yet some studies provide evidence on the effectiveness of Fintech-based innovations to help increase the performance (Karim et al., 2020a, 2020c). In this stream, Finocracy and Mirakhor (2017) presented a research study on how Fintech solutions and inventions can accelerate the risk-sharing mechanism of Islamic finance and concluded that blockchain technology with its effective and efficient processes tends to speed up the risk sharing in the Islamic finance. Similarly, Lacasse et al. (2017) evidenced on blockchain technology and provided grounds that the technology provides surety of the Shari'a compliance in Islamic financial industry.

Like blockchain technology, there are several other Fintech innovations that are being implemented in the Islamic banking industry. To name a few, there are smart contracts, biometric systems, personalized identification, Big Data, Artificial Intelligence, and crowdfunding. Literature suggests that Fintech operations and innovations provide significant challenges and opportunities for Islamic finance. Taking the consumer perspective, Fintech offers unique enabling opportunities to the individuals which are aligned with their choices. Based on current technologies, the consumers have experienced user-friendly and convenient modes of transactions that have accelerated their satisfaction (Global Islamic Finance Report, 2017). Contrarily, on the supplier perspective, the traditional Islamic financial institutions are faced with intense competitors who are leading in adopting the Fintech innovations. As a solution to this competition, Islamic banks and financial institutions must focus on developing collaborations with major Fintech players and technology providers.

In sum, there are significant developments observed by the Islamic banks and Islamic financial institutions in terms of Fintech innovations. In this way, the current study provides fresh insights on the application of Fintech innovations in the Islamic banks of Pakistan to reveal the real-time implementation.

3 Methodology

This study employed the data of Islamic banks from Pakistan for the period 2006–2020. The content analysis approach is used to extract the desired information on digital advancements and adoption of financial technologies in the Islamic banks. For this purpose, content analysis was performed on the annual report of Islamic banks with particular keywords and themes used in the annual reports to denote their developments in Fintech innovations. There are mainly five Islamic banks in Pakistan under the supervision of State Bank of Pakistan (SBP) and data covered a period of 10 years. In this way, a total of 50 observations were estimated for examining the technology adoption in these banks. The keywords used to extract the information were technology/technologies, financial technology, Fintech, digital progress, digital advancements, Islamic Fintech, Islamic banking industry, awareness of Fintech solutions, investment in Fintech, Industrial Revolution (4.0), and performance impact of Fintech. Moreover, the thematic analysis based on content analysis was conducted on five main technologies widely used in the Pakistani Islamic banks. Table 1 presents both keywords selection method and thematic approach with specific coding to investigate the application of Fintech innovations in the Islamic banking sector.

Each of the keywords and themes was coded in the Microsoft Excel Sheet and the responses were added as '1' if the relevant information was found and at least one sentence was attributed to a particular keyword and theme. Moreover, the responses were coded as '0' if no or very little information was available based on the keywords searched and themes applied. The arranged data sheet was analyzed using the STATA software and dynamic estimator named system Generalized Method of Moments (S-GMM) to obtain which Fintech innovations have been widely adopted by the Islamic banks. Table 1 presents the list of keywords and themes

Table 1 Keywords and theme selection

Sr. No	Keywords	Proxy	Coding
Panel A: Content analysis using keywords method			
1	Technology/Technologies	TECH	Coded as '1' if information available and '0' otherwise
2	Financial Technology	FTECH	Coded as '1' if information available and '0' otherwise
3	Digital Progress	DP	Coded as '1' if information available and '0' otherwise
4	Digital Advancements	DA	Coded as '1' if information available and '0' otherwise
5	Islamic Fintech	IFT	Coded as '1' if information available and '0' otherwise
6	Islamic Banking Industry	IBI	Coded as '1' if information available and '0' otherwise
7	Awareness of Fintech Solutions	AWR	Coded as '1' if information available and '0' otherwise
8	Investment in Fintech	INV	Coded as '1' if information available and '0' otherwise
9	Industrial Revolution (4.0)	IR4	Coded as '1' if information available and '0' otherwise
10	Performance Impact of Fintech	PER	Coded as '1' if information available and '0' otherwise
Panel B: Content analysis using thematic approach			
1	Digital Wallets	DWAL	Coded as '1' if information available and '0' otherwise
2	Biometrics	BIO	Coded as '1' if information available and '0' otherwise
3	Smart Contracts	SC	Coded as '1' if information available and '0' otherwise
4	Distributed Ledger	DL	Coded as '1' if information available and '0' otherwise
5	Machine Learning	ML	Coded as '1' if information available and '0' otherwise

along with specific technologies to reach a significant set of technologies widely applied by the Islamic banks in Pakistan.

4 Results and Discussion

The arranged data on selected keywords and themes were estimated and analyzed using the STATA software. Table 2 gives the descriptive statistics of keywords and themes used in the study.

Table 2 Descriptive statistics of variables over the period (2006–2020)

Variable	Unit	Obs	Mean	Std. Dev	Minimum	Maximum
Panel A: Descriptive statistics of keywords method						
TECH	(%)	75	0.6327	0.5181	0	1
FTECH	(%)	75	0.3081	0.2856	0	1
DP	(%)	75	0.5029	0.4256	0	1
DA	(%)	75	0.4152	0.3287	0	1
IFT	(%)	75	0.2037	0.1849	0	1
IBI	(%)	75	0.5362	0.4852	0	1
AWR	(%)	75	0.4058	0.3261	0	1
INV	(%)	75	0.6239	0.5327	0	1
IR4	(%)	75	0.2384	0.1934	0	1
PER	(%)	75	0.8862	0.8457	0	1
Panel B: Content analysis using thematic approach						
DWAL	(%)	75	0.8251	0.6217	0	1
BIO	(%)	75	08,859	0.7489	0	1
SC	(%)	75	0.7842	0.6578	0	1
DL	(%)	75	0.3218	0.2015	0	1
ML	(%)	75	0.2898	0.1953	0	1

The descriptive statistics in Panel A give the information on the keywords selected for the study. The mean value of word technology and technologies show that Islamic banks in Pakistan have reported information related to the technology of about 63%. Similarly, for the keyword financial technology the average value is 30% indicating the focus of banks toward financial technologies. The term technology includes all the technologies incorporated in the banks to facilitate its customers whereas Fintech is particularly used for the technologies specified for Fintech operations of the banks. Digital progress shows the average value of 50% and digital awareness is about 41% in the Islamic banks of Pakistan. These average values suggest that Pakistani Islamic banks report on digital progress quite frequently than digital awareness of banks. A very low average value of Islamic Fintech of about 20% is reported by the banks revealing a minor focus of banks toward Islamic Fintech. Moreover, on average Fintech awareness is about 40% corresponding to the digital awareness where the average value is 41%. Further, the investment in the Fintech operations reveals remarkable developments with an average value of 60%. Industrial revolution 4.0 showed the average value of about 20% indicating relatively lower concerns toward IR4.0. Interestingly, the performance effects of Fintech on operations of banks reveal a significant mean value of 88% indicating that Islamic banks, through having lower applications of Fintech in their organizations, tend to have a significant impact of Fintech on performance. Overall, the keyword selection criterion suggests that Islamic banks in Pakistan are still evolving in the latest technologies and its awareness with substantial investments in the technology-backed operations.

Panel B of Table 2 reveals the descriptive statistics of themes selected for the study to examine the application of Fintech in the Islamic banks of Pakistan. There are a total of five themes selected which are different financial technologies widely applicable in the Islamic banks. Digital wallets reveal the average value of 82% denoting the wide application of this technology in the Islamic banks of Pakistan. Biometrics, on the other hand, showed a significant average value of 88% and marked itself as the most applicable technology in the Islamic banks. Smart contracts show the mean value of 78% reiterating this technology as widely applicable technology in the Islamic banks of Pakistan during the given period. However, distributed ledger, considered as one of the significant technologies of blockchain, showed the average value of 32% recalling the arguments that the latest technologies are yet to be applied in the Islamic banks. Meanwhile, machine learning, again one of the blockchain technologies, is also revealing the mean value of 28% suggesting that blockchain technologies are evolving over the time with recent modifications in the financial technologies.

In sum, the mean values of the keywords and themes selected for the study showed that Islamic banks have shown progress in digital literacy and adopted some of the financial technologies to facilitate their customers. However, there are few technologies that need to be incorporated in the banking operations to speed up the processes and enhance firm value. In this way, Islamic banks can compete with their conventional bank's competitors. Moreover, following the guidelines of Shari'a and Quran and Hadith, Islamic banks can develop themselves on the basis of financial technologies to reap its fruits in the long run.

Additional Analysis

The study conducted some additional analysis where all of the selected keywords and themes of Fintech were regressed against the return on assets of Islamic banks to examine whether these technologies impact profitability of banks or not. Table 3 presents the impact of significant keywords on profitability.

The results of additional analysis in Table 3 indicate that most of the keywords are significant with the profitability of the banks. Contrarily, some of the keywords, for instance, Islamic banking industry, investment, industrial revolution 4.0, and performance impact are relatively less significant with return on assets for Islamic banks in Pakistan. In addition, control variables are also significantly related to bank profitability (Sheikh & Karim, 2015). The Sargan test is used to test whether the regression results are not catering to the problems of misspecification (Karim et al., 2020a, 2020b) and Arellano-Bond test is used to identify the autocorrelation problem (Karim, 2021a, 2021b). The p-values of both post-estimation specification tests indicate that there is no problem of misspecification and autocorrelation.

The findings have significant implications for Islamic banks and Islamic financial institutions to include the technological advancements in their business processes to enhance the profitability and performance of banks. Since Islamic finance is based on the principles of Shari'a and pre-settled rules and regulations of Islam, thus, adopting different kinds of technologies to accelerate the banking process and increase performance is not

Table 3 The impact of selected keywords on profitability (ROA)

Keywords	Coefficient	z-score	Significance
L1	0.1254	0.18	0.000
TECH	0.5418	0.21	0.007
FTECH	0.3635	0.87	0.021
DP	0.2458	0.98	0.005
DA	1.2884	1.29	0.012
IFT	1.2998	1.32	0.003
IBI	1.9857	0.32	0.028
AWR	1.6988	1.28	0.009
INV	1.2879	1.30	0.052
IR4	1.9562	0.27	0.089
PER	1.2879	1.23	0.095
BAGE	0.9856	2.84	0.002
BSIZE	1.9823	1.23	0.008
Sargan-test of misspecification (p-value)			0.1287
Arellano-Bond first order test (AR(2)) p-value			0.2192

prohibited in Islam (Rabbani et al., 2021c, 2021d). Moreover, the significant values of coefficients highlight the need to welcome different types of technologies in their Islamic finance operations and maximize their value.

Table 4 presents the impact of different Islamic Fintech themes on profitability. The results of the regression analysis indicate that biometrics technology is the most significantly related to return on assets as compared to other technologies. Digital wallets and smart contracts are significant at 95% whereas distributed ledger and machine learning are insignificant with profitability. The probable explanation for significant relationships is that the Islamic banks adopt few of the technologies to facilitate their customers and the trend of adopting several innovations is quite low. For this reason, the widely adopted technologies have a significant impact on the bank profitability whereas the technologies that are still evolving and being adopted at a slower pace are insignificant to the profitability of Islamic banks. Additionally, control variables, bank age, and bank size are significantly related to the profitability of Islamic banks in Pakistan. The post-estimation tests reveal that p-values are greater than the threshold value of 0.05, thus, there is no problem of misspecification and autocorrelation.

Overall, the findings of the study inculcate that Islamic bank of Pakistan reveals significant modifications in terms of application of Fintech in their organizations. There is an increasing trend in the adoption of Fintech innovations to accelerate the organizational performance and provide customers with the best services. The additional analysis using

Table 4 The impact of selected themes on profitability (ROA)

Keywords	Coefficient	z-score	Significance
L1	1.0582	1.28	0.000
DWAL	1.9856	0.29	0.008
BIO	2.0684	1.84	0.000
SC	1.3882	0.41	0.005
DL	0.8799	1.36	0.245
ML	0.9759	1.67	0.184
BAGE	2.0570	2.32	0.000
BSIZE	1.9890	1.28	0.000
Sargan-test of misspecification (p-value)			0.1523
Arellano-Bond first order test (AR(2)) p-value)			0.2685

the S-GMM indicates that technological innovations of Islamic banking industry are having a remarkable impact on the profitability of the banks. Meanwhile, the findings of the study are significant for policymakers, regulators, and Islamic banks to adopt the Islamic Fintech solutions in their business operations to augment the process of services to their customers. More awareness, increased investments, introducing new technologies in their banks, creating training for the employees and customers, and initiating technological developments to speed up the banking operations will ultimately increase the performance of banks. Based on Islamic finance, the findings generate several outcomes in terms of successful processes to be initiated and promote industrial revolution 4.0 to sustain the competitive global environment on the fundamentals of Islamic principles and rules.

5 Conclusion

This study aimed to investigate the application of Fintech innovations on the Islamic banking industry in Pakistan. The data of five Islamic banks were used to obtain the required information on the adoption of Fintech solutions during 2006–2020. The primary analysis was carried out using the content analysis of annual reports where 10 keywords and 5 themes based on Fintech were selected. The average values show that some keywords are not very well established in the annual reports of Pakistani Islamic banks whereas few keywords such as technology, financial technology, digital progress, investments, etc., are well occupied and equally applied in the Islamic banking sector. Out of 5 themes of Fintech, only 3 are widely adopted and 2 are still emerging and need more concentration on the matter.

Additional analysis using system GMM suggests that almost all the keywords are significantly related to the profitability of the Islamic banking industry. Corresponding to the descriptive statistics, out of five Fintech themes only three were significant with return on assets. Meanwhile, control variables were significant and positive with profitability.

The results of the study have substantial implications for academics and practitioners of Islamic finance. Academically, the upcoming researchers can set this study as a benchmark to further evaluate its validity in the context of other Islamic banks and Islamic countries. The novel results can provide fresh insights to the academia for carrying out their future research endeavors. On practical grounds, the study is significant for regulators, policymakers, Islamic banking industry, Islamic financial institutions, and Shari'a-compliant banks and firms. The technological advancements in the current competitive environment have fetched the attention of regulators to issue the adoption of Fintech innovations and implement them in their business operations to achieve fast and resilient mechanisms for facilitating customers. Islamic finance, having fundamentals of Islamic principles and ethics, provide a guiding light for its followers to adopt the Fintech innovations provided that they do not violate the Islamic Shari'a (Karim et al., 2021a, 2021b; Rabbani et al., 2021a, 2021b). Given this situation, this study provides empirical evidence on the adoption of Fintech innovations in the Islamic banks of Pakistan. The study is unique in its contribution where Pakistani Islamic banks have revealed an evolving trend in the adoption and application of Islamic Fintech innovations by maintaining the boundaries of Islamic Shari'a. The study is a guideline to motivate other Islamic financial institutions to comply with the recent developments of Islamic Fintech.

Fig. 1 Evolution of digital banking system (*Source* Adapted from Rahim et al., 2018)

REFERENCES

Abdullah, Y., & Rabbani, M. R. (2021, December). COVID-19 and GCC Islamic market Indices. In *2021 International conference on sustainable Islamic business and finance (SIBF)*. (pp. 56–60). IEEE. University of Bahrain.
Ali, H., Abdullah, R., & Zaini, M. Z. (2019). Fintech and its potential impact on Islamic banking and finance industry: A case study of Brunei Darussalam and Malaysia. *Interntaional Journal of Islamic Economics and Finance, 2*(1), 73–108.
Bashar, A., & Rabbani, M. R. (2021). Exploring the role of web personalization in consumer green purchasing behavior: A conceptual framework. In *2021 third international sustainability and resilience conference: Climate change* (pp. 23–28).
Bashar, A., Rabbani, M., Khan, S., & Ali, M. A. M. (2021, October). Data driven finance: A bibliometric review and scientific mapping. In *2021 international conference on data analytics for business and industry (ICDABI)* (pp. 161–166). IEEE. University of Bahrain.
CB Insights. (2018). *Fintech trends to watch in 2018*. CB Insights
Dharani, M., Hassan, M. K., Rabbani, M. R., & Huq, T. (2022). Does the Covid-19 pandemic affect faith-based investments? Evidence from global sectoral indices. *Research in International Business and Finance, 59*, 101537.
Deloitte, G. (2017). *AI and you: Perceptions of artificial intelligence from the EMEA financial services industry*. Deloitte.
Finocracy, A. A., & Mirakhor, A. (2017). Accelerating risk sharing finance via Fintech: Nextgen Islamic finance. https://www.sid.ir/en/seminar/ViewPaper.aspx?FID=433e20170101
Global Islamic Finance Report. (2017). *Islamic finance in the digital age: Fintech revolution*.
Hassan, M. K., Rabbani, M., & Daouia, C. (2021a). Integrating Islamic finance and Halal industry: Current landscape and future forward. *International Journal of Islamic Marketing and Branding, 6*(1), 60–78.
Hassan, M. K., Rabbani, M. R., & Abdullah, Y. (2021b). Socioeconomic Impact of COVID-19 in MENA region and the Role of Islamic Finance. *International Journal of Islamic Economics and Finance (IJIEF), 4*(1), 51–78.
Hassan, M. K., Rabbani, M. R., & Ali, M. A. (2020a). Challenges for the Islamic Finance and banking in post COVID era and the role of Fintech. *Journal of Economic Cooperation and Development, 43*(3), 93–116.
Hassan, M. K., Rabbani, M. R., & Ali, M. A. (2020b). Challenges for the Islamic Finance and banking in post COVID era and the role of Fintech. *Journal of Economic Cooperation and Development, 43*(3), 93–116.
Insights, C. B. (2019). Global Fintech Report Q2 2019. CB Insights.
Karim, S. (2021). Do women on corporate boardrooms influence the remuneration patterns and socially responsible practices? Malaysian evidence. *Equality,*

Diversity, and Inclusion: An International Journal. https://doi.org/10.1108/EDI-07-2020-0213

Karim, S., Akhtar, M. U., Tashfeen, R., Raza Rabbani, M., Rahman, A. A. A., & AlAbbas, A. (2021b). Sustainable banking regulations pre and during coronavirus outbreak: The moderating role of financial stability. *Economic Research-Ekonomska Istraživanja.* https://doi.org/10.1080/1331677X.2021.1993951

Karim, S., Manab, N. A., & Ismail, R. B. (2019). Legitimising the role of corporate boards and corporate social responsibility on the performance of Malaysian Listed Companies. *Indian Journal of Corporate Governance, 12*(2), 125–141.

Karim, S., Manab, N. A., & Ismail, R. B. (2020a). Assessing the governance mechanisms, corporate social responsibility and performance: The moderating effect of board independence. *Global Business Review.* DOI:https://doi.org/10.1177/0972150920917773

Karim, S., Manab, N. A., & Ismail, R. B. (2020b). The interaction effect of independent boards on CG-CSR and performance nexus. *Asian Academy of Management Journal, 25*(1), 61–84.

Karim, S., Manab, N. A., & Ismail, R. B. (2020c). The dynamic impact of board composition on CSR practices and their mutual effect on organizational returns. *Journal of Asia Business Studies, 14*(4), 463–479.

Karim, S., Rabbani, M. R., & Bawazir, H. (2022). Applications of blockchain technology in the finance and banking industry beyond digital currencies. In *Blockchain technology and computational excellence for society 5.0* (pp. 216–238). IGI Global.

Karim, S., Rabbani, M. R., & Khan, M. A. (2021a). Determining the key factors of corporate leverage in Malaysian service sector firms using dynamic modeling. *Journal of Economic Cooperation and Development, 42*(3), 1–20.

Khan, S., & Rabbani, M. R. (2020a). Chatbot as Islamic finance expert (CaIFE) When finance meets artificial intelligence. In *proceedings of the 2020 4th international symposium on computer science and intelligent control* (pp. 1–5).

Khan, S., & Rabbani, M. R. (2020b). Agility and fintech is the future of Islamic finance: A study from Islamic banks in Bahrain. *International Journal of Scientific and Technology Research, 9*(3).

Khan, M. S., Rabbani, M. R., Hawaldar, I. T., & Bashar, A. (2022). Determinants of behavioral intentions to use islamic financial technology: An empirical assessment. *Risks, 10*(6), 114.

Lacasse, R.-M., Lambert, B., & Khan, N. (2017). Blockchain technology-arsenal for a Shariah compliant financial ecosystem. http://publications.uni.lu/bitstream/10993/33529/1/Research%20Paper%20Blockchain.pdf

Lajis, S. M. (2017). Risk-sharing securities: Accelerating finance for SMEs. *Islamic Economic Studies, 25*(2), 35–55.

Lutfi, M. A., & Ismail, M. A. (2016). Sadaqah-based crowdfunding model for microfinancing and health care. http://ddms.usim.edu.my/handle/123456 789/14853

Ng, A., Mirakhor, A., & Ibrahim, M. H. (2015). Risk sharing and crowdfunding. In *Social capital and risk sharing* (pp. 115–131). Springer.

Rabbani, M. R. (2021). COVID-19 and its impact on supply chain financing and the role of Islamic Fintech: Evidence from GCC countries. *International Journal of Agile Systems and Management (IJASM)* (In press).

Rabbani, M. R. (2022). Fintech innovations, scope, challenges, and implications in Islamic Finance: A systematic analysis. *International Journal of Computing and Digital Systems, 11*(1), 1–28.

Rabbani, M. R., Abdulla, Y., Basahr, A., Khan, S., & Moh'd Ali, M. A. (2020, November). Embracing of fintech in islamic finance in the post COVID era. In *2020 international conference on decision aid sciences and application (DASA)* (pp. 1230–1234). IEEE. University of Bahrain.

Rabbani, M. R., Sarea, A., Khan, S., & Abdullah, Y. (2021a, September). Ethical concerns in artificial intelligence (AI): The role of RegTech and Islamic finance. *In the international conference on global economic revolutions* (pp. 381–390). Springer.

Rabbani, M. R., Ali, M. A. M., Rahiman, H. U., Atif, M., Zulfikar, Z., & Naseem, Y. (2021b). The response of Islamic financial service to the COVID-19 pandemic: The open social innovation of the financial system. *Journal of Open Innovation: Technology, Market, and Complexity, 7*(1), 1–18.

Rabbani, M. R., Bashar, A., Nawaz, N., Karim, S., Ali, M. A. M., Rahiman, H. U., & Alam, M. S. (2021c). Exploring the role of Islamic Fintech in combating the aftershocks of COVID-19: The open social innovation of the islamic financial system. *Journal of Open Innovation: Technology, Market & Complexity, 7*, 136. https://doi.org/10.3390/joitmc7020136

Rabbani, M. R., Bashar, A., Atif, M., Jreisat, A., Zulfikar, Z., & Naseem, Y. (2021d). Text mining and visual analytics in research: Exploring the innovative tools. In *2021d international conference on decision aid sciences and application (DASA).* (pp. 1087–1091). IEEE. University of Bahrain.

Rabbani, M. R., Jreisat, A., AlAbbas, A., Bashar, A., & Ali, M. A. M. (2021e). Whether Cryptocurrency is a threat or a revolution? An ESG perspective. In *2021e international conference on sustainable islamic business and finance (SIBF).* (pp. 103–108). IEEE. University of Bahrain.

Rabbani, M. R., Kayani, U., Bawazir, H. S., & Hawaldar, I. T. (2022). A commentary on emerging markets banking sector spillovers: Covid-19 vs GFC pattern analysis. *Heliyon, 8*(3), e09074.

Rabbani, M. R., Khan, S., & Atif, M. (2021a). Machine learning based P2P lending Islamic FinTech model for small and medium enterprises (SMEs) in

Bahrain. *International Journal of Business Innovation and Research*.https://doi.org/10.1504/IJBIR.2021a.10040857

Rahim, S. R., Mohamad, Z. Z., Abu Bakar, J., Mohsin, F. H., & Md Isa, N. (2018). Artificial intelligence, smart contract, and Islamic finance. *Asian Social Science*, *14*(2), 145.

Saba, I., Kouser, R., & Chaudhary, I. S. (2019). FinTech and Islamic finance-challenges and opportunities. *Review of Economics and Development Studies*, *5*(4), 581–590.

Sarea, A. M. (2016). The impact of AAOIFI accounting standards on earnings quality: The case of Islamic banks in Bahrain. *Corporate Ownership and Control*, *13*(41), 160–164. https://doi.org/10.22495/cocv13i4c1p1

Selim, M., & Hassan, M. K. (2019). Interest-free monetary policy and its impact on inflation and unemployment rates. *ISRA International Journal of Islamic Finance*. https://doi.org/10.1108/IJIF-06-2018-0065

Sheikh, N. A., & Karim, S. (2015). Effects of internal governance indicators on performance of commercial banks in Pakistan. *Pakistan Journal of Social Sciences*, *35*(1), 77–90.

Torabi, O. (2017). Using reputation (fame) to reduce information asymmetry in Islamic risk sharing crowdfunding models: A game theory approach.

Wahjono, S. I., & Marina, A. (2017). *Islamic crowdfunding: Alternative funding solution*. Editors, 30.

World Bank. (2019). *Global economic prospects, June 2019: Heightened tensions, subdued investment*. The World Bank.

Fintech in the Islamic Banking Sector and Its Impact on the Stakeholders in the Wake of COVID-19

M. Kabir Hassan, Rabab Hasan Ebrahim, Mustafa Raza Rabbani, and Hasanul Banna

1 Introduction

Throughout history, the industrial revolution has gone through different stages. The first stage was based on steam power and water to enhance production; the second one depended on electricity to generate mass production; and the third one employed new electronics and information technologies to automate production (Mackenzie, 2015; Omarova, 2020). Currently, we are in the fourth stage of industrial revolution,

---

M. K. Hassan
University of New, Orleans, New Orleans, LA 70148, USA
e-mail: mhassan@uno.edu

R. H. Ebrahim (✉)
Department of Economics and Finance, College of Business Administration, University of Bahrain, Sakhir, Bahrain
e-mail: rhasan@uob.edu.bh

M. R. Rabbani
Department Economics and Finance, College of Business Administration, University of Bahrain, Bahrain, Kingdom of Bahrain

© The Author(s), under exclusive license to Springer Nature Switzerland AG 2022
M. K. Hassan et al. (eds.), *FinTech in Islamic Financial Institutions*, https://doi.org/10.1007/978-3-031-14941-2_9

which is grounded on the digital transformation that began in the middle of last century and is still ongoing (Zezulka et al., 2019). It is characterized by a convergence of technologies that have grown inextricably and have created havoc on every aspect of business. The financial services business is no exception as along with the fourth industrial revolution, a new industry known as "Fintech" has emerged (Jreisat et al., 2021; Rabbani, 2022a, 2022b).

Fintech is growing in popularity in banking and finance business through offering more creative financial services as those offered in traditional financial institutions (Bashar & Rabbani, 2021; Khan & Rabbani, 2020). Fintech is defined as the merging of technological revolution and finance industry with the aim of boosting business models in the finance industry services business (Hassan et al., 2020, 2022). Zavolokina et al. (2016) describe Fintech as the wedding of technology with the finance industry that has the potential to take finance industry to new heights with innovative financial services (Zavolokina et al., 2016). Fintech can increase operational efficiency, customer-centric services, and transparency in the financial services industry (Gomber et al., 2018). Van Loo (2018), argues that Fintech can help financial services industry to bring efficiency, transparency and minimize the risk of financial meltdowns.

Fintech is expanding at a rapid pace, resulting in the development of innovative business models. In 2020, the Islamic Fintech market size in the OIC was $49 billion which represents 0.72% of the current global Fintech market size, based on transaction volumes. This market size is projected to grow at 21% CAGR to $128 billion by 2025 (DinarStandard, 2021). Islamic financial institutions and banks have already embraced the Fintech disruption and have started to treat it as an opportunity to extend its services to unreachable (Ali et al., 2019; Oseni et al., 2019). Islamic banks are taking this opportunity to position themselves as a new generation banking of millennial consumers (Miskam et al., 2019; Rabbani et al., 2020). As Fintech has already entered its third phase of revolution, Islamic

---

e-mail: mrabbani@uob.edu.bh

H. Banna
Department of Accounting, Finance and Banking, Business School,
Manchester Metropolitan University, Manchester, UK
e-mail: b.banna@mmu.ac.uk

banks have started to maximize the use of Fintech-based innovations such as Blockchain and artificial intelligence for operational efficiency and cost savings (Firmansyah & Anwar, 2019; Lajis, 2019; Shaikh, 2020).

The use of Fintech technologies in Islamic finance, which is based on Shariah rules, can be beneficial (Hendratmi et al., 2019). Recent research including Biancone et al. (2019), Abubakar et al. (2018) and Todorof (2018) have investigated the Shariah compliance aspect of Fintech products and found that Fintech has numerous uses in the Islamic finance business. Khan and Rabbani (2020) and Rabbani et al. (2021a), provided an overview of the sharia compliance of the cryptocurrency and concluded that, although it sharia scholars are divided over the permissibility of the cryptocurrency but it can be used as a financial investment with certain limitations. Karim et al. (2022), provided an overview of the use of blockchain technology in the Islamic finance and banking sector beyond cryptocurrency and concluded the Blockchain is one of the most significant innovations of the twenty-first century and it has multiple application in Islamic finance and banking industry other than cryptocurrency. Blockchain has multiple applications such as, smart contracts, electronic voting, employee payment, supply chain communication and cloud storage etc.

In November of 2019, COVID-19, was discovered in the Wuhan province of China and since then it made huge impacts in every country around the world (Furlow, 2020; Sachs et al., 2020). This health issue has transformed into a financial crisis, primarily because of the high spread of the virus, which has prompted governments throughout the world to impose lockdowns, quarantines, and social distancing, leading to the shutdown of commercial operations, financial markets, and other services (Dharani et al., 2022; Habeeb et al., 2021; Panakaje et al., 2022). Recent studies have highlighted the importance of Islamic Fintech in tackling the various economic difficulties that the pandemic has created. According to Al-Nawayseh (2020), Islamic Fintech has helped several countries to create economic resilience in the face of pandemic unanticipated situations. Furthermore, because it improves ethical financial inclusion during this difficult time, financial technology is consistent with the sustainability needs to manage this unforeseeable crisis (Fakhrunnas et al., 2021).

In the new environment created by the COVID-19 outbreak, collaboration between Islamic financial institutions and Fintech could be vital to finding solutions (Hassan et al., 2020). The recovery after this pandemic will be massive, and Islamic Financial Institutions will play a vital role, just as they did after the 2008 financial crisis (Rabbani et al., 2021b). Therefore, the present study aims to explore and discuss the different aspects of Islamic Fintech and its role in Islamic banking sector and contributes by highlighting its potential impact on the different stakeholders in the wake of COVID-19. Currently, several expectations and assumptions have been made regarding the impact of Fintech on Islamic finance and banking. Existing literature, however, does not provide an obvious picture of this. As a result, this study adds to the current literature and expands our knowledge by shedding the light on the most common uses of Fintech in Islamic institutions and banks as well as its impact on the different stakeholders during and after the COVID-19 pandemic.

The present study is divided into four parts. The first part presents an overview of Islamic Fintech, the second part provides an overview of the use of Islamic Fintech in the Islamic banking industry whereas, the third part highlights the impact of Islamic Fintech on the different stakeholders during the COVID-19 pandemic and beyond. In the last part, we conclude and provide some recommendations.

2 Islamic Fintech and Its Application in Islamic Banking Industry

Financial Technology, or "Fintech," has emerged as the fastest developing sector in the information technology industry. This industry is born out of the marriage of technology and traditional financial services (Hassan et al., 2021a, 2021b; Rabbani et al., 2021b). Innovations in cybersecurity, data analytics, and software platforms, combined with new consumer demands, have urged financial services to become more modern and efficient. Although Fintech is innovative, frictionless, faster, and user-friendly, it can also deliver financial services at a low cost. Fintech is a relatively new concept. However, it has shown to be an advantage innovation for the financial services business. Fintech has proved to be an advantageous to everyone including banks and its customers. It has empowered customers to take charge of its financial operation from the comfort of their drawing room, leading to much greater financial literacy as well as financial inclusion. On the other hand, banks and financial institutions have multiple product options to offer and attract customers with new, innovative, responsive, efficient and transparent offerings (Henderson, 2017; Pwc, 2017; WorldBank, 2020).

Fintech has been described in a variety of ways by many authors. For example, Hassan et al. (2020) said that "Fintech is the collaboration between finance and technology industry for the mutual benefit and to provide the tech-based innovative financial services with more efficiency and less cost." Financial technology (Fintech) can be described as the application of modern innovative technology to provide financial services, such as artificial intelligence, Blockchain, smart contracts, peer-to-peer lending, RegTech, crowdfunding, digital currency, and so on (Rabbani et al., 2021b).

Traditionally, Fintech-based financial innovations are primarily interest bearing innovations, and Islamic finance clearly forbids transactions containing elements of *Riba* (interest-based transactions), *Maisir* (transactions involving a great amount of speculation or gambling), or *Gharar* (extreme ambiguity, fraud, and ribbing) (Samsudeen et al., 2020). This encouraged Islamic financial institutions and banks to search for different ways and offer financial services that comply with Islam principles. Islamic fintech is a subset of financial technology that adheres to shariah principles (Jreisat et al., 2021; Rabbani et al., 2022a, 2022b).

Islamic Fintech differs from traditional Fintech in that it is more inclusive, ethical, transparent, and adheres to shariah standards. Islamic Fintech is a quite new idea, with only limited studies having been undertaken in this area (Rabbani et al., 2022a, 2022b). It is important to emphasize that in Islam, every invention or innovation is allowed unless there is strong evidence to the contrary (Banna et al., 2021; Yussof & Al-Harthy, 2018).

The rise of Islamic Fintech has cleared the opportunity for the creation of novel Shariah-compliant products for Islamic consumers, potentially giving the Islamic financial sector a competitive advantage. Islamic Fintech achieved remarkable growth in the Islamic finance business between 2016 and 2017, even though it was not widely used in the industry until 2015. It aids in the transition of financial systems and services to more creative financial technology in conformity with Islamic Shariah values and principles (Saba et al., 2019). Saba et al. (2019) emphasize that using Fintech, including Islamic fintech, results in cost-effective financial solutions, enhances the quality of financial or banking services and products, improves customer retention, and enhances the overall customer experience.

According to the global Islamic Fintech report (2019), 87% of Islamic economy institutions prefer to engage with Islamic FinTech's and that

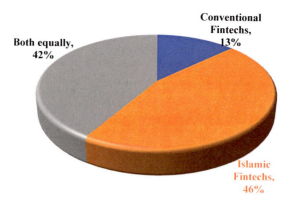

Fig. 1 Islamic versus conventional Fintech (*Source* Adapted from DinarStandard (2020))

46% expect to entirely engage with Islamic FinTech's compared to conventional FinTech's (see Fig. 1).

Islamic Fintech has continued to grow, with around 240 Islamic FinTech's globally now, covering a wide range of customers and financial needs through several emerging technologies. Peer-to-peer and Crowdfunding, deposits and lending, payments, wealth management and alternative finance are the most popular types among these Islamic FinTech's, accounting for 77% (see Fig. 2).

Recently, various academic researchers and Islamic Fintech reports have concluded that the variety of financial services used by the Islamic financial services has increased and most of it includes the Fintech-based services (Dinar Standard, 2020; Rabbani et al., 2021b). Fintech was a muchneeded boost for the Islamic finance industry as it would give them aid in achieving its objective of social justice and equal distribution of income. Saad et al. (2019), investigate the potential customers' tendency to adopt Fintech services and that awareness theory is appropriate for explaining behavior toward Fintech-based services provided by Islamic financial institutions.

It is to be noted that the Islamic and conventional Fintech share completely different characteristics in terms of sharia compliance. Islamic Fintech must adhere to the requirements of the sharia in every situation (Abdullah & Rabbani, 2021). Fintech solutions have given Islamic financial institutions more opportunity to improve their infrastructure

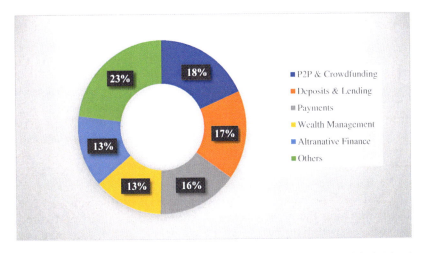

Fig. 2 Islamic Fintech by sector (*Source* Adapted from The Global Islamic Fintech Report, DinarStandard, 2021)

and services (Khan & Ismail, 2011; Khan et al., 2022). As a result, the number of academic and other research are growing on Islamic fintech field (Buerhan Saiti et al., 2018a, 2018b; Mustafa Raza Rabbani, 2022a, 2022b; Oseni et al., 2019; Saiti et al., 2018a, 2018b).

Some researchers including Mohamed and Ali (2018), had documented the Fintech's potentials of increased effectiveness across the operations of Islamic financial institutions. At present, not only Islamic financial institutions adjust for the demand for digitalization, but also other institutions and digital platforms are offering Shariah-compliant financial products and services. Islamic Fintech broadens access to Shariah-compliant financial services and creates investment opportunities (Glavina et al., 2021).

Although Islamic banks are relatively new and small, they are able to compete with well-established traditional banks. The dawn of the Fintech industry has granted these institutions the opportunity to compete on an equal footing with traditional banks. Using blockchain-based technologies, Islamic banks manage profit-sharing agreements and minimize the rising cost of transactions. Abojeib and Habib (2021) examine how blockchain may be utilized for charitable uses, mainly in the collection of zakat. Similarly, Fintech may be used to make the usage of waqf better.

Furthermore, the significance of blockchain as a solution for the halal sector challenge was discussed by Karim et al. (2022).

The COVID-19 pandemic has caused several disruptions to the economy as well as to all aspects of our daily lives, including financial markets (Baber, 2020). A new approach is required in response to recurring crises and pandemic-induced global economic downturns. Institutionalized risk-sharing can help the global economy withstand shocks and stimulate declining demand. Islamic finance can deal with any economic interruption, like financial crises and COVID-19 at both individual and company levels (Hassan et al., 2021a, 2021b; Rabbani, 2022a, 2022b; Rabbani et al., 2021b).

COVID-19's outcomes could pave the road for Islamic banking, especially considering the increasing significance of sustainability and corporate social responsibility. Prior to the pandemic, global data predicted that Islamic financial deposits would have climbed by 5% in 2020. Islamic banking rules can aid the economy to avoid endogenous crises like the global financial crisis and provide a robust safety net against exogenous crises like the COVID-19 disaster (Mohd. Yusof & Bahlous, 2013). Putting these ideas into effect requires a diversified range of well-functioning institutions. However, several important elements of this spectrum are now absent from the Islamic finance industry and hence the crisis should be used to fill in the blanks and diversify the sector. Islamic financial instruments such as Zakat, Qardh-Al-Hasan, Waqf and Sukuk are good choices for Islamic banks to use during COVID-19 and beyond to assist affected individuals and corporations through offering direct cash transfers and providing access to education and health care services (Khan et al., 2021).

However, the COVID-19 pandemic had put both traditional and Islamic financial institutions in jeopardy. In the second quarter of 2020, many Islamic banks recorded losses or declined profits when compared to the same period of the previous year (Hasan et al., 2021a, 2021b), due mainly to an increase in loan defaults and a decline in asset quality. According to (Glavina et al., 2021), the activities of Islamic financial institutions are driven by demand from small and medium-sized firms and thus, the Islamic finance industry is expected to lose much more during Covid. In this light, the pandemic is being viewed as a watershed moment in the industry's digitalization. The adoption of Fintech was increased across the board as it assisted in facilitating the consumption during the pandemic and decreased the risks of contact with others

(Vasenska & Koyundzhiyska-Davidkova, 2021), The Islamic financial industry, like other industries, has quickly responded to demand from remote customers by offering a huge range of high-quality digital financial services.

The global Fintech business is expanding. By 2024, more than 1.7 billion individuals are projected to be using mobile wallets (Almuhammadi, 2020). The Islamic Fintech industry has not lagged, having grabbed the opportunity, and adopted Fintech-based novel financial services. Fintech innovations are estimated to attract 150 million new clients to Islamic banking (Baber, 2020).

3 Islamic Fintech and Its Impact on Banking Stakeholders Following COVID-19

Similar to conventional financial technologies, Islamic fintech enables financial inclusion, provides access to Islamic financial services, expands prospects for ethical investments, reduces poverty, and promotes gender equality (Glavina et al., 2021). Therefore, Islamic Fintech has emerged as a critical tool for mitigating the negative consequences of the COVID-19 pandemic on the economy and society during and after this difficult time. Rabbani et al. (2020) suggest that Islamic Fintech can help in minimizing the COVID-19 pandemic effects in the short, medium, and long term. They also state that combining Islamic financial services with Islamic Fintech can accelerate the recovery process from the economic destruction caused by the pandemic. The pandemic has uncovered the need for digital services that decrease or eliminate direct human contact. Throughout the financial crisis, e-commerce businesses thrived. Furthermore, digital money is becoming increasingly crucial to reduce disease transmission via paper money. Khan et al. (2021) show that during the pandemic, the use of Islamic Fintech-based apps increased by 70%. This increase demonstrates that the pandemic has elevated the importance of Islamic Fintech, and that individuals, businesses, and governments becoming more conscious of its significance. Figure 3 shows the most common uses of Islamic Fintech following COVID-19 pandemic. As shown in the figure, these uses can be classified into three categories:

Following the COVID-19 pandemic, Hassan et al. (2020) expect a considerable growth in the use of Islamic Fintech for providing financial services. They also state that Islamic Fintech will have a massive role in the

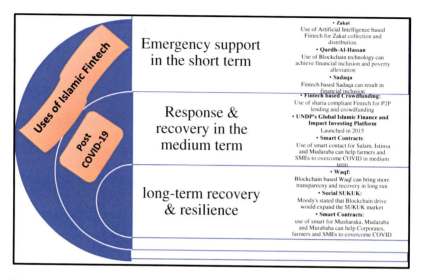

Fig. 3 Uses of Islamic Fintech following COVID-19 (*Source* Adapted from Hassan et al., 2020, p. 108)

recovery of the economy following the pandemic through several Islamic financial services, such as Zakat, Waqf, and crowdfunding.

The global pandemic has brought every section of the society together on the same platform to provide help and support. It was seen for the first time that governments, civil society, corporates startups and financial institutions came together and provided the valuable services to the covid affected individuals and SMEs. Every government across the globe came up with some stimulus and help packages for the COVID affected people highly afflicted industries to reduce the impact of the covid brought disaster and lockdowns. Central banks are loosening their monetary policies, and asset purchase programs and tax relief procedures are being revealed. FinTech played a key role in reaching out to the customers in terms of providing instant cash and relief packages. Several countries have launched sponsored lending schemes for COVID affected SMEs to minimize the damages caused by the pandemic and allowing the economy to return to the same mode as before the pandemic. Furthermore, since the start of the COVID-19 pandemic, authorities have taken several actions including: restructuring and/or rescheduling of loans, offering government guarantees, providing liquidity through different tools, and ensuring that the public has continuous access to the financial services. Islamic Fintech has brought Islamic economies closer to their goals of social justice and inclusion, as evidenced by "Ehsaas Emergency cash relief program" that has been launched by the government of Pakistan. This program was able to reach 6.8 million families within a week through using mobile money transfer (Asif Javed et al., 2021).

With regards to customers, their behavior, and intentions toward adopting Islamic Fintech have been favorably impacted during COVID-19 pandemic, due to demonstrated evidence of the technology's value at this difficult time, ease of use, and government endorsement of this technology (Nurfadilah & Samidi, 2021). The pandemic had an impact on how individuals use technology for financial operations like payments and lending. Consumer behavior is shifting away from cash transactions and toward an advanced mobile system, which is a positive indicator for the Islamic FinTech business. One of the effects of COVID-19 pandemic is that it requires customers to use an online banking platform as a new way to transact with the bank. Another effect of COVID-19 outbreak is the firing of employees because of companies' closure, which places a financial burden on consumers in terms of debt repayment (Jamaruddin & Markom, 2020).

Financial institutions can help alleviate the social-financial implications of the COVID-19 pandemic by using Islamic Fintech as a social finance tool. According to Rabbani et al. (2020), this would be a great way to approach affected individuals and SMEs and provide the necessary financial assistance. Several small firms and young entrepreneurs who are having trouble obtaining traditional bank finance are looking for the reliable sharia compliant Fintech platform such as crowdfunding and P2P lending digital platforms to get their financing needs. Furthermore, Khan et al. (2021) propose that integrating Qardh Al-Hassan loans with AI-based Islamic Fintech can aid individuals and SMEs that have been adversely impacted by COVID-19 pandemic in their recovery. This can be achieved by making it easier to receive Zakat and financial aids without encountering additional hurdles or violating social distance norms. Smart Contract is another Islamic Fintech solution that is utilized in financial transactions to record financial transactions between parties. The use of smart contracts that are based on Blockchain solutions will help farmers and SMEs to overcome the damages caused by the pandemic (Rabbani et al., 2020).

The pandemic has also affected Fintech developers as they can use big data analytics, cloud computing, cryptocurrencies, and other technologies to provide new and inventive solutions to existing problems (Khan et al., 2021; Sun et al., 2020). Moreover, Fintech startups are gradually developing to be the new financial services, and they will play an increasingly crucial role in the incorporation of financial institutions with Fintech firms, Islamic banks, and other Islamic financial institutions in the future (Sun et al., 2020). After the COVID-19 pandemic, a new opportunity has arisen for some Fintech organizations to embrace this opportunity by leveraging their assets and abilities. It also opens the possibility of Islamic financial institutions seizing this opportunity and using Fintech to deliver a long-term and sustainable financial service. During this challenging time, fintech startups have been able to alter their services to become crucial agents of support. It is expected that fintech startups will be able to expand their services to more users and provide additional support to their current users, providing the digital financial services that will be crucial to helping countries recover better after COVID-19. Fu and Mishra (2022) show that during COVID-19, fintech startups witnessed significant growth in their adoption of financial app and that modern and more inventive fintech firms may have a competitive advantage in generating new services as time goes on.

4 Conclusion

Fintech has brought significant changes to nearly every sector all over the world, and the financial and banking sector is no exception. This study explores the distinct aspects of Islamic Fintech and its role in the Islamic Banking industry as well as its impact on the stakeholders in the wake of COVID-19. We conclude that Islamic fintech products had the ability to help Islamic financial institutions and banks during COVID-19 pandemic and currently Islamic Fintech has emerged as the much-needed boost for the Islamic financial institutions to provided aid during crisis like situation such as ongoing pandemic. Islamic finance, in tandem with financial technology, will be the most effective instrument in combating the Covid 19's economic implications (Hassan et al., 2020). We also conclude that during the COVID-19 pandemic, everyone has been impacted including governments, customers, Fintech developers, Fintech startups, and Islamic financial institutions.

Future researchers are recommended to perform empirical research through conducting, for example, interviews and questionnaires which may help other researchers and interested parties in getting a better understanding of the role of Islamic Fintech during and following COVID-19 pandemic.

References

Abubakar, Y. S., Ogunbado, A. F., & Saidi, M. A. (2018). Bitcoin and its Legality from Shari'ah Point of View. *SEISENSE Journal of Management, 1*(4), 13–21.

Abdulla, Y., & Rabbani, M. R. (2021, December). COVID-19 and GCC Islamic market Indices. In *2021 international conference on sustainable Islamic business and finance* (pp. 56–60). IEEE. at University of Bahrain.

Abojeib, M., & Habib, F. (2021). Blockchain for Islamic social responsibility institutions. In *Research anthology on blockchain technology in business, healthcare, education, and government* (pp. 1114–1128). IGI Global.

Al-Nawayseh, M. K. (2020). Fintech in COVID-19 and beyond: What factors are affecting customers' choice of FinTech applications? *Journal of Open Innovation: Technology, Market, and Complexity, 6*(4), 1–15.

Ali, H., Abdullah, R., & Zaki Zaini, M. (2019). Fintech and its potential impact on islamic banking and finance industry: A case study of Brunei Darussalam and Malaysia. *International Journal of Islamic Economics and Finance (IJIEF)*. https://doi.org/10.18196/ijief.2116

Almuhammadi, A. (2020). An overview of mobile payments, fintech, and digital wallet in Saudi Arabia. In *7th international conference on computing for sustainable global development*, INDIACom 2020 (pp. 271–278). https://doi.org/10.23919/INDIACom49435.2020.9083726

Asif J., Ahmed, V. & Amal, B. K. (2021). The social safety nets and poverty alleviation in Pakistan: An evaluation of livelihood enhancement and protection programme. *Britain International of Humanities and Social Sciences (BIoHS) Journal*. https://doi.org/10.33258/biohs.v3i1.357

Atif, M., Rabbani, M. R., Bawazir, H., Hawaldar, I. T., Chebab, D., Karim, S., & Alabbas, A. (2022). Oil price changes and stock returns: Fresh evidence from oil exporting and oil importing countries. *Cogent Economics & Finance, 10*(1), 2018163.

Baber, H. (2020). FinTech, crowdfunding and customer retention in Islamic banks. *Vision*. https://doi.org/10.1177/0972262919869765

Banna, H., Kabir Hassan, M., & Rashid, M. (2021). Fintech-based financial inclusion and bank risk-taking: Evidence from OIC countries. *Journal of International Financial Markets, Institutions and Money, 75*(October), 1–20. https://doi.org/10.1016/j.intfin.2021.101447

Bashar, A., & Rabbani, M. R. (2021, November). Exploring the role of web personalization in consumer green purchasing behavior: A conceptual framework. In *2021 third international sustainability and resilience conference: Climate change* (pp. 23–28). IEEE. at University of Bahrain.

Beik, I. S., & Arsyianti, L. D. (2008). Why the rate of financing in Islamic banks is high? An analysis based on Malaysian case. *Tazkia Islamic Finance and Business Review, 3*, 1.

Biancone, P. P., Secinaro, S., & Kamal, M. (2019). Crowdfunding and Fintech: business model sharia-compliant. *European Journal of Islamic Finance, 12*.

Dharani, M., Hassan, M. K., Rabbani, M. R., & Huq, T. (2022). Does the COVID-19 pandemic affect faith-based investments? Evidence from global sectoral indices. *Research in International Business and Finance, 59*, 101537.

DinarStandard. (2020). *State of the global Islamic economy report 2020/21.* Dubai International Financial Centre. https://haladinar.io/hdn/doc/report2018.pdf

DinarStandard. (2021). *Islamic Fintech report 2018: Current landscape and path forward.* Dubai Islamic Economy Development Centre. https://www.dinarstandard.com/wp-content/uploads/2018/12/Islamic-Fintech-Report-2018.pdf

Fakhrunnas, F., Tumewang, Y. K., & Anto, M. B. H. (2021). The impact of inflation on Islamic banks' home financing risk: Before and during the COVID-19 outbreak. *Banks and Bank Systems, 16*(2), 78–90. https://doi.org/10.21511/bbs.16(2).2021.08

Firmansyah, E. A., & Anwar, M. (2019). Islamic financial technology (Fintech): Its challenges and prospect. https://doi.org/10.2991/assdg-18.2019.5

Fu, J., & Mishra, M. (2022). Fintech in the time of COVID-19: Technological adoption during crises. *Journal of Financial Intermediation, 50*. https://doi.org/10.1016/j.jfi.2021.100945

Furlow, B. (2020). US NICUs and donor milk banks brace for COVID-19. *The Lancet Child and Adolescent Health, 4*(5), 355. https://doi.org/10.1016/S2352-4642(20)30103-6

Glavina, S., Aidrus, I., & Trusova, A. (2021). Assessment of the competitiveness of Islamic Fintech implementation: A composite indicator for cross-country analysis. *Journal of Risk and Financial Management, 14*(12), 602.

Gomber, P., Kauffman, R. J., Parker, C., & Weber, B. W. (2018). On the Fintech revolution: Interpreting the forces of innovation, disruption, and transformation in financial services. *Journal of Management Information Systems, 35*(1), 220–265. https://doi.org/10.1080/07421222.2018.1440766

Habeeb, S., Rabbani, M. R., Ahmad, N., Ali, M. A. M., & Bashar, A. (2021, December). Post COVID-19 challenges for the sustainable entrepreneurship. In *2021 International Conference on Sustainable Islamic Business and Finance* (pp. 154–158). IEEE. at University of Bahrain, Bahrain.

Hasan, M. B., Mahi, M., Hassan, M. K., & Bhuiyan, A. B. (2021a). Impact of COVID-19 pandemic on stock markets: Conventional vs. Islamic indices using wavelet-based multi-timescales analysis. *The North American Journal of Economics and Finance, 58*, 101504.

Hassan, M. K., Djajadikerta, H. G., Choudhury, T., & Kamran, M. (2021b). Safe havens in Islamic financial markets: COVID-19 versus GFC. *Global Finance Journal*.

Hassan, M. K., Rabbani, M. R., & Abdullah, Y. (2021a). Socioeconomic Impact of COVID-19 in MENA region and the Role of Islamic finance. *International Journal of Islamic Economics and Finance (IJIEF), 4*(1), 51–78.

Hassan, M. K., Rabbani, M. R., & Ali, M. A. (2020). Challenges for the Islamic finance and banking in post COVID era and the role of Fintech. *Journal of Economic Cooperation and Development, 43*(3), 93–116.

Hassan, M. K., Rabbani, M. R., Brodmann, J., Bashar, A., & Grewal, H. (2022). Bibliometric and scientometric analysis on CSR practices in the banking sector. *Review of Financial Economics.* https://doi.org/10.1002/rfe.1171

Henderson, H. (2017). Fintech: Good and bad news for sustainable finance. *Pesquisa & Debate. Revista Do Programa de Estudos Pós-Graduados Em Economia Política, 28*(51), 6–15.

Hendratmi, A., Ryandono, M. N. H., & Sukmaningrum, P. S. (2019). Developing Islamic crowdfunding website platform for startup companies in Indonesia. *Journal of Islamic Marketing.* https://doi.org/10.1108/JIMA-02-2019-0022

Ibrahim, M. A., Fisol, W. N. M., & Haji-Othman, Y. (2017). Customer intention on Islamic home financing products: An application of theory of planned behavior (TPB). *Mediterranean Journal of Social Sciences, 8*(2), 77.

Jamaruddin, W. N., & Markom, R. (2020). The application of Fintech in the operation of Islamic banking focussing on Islamic documentation: Post-COVID-19. *INSLA E-Proceedings, 3*(1), 31–43.

Jreisat, A., Bashar, A., Alshaikh, A., Rabbani, M. R., & Moh'd Ali, M. A. (2021, December). Is Fintech valuation an art of science? Exploring the innovative methods for the valuation of fintech startups. In *2021 international conference on decision aid sciences and application (DASA)* (pp. 922–925). IEEE.

Karim, S., Rabbani, M. R., & Bawazir, H. (2022). Applications of blockchain technology in the finance and banking industry beyond digital currencies. In *Blockchain technology and computational excellence for society 5.0* (pp. 216–238). IGI Global.

Khan, M., & Ismail, N. A. (2011). The level of internet financial reporting of Malaysian companies. *Asian Journal of Accounting and Governance, 2*(1), 27–39.

Khan, S., Hassan, M. K., & Rabbani, M. R. (2021). An artificial intelligence-based Islamic FinTech model on Qardh-Al-Hasan for COVID 19 affected

SMEs. In *Islamic perspective for sustainable financial system*. Istanbul University Press.

Khan, M. S., Rabbani, M. R., Hawaldar, I. T., & Bashar, A. (2022). Determinants of behavioral intentions to use islamic financial technology: An empirical assessment. *Risks, 10*(6), 114.

Khan, S., & Rabbani, M. R. (2020). In depth analysis of blockchain, cryptocurrency and sharia compliance. *International Journal of Business Innovation and Research, 1*(1), 1. https://doi.org/10.1504/ijbir.2020.10033066

Lajis, S. M. (2019). Fintech and risk-sharing: A catalyst for islamic finance. In *Islamic finance, risk-sharing and macroeconomic stability* (pp. 237–254). Palgrave Macmillan. https://doi.org/10.1007/978-3-030-05225-6-12

Mackenzie, A. (2015). The fintech revolution. *London Business School Review, 26*(3), 50–53. https://doi.org/10.1111/2057-1615.12059

Miskam, S., Yaacob, A. M., & Rosman, R. (2019). Fintech and its impact on islamic fund management in Malaysia: A legal viewpoint. In *Emerging issues in Islamic Finance Law and Practice in Malaysia*. Emerald. https://doi.org/10.1108/978-1-78973-545-120191019

Mohamed, H., & Ali, H. (2018). Blockchain, Fintech, and Islamic finance. *Blockchain, Fintech, and Islamic Finance*. https://doi.org/10.1515/9781547400966

Mohd. Yusof, R., & Bahlous, M. (2013). Islamic banking and economic growth in GCC & East Asia countries: A panel cointegration analysis. *Journal of Islamic Accounting and Business Research*. https://doi.org/10.1108/JIABR-07-2012-0044

Nurfadilah, D., & Samidi, S. (2021). How the COVID-19 crisis is affecting customers' intention to use Islamic fintech services: evidence from Indonesia. *Journal of Islamic Monetary Economics and Finance*. https://doi.org/10.21098/jimf.v7i0.1318

Omarova, S. T. (2020). Technology versus technocracy: Fintech as a regulatory challenge. *Journal of Financial Regulation, 6*(1), 75–124. https://doi.org/10.1093/jfr/fjaa004

Oseni, U. A., Ali, S. N., & de Anca, C. (2019). Fintech in Islamic finance. *Fintech in Islamic Finance*. https://doi.org/10.4324/9781351025584-4

Panakaje, N., Rahiman, H. U., Rabbani, M. R., Kulal, A., Pandavarakallu, M. T., & Irfana, S. (2022). COVID-19 and its impact on educational environment in India. *Environmental Science and Pollution Research, 29*, 27788–27804.

Pikin, M., & Ku, M. C. (2019). Islamic online P2P lending platform. *Procedia Computer Science, 158*, 415–419.

PWC. (2017). *FinTech's growing influence on financial services*. Global Fintech Report.

Rabbani, M. R. (2022a) (in press). COVID-19 and its impact on supply chain financing and the role of Islamic Fintech: Evidence from GCC countries. *International Journal of Agile Systems and Management (IJASM)*. Available online at: https://www.inderscience.com/info/ingeneral/forthcoming.php?jcode=ijasm

Rabbani, M. R. (2022b). Fintech innovations, scope, challenges, and implications in Islamic Finance: A systematic analysis. *International Journal of Computing and Digital Systems, 11*(1), 1–28.

Rabbani, M. R., Abdulla, Y., Basahr, A., Khan, S., & Moh'd Ali, M. A. (2020). Embracing of fintech in Islamic finance in the post COVID era. In 2020 International conference on decision aid sciences and application. *DASA, 2020*, 136. https://doi.org/10.1109/DASA51403.2020.9317196

Rabbani, M. R., Bashar, A., Nawaz, N., Karim, S., Ali, M. A. M., Khan, A., Rahiman, H., & Alam, S. (2021a). Exploring the role of Islamic Fintech in combating the after-shocks of COVID-19: The open social innovation of the Islamic financial system. *Journal of Open Innovation: Technology, Market, and Complexity, 7*, 136.

Rabbani, M. R., Alshaikh, A., Jreisat, A., Bashar, A., & Moh'd Ali, M. A. (2021b, December). Whether Cryptocurrency is a threat or a revolution? An analysis from ESG perspective. In *2021 international conference on sustainable Islamic business and finance* (pp. 103–108). at University of Bahrain.

Saad, M. A., Fisol, W. N., & Bin, M. (2019). Financial technology (Fintech) services in Islamic financial institutions. In *International postgraduate conference* (pp. 1–10). at UniSHAMS.

Saba, I., Kouser, R., & Chaudhry, I. S. (2019). FinTech and Islamic finance-challenges and opportunities. *Review of Economics and Development Studies, 5*(4), 581–890.

Sachs, J. D., Horton, R., Bagenal, J., Ben Amor, Y., Karadag Caman, O., & Lafortune, G. (2020). The lancet COVID-19 commission. *The Lancet, 396*(10249), 454–455. https://doi.org/10.1016/S0140-6736(20)31494-X

Saiti, B, Musito, M. H., & Yucel, E. (2018a). Islamic crowdfunding: Fundamentals, developments and challenges. *Islamic Quarterly, 62*(3), 469–485. https://www.scopus.com/inward/record.uri?eid=2-s2.0-85062840918&partnerID=40&md5=c90f190a304de6e7479ea5f3171b4af7

Saiti, B., Musito, M. H., & Yucel, E. (2018b). Islamic crowdfunding: Fundamentals, developments and challenges. *Islamic Quarterly, 62*, 469–485.

Samsudeen, S. N., Hilmy, M. H. A., & Gunapalan, S. (2020). Islamic banking customers' intention to use mobile banking services: A Sri Lankan study. *Journal of Advanced Research in Dynamical and Control Systems, 12*(2), 1610–1626.

Sari, D. W. (2019). Ratio analysis of financial performance of companiesl Q45 index listed. *Humanities and Social Sciences Reviews*, 7(3), 419–423. https://doi.org/10.18510/hssr.2019.7361

Shaikh, S. A. (2020). Using Fintech in scaling up Islamic microfinance. *Journal of Islamic Accounting and Business Research*. https://doi.org/10.1108/JIABR-10-2019-0198

Sun, H., Rabbani, M. R., Sial, M. S., Yu, S., Filipe, J. A., & Cherian, J. (2020). Identifying big data's opportunities, challenges, and implications in finance. *Mathematics*, 8(10). https://doi.org/10.3390/math8101738

Todorof, M. (2018). Shariah-compliant FinTech in the banking industry. *ERA Forum*, 19(1). https://doi.org/10.1007/s12027-018-0505-8

Van Loo, R. (2018). Making innovation more competitive: The case of fintech. *UCLA Law Review*, 65(1), 232–279. https://www.scopus.com/inward/record.uri?eid=2-s2.0-85044523825&partnerID=40&md5=0134a708670ab7fa2c9555b31b655da9

Vasenska, I., & Koyundzhiyska-Davidkova, B. (2021). Tourism customer attitudes during the COVID-19 crisis. In *culture and tourism in a smart, globalized, and sustainable world* (pp. 295–309). Springer.

WorldBank. (2020). Leveraging Islamic Fintech to improve financial inclusion. https://doi.org/10.1596/34520

Yussof, S. A., & Al-Harthy, A. (2018). Cryptocurrency as an alternative currency in Malaysia : Issues and challenges. *Islam and Civilisational Renewal*, 9(1), 48–65. https://doi.org/10.12816/0049515

Zavolokina, L., Dolata, M., & Schwabe, G. (2016). FinTech transformation: How IT-enabled innovations shape the financial sector. *FinanceCom, 2016*, 75–88.

Zezulka, F., Marcon, P., Bradac, Z., Arm, J., & Benesl, T. (2019). Time-sensitive networking as the communication future of industry 4.0. *IFAC-PapersOnLine*, 52(27), 133–138. https://doi.org/10.1016/j.ifacol.2019.12.745

Fintech and Islamic Financial Institutions: Applications and Challenges

Islam Abdeljawad, Shatha Qamhieh Hashem, and Mamunur Rashid

1 Introduction and Theoretical Background

The financial system is the lifeblood of an economy. Traditional financial institutions that run on limited use of technology have experienced steeper competition from technology-based start-ups. These relatively newer financial institutions are using a battery of services that rely on new technology, often dubbed "financial technology " or "Fintech". Fintech is a technology-based channel to plan, process, and deliver financial products and services, and a modern non-tangible way of engaging with customers in the financial industry (Knewtson & Rosenbaum, 2020). Global investments in the forms of mergers and acquisitions, private

---

I. Abdeljawad · S. Q. Hashem (✉)
An-Najah National University, Nablus, Palestine
e-mail: shatha.qamhieh@najah.edu

I. Abdeljawad
e-mail: islamjawad@najah.edu

M. Rashid
Canterbury Christ Church University, Canterbury, UK
e-mail: Mamunur.Rashid@canterbury.ac.uk

© The Author(s), under exclusive license to Springer Nature
Switzerland AG 2022
M. K. Hassan et al. (eds.), *FinTech in Islamic Financial Institutions*,
https://doi.org/10.1007/978-3-031-14941-2_10

equity, and venture capital in Fintech innovations exhibit a remarkable growth to $98 billion only in the first half of 2021 compared to $121.5 billion in the entire 2020 (KPMG, 2021).

Despite the initial thoughts around mobile-based financial services, preferably using an app, Fintech encompasses a wide range of areas and channels, including banking, asset and wealth management, credit (crowdfunding and P2P lending), electronic payment services, use of virtual currencies (such as the bitcoin), and integrated advisory services using robotics, as well as the decentralized transaction management system using the distributed ledger technology and blockchain), biometric recognition using retina, fingerprint, and facial recognition, and support for service analysis and delivery (cloud computing and big data) (Lim et al., 2019; Oseni & Ali, 2019). Consequently, we have seen massive investment in Fintech in all aspects of the banking and financial services industries (Thakor, 2020). As demand drives the market, Fintech has taken the centre stage while developing new products and business models having a significant impact on financial and non-financial markets and institutions (Frame & White, 2014).

There are several benefits of Fintech as explored in the academic as well as policy literature. Among several of these, innovative business solutions, reduced cost of operation, better customer engagement, financial stability, and growth and expansion opportunities are commonly cited (Banna et al., 2021; Barbu et al., 2021; Daqar et al., 2020; Khan et al., 2022; KPMG, 2018; Mention, 2019; Ryu & Ko, 2020; Sangwan et al., 2020). When merged with finance, the technologies are modified for delivering services such as the cryptocurrencies, digital payments and digital wallets, smart contracts, robotics, consumer data analysis and predictive techniques, internet banking, and mobile banking. Fintech innovations provide customized financial services with improved quality in a cost-effective manner. Shiau et al. (2020) have found that the perceived usefulness and satisfaction in Fintech carry a positive influence on the growth of the Fintech firms. Investment in Fintech, thus, can help ensure competitive advantage (Wigglesworth, 2016).

Fintech has experienced significant growth since the year 2019. The industry has expanded across a variety of technology foundations, including Artificial Intelligence (AI), blockchain, digital banking, cryptography, APIs, biometric sensors, the internet of things, and mobile-based businesses. Higher consumer demand for Fintech-based services has forced traditional financial services providers to modify business models

(Fisher, 2001; Lee et al., 2012). The biggest change so far in financial sector has been recorded in facilitation of payment, risk management, exchanges, and financial regulation (Haddad & Hornuf, 2019).

Despite growing awareness, there are several grey areas surrounding the most common questions—how does Fintech interact with the traditional financial system? How big is the change expected to be? What is the cost of that change? What impact will it have on banks as we know them today? We address these questions from the standpoint of the disruptive innovation theory. There are two types of Fintech in relevance to financial institutions. First comes the sustainable Fintech, and second comes the disruptive Fintech (Christensen, 1997, 2013; Christensen & Raynor, 2003). Sustainable Fintech refers to structured traditional financial institutions that use technology outputs to improve and protect their established businesses. The disruptive Fintech includes business providers such as the IT companies and start-ups that offer financial services and products that compete with the established business. The banking industry is the main structured financial component within the financial system that is being challenged by the disruptive creative technical financial services and products (Berger, 2003; Dapp, 2014; DeYoung, 2005; Schueffel, 2016).

As the core business of the financial institutions involves trust, Fintech must help solve the moral hazard and asymmetric information puzzles. The current institutional setting has resulted in extremely disproportionate wealth concentration as well as the exclusion of most of the people from the financial system. The bank credit models do not offer direct solutions for the most significant economic institutions, such as the micro, small, and medium enterprises (MSMEs). Over the years, banks have established a "minimum" for their business, which includes a minimum cost, minimum age limit, a minimum credit limit, and so on. With the traditional models, banks cannot go below this minimum level. As a result, inclusivity is in jeopardy.

Fintech is designed not only to address the inclusivity issue but also to take care of the asymmetric information and moral hazard. Despite being noted as one of the significant disruptors in the history of finance, Fintech offers a wide range of technology-based services for the previously unbanked population. Fintech offers a business model where there are opportunities for the lenders and the borrowers to reduce information gap. With the implementation of blockchain technology, fraud detection is becoming easier. Fintech requires firms to report their statements properly, which leads to an adequate collection of revenues for the government. Credit agency data is also being used to build a more comprehensive consumer profile. Fintech has aided in the reduction of information asymmetry, allowing for improved credit appraisal and risk management. As a result, banks will be able to reduce their monitoring cost, face-to-face customer engagement cost, and marketing cost. In a study of five successful Fintech firms in Switzerland, Zavolokina et al. (2017) have discovered a substantial financial flow from large banking institutions to smaller Fintech start-ups, indicating the presence of cooperative rather than competitive activities between them, which leads to improved services at lower costs and fees.

Fintech is also helping banks to offer finance based on risk-sharing method. Due to agency problem, banks accept collateral while financing a project, which results in money going exclusively to the wealthiest echelon of the society. Also, as collateral is hard to manage, small entrepreneurs, with better ideas, fail to obtain credit. This problem stifles broader investments and employment generation.

Similar to their conventional peers, Islamic banks are also impacted by the Fintech. While there is no direct conflict with the Shariah—Islamic law that govern the Islamic financial institutions, Fintech still poses threats to Islamic financial institutions (Hassan et al., 2020, 2022). Fintech is expected to impact Islamic financial industry from several grounds, such as the wide-spread automation, disintermediation that has resulted in open access to financial services such as the peer-to-peer (P2P) lending and banking using mobile devices, and decentralization and security, which includes blockchain and cloud-based technology (Hasan et al., 2020).

Given the diversity of the developments surrounding Fintech, this chapter summarizes the key factors as well as strategic reaction by Islamic financial institutions, with a particular emphasis on Islamic banks. The chapter is divided into the following sections. Section two delves into the history and current state of Fintech and Islamic Fintech. Section three discusses Fintech applications for Islamic bank operations. Section Four explores the link between Islamic banking and Islamic Fintech. Section Five concludes the chapter.

2 Growth of Fintech

History

How have we arrived at the current point of Fintech revolution? Most cite the introduction of the Diner's club credit card during 1950 as the technology starting point in finance, which is, at a lag, followed by the first automated teller machine (ATM) card by Barclays Bank in 1967, introduction of NASDAQ in 1971 as the first electronic stock trading platform, and cross-border payment system using SWIFT in 1973. While there has been gradual movement towards partial electronic trading, for instance, the start of E-Trade as the first online brokerage firm in 1982, the first big step towards online banking activities started in 1983 (Bagadi, 2019; Sharma, 2014). By 1998, most banks in the US started offering online payment systems and transactions through websites. The same year we have seen the start of PayPal as the first electronic payment system. Another major landmark was in 2008, which witnessed the creation of Bitcoin cryptocurrency (Fauzi et al., 2020; Murugeswari et al., 2020).

Global Fintech universe started taking a new shape since the year 2010. Google Pay Send, which was later renamed as Google Pay, was introduced in 2011 (Majumder et al., 2017). Stripe was the other payment vehicle that attracted a growing customer base (Markovich, 2017). There has been an obvious outbreak of many Fintech channels, tools, and institutions that appear in consumer pastimes. E-commerce giant Alibaba group introduced a cloud-based facial recognition—"smile to pay"—to replace passwords. Perhaps the biggest jump in the Fintech universe happens during the COVID-19 period, which started in 2019–2020 (Kauflin, 2020; Talwar, 2020). A sheer portion of these recent developments is not only contributed by the technological innovations but also the restrictions placed on face-to-face interactions at the trading points, which necessitates an online or non-physical transaction mode. Salz (2020) pointed out that financial applications were accessed by consumers more than 1 trillion times during 2019, which was an increase of more than 71% in registration rates in comparison to the previous year.

Le (2021) reported that COVID-19 spread and the governmental lockdowns caused an increase in the daily download rate of Fintech service applications by a range of 24–32%. As a result, the users that choose to use Fintech applications during lockout times to purchase products and services were able to realize the useful value of Fintech in their daily lives (Fu & Mishra, 2020), this realization of Fintech usefulness may increase the opportunities to continue using Fintech by customers after COVID-19 (Revathy & Balaji, 2020).

Users' Perception: EY Fintech Global Adoption Index (2019)

In a report by Statista (2020) on digital banking users in the US, 75% of the young generation use digital banking, and this percentage is expected to reach 77.6% in 2022. Based on the EY Global Fintech Adoption Index (2019) presented in Fig. 1, the Fintech application development rate witnessed a large growth over the past years as the global consumer adoption rate of Fintech reached 64%. In addition, the consumer survey of the EY report shows that 94% of the global consumers included in the survey reported their awareness of at least one Fintech money transfer and payment services, the survey also shows the rate per Fintech category as it shows that 75% of consumers used at least once a payment service, 34% took savings and investment plans, 29% use budgeting and financial planning, 27% use Fintech borrowing services, and 48% use insurance Fintech services. Furthermore, the SME Fintech adoption survey section in the EY Global Fintech Adoption Index (2019) shows a 25% growth rate in the SMEs market adoption of Fintech services, out of which 56% use banking and payment Fintech services and 46% of them use a Fintech financing services.

Figure 2 shows the changes in reasons behind using the services of a Fintech challenger.[1] Rates and fees become important determinants of Fintech adoption (grew from 13% in 2017 to about 27% in 2019). Almost 10% increase in consumer preference for easiness of opening an account that has seen a growth from 20% in 2017 to 30% in 2019.

The EY global Fintech Adoption Index (2019) also shows reasons for small and medium enterprises (SME) to adopt Fintech solutions (Fig. 3). The top reason based on SMEs preferences is Fintech functionality and features (66%), next rank is service availability for 24 h a day for all weekdays which gained 55%, next is the ease of setting up, configuring, and

---

[1] A Fintech challenger is focused on consumer preference, offer more innovative products, and provide a better overall experience than traditional financial institutions (Girling, 2020).

using the service at 53%, followed by favourable rates and fees at 39%, while compatibility with daily operations and infrastructure gained 38%, and last 31% is for trust in the provider's team and their reputation.

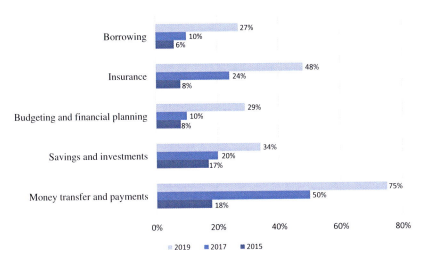

Fig. 1 Global consumer Fintech adoption rates for the years 2015, 2017, and 2019 (*Source* EY Global Fintech Adoption Index [2019])

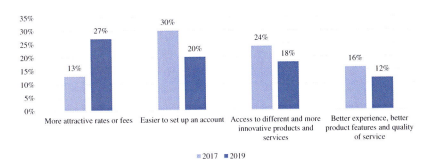

Fig. 2 Changes in reasons for using a Fintech challenger for the years 2017 and 2019 (*Source* EY global Fintech Adoption Index [2019])

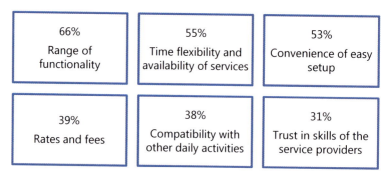

Fig. 3 Top reasons for SMEs to use Fintech globally for the year 2019 (*Source* EY global Fintech Adoption Index [2019])

Fintech Unicorns

Bruene (2021) provides a list of the twenty-first-century Fintech Unicorns[2] that are launched since 1999. The list shows that as of 9 September 2021, there are 288 Fintech unicorns. Total investment value of all Fintech Unicorns in the list is US $2249.4 billion. The largest component within the total is Fintech which has US $1838.9 billion, followed by Cryptos at US $185.3 billion, E-commerce at US $183 billion, Insurtech at US $22.8 billion, and Healthtech at US $19.4 billion.

Analysing only the top 100 of the Fintech categories reported in Fig. 4, we find that 41% of the firms are categorized as payment firms with a total investment value of US $1129.2 billion, 11% are categorized as lending firms at a value of US $181.8 billion, 13% are categorized as banking at a value of US $133.3 billion, 12% are categorized as investing at a value of US $99.1 billion, and 6% are categorized as insurance with an investment

---

[2] The "Unicorn" is a term used in the venture capital industry to describe a privately held startup company with a value of over $1 billion. The term was first popularized in 2013 by venture capitalist Aileen Lee. (https://www.investopedia.com/terms/u/unicorn.asp).

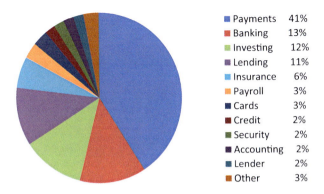

Fig. 4 Subcategories of the Top 100 Fintech Unicorns as of September 2021 (*Source* Researchers calculation based on fintechlabs.com)

value of US $39.3 billion. The global investment in Fintech is expected to reach a compounded growth rate (CAGR) of around 27% by the end of 2026.[3]

Islamic Fintech Worldwide

The Global Islamic Fintech Report (2021) points out the presence of US $49 billion Islamic Fintech transactions of 241 Islamic Fintech firms, in the Organization of Islamic Cooperation countries (OIC). The main categories that represent 77% of the Islamic Fintech firms are payments, lending, wealth management, deposits, raising funds, and alternative finance. Even though Islamic Fintech represents nearly 0.72% of the global Fintech transaction, it is expected to grow at 21% CAGR to become US $128 billion industry by 2025 in the OIC countries, which is higher than the 15% CAGR expected for the conventional Fintech over the same period. The top five markets among the OIC countries based on the transaction volume of Islamic Fintech services are Kingdom of Saudi Arabia, United Arab Emirates, Islamic Republic of Iran, Malaysia,

---

[3] Data is based on the Globe Newswire "Global Fintech Market, By Technology, By Service, By Application, By Region, Competition Forecast and Opportunities, 2026", published by "Researchandmarkets.com" October 13, 2021.

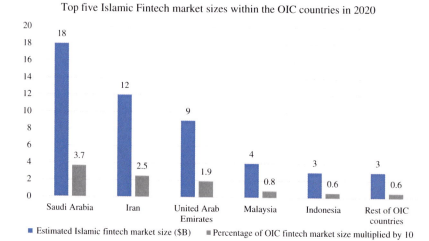

Fig. 5 The top five Islamic Fintech market sizes within the OIC countries (*Source* Global Islamic Fintech Report [2021])

and Indonesia. These countries accumulate three-fourths of the Islamic Fintech market in OIC region. Figure 5 provides details on the market size.[4]

The Global Islamic Fintech Index (GIFT Index) is a composite index including 32 indicators that are categorized into 5 main areas which are Islamic Fintech markets & ecosystems, talent, regulation, infrastructure and capital.[5] The initial list includes 64 Islamic Fintech jurisdictions. Figure 6 shows the GIFT index.

The GIFT Index includes sixty-four countries including the likes of Malaysia, Kingdom of Saudi Arabia, UAE, Indonesia, and the UK in the top-5 strongest ecosystems. The GIFT index also shows that there are fast maturing ecosystems which include Bahrain, Kuwait, Pakistan, Qatar, and Jordan. The survey conveyed the main hurdles in front of the Islamic

---

[4] The complete list of the OIC countries and other related information is available on https://www.oic-oci.org/states/?lan=en.

[5] To obtain more information on the index scores of the GIFT, the methodology and rankings are provided in appendix 1 of the global Islamic Fintech Report (2021).

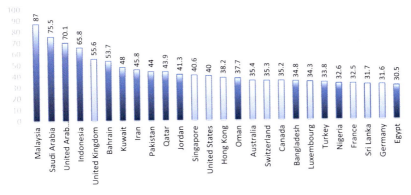

Fig. 6 The Global Islamic Fintech (GIFT) Index (*Source* Global Islamic Fintech Report [2021]; *Note* OIC countries are distinguished using the darker colour)

Fintech growth which are the education level of consumers, the capital shortage, and the availability of talent. On the other hand, the top rank Islamic Fintech growth segments for 2021 are found to be payments, deposits, lending, and fundraising.

3 Applications of Fintech in Islamic Finance

Payments and Remittances

Fintech firms employed technology to incorporate a variety of payment methods into consumer-friendly applications and financial gateways having mobile and internet technologies in the backdrop. Customers can use electronic cards, bitcoins, and digital wallets to make purchases. These transaction facilities are integrated into major mobile, transportation, and retail chains for day-to-day transactions. Traditional banks charge a high price to execute transactions using any of these alternative payment methods, making them unviable for merchants. Instead of credit cards, people can utilize mobile wallets. Individuals can send money without using traditional banks and process payments more efficiently with digital banking.

Fintech-enabled remittance, on the other hand, makes money transfer far more affordable. Remittance is possible even if remitters do not have a bank account. According to Tarique and Ahmed (2021), Fintech facilitates money transfers and banking transactions for Islamic finance consumers, resulting in greater investment in Fintech services by top Islamic finance organizations.

Deposits and Lending

Challenger Banking
A "challenger bank" is a bank or a Fintech (financial technology) non-banking start-up that uses digital technologies to compete with big, traditional banks (Polasik et al., 2021). Challenger banks are focusing on providing a better user experience and appealing costs for certain financial services to their consumers because of their branchless and often mobile operations. Challenger banks are referred to as "mobile-only banks" or "neobanks" (Gomber et al., 2018; Hopkinson et al., 2019) to emphasize their radical rejection of traditional distribution channels like branches, phone banking, and even web-transaction applications. Customers can use their smartphones to not only open an account, but also to perform a variety of additional financial transactions (Capgemini & Efma, 2020). Challenger banks often operate on a monthly subscription model that provides a set of services.

Open Banking
Open banking is a blockchain-based concept that proposes that external parties are given access to the consumer data collected by the banks and other financial institutions to build applications that connect financial institutions and third-party providers. Explicitly, this provides third party access to Know-Your-Customer information system held by the bank and other relevant risk management and credit review system to be available on an "open innovation" platform. There are rules and regulations that govern how and what data can be shared, focusing on the end-benefit users without jeopardizing data integrity, sensitive data leaks, or data volatility. Open banking services will not be activated unless the customers express approval, and there is complete security and integrity. According to Juniper Research (2020), open banking users are predicted to double from 2019 to 2021, from 18 million in 2019 to 40 million in 2021, because of increased consumer demand for information on financial health during COVID-19, which enhances open banking usage.

To provide a uniform perspective, open banking models employ application programming interfaces (APIs) to aggregate consumers' financial information across many financial institutions. Open banking's development and expanding adoption will help banks to have a better understanding of client behaviour and requirements, allowing them to provide highly tailored services and products. Open banking's guarantee of real-time data access can be augmented by intuitive business and data analytics tools.

Unbanked/Under-Banked Facilities
Unbanked population is a threat to financial stability due to two reasons: first, there is no record of their financial transaction, and second, they primarily use cash and fund from friends and family, bypassing the financial systems. Under-banked population does not get the full package of financial services, primarily because of the limited infrastructure and skill set. Due to the minimum requirement set by the traditional financial institutions, it is not easy for both unbanked and under-banked to apply for financial services. Fintech companies can be a good solution in this regard, as they are not limited by regulatory requirements similar to traditional banks. Non-bank financial institutions also cater to customers with lower credit scores than banks, and Fintech lenders have a larger market share in places where credit scores are lower and mortgage rejection rates are higher.

Alternative Finance
Micro, Small, and Medium Enterprises (MSMEs) are the true engines of global growth and employment that frequently experience capital shortages. Because a large percentage of these businesses lack sufficient collateral to receive a loan, as the risk of unsecured lending is considerable to the financial institutions. Due to a lack of Shariah-compliant borrowing options, most MSMEs must rely on their own funds, which can impede their growth and expansion plans. Fintech, on the other hand, has the potential to reverse this trend. MSMEs can raise financing via technology-enabled innovative models such as crowdfunding and P2P platforms.

Alternative financing, which refers to funding sources other than banks, such as the internal capital (retained earnings) and working capital (trade credit) may be able to alleviate financial constraints for these businesses (Ferrando et al., 2019). Alternative financing is the most common source of external funding, according to Allen et al. (2012), and enterprises having access to bank or market credit do not have greater growth rates than firms that rely on alternative finance. Bank funding difficulties for SMEs may have come from high capital requirements for banks (Bams et al., 2019). Alternative finance could help SMEs overcome the financial limits caused by rising bank capital requirements.

Bilan et al. (2019) defines alternative finance in the Fintech era as the ability to raise funds and conduct borrowings using online platforms. There are several common methods and channels of P2P and crowdfunding models. These can take the structure of an equity- and/or reward-based crowdfunding, P2P, or Peer-to-Business (P2B) finance (Coakley & Lazos, 2021; Rossi et al., 2021). Alternative financing arranges financial services for individuals and businesses, preferably the SMEs, using P2P lending platforms or crowdfunding channels. P2P and crowdfunding platforms help save time and cost as these bypass the regular banking system and do not have the prerequisites of legal documentations and supervision. Because of recent breakthroughs in Fintech, alternative financing has grown dramatically in recent years (Fuster et al., 2019).

(a) Peer-to-Peer Financing

P2P lending connects borrowers and lenders in a very profitable way. There is practically no intermediation in this case. Hence, a direct contact between the borrower and the lender has been possible. Borrowers that use peer-to-peer lending can get finance from a variety of people. When compared to traditional banks, the process of obtaining a loan is much easier. Lenders on peer-to-peer consumer lending platforms are typically investors wishing to park their money with institutions that help them maximize their wealth. The platform handles the vetting and pre-approval of applicants, making it simple for lenders to identify the suitable borrower for them. The same principle applies to P2B or P2P commercial lending. The platform is responsible for creating a pool of lenders and connecting them to a pool of borrowers using technology. There are endless opportunities provided by P2P financing methods, especially to the new charters and start-ups, often with very risky ideas, that are not financed by the banks.

(b) Crowdfunding

As the name suggests, crowdfunding is an alternative but less structured and open stock market system for limited time funding. Ideas in need of short-term funding come to crowdfunding marketplace presenting their ideas for funding, generally to non-professional investors. Aside from financial causes, crowdfunding is often used for social causes, like raising funds for charitable donations. Crowdfunding platforms are often used to finance green and sustainable projects that help preserve environment (Pimonenko et al., 2017). Crowdfunding, in theory, connects a borrower and a creditor without requiring them to live in the same nation or even know one other. Fintech innovations have resulted in crowdfunding platforms such as Kickstarter, GoFundMe, and Patreon. Entrepreneurs and early-stage enterprises can use the platforms to raise cash from all over the world, bypassing geographical barriers and reaching international markets and investors.

Crowdsourcing can have several models. Yang and Zhang (2016) forward that there are at least six types of crowdfunding models suitable for Shariah applications. These are (1) equity-based, (2) reward-based, (3) real estate, (4) profit-sharing, (5) donation-based, and (6) invoice trading crowdfunding. Additionally, some Shariah-compliant products appear to be eligible for crowdfunding. Examples include Murabaha (profit margin) for purchasing an asset and the profit-and-loss sharing models, such as the Musharakah- or Mudharabah-based strategies. Fintech (along with other digital breakthroughs like social media) looks logical for such transactions because it lowers transaction costs.

A lion's share of the global Islamic banking instruments is based on non-PLS-based contracts, such as the Murabahah and Ijarah. Muslims traditionally exclude themselves from the conventional financial system due to interest-based (Riba) and uncertain risk-taking financial transactions (Gharar and Mysir). Islamic banks also partly failed to attract many Muslims due to their bank-like financial and regulatory structure. Fintech can help to attract more people into the financial services area through novel payment options, Distributed Ledger Technology (DLT), and smart contracts. Use of crowdfunding and P2P lending will promote financial inclusion among Muslim investors and entrepreneurs in the coming future (Al-Amine, 2019).

(c) SME Finance

Traditional credit scoring system demotes individuals and SMEs with limited financial liquidity. Fintech-based credit scoring replaces the standard credit scoring system by employing algorithms that improve the credit management system over time. The amount of information the Fintech scoring system uses provides a much deeper analysis of credit acceptability, percentile credit scoring, and social signalling. While the alternative scoring system is flexible, it improves the credit judgement system using machine learning. These credit scoring algorithms have also reduced the cost of underwriting loans, allowing Fintech to pass the savings on to borrowers and therefore expand their client base.

Because of the poor profits and high underwriting expenses on small loans, traditional banks often do not accept loan proposals from MSMEs. Fintech offers two major benefits to these borrowers. First, their loans are underwritten at no cost. Second, they are provided with facilities like Buy Now Pay Later (BNPL), which is helping not only in higher sales but also in higher loans.

(d) Trade Finance

Trade finance is a strong working capital finance tool, mostly for the benefits of the large firms. Traditionally, small firms do not have the arbitrage of engaging into receivable or inventory securitization, primarily due to risk. Even though they get a factor or a bank in the securitization process, the cost has been extremely high. SMEs suffer high price due to lack of technology orientation in trade financing (Cornelli et al., 2019). Fintech helps with inventory and receivable financing systems using distribute ledger technology that uses no middlemen in the process, reducing the cost of transaction.

Fintech help reduce "overpricing" cost of the supplier as the bank premium drops in the baseline trade finance model (Wang & Xu, 2021). When invoice trading is used as a post-shipment finance plan, digitalization benefits the supply chain. The supply chain always benefits from smart contracts (both the supplier and the retailer). According to the findings of Lee et al. (2022), reducing financial friction through contract innovation and Fintech leads to larger order quantities, higher supply chain profit, and higher consumer surplus.

Digital Wallets: Most Common Fintech Product

Under the traditional system, payments for utilities were cleared after a physical visit to the bank branch. Customers have to carry documents of past payments and records of utility bills. Using Fintech and mobile wallets, paying for household services and utility bills becomes easier. Financial institutions are working with application-developing Fintech firms to come up with an intuitive, user-friendly, and secured payment system that can be used to settle day-to-day transactions. These apps do not only offer convenience, but they also reduce costs.

Asset Management and Robo-Advisory

With high-frequency robotics trading in the corner, personal wealth and consultative asset management functions have seen significant growth in recent years. Sophisticated algorithms and machine learning techniques are used to replace human labour on the trading floor, which has seen a significant reduction in trading costs (Lee & Shin, 2018). As the decision turnout time is much faster for a Fintech-enabled trading platform, which also comes with lesser mistakes than the human-controlled system, there is growing popularity of the Fintech-based asset management system among the young as well as rich investors (Imerman & Fabozzi, 2020). Investors now can build their portfolios at a much lesser cost to pay to the brokers and asset managers. High-frequency traders manipulate investor information collected from the asset managers and provide cloud-based bot-enabled investment advice.

This is demonstrated by the wide range of Fintech-creating financial planning skills. These allow wealth managers to efficiently capture, monitor, and assess their clients' needs, assisting in the improvement and automation of advice-giving. Fintech-driven innovation is also improving client engagement from the start with prospecting and on-boarding, as well as providing operational efficiencies for wealth managers through workflow management and automation.

Robo-advisors provide automated self-controlled cloud-based personal wealth management services to clients at a low cost than the traditional wealth managers. Because of the use of sophisticated machine learning techniques, Robo-advisors can allocate assets much faster and achieve better risk-return balance, even though the investors may not have minimum investment skills (Gomber et al., 2018). They enable consumers of all ages to participate in low-cost investment activities with minimal manual effort. Fintech Robo-advisors can estimate and predict how a customer's portfolio balance will look if they invest according to their strategies. Robo-advisors do this by analysing investing strategies and potential risks to see how they may affect personal finances in the future.

Robo-advisor poses a significant threat to traditional financial service providers (Seiler & Fanenbruck, 2021). Using an automated trading system, individual investors take the benefits of the rights choice made at the fastest possible time, which is otherwise poorly done in a traditional trading platform (Giudici, 2018). There are, however, bigger risks that require regulators to step in. In the words of Elon Musk, "AI is our biggest existential threat".[6] Market risk and compliance risks are the other major risks that must be closely monitored. Adverse movements in the Fintech market (such as the one from Bitcoin market as an example), may see regulatory footprints reducing the benefits of Fintech soon. Tech veteran Bill Gates once commented on investing in Bitcoin, "if you have less money than Elon (Elon Musk), watch out".[7] The recent abrupt movement in the Crypto market provides ample evidence to support the aggravated risk in the Fintech market, which might result in lower consumer confidence and a rise in the cost of trading.

Smart Sukuk

Unlike cryptocurrencies, Smart Sukuk manages finance based on a blockchain technology, which is also not speculative in nature (Chong, 2021; Mohamed & Ali, 2019). The system uses profit-and-loss sharing method in the backdrop. Smart Sukuk offers a smart connection between a domestic microfinance company and a foreign bank, while the foreign bank arranges the blockchain to exchange funds across borders. This collaboration saves cost and time. Blockchain technology also allows for the screening of the compliance to Shariah and religious underpinning of the fund transfer. Islamic financial institutions are also taking part in developing similar Smart Sukuk issuance based on blockchain technology to meet global demand of funds (Foglie et al., 2021).

---

[6] https://www.theguardian.com/technology/2014/oct/27/elon-musk-artificial-intelligence-ai-biggest-existential-threat.

[7] https://www.cnbc.com/2022/03/09/bill-gates-on-bitcoin-if-you-have-less-money-than-elon-watch-out.html.

InsureTech and TakaTech

InsurTech is developed to add better client experience using technology in the insurance industry (Hargrave, 2020; Milanovic et al., 2021). Efficiency of the insurance industry is a by-product of the system. Computer and mobile applications are used by customers to apply for new products and services, and to apply for claims. Fintech is expected to have a massive impact on the Takaful market soon (Hasan et al., 2020). Fintech companies that offer insurance products, if they have access to customer data, can pair the data with algorithms and analytics, to deliver highly personalized insurance rates to their applicants, as well as alternative payment methods, based on their individual needs and qualifications.

4 FINTECH AND ISLAMIC FINANCE: COMPLEMENTARY OR COMPETITIVE

Fintech innovations can be regarded as either complementary or competitive to the Islamic banking market. Fintech firms that provide services or products that are complementary to those given by banks are candidates to become business partners with banks, whereas Fintech firms that provide services and goods that are identical to those supplied by banks are classed as competitors. According to Muda et al. (2021), Islamic banks must embrace Fintech to avoid financial disintermediation and provide value to their stakeholders. Banks have the option of collaborating with Fintechs, acquiring Fintechs, or developing their own Fintech firm. According to Rabbani et al. (2021a, 2021b), Islamic banks must partner with Fintech companies. Furthermore, according to Alam and Ali (2021), a complementary relationship between IFIs and Shariah-compliant Fintechs allows IFIs to reach international markets while also lowering operating costs.

While there are strong possibilities that the Fintech platforms and the Islamic financial institutions work together (Irfan & Ahmed, 2019), there exists a threat that these Fintech firms will take over an important, and rather lucrative, section of the traditional financial institutions. Moreover, in a general sense, the Islamic Fintech institutions might need to be directly under the preview of the Shariah supervisory board in order to ascertain the Shariah compliance risks products and services offered by them. This monitoring by the supervisory board might go against the entire foundation of Fintech.

There is a growing list of literature on complementarity between the Fintech companies with the Islamic financial institutions, as these institutions are found to assist each other in shared goals (Abojeib & Habib, 2021; Jamil & Seman, 2019). When Shariah screening is the central activity that determines the compliance to Shariah, Islamic Fintech firms are found to be equally Shariah-compliant to the Islamic banks while offering investment in compliant products and services that reduce risk and do not use "Riba" (Biancone et al., 2019). However, the constant monitoring to maintain compliance might jeopardize the level of privacy promised by the Fintech operation. Therefore, while compliance to Shariah is a key challenge in a Fintech-based business model (Biancone & Radwan, 2019), the same can be a major disruption as well.

Islamic banks have specific characteristics that limit the large adoption of Fintechs. Islamic finance operates on profit-sharing models that help diversify risks. Some of these models include the Musharakah and the Mudarabah models. There are extremely limited profit-sharing instruments when it comes to short-term investment. Fintech companies might find it challenging. Also, since the Shariah-compliant investment and financing avoid engaging with interest payment and receipts, Fintech companies may find it difficult to engage in cross-border trading, financing, and investment. Islamic financial institutions also prefer equity over debt, as debt is strictly controlled in Islamic system. Therefore, having an Islamic financial system might be important to establish Islamic Fintech organization.

Fintech has become a challenge for financial institutions, but it may be converted into an opportunity by collaborating with Fintech companies to provide innovative services rather than considering them as competitors. If an Islamic bank considers partnering with a Fintech provider, it may have access to benefits such as a low-cost technical financial solution that is focused on the consumer. According to Ahmad et al. (2021), Islamic banks and Islamic banking windows in Pakistan use a variety of financial technology to provide customer-oriented products and services, which has an impact on their business strategy, product transparency, and efficiency.

In this light, Islamic banking is under pressure to strategize its growth potential around Fintech solutions to avoid a loss of market share and a squeeze on margins. However, while using Fintech solutions, Islamic banking faces the potential of increasing operational and fraud risk. Another factor to consider is whether the Fintech solution adheres to Islamic Shariah rules and regulations. Abd Rani et al. (2021) illustrate that it is vital to have a strong partnership in producing iFintech products and services between Shariah scholars and technology professionals to deal with the problem of shariah compliance. Furthermore, Khudhori and Hendri (2021) demonstrate that collaboration between Islamic Banking and Syariah Fintech is the most valuable for expanding financing services because it allows Islamic Banking to reach out to its customers through the Syariah Fintech network; however, this perceived value obstructs the availability of detailed regulations and protection policies.

Islamic Fintech may target the financial exclusion problem in many Muslim countries; the exclusion which might be due to lack of protection and limited knowledge of Islamic finance principles. Gulrez (2021) points out those advocating worldwide consumer protection policies, laws, understanding of Islamic Fintech's viability and trustworthiness are the essential elements for GCC's Islamic Fintech to reach out to global clients. Islamic Fintech can help financing Islamic SMEs using crowdfunding. The ideas that are often risky for conventional banks to finance, these are few clicks away for an Islamic Fintech firm that uses crowdfunding.

When it comes to integrating Fintech advances, Islamic banks can profit from several qualities. For starters, they may save money by delivering Fintech services and products that are based on data standards. Second, Fintech developments are primarily internet-based, allowing service providers to circumvent regional boundaries. Third, Islamic banks can benefit from reaching out to a larger diversified number of customers, which increases the potential market size without incurring additional costs, thanks to lower costs and the ability to reach out to non-geographically limited areas via the internet. This is also aided by increased customer awareness of technological solutions in meeting their needs. Fourth, Fintech companies that provide loan platforms may allow decreasing maturity and defaulting risk since they mainly link borrowers and lenders, Islamic banks might leverage such benefit. Fifth, Islamic banks cooperation with Fintechs may provide profits from the lower regulatory expenses and barriers that Fintech firms and start-ups have as they are regarded non-bank firms (Dapp, 2014). Sixth, Fintechs data analysis techniques may assist Islamic banks to have greater risk assessment skills and get higher understanding of their business.

Fintech is broadly responsible for cheap deposits and easy loans, while banks capitalize on robust financial technology superstructure (Banna et al., 2021). However, there is a bigger challenge for Islamic banks in this regard, as they charge their customers slightly higher than their conventional peers. Due to high competition or adverse monetary policy shocks, Islamic banks may lose, otherwise, good customers to the conventional banks (Saeed et al., 2021). This gap in quality customers might be replaced with bad clients as Fintech might find more customers for banks. In addition to this, Islamic banks are relatively smaller in terms of their investment in Fintech, when compared to their conventional counterparts. Hence, to gain higher benefits, Fintech innovations might be more attracted by conventional banks.

Despite these challenges, Islamic Fintech remains an important niche for new investment. Thanks to the technology, Islamic financial institutions can design new products that are not only cheaper, but also help ensure stability, financial inclusion, and customer satisfaction (Banna et al., 2021). If some core challenges related to the Shariah supervision are managed effectively, Fintech can become a complementary force that drives Islamic finance forward.

5 Conclusion

Islamic finance is around seventy years old. Its primary markets are growing in Asian and African countries, with Muslim majority population. Some of these countries, such as Malaysia, Indonesia, Bangladesh, Pakistan, most countries from the Middle East and North African region, and some central Asian countries, are home to massive domestic market changes. In recent years, these jurisdictions are investing a lot in developing technology infrastructure, with a view to boost private sector participation in economic activity. These countries are home to Islamic finance as well. Therefore, from the perspectives of both survival and growth, Islamic financial institutions must embrace Fintech activities that bring several mutual benefits.

Aside from typical growth factors and pockets of development, we review specific applications of Fintech in Islamic finance. While other studies cover Islamic banks and Fintech, we widen the coverage of our discussion to Islamic financial institutions. While we have seen, overall, Fintech and Islamic finance will be complementary to each other, there exist several core challenges.

Shariah compliance, screening, and supervision are major challenges. Fintech companies work freely, most without any control from Central Banks or other regulatory institutions. Islamic banks cannot work in isolation. One of the reasons why customers like Islamic banking is because this banking system is supervised and audited on multiple levels (Iqbal et al., 2018). Hence, there has to be a mechanism of supervision before Islamic Fintech can flourish. Another problem is with the availability of instruments that fit the need of both Islamic finance and the Fintech companies. More research is needed to investigate the marriage between the Fintech firms and Islamic banks on their use of profit-sharing contracts.

There are still several questions that remain unresolved. Essentially, the most important question is whether Fintech can solve some of the growing problems with Islamic finance. Say for instance, researchers can explore whether Fintech can help Islamic banks to bring back the profit-and-loss sharing contracts. At this moment, a minor proportion of Islamic banks' activities are based on profit-and-loss sharing (PLS) method. It would be ground-breaking if Fintech models could be employed to ensure PLS-based transaction. Also, technology is evolving fast, and every new dimension of technology has been expensive, for banks as well as for the customers. Question remains, to what extent, Fintech is really cost efficient in the long term. There is growing evidence of short-term cost efficiency. However, we need to wait longer to analyse its long-term viability.

References

Abd Rani, N. F., Seman, A. C., Ab Rahman, A., & Z'aba, M. R. (2021). A viewpoint of Islamic financial technology (i-fintech) in Malaysia. *Labuan e-Journal of Muamalat and Society (LJMS), 15*, 97–110.

Abojeib, M., & Habib, F. (2021). Blockchain for Islamic social responsibility institutions. In *Research anthology on blockchain technology in business, healthcare, education, and government* (pp. 1114–1128). IGI Global.

Ahmad, A., Sohail, A., & Hussain, A. (2021). Emergence of financial technology in Islamic banking industry and its influence on bank performance in covid-19 scenario: A case of developing economy. *Gomal University Journal of Research, 37*(1), 97–109.

Alam, N., & Ali, S. N. (2021). Introduction: Fintech and Islamic finance in the Gulf Cooperation Council (GCC). In N. Alam and S. Nazim Ali (Eds.), *Fintech, digital currency and the future of Islamic Finance: Strategic, regulatory and adoption issues in the Gulf Cooperation Council* (pp. 1–8). Cham: Springer.

Al-Amine, M. A. B. M. (2019). Crowdfunding in Islamic Finance: Ensuring proper Sharī 'ah oversight. In *Fintech in Islamic Finance* (pp. 132–155). Routledge.

Allen, F., Chakrabarti, R., De, S., & Qian, M. (2012). Financing firms in India. *Journal of Financial Intermediation, 21*(3), 409–445.

Bagadi. S. M. B. (2019). Challenges and opportunities of E-banking system in nationalized banking. *International Journal of Research and Analytical Reviews, 6*(4), 260–267. http://www.ijrar.org/IJRAR19D1315.pdf

Bams, D., Pisa, M., & Wolff, C. C. (2019). Are capital requirements on small business loans flawed? *Journal of Empirical Finance, 52*, 255–274.

Banna, H., Hassan, M. K., & Rashid, M. (2021). Fintech-based financial inclusion and bank risk-taking: Evidence from OIC countries. *Journal of International Financial Markets, Institutions and Money, 75*, 101447.

Barbu, C. M., Florea, D. L., Dabija, D.-C., & Barbu, M. C. R. (2021). Customer Experience in Fintech. *Journal of Theoretical and Applied Electronic Commerce Research, 16*(5), 1415–1433. https://doi.org/10.3390/jtaer16050080

Berger, A. N. (2003). The economic effects of technological progress: Evidence from the banking industry. *Journal of Money, Credit and Banking, 35*, 141–176. https://doi.org/10.1353/mcb.2003.0009

Biancone, P. P., & Radwan, M. (2019). Social finance and financing social enterprises: An Islamic finance prospective. *European Journal of Islamic Finance, Special Issue*, 1–7.

Biancone, P. P., Secinaro, S., & Kamal, M. (2019). Crowdfunding and Fintech: Business model sharia-compliant. *European Journal of Islamic Finance, 12*. https://doi.org/10.13135/2421-2172/3260

Bilan, Y., Rubanov, P., Vasylieva, T. A., & Lyeonov, S. (2019). The influence of industry 4.0 on financial services: Determinants of alternative finance development. *Polish Journal of Management Studies.19*(1), 70–93

Bruene, J. (2021, February 2). *The 134 Fintech unicorns of the 21st century*. FintechLIVE. https://Fintechlabs.com/the-134-Fintech-unicorns-of-the-21st-century-feb-2021-update/

Capgemini and EFM. (2020). *World Fintech Report 2020*. https://Fintechworldreport.com/resources/world-Fintech-report-2020/

Chong, F. H. L. (2021). Enhancing trust through digital Islamic finance and blockchain technology. *Qualitative Research in Financial Markets, 13*(3), 328–341. https://doi.org/10.1108/QRFM-05-2020-0076

Christensen, C. M. (1997). *The innovator's dilemma: When new technologies cause great firms to fail*. Harvard Business School Press.

Christensen, C. M. (2013). *The innovator's dilemma: When new technologies cause great firms to fail*. Harvard Business Review Press.

Christensen, C., & Raynor, M. (2003). *The innovator's solution: Creating and sustaining successful growth*. Harvard Business School Press.

Coakley, J., & Lazos, A. (2021). New developments in equity crowdfunding: A review. *Review of Corporate Finance*, 1(3–4), 341–405.

Cornelli, G., Davidson, V., Frost, J., Gambacorta, L., & Oishi, K. (2019). *SME finance in Asia: Recent innovations in Fintech Credit, trade finance, and beyond* (ADBI Working Paper No. 1027). Asian Development Bank. https://www.adb.org/publications/sme-finance-asia-innovations-Fintech-credit-trade-finance-beyond

Daqar, M. A. M. A.; Arqawi, S. & Karsh, S. A. (2020). Fintech in the eyes of millennials and generation Z (the financial behavior and Fintech perception). *Banks and Bank Systems, LLC CPC Business Perspectives*, 15, 20–28. https://doi.org/10.21511/bbs.15(3).2020.03

Dapp, T. (2014). *Fintech: The digital (r) evolution in the financial sector* (Deutsche Bank Res 39). https://goo.gl/UcZJFz.

DeYoung, R. (2005). The performance of internet based business models: Evidence from the banking industry. *Journal of Business*, 78, 893–948. https://doi.org/10.1086/429648

DinarStandard and Elipses. (2021). *Global Islamic Fintech report 2021*. Salaam Gateway. https://salaamgateway.com/specialcoverage/islamic-Fintech-2021

Foglie, D., Andrea, P., Claudia, I., Boukrami, E., & Vento, G. (2021). The impact of the Blockchain technology on the global Sukuk industry: Smart contracts and asset tokenisation. *Technology Analysis & Strategic Management*, 1–15. https://doi.org/10.1080/09537325.2021.1939000

Ernst and Young Global Limited. (2017). *EY Fintech Adoption Index 2017* (EYG No. 03893–174Gbl, ED 0619). https://startup.ey.com/ey-Fintech-adoption-index-2017

Ernst and Young Global Limited. (2019). *EY global Fintech adoption index 2019* (EYG No. 002455–19Gbl). https://www.ey.com/en_gl/ey-global-Fintech-adoption-index

Fauzi, M. A., Paiman, N., & Othman, Z. (2020). Bitcoin and cryptocurrency: Challenges, opportunities and future works. *The Journal of Asian Finance, Economics and Business*, 7(8), 695–704.

Ferrando, A., Popov, A., & Udell, G. F. (2019). Do SMEs benefit from unconventional monetary policy and how? Microevidence from the eurozone. *Journal of Money, Credit and Banking*, 51(4), 895–928.

Fisher, A. (2001). Winning the battle for customers. *Journal of Financial Services Marketing*, 6(1), 77–83.

Frame, W. S., & White, L. J. (2014). Technological change, financial innovation, and diffusion in banking. In N. Allen, P. M. Berger and O. S. John Wilson (Eds.), *The Oxford handbook of banking* (2nd ed.). http://ssrn.com/abstract=2380060.

Fu, J., & Mishra, M. (2020). *The global impact of COVID-19 on Fintech adoption* (Swiss Finance Institute Research Paper 20–38). Swiss Finance Institute.

Fuster, A., Plosser, M., Schnabl, P., & Vickery, J. (2019). The role of technology in mortgage lending. *The Review of Financial Studies, 32*(5), 1854–1899.

Girling, W. (2020, November 13). The battle between challenger and incumbent banks continues. *Fintech Magazine.* https://Fintechmagazine.com/banking/battle-between-challenger-and-incumbent-banks-continues

Giudici, P. (2018). Fintech risk management: A research challenge for artificial intelligence in finance. *Frontiers in Artificial Intelligence, 1*(1). https://doi.org/10.3389/frai.2018.00001

Gomber, P., Kauffman, R. J., Parker, C., & Weber, B. W. (2018). On the Fintech revolution: Interpreting the forces of innovation, disruption, and transformation in financial services. *Journal of Management Information Systems, 35*(1), 220–265.

Gulrez, T. (2021). Strategic assessment of Islamic Fintech in GCC countries. In N. Alam and S. Nazim Ali (Eds.), *Fintech, digital currency and the future of Islamic finance: Strategic, regulatory and adoption issues in the Gulf Cooperation Council* (pp. 223–241). Springer.

Haddad, C., & Hornuf, L. (2019). The emergence of the global Fintech market: Economic and technological determinants. *Small Business Economics, 53,* 81–105.

Hargrave, M. (2020). *Insurtech.* https://www.investopedia.com/terms/i/insurtech.asp.

Hasan, R., Hassan, M. K., & Aliyu, S. (2020). Fintech and Islamic finance: Literature review and research agenda. *International Journal of Islamic Economics and Finance, 3*(1), 75–94.

Hassan, M. K., Rabbani, M. R., & Ali, M. A. (2020). Challenges for the Islamic Finance and banking in post COVID era and the role of Fintech. *Journal of Economic Cooperation and Development, 41*(3), 93–116.

Hassan, M. K., Rabbani, M. R., Brodmann, J., Bashar, A., & Grewal, H. (2022). Bibliometric and Scientometric analysis on CSR practices in the banking sector. *Review of Financial Economics,* 1–20. https://doi.org/10.1002/rfe.1171

Hopkinson, G. G., Klarova, D., Turcan, R. & Gulieva, V. (Eds.). (2019). *How neobanks' business models challenge traditional banks.* https://www.ibc.aau.dk/collaboration/Young+Graduate+News/

Imerman, M. B., & Fabozzi, F. J. (2020). Cashing in on innovation: A taxonomy of Fintech. *Journal of Asset Management, 21*(3), 167–177.

Irfan, H., & Ahmed, D. (2019). Fintech: The opportunity for Islamic finance. In *Fintech in Islamic Finance: Theory and Practice* (pp. 19–30). Routledge.

Iqbal, M., Nisha, N., & Rashid, M. (2018). Bank selection criteria and satisfaction of retail customers of Islamic banks in Bangladesh. *International Journal of Bank Marketing, 36*(5), 931–946.

Jamil, N. N., & Seman, J. A. (2019). The impact of Fintech on the sustainability of Islamic accounting and finance education in Malaysia. *Journal of Islamic, Social, Economics and Development, 4*(17), 74–88.

Juniper Research. (2020). *Open banking users to double by 2021, as consumers seek deeper financial insights.* Juniper Research.

Kauflin, J. (2020). The 10 biggest Fintech companies in America 2020. *Forbes.* https://www.forbes.com/sites/jeffkauflin/2020/02/12/the-10-biggest-Fintech-companies-in-america-2020/#7e7279691259

Khudhori, K. U., & Hendri, L. (2021). Islamic banking and Fintech: Sustainable collaboration. *Al-Intaj: Journal Ekonomi dan Perbankan Syariah, 7*(2), 172–182.

Khan, M. S., Rabbani, M. R., Hawaldar, I. T., & Bashar, A. (2022). Determinants of behavioral intentions to use islamic financial technology: An empirical assessment. *Risks, 10,* 114.

Knewtson, H. S., & Rosenbaum, Z. A. (2020). Toward understanding Fintech and its industry. *Managerial Finance, 46*(8), 1043–1060. https://doi.org/10.1108/MF-01-2020-0024

KPMG. (2018). *The pulse of Fintech 2018: Global report on Fintech investment trends.* KPMG. https://home.kpmg/au/en/home/insights/2017/04/pulse-of-Fintech.html

KPMG Global. (2021). *Record-breaking VC investment in Fintech in first half of 2021.* https://home.kpmg/xx/en/home/media/press-releases/2021/08/record-breaking-vc-investment-in-Fintech-in-first-half-of-2021.html.

Le, M. T. (2021). Examining factors that boost intention and loyalty to use Fintech post-COVID-19 lockdown as a new normal behavior. *Heliyon, 7*(8), e07821.

Lee, H. L., Tang, C. S., Yang, S. A., & Zhang, Y. (2022). Dynamic trade finance in the presence of information frictions and Fintech. *Manufacturing & Service Operations Management.*

Lee, I., & Shin, Y. J. (2018). Fintech: Ecosystem, business models, investment decisions, and challenges. *Business Horizons, 61*(1), 35–46.

Lee, Y. K., Park, J. H., Chung, N., & Blakeney, A. (2012). A unified perspective on the factors influencing usage intention toward mobile financial services. *Journal of Business Research, 65*(11), 1590–1599.

Lim, S. H., Kim, D. J., Hur, Y., & Park, K. (2019). An empirical study of the impacts of perceived security and knowledge on continuous intention to use mobile Fintech payment services. *International Journal of Human-Computer Interaction, 35*(10), 886–898.

Majumder, A.; Goswami, J.; Ghosh, S.; Shrivastava, R.; Mohanty, S. P. & Bhattacharyya, B. K. (2017). Pay-Cloak: A biometric back cover for smartphones: Facilitating secure contactless payments and identity virtualization at low cost to end users. *IEEE Consumer Electronics Magazine, Institute of Electrical and Electronics Engineers (IEEE)*, 6, 78–88.

Markovich, S., Achwal, N., & Queathem, E. (2017). Stripe: Helping money move on the internet. *Kellogg school of management cases.* https://doi.org/10.1108/case.kellogg.2021.000073

Mention, A.-L. (2019). The Future of Fintech. *Research-Technology Management*, 62(4), 59–63. https://doi.org/10.1080/08956308.2019.1613123

Milanovic, N., Milosavljevic, M., & Joksimovic, N. Z. (2021). The emergence of insurtech: A bibliometric survey. In *Economic and social development: Book of proceedings* (pp. 1124–1133). VADEA

Mohamed, H., & Ali, H. (2019). *Blockchain, Fintech, and Islamic finance: Building the future in the new Islamic digital economy.* Walter de Gruyter GmbH and Co KG.

Muda, R., Lateff, M. S. M., Arshad, R., Rashdan, A. A., Oladapo, I. A. and Othman, J. (2021). Does Fintech revolution lead to the disintermediation of banks? A study into Islamic Bank income. In N. Alam and S. Nazim Ali (Eds.) *Fintech, digital currency and the future of Islamic Finance: Strategic, regulatory and adoption issues in the Gulf Cooperation Council* (pp. 169–185). Cham: Springer International Publishing.

Murugeswari, K., Balamurugan, B., & Ganesan, G. (2020). Blockchain and bitcoin security. In G. Shrivastava, D.-N. Le, and K. Sharma (Eds.), *Cryptocurrencies and blockchain technology applications.* https://doi.org/10.1002/9781119621201.ch8

Oseni, U. A., & Ali, S. N. (2019). *Fintech in Islamic finance: Theory and practice* (1st ed.). Routledge. https://doi.org/10.4324/9781351025584

Pimonenko, T., Prokopenko, O., & Dado, J. (2017). Net zero house: EU experience in Ukrainian conditions. *International Journal of Ecological Economics and Statistics*, 38(4), 46–57.

Polasik, M., Widawski, P., & Lis, A. (2021). Challenger bank as a new digital form of providing financial services to retail consumers in the EU Internal Market: The case of Revolut. In *The digitalization of financial markets: The socioeconomic impact of financial technologies* (pp. 175–193). https://doi.org/10.4324/9781003095354-10

Rabbani, M. R. (2022). Fintech innovations, scope, challenges, and implications in Islamic Finance: A systematic analysis. *International Journal of Computing and Digital Systems*, 11(1), 1–28.

Rabbani, M. R., Bashar, A., Nawaz, N., Karim, S., Ali, M. A. M., Rahiman, H. U., & Alam, M. S. (2021a). Exploring the role of islamic fintech in combating the aftershocks of covid-19: The open social innovation of the islamic financial system. *Journal of Open Innovation: Technology, Market, and Complexity*, 7(2). https://doi.org/10.3390/joitmc7020136

Rabbani, M. R., Alshaikh, A., Jreisat, A., Bashar, A., & Moh'd Ali, M. A. (2021b). Whether Cryptocurrency is a threat or a revolution? An analysis from ESG perspective. In *2021 international conference on sustainable Islamic business and finance* (pp. 103–108). IEEE.
Revathy, C., & Balaji, P. (2020). Determinants of behavioural intention on E-wallet usage: An empirical examination in amid of Covid-19 lockdown period. *International Journal of Management, 11*(6), 92–104.
Rossi, A., Vanacker, T. R., & Vismara, S. (2020). *Equity Crowdfunding: New Evidence from US and UK Markets.* https://doi.org/10.2139/ssrn.3752616
Ryu, H.-S., & Ko, K. S. (2020). Sustainable development of Fintech: Focused on uncertainty and perceived quality issues. *Sustainability, 12*(18), 7669. https://doi.org/10.3390/su12187669
Saeed, S. M., Abdeljawad, I., Hassan, M. K., & Rashid, M. (2021). Dependency of Islamic bank rates on conventional rates in a dual banking system: A trade-off between religious and economic fundamentals. *International Review of Economics & Finance.* https://doi.org/10.1016/j.iref.2021.09.013
Sangwan, V., & H., Prakash, P., & Singh, S. (2020). Financial technology: A review of extant literature. *Studies in Economics and Finance, 37*(1), 71–88. https://doi.org/10.1108/SEF-07-2019-0270
Salz, P. A. (2020). Mobile marketing experts show how Fintech apps will emerge fighting fit from the COVID-19 crisis. *Forbes.* https://www.forbes.com/sites/peggyannesalz/2020/05/04/mobile-marketing-experts-show-how-Fintech-apps-will-emerge-fighting-fit-from-the-covid-19-crisis/#4136976c4d50
Schueffel Mname, P. (2016). Taming the beast: A scientific definition of Fintech. *SSRN Electronic Journal, 4*, 32–54. https://doi.org/10.2139/ssrn.3097312
Seiler, V., & Fanenbruck, K. M. (2021). Acceptance of digital investment solutions: The case of robo advisory in Germany. *Research in International Business and Finance, 58*, 101490. https://doi.org/10.1016/j.ribaf.2021.101490
Sharma, S. (2014). The pragmatic review on internet banking and associated services in India. *International Journal of Computing and Corporate Research, 4*(4). http://ijccr.com/index.php/-vol-4-issue-4-july-2014
Shiau, W.-L., Yuan, Y., Pu, X., Ray, S., & Chen, C. C. (2020). Understanding Fintech continuance: Perspectives from self-efficacy and ECT-IS theories. *Industrial Management & Data Systems, 120*(9), 1659–1689. https://doi.org/10.1108/IMDS-02-2020-0069
Statista. (2020). *Digital banking users in the U.S. 2018–2022, by generation.* https://www.statista.com/statistics/946104/digital-banking-users-by-generation-usa/
Talwar, S., Dhir, A., Khalil, A., Mohan, G., & Islam, A. N. (2020). Point of adoption and beyond. Initial trust and mobile-payment continuation intention. *Journal of Retailing and Consumer Services, 55*, 102086.

Tarique, K. M. & Ahmed, M. U. (2021). The direction of future research on i-Fintech. In M. M. S. Billah (Ed.), *Islamic Fintech: Insights and solutions*. Springer.

Thakor, A. V. (2020). Fintech and banking: What do we know? *Journal of Financial Intermediation, 41*, 100833. https://doi.org/10.1016/j.jfi.2019.100833

Wang, X., & Xu, F. (2021). *A theory of Fintech and trade finance*. https://doi.org/10.2139/ssrn.37772

Wigglesworth, R. (January 20, 2016). Fintech: Search for a super-algo. *Financial Times*. https://www.ft.com/content/5eb91614-bee5-11e5-846f-79b0e3d20eaf

Yang, D. F., & Zhang, X. L. (2016). Review of the domestic crowdfunding industry development. *Journal of Service Science and Management, 9*(1), 45–49. https://doi.org/10.4236/jssm.2016.91006

Zavolokina, L., Dolata, M., & Schwabe, G. (2017). Fintech transformation: How IT-enabled innovations shape the financial sector. In S. Feuerriegel and D. Neumann (Eds.), *Enterprise applications, markets and services in the finance industry. Lecture notes in business information processing* (Vol. 276). FinanceCom 2016. Springer. https://doi.org/10.1007/978-3-319-52764-2_6

An Assessment of Level of Adoption of Fintech in Islamic Banks in the MENA Region

M. Kabir Hassan, Somar Al-Mohamed, Mustafa Raza Rabbani, and Ammar Jreisat

1 Introduction

The revolution in financial technology, which is often termed as Fintech, is considered as a conspicuous feature of the contemporaneous technological advancement in this century (Buchak et al., 2018; Hasan et al., 2021; Mackenzie, 2015; Qi & Xiao, 2018). The rise of Fintech has also disrupted the Islamic finance sector as Islamic banks and financial institutions started utilizing a segment of financial technology that adheres to the Shariah principles. It has similar ethics and values of Islamic finance. Islamic finance technology has grown tremendously with a primary focus on peer-to-peer lending and digital financial inclusion.

M. K. Hassan
Department of Economics and Finance, University of New Orleans, New Orleans, LA, USA
e-mail: mhassan@uno.edu

S. Al-Mohamed
Department of Finance, College of Business Administration, American University of the Middle East, Eqaila, Kuwait
e-mail: somar.al-mohamad@aum.edu.kw

© The Author(s), under exclusive license to Springer Nature Switzerland AG 2022
M. K. Hassan et al. (eds.), *FinTech in Islamic Financial Institutions*, https://doi.org/10.1007/978-3-031-14941-2_11

The Fintech market has grown rapidly in MENA region with an annual growth rate of almost 30%. As half of the region's population (almost 200 million) are under the age of 25, the number of Fintech hubs in the region is expected to expand significantly in near future. The level of awareness in financial sector to the unprecedented boost in financial inclusion and digital access has derived banks in MENA region to embrace Fintech-based products and services. Although the scale of Fintech application and adoption still lagged behind in MENA region as compared to developed countries, however there has been an evidence for further increase in Fintech adoption in the region in the wake of the corona pandemic, the adoption of Fintech-based applications enables Islamic banks to reduce their costs in different aspects, for instance, the Islamic banks can reduce the cost of products offering by enhancing Fintech technologies adoption (Alam et al., 2019; Nguyen et al., 2021).

A handful number of academic research on Fintech in Islamic financial institutions has come to the fore in the last few years. Researchers in this field have investigated the implication of Fintech to advance the Islamic finance. The potential benefits of Fintech to the Islamic banking sector in MENA region include funds raising, and wealth management, equity investment, and accounts payments. Additionally, other types of Islamic financial institutions such as investment funds, takaful institutions, and project finance companies also have prospects to benefit from the growing diversity of Fintech. This chapter aims at assessing the potential benefits of adoption on Fintech to Islamic banks' performance in MENA region (Hassan et al., 2020). The use of Fintech in Islamic financial institutions is believed to be imperative to Islamic banks in the region. The adoption of Fintech-based applications enables Islamic banks to reduce their costs and increase their market shares by enhancing the awareness of customers of Islamic finance products and promoting financial inclusion in the region (Hassan et al., 2021; Rabbani et al., 2021d).

M. R. Rabbani · A. Jreisat (✉)
Department of Economics and Finance, College of Business Administration, University of Bahrain, Zallaq, Kingdom of Bahrain
e-mail: abarham@uob.edu.bh

M. R. Rabbani
e-mail: mrabbani@uob.edu.bh

The chapter aims to contribute to the academic literature on Fintech in Islamic financial institutions in the following ways. First, this chapter provides evidence on the imperativeness of Fintech to Islamic financial sector, in general, and the Islamic banking sector, in particular, in the MENA region. Second, the chapter sheds light on the level of readiness of the financial infrastructure in the MENA region for further incorporation of the Fintech with the Islamic banking activities. Third, the chapter assesses the potential opportunities for Islamic banks in the MENA region to enhance financial inclusion of the unbanked population in the MENA region, and to facilitate and promote social finance to alleviate the repercussions of potential financial and non-financial crises.

Remaining chapter proceeds as follows: Section 2 provides an overview of Fintech and its core technologies. Section 3 introduces the concept of Fintech in Islamic financial institutions and displays the interconnectedness among Fintech technologies and Islamic finance. Section 4 discusses Fintech in Islamic finance sector in the MENA region. Section 5 evaluates the level of Fintech adoption by Islamic financial institutions and its benefits to Islamic banks in the MENA region. Section 6 concludes the chapter.

2 The Rise of Financial Technology (Fintech)

The revolution in financial technology is considered as a main conspicuous feature of the contemporaneous technological advancement in this century (Khan et al., 2022). The ascending trajectory of financial technology (Fintech) is mainly propelled by the enhancement in high-speed internet connections and the noticeable increase in mobile applications among youth who became magnificent gurus of technological innovations (Arslan et al., 2021; Mackenzie, 2015; Zavolokina et al., 2016). The use of technology in financial services industry has gone through gradual stratums of improvements, starting with computers networks and ATMs, until a comprehensive digital transformation of financial products and services that helps financial institutions and banks deliver their products to their customers in faster and more efficient means than the past (Bashar & Rabbani, 2021; Rabbani et al., 2021e). Fintech is the lucid marriage of finance and technology that provides more personalized and cheaper services and offerings to individuals and businesses (Ernst & Newswire, 2016; Young, 2019). Among other ramifications, the digital financial inclusion (DFI) has come to the fore as a main aspect of the

Fintech. The DOI democratizes the accessibility of financial services by enabling unbanked population, mainly adults due to lack of sufficient documentations, lack of purchasing power, and inaccessibility of financial institutions in their geographic areas (Mahalle et al., 2021; Omodero, 2021).

The evolution of contemporaneous Fintech has also brought a variety of benefits to business enterprises. There is unanimity among business participants and research scholars alike on the impact of Fintech on enhancing the capital availability for emerging enterprises and entrepreneurs, also, it helps reducing the cost of intermediation among sources and uses of money and this leads to faster movement of capital from savers to users of funds. The Fintech has recently gained an increased traction of different types of businesses, who initially considered it as a threat, since it provides opportunities to financial services providers to look up for potential partnership opportunities to enhance customer relationships through the thriving business to customer (B2C) financial services ecosystem (Meero et al., 2021). The Fintech also promotes an automation of different business activities, and this leads to lower the customer service costs due to less physical presence is required (Ernst and Moccia et al., 2018; Young, 2019). Moreover, the Fintech paves the road for smooth and correct direction of venture capitals to fuel new start-up businesses, especially in countries with inefficient and shallow financial systems, as it can support rural areas and low-income households (Demirguc-Kunt et al., 2018). The current framework of the global Fintech encompasses nine core technologies divided up into three main categories of disintermediation leading to open access to services, automation from insights to activity, and the decentralization and security (World Bank, 2020). According to The World Bank Group, the core technologies of global Fintech can be summarized as per Table 1:

In fact, Fintech can be thought of as an umbrella under which a diverse range of platforms exists. The most prevalent services offered for both individuals and businesses can be summarized as:

- Crowdfunding, lending, and peer-to-peer platforms that enable money transfer (borrow/lend) among savers and users of funds through a wide variety of internet applications (Kontogiannidis et al., 2017; The World Bank, 2013).
- Subscription billing software (such as Uber and Netflix), and payment processing system (such as Stipes, Pay Tabs, and PayPal).

Table 1 Overview of the nine core Fintech technologies

Core Fintech technology	Description	Category
Big Data Analytics	The process of reading, checking, and analyzing data stored on the internet (server). It includes every click for online transactions (Sun et al., 2020)	Category 1: Disintermediation leading to open access to services
Artificial Intelligence	A machine education technology in which the human teaches robots to handle different activities starting with daily personal an arriving to anti money laundering duties (Khan & Rabbani, 2020)	
Quantum Computing	Utilizes the principles of quantum theory to create more advanced computer software's power. It enables solving more complex problems than the ones solved by convectional PCs (Rabbani et al., 2021a)	
Mobile Payment	Payment using mobile applications and technologies to access bank personal and business bank accounts, and execute convectional transactions anytime and anywhere if they have internet connections (Kim et al., 2016; Liu et al., 2020)	Category 2: Automation from insights to activity
P2P Finance	Peer-to-peer finance enables through specific websites where lenders have direct connection with borrowers. This technology is considered as an alternative to traditional banking activities (Rabbani et al., 2022a, 2022b, 2021c)	

(continued)

Table 1 (continued)

Core Fintech technology	Description	Category
Open Banking	A technological innovation that enables banks' customers to monitor their cash flows through third-party application (Open Banking Implementation Entity, 2019)	
Blockchain	Blockchain is a digital ledger of transactions and recording information. The data sequence is disseminated to global servers for decentralization and cross-verification check (Karim et al., 2022)	Category 3: Decentralization and security
Cybersecurity	Specific data protection technology that aims at protecting the privacy of all users (Bendovschi, 2015; Rehman et al., 2020)	
Cloud Adoption	A storage system used to upload and retrieve data (Hu et al., 2019)	

- Regulatory Compliance Software (RegTech): to monitor the businesses compliance with regulatory requirements and standards (such as anti-money laundering, detection, and fraud screening) (Rabbani et al., 2021b).
- Investment management and stock trading applications: which enables less experienced investors to execute, relatively inexpensive, transactions and increase their participation in financial markets (e.g. Alvexo, and etoro) (Marcelin et al., 2019; Mishra, 2007).
- InsurTech: enables insurance companies to offer digital insurance policies tailored to fit specific market segments such as low-income households.

3 Imperatives of Fintech Technologies to Islamic Finance

The Fintech in Islamic financial institutions is a segment of financial technology that obey to the Sharia law. It has the same ethics and values of Islamic finance. The Fintech adoption and utilization by Islamic institutions has experienced a high level of growth in recent years, the main advantages of Islamic Fintech are enhancing financial inclusion transparency, and accessibility and usage, and cost effectives. The Fintech in Islamic financial institutions can be categorized as a division of Fintech that enables and facilitates all activities and transactions that adhere to Sharia principles (Hassan et al., 2020, 2021). It comprises a variety of markets and sectors such as Islamic banking, Sukuk market, Takaful, and Islamic capital market. The value of Islamic finance assets is expected to reach USD $3.5 trillion in 2024 as compared to USD 2.5 trillion in 2018 (World Bank, 2020). Fintech is expected to promote the application of Islamic finance and enhance the awareness of the investment society to Islamic finance products. Briefly, the essential contribution of Fintech technology to Islamic financial industry can be categorized into three core divisions: First, a group of Fintech technologies focuses on decentralization and security including the cloud-based and blockchain. Second, the Big Data and Artificial Intelligence technologies that promote automation of Islamic finance products (Sun et al., 2020). Last, the Fintech technologies focus on disintermediation for open access of mobile banking and P2P finance. Consequently, there are potentials for increase in availability and market share of Islamic financial products and services including wealth management, Takaful, enterprises funding, and trade finance.

A handful number of academic research on FinTech in Islamic financial institutions has come to the fore in the last few years. A main strand in literature has also investigated the implication of Fintech technologies to advance the Islamic finance. For instance, Abojeib and Habib (2021), provided evidence of the importance of Fintech, blockchain particularly, on improving the mechanism through which the charitable utility of waqf. Elasrag (2016), recommended the utilization of smart contracts to enhance the compliance of the Islamic financial products and services with Sharia law. Gomber et al. (2018), affirmed on the role of Fintech in advancement of transparency and customer-centric of Islamic finance products. Todorof (2019), investigated whether Fintech technologies comply with Sharia principles, and he concludes that the adoption of

Fintech by Islamic banks could enhance the efficiency of their products and services and increase their market shares. In a different work, Suzuki et al. (2018), critically examined the dynamic changes in SWOT analysis dimension in Islamic banks in Indonesia following the Fintech adoption. They find that Fintech technologies will, surely, enhance the quality of Islamic banks' activities including customer relationship management. A growing stratum of literature assessed the potential advantages of blockchain utilization for Islamic finance. Fernandez-Vazquez et al. (2019), evaluated the role of blockchain in leveraging the usage Islamic finance products in crises periods. They conclude that blockchain enables for swift and more efficient collection of *Zakat* and *Sadaqah* money to provide social aids during pandemics and crises. Richard-Marc et al. (2017), affirmed on the potential role of blockchain in enhancing the transparency in the Islamic financial system, especially for Islamic banks contracts and operations. Isik and Uygur (2021), investigated the possibility of blockchain technology utilization to initiate a digital Islamic currency that complies with Sharia law. Habib and Ahmad (2019) studied the potential impact of blockchain on enhancing the Waqf institutions' performance, their study proposed that blockchain could enhance the image and efficiency of the Islamic Waqf institutions. Elasrag (2012), highlighted the main challenges for blockchain usages in the context of Islamic finance. The study concluded that the technical and legal obstacles represent main obstacles for the blockchain application in Islamic financial products and services. Wulan et al. (2018), shed the light on the potential application of Fintech technologies to improve the *Zakat* collection process. They claim that the digital collection of *Zakat* through Fintech technologies can enhance the collection process, in addition to ensuring the efficiency of *Zakat* distribution. Analogously, Yahaya and Ahmad (2019), proposed that Fintech enables for digital collection, allocation, and distribution of zakat money. The use of mobile banking is also believed to be an efficient and transparent means for zakat collection and distribution (Yahaya et al., 2019).

An emerging strand in literature investigates the applicability and importance of different aspects of Fintech technology to Islamic finance topics, for instance, Abdullah and Oseni (2017), investigate the advantage of combining the crowdfunding and Halal industry in Malaysia. They found that further improvements are needed toward making the equity-based crowdfunding more compliant with Sharia principles. Fatturroyhan (2018), on the other hand found that Fintech platform can be utilized to advance "Mudarabah" that represents the Islamic implication of crowdfunding to provide solutions for lack of funds among SMEs in Islamic financial system. In a different work, Miskam and Eksan (2018), investigated the potential utilization of the Bog Data technology by Islamic financial institutions to enhance the decision-making process. They found that Big Data can improve the decision-making by better understanding of consumer habits and market trends. Lajis (2019), also provided evidence on the impact of Fintech-based platform on enhancing the risk sharing aspects in the Islamic financial model. Similar results were reported by Manaf and binti Amiruddin (2019), who found that Fintech technology can improve the financial performance of Takaful companies in Malaysia.

4 Overview of Fintech in Islamic Financial Institutions in Middle East and North Africa (MENA) Region

Over the last few years, the Fintech market has grown significantly in MENA region. The financial systems in the region are marked by the dominance of banking sector in general. The financial markets in the MENA region are at their early stage in many countries, with exception of countries with well-established stock and bond markets such as Egypt, Kuwait, Morocco, and Saudi Arabia (Allen, 2021). These factors make the MENA region a fertile destination for Fintech applications, accompanied by the rising number of start-ups and high number of youths as a percentage of total population (Chinnasamy et al., 2021; Kammoun et al., 2019; Loukil et al., 2021; Wang et al., 2021). The financial inclusion in the region is historically limited to large or state-owned companies, and this was to the detriment of small and medium enterprises and deterred them from good access to formal types of finance such as bank loans and lines of credit (Demir et al., 2020; Kandpal & Mehrotra, 2019). The adoption of Fintech in MENA region is heavily dependent of the countries' readiness for Fintech technologies' infrastructure as well as the magnitude of Islamic financial capital and current legal frameworks (Chinnasamy et al., 2021). To compare, there is a prevalent clue on advancement of GCC countries in the region to adopt Islamic Fintech as compared to non-GCC ones. For instance, UAE, Bahrain, Saudi Arabia, and Qatar are more equipped than other MENA countries with proper regulatory environment, capital availability, and long-established financial sector with upgraded ranking in Global Competitive indicators (Meero et al., 2021). The Fintech in Islamic financial institutions is believed to be imperative to the MEAN region as it is expected to carry promising improvements in the following areas:

Financial Inclusion

The increased digitalization of Islamic products and services will give access for individuals and small enterprises for cheaper and more Sharia compliant sources of finance including the financing platforms such as private equity, venture capital, peer-to-peer financing, and crowdfunding. According to the Arab Monetary Fund (2021), there are almost 13 million startup companies suffer from financial shortages, in addition to approximately 140 million adults are financially excluded in the Arab region. As such, the Fintech-based Islamic financial products and services have an immense opportunity to fill this gap by enhancing the financial inclusion and capital accessibility in the region (Demir et al., 2020; Kandpal & Mehrotra, 2019; Kim et al., 2018).

Islamic Social Finance

In the wake of COVID-19 pandemic, the financial innovations and technological advancements have been notoriously important for addressing and handling the issues pertinent to social aids, administration, and collection (Bashar et al., 2021; Rabbani et al., 2022a, 2022b). Also, the mobilization of social funds provided by Islamic institutions such as *sadaqah, Zakat, and awqaf* has grown tremendously in MENA region to support individuals and families who were standing in need for these supports. The Fintech in Islamic financial institutions is expected to play a key role in alleviating the repercussions of future financial, health, or other crises (Hamidi & Worthington, 2017; Syed Azman & Engku Ali, 2019).

Improve Regulations and Promote Transparency

The MENA region has been historically marked by its tenuous legal financial infrastructure. There was a lack of unanimity on the degree of financial transparency and crony over the last decades. The regulatory authorities in the MENA region should assiduously attempt to enhance the legal infrastructure that falls within the ambit of digital finance. The adoption of advanced and standardized Islamic financial products and services would be of great help to regulatory authorities in the MENA region to enhance the integrity and stability of financial transactions through promoting Fintech-related regulations pertinent to electronic banking, pre-paid cards, crowdfunding, cyber-security monitoring, cloud computing sandboxes, and outsourcing (Buchak et al., 2018; Jagtiani & John, 2018; Rabbani et al., 2021a).

5 Fintech in Islamic Financial Institutions and Banking Industry in MENA Region

The Islamic banking sector in MENA region is dominated by private sector. They operate along with conventional commercial banks and financial institutions. The most developed Islamic banking sectors among MENA countries are mainly located in UAE, Bahrain, Kuwait, Saudi Arabia, and Qatar. The banking activities in this sector are compliant with Sharia principles and include investments financing, and trading. The adoption of Fintech-based applications enables Islamic banks to reduce their costs in different aspects, for instance, the Islamic banks can reduce the cost of products offered by enhancing Fintech technologies adoption (Rabbani et al., 2021a, 2021b, 2021c, 2021d, 2021e; Rabbani, 2022). The Big Data solution could enable this sector for better funds allocation in one hand, the Big Data can also enhance the banks awareness of customers' preferences of various types of Fintech services on the other hand. However, the incorporation of Fintech technology with the Islamic banking activities in MENA region would require more improvement of legal structure and increase the financial inclusion on the non-banked population (Allen, 2021; Chinnasamy et al., 2021; Kukreja et al., 2021). The potential opportunities for Islamic banking sector in MENA region include, but not limited to, the following areas:

- Saving and Deposit Accounts

The nature and specifications of accounts and contracts in Islamic finance are different from their counterparts of traditional commercial banking sectors. In traditional Fintech banking, the current accounts for instance are used through smart phones application to pay for daily expenses. On the other hand, funds deposited in Islamic banking accounts need to be invested in profit sharing model. As such, an investment account contract is required with collaboration of both investors and financial institutions through which the funds can be transferred to small and medium enterprises. The IAP (Investment Account Platform) in Malaysia represents a good example for Islamic bank's adoption of Fintech Technology. Islamic banks also have opportunities to attract funds through credit associations and savings rotations, in which a group of entities contributes periodic payments to a special Islamic saving scheme offered by Islamic banks (Hasan et al., 2020; Saba et al., 2019). The contributions are then pooled and directed to SMEs of start-ups periodically. "el Gameya" in Egypt, is a clear example of this financing mechanism.

- Equity Investment and Wealth Management

The Islamic banking sector in MENA countries has a potential opportunity to provide their customers with investment advice pertinent to Sharia compliant equities for long-term investment purposes. Through their bank-specific mobile applications, Islamic banks can enhance the customer's awareness and accessibility to appropriate Islamic financial instruments. The Robo advisor application offered by Wahed Invest enables customers from over 100 countries to access investment instruments that are supervised by the Shariah Review Board. In MENA, "Sarwa" in UAE is one of the few Islamic Fintech investment advisor platforms that offer Sharia compliant investment alternatives (Thiele, 2017).

- Accounts and Payments

The Sharia law prohibits interest charges on accounts. Islamic banks have an opportunity to offer an interest-free account to their clients with electronic debit bank cards from international providers such as Master cards and Visa. These cards can be used and controlled via smart phone applications for seamless access and transfer of money. In UK, the *Niyah and RIZQ* are digital Islamic banks that offer e-debit cards to customers issued by Master cards and Visa. There are very few digital banks in MENA region now, with few exceptions such as the digital Islamic bank initiated by Zurich Capital Funds Group (Ismon, 2012; Mokni et al., 2016; Naz & Gulzar, 2020). Hence, Islamic bans in MENA are required to initiate the evolution of digitalization of their banking institutions with complete online platforms to enhance the digital financial inclusion of unbacked population in MENA region.

6 Conclusion

The Islamic financial industry is one of the most rapidly expanding divisions of the global financial sector. When it comes to global social financing needs, it is becoming increasingly important. Technology and automation have long been important aspects of global financial services. Fintech (financial technology) has been undergoing a technological revolution in the financial sector over the last few years. The artificial intelligence, blockchain technology, robotics, and other developing technologies have all gradually made their way into the world in recent years. There is little doubt that these developments will have an impact on the Islamic banking sector. The MENA region is a fertile destination for Fintech applications, accompanied by the rising number of start-ups and high number of youths as a percentage of total population. The adoption of Fintech in Islamic financial institutions in the MENA region is heavily dependent of the countries' readiness for Fintech technologies' infrastructure as well as the magnitude of Islamic financial capital and current legal frameworks. The Fintech in Islamic financial institutions enables the Islamic banking sector in MENA countries to gain the opportunity to provide their customers with investment advice pertinent to Sharia compliant equities for long-term investment purposes.

References

Abdullah, S., & Oseni, U. A. (2017). Towards a sharī'ah compliant equity-based crowdfunding for the halal industry in Malaysia. *International Journal of Business and Society*, *18*(S1), 223–240. https://www.scopus.com/inward/record.uri?eid=2-s2.0-85032496111&partnerID=40&md5=6be491893722ce73c9fed2aa1b0a7dd4

Abojeib, M., & Habib, F. (2021). Blockchain for Islamic social responsibility institutions. In *Research anthology on blockchain technology in business, healthcare, education, and government* (pp. 1114–1128). IGI Global.

Alam, N., Gupta, L., & Zameni, A. (2019). Fintech and Islamic finance: Digitalization, development and disruption. In *Fintech and Islamic finance: Digitalization, development and disruption*. Springer. https://doi.org/10.1007/978-3-030-24666-2

Allen, F. (2021). *Globalization of finance and Fintech in the MENA region*.

Arab Monetary Fund. (2021, November). *Islamic fintech in the Arab region: Imperatives, challenges, and the way forward*. Arab Regional Fintech Working Paper No. 173.

Arslan, A., Buchanan, B. G., Kamara, S., & Al Nabulsi, N. (2021). Fintech, base of the pyramid entrepreneurs and social value creation. *Journal of Small Business and Enterprise Development*. https://doi.org/10.1108/JSBED-10-2020-0370

Bashar, A., & Rabbani, M. R. (2021). Exploring the role of web personalization in consumer green purchasing behavior: A conceptual framework. In *2021 third international sustainability and resilience conference: Climate change* (pp. 23–28). (Online).

Bashar, A., Rabbani, M., Khan, S., & Ali, M. A. M. (2021). Data driven finance: A bibliometric review and scientific mapping. In *2021 international conference on data analytics for business and industry (ICDABI)* (pp. 161–166). (Online).

Bendovschi, A. (2015). Cyber-attacks: Trends, patterns and security countermeasures. *Procedia Economics and Finance*. https://doi.org/10.1016/s2212-5671(15)01077-1

Buchak, G., Matvos, G., Piskorski, T., & Seru, A. (2018). Fintech, regulatory arbitrage, and the rise of shadow banks. *Journal of Financial Economics*, 130(3), 453–483. https://doi.org/10.1016/j.jfineco.2018.03.011

Chinnasamy, G., Madbouly, A., & Reyad, S. (2021). Fintech: A pathway for MENA region. In *Studies in computational intelligence* (Vol. 935, pp. 135–151). Springer. https://doi.org/10.1007/978-3-030-62796-6_7

Demir, A., Pesqué-Cela, V., Altunbas, Y., & Murinde, V. (2020). Fintech, financial inclusion and income inequality: A quantile regression approach. *European Journal of Finance*. https://doi.org/10.1080/1351847X.2020.1772335

Demirguc-Kunt, A., Klapper, L., Singer, D., Ansar, S., & Hess, J. (2018). The global findex database 2017: Measuring financial inclusion and the Fintech revolution. In *The global findex database 2017: Measuring financial inclusion and the Fintech revolution*. https://doi.org/10.1596/978-1-4648-1259-0

Elasrag, H. (2012). Principals of the Islamic finance: A focus on project finance. *SSRN Electronic Journal*. https://doi.org/10.2139/ssrn.1806305

Elasrag, H. (2016). Islamic finance for SMES. *SSRN Electronic Journal*. https://doi.org/10.2139/ssrn.2842160

Ernst & Young. (2019). *Global FinTech adoption index 2019*. Ernst & Young.

Fatturroyhan, F. (2018). Go-Mudaraba: The solution of poverty and unemployment in the digital era. In *3rd international conference of integrated intellectual community (ICONIC)*, Hannover, Germany.

Fernandez-Vazquez, S., Rosillo, R., De La Fuente, D., & Priore, P. (2019). Blockchain in FinTech: A mapping study. *Sustainability (Switzerland)*, *11*(22). https://Doi.org/10.3390/su11226366

Gomber, P., Kauffman, R. J., Parker, C., & Weber, B. W. (2018). On the Fintech revolution: Interpreting the forces of innovation, disruption, and transformation in financial services. *Journal of Management Information Systems*, *35*(1), 220–265. https://doi.org/10.1080/07421222.2018.1440766

Habib, F., & Ahmad, A. U. F. (2019). Using blockchain and smart contracts for waqf institutions. *Financial technology and disruptive innovation is ASEAN* (pp. 225–244). IGI Global.

Hamidi, M. L., & Worthington, A. C. (2017). Islamic banking plus social banking equals Islamic social banking: An equation in the making. In *Banking: services, opportunities and risks* (pp. 15–39). Nova Science. https://www.scopus.com/inward/record.uri?eid=2-s2.0-85044061698&partnerID=40&md5=969290cdc2037aaa047d37a7835dce10

Hasan, R., Ashfaq, M., & Shao, L. (2021). Evaluating drivers of fintech adoption in the Netherlands. *Global Business Review*. https://doi.org/10.1177/09721509211027402

Hasan, R., Hassan, M. K., & Aliyu, S. (2020). Fintech and Islamic finance: Literature review and research agenda. *International Journal of Islamic Economics and Finance*, *1*(2), 75–94. https://doi.org/10.18196/ijief.2122

Hassan, M. K., Rabbani, M. R., & Ali, M. A. (2020). Challenges for the Islamic finance and banking in post COVID era and the role of Fintech. *Journal of Economic Cooperation and Development*, *43*(3), 93–116.

Hassan, M. K., Rabbani, M. R., & Abdullah, Y. (2021). Socioeconomic impact of COVID-19 in MENA region and the role of Islamic finance. *International Journal of Islamic Economics and Finance*, *4*(1), 51–78.

Hu, Z., Ding, S., Li, S., Chen, L., & Yang, S. (2019). Adoption intention of fintech services for bank users: An empirical examination with an extended technology acceptance model. *Symmetry*, *11*(3). https://doi.org/10.3390/sym11030340

Isik, I., & Uygur, O. (2021). Financial crises, bank efficiency and survival: Theory, literature and emerging market evidence. *International Review of Economics and Finance*, *76*, 952–987. https://doi.org/10.1016/j.iref.2021.07.016

Ismon, N. Y. (2012). Legality of Tawarruq in Islamic finance. *Tazkia Islamic Finance and Business Review*, *7*(1), 81–108.

Jagtiani, J., & John, K. (2018). Fintech: The impact on consumers and regulatory responses. *Journal of Economics and Business, 100*, 1–6. https://doi.org/10.1016/j.jeconbus.2018.11.002

Kammoun, S., Loukil, S., & Loukil, Y. B. R. (2019). The impact of fintech on economic performance and financial stability in mena zone. In *Impact of financial technology (FinTech) on Islamic finance and financial stability* (pp. 253–275). IGI Global. https://doi.org/10.4018/978-1-7998-0039-2.ch013

Kandpal, V., & Mehrotra, R. (2019). Financial inclusion: The role of fintech and digital financial services in India. *Indian Journal of Economics and Business, 18*(1), 95–104. https://www.scopus.com/inward/record.uri?eid=2-s2.0-85078895210&partnerID=40&md5=9e64e01e4a9fa4ca88ba1291b319ad9d

Karim, S., Rabbani, M. R., & Bawazir, H. (2022). Applications of blockchain technology in the finance and banking industry beyond digital currencies. In *Blockchain technology and computational excellence for society 5.0* (pp. 216–238). IGI Global.

Khan, S., & Rabbani, M. R. (2020). In depth analysis of blockchain, cryptocurrency and Sharia compliance. *International Journal of Business Innovation and Research, 1*(1), 1. https://doi.org/10.1504/ijbir.2020.10033066

Khan, M. S., Rabbani, M. R., Hawaldar, I. T., & Bashar, A. (2022). Determinants of behavioral intentions to use Islamic financial technology: An empirical assessment. *Risks, 10*(6), 114.

Kim, D. W., Yu, J. S., & Hassan, M. K. (2018). Financial inclusion and economic growth in OIC countries. *Research in International Business and Finance.* https://doi.org/10.1016/j.ribaf.2017.07.178

Kim, Y., Choi, J., Park, Y.-J., & Yeon, J. (2016). The adoption of mobile payment services for "fintech." *International Journal of Applied Engineering Research, 11*(2), 1058–1061. https://www.scopus.com/inward/record.uri?eid=2-s2.0-84959530641&partnerID=40&md5=01ffedcecd6b6f0ccc874643fa172510

Kontogiannidis, P., Theriou, G., & Sarigiannidis, L. (2017). Crowdfunding: Exploring the factors associated with the users' intention to finance a project online. *International Journal of Web Based Communities, 13*(1), 73–101. https://doi.org/10.1504/IJWBC.2017.082721

Kukreja, G., Gupta, R., & Gupta, A. (2021). Fintech in oman: Present and future scenario. In *Studies in computational intelligence* (Vol. 954, pp. 173–183). Springer. https://doi.org/10.1007/978-3-030-72080-3_10

Lajis, S. M. (2019). Fintech and risk-sharing: A catalyst for islamic finance. In *Islamic finance, risk-sharing and macroeconomic stability* (pp. 237–254). Palgrave Macmillan. https://doi.org/10.1007/978-3-030-05225-6-12

Liu, T., Pan, B., & Yin, Z. (2020). Pandemic, mobile payment, and household consumption: Micro-evidence from China. *Emerging Markets Finance and*

Trade, 56(10), 2378–2389. https://doi.org/10.1080/1540496X.2020.178 8539

Loukil, Y. B. R., Kammoun, S., & Loukil, S. (2021). Fintech development, digital infrastructure and institutions in the MENA Zone. In *Financial and economic systems: Transformations and new challenges* (pp. 481–506). World Scientific Publishing Co. https://doi.org/10.1142/9781786349507_0017

Mackenzie, A. (2015). The Fintech revolution. *London Business School Review, 26*(3), 50–53. https://doi.org/10.1111/2057-1615.12059

Mahalle, A., Yong, J., & Tao, X. (2021). Regulatory challenges and mitigation for account services offered by FinTech. In *24th IEEE international conference on computer supported cooperative work in design, CSCWD 2021* (pp. 280–287). Institute of Electrical and Electronics Engineers Inc. https://doi.org/10.1109/CSCWD49262.2021.9437631

Manaf, A. W. A., & Binti Amiruddin, N. (2019). Fintech and the challenge of digital disruption in takaful operation. *Asia Proceedings of Social Sciences, 4*(1), 1–3.

Marcelin, I., Stephen, S.-A.K., Fanta, F., & Tecklezion, M. (2019). Political regimes, investment and electoral uncertainty. *Research in International Business and Finance, 47*, 580–599. https://doi.org/10.1016/j.ribaf.2018.10.003

Meero, A., Rahiman, H. U., & Rahman, A. A. A. (2021). The prospects of Bahrain's entrepreneurial ecosystem: An exploratory approach. *Problems and Perspectives in Management, 18*(4), 402.

Mishra, A. V. (2007). International investment patterns: Evidence using a new dataset. *Research in International Business and Finance, 21*(2), 342–360. https://doi.org/10.1016/j.ribaf.2006.09.002

Miskam, S., & Eksan, S. H. R. (2018). Big Data and Fintech in Islamic finance: Prospects and challenges. In *4th Muzakarah Fiqh and international Fiqh conference (MFIFC 2018)*, Malaysia.

Moccia, S., Passerini, K., & Tomic, I. (2018). Fintech: Challenges, drivers, and future opportunities. *Cutter Business Technology Journal, 31*(11–12), 6–11. https://www.scopus.com/inward/record.uri?eid=2-s2.0-85064404797&partnerID=40&md5=e3909c43b06c2bb469d7f0f08d2c1ec0

Mokni, R. B. S., Rajhi, M. T., & Rachdi, H. (2016). Bank risk-taking in the MENA region: A comparison between Islamic banks and conventional banks. *International Journal of Social Economics, 43*(12), 1367–1385. https://doi.org/10.1108/IJSE-03-2015-0050

Naz, S. A., & Gulzar, S. (2020). Impact of Islamic finance on economic growth: An empirical analysis of muslim countries. *Singapore Economic Review.* https://doi.org/10.1142/S0217590819420062

Newswire, P. R. (2016). *Global FinTech investment market 2016–2020.* Lon-Reportbuyer.

Nguyen, L., Tran, S., & Ho, T. (2021). Fintech credit, bank regulations and bank performance: A cross-country analysis. *Asia-Pacific Journal of Business Administration*. https://doi.org/10.1108/APJBA-05-2021-0196

Omodero, C. O. (2021). Fintech innovation in the financial sector: Influence of E-money products on a growing economy. *Studia Universitatis Vasile Goldis Arad, Economics Series*, 31(4), 40–53. https://doi.org/10.2478/sues-2021-0018

Open Banking Implementation Entity. (2019). *Open banking, preparing for lift off*. The Open Data Institute.

Qi, B. Y., & Xiao, J. (2018). Fintech: AI powers financial services to improve people's lives. *Communications of the ACM*, 61(11), 65–69. https://doi.org/10.1145/3239550

Rabbani, M. R., Abdullah, Y., Bashar, A., Khan, S., & Ali, M. A. M. (2020). Embracing of Fintech in Islamic finance in the post COVID era. in *2020 International Conference on Decision Aid Sciences and Application (DASA)*, (pp. 1230–1234) Sakheer, Bahrain, 2020.https://doi.org/10.1109/DASA51403.2020.9317196

Rabbani, M. R., Bashar, A., Atif, M., Jreisat, A., Zulfikar, Z., & Naseem, Y. (2021a). Text mining and visual analytics in research: Exploring the innovative tools. In *2021 International Conference on Decision Aid Sciences and Application (DASA)* (pp. 1087–1091). IEEE. https://doi.org/10.1109/DASA53625.2021.9682360

Rabbani, M. R., Jreisat, A., AlAbbas, A., Bashar, A., & Ali, M. A. M. (2021b). Whether Cryptocurrency is a threat or a revolution? An ESG perspective. In *2021 international conference on sustainable Islamic business and finance (SIBF)*. (Online).

Rabbani, M. R., Ali, M. A. M., Rahiman, H., Atif, M., Zulfikar, Z., & Naseem, Y. (2021c). The response of Islamic financial service to the Covid-19 pandemic: The Open Social Innovation of financial system. *Journal of Open Innovation: Technology, Market, and Complexity*, 7(1), 85. https://doi.org/10.3390/joitmc7010085

Rabbani, M. R., Bashar, A., Nawaz, N., Karim, S., Ali, M. A. M., Khan, A., Rahiman, H., & Alam, S. (2021d). Exploring the role of Islamic Fintech in combating the after-shocks of COVID-19: The open social innovation of the Islamic financial system. *Journal of Open Innovation: Technology, Market, and Complexity*, 7, 136.

Rabbani, M. R., Sarea, A., Khan, S., & Abdullah, Y. (2021e). Ethical concerns in artificial intelligence (AI): The role of RegTech and Islamic finance. In *The international conference on global economic revolutions* (pp. 381–390).

Rabbani, M. R. (2022). Fintech innovations, scope, challenges, and implications in Islamic Finance: A systematic analysis. *International Journal of Computing and Digital Systems*, 11(1), 1–28.

Rabbani, M. R., Khan, S., & Atif, M. (2022a). Machine learning based P2P lending Islamic FinTech model for small and medium enterprises (SMEs) in Bahrain. *International Journal of Business Innovation and Research* (in press)..

Rabbani, M. R., Kayani, U., Bawazir, H. S., & Hawaldar, I. T. (2022b). A commentary on emerging markets banking sector spillovers: Covid-19 vs GFC pattern analysis. *Heliyon, 8*(3), e09074.

Rehman, M. M. U., Rehman, H. Z. U., & Khan, Z. H. (2020). Cyber-attacks on medical implants: A case study of cardiac pacemaker vulnerability. *International Journal of Computing and Digital Systems, 9*(6), 1229–1235. https://doi.org/10.12785/ijcds/0906020

Richard-Marc, L., Berthe, L., & Nida, K. (2017). *Blockchain technology-Arsenal for a Shariah-compliant financial ecosystem?* Université du Québec, Canada Berthe Lambert Université du Québec, Canada Nida Khan Université du Luxembourg, Luxembourg.

Saba, I., Kouser, R., & Sharif Chaudhry, I. (2019). Fintech and Islamic finance-challenges and opportunities. *Review of Economics and Development Studies, 5*(4), 581–590. https://doi.org/10.26710/reads.v5i4.887

Sun, H., Rabbani, M. R., Sial, M. S., Yu, S., Filipe, J. A., & Cherian, J. (2020). Identifying big data's opportunities, challenges, and implications in finance. *Mathematics, 8*(10). https://doi.org/10.3390/math8101738

Suzuki, Y., Hasan, A. K. M. K., & Pramono, S. (2018). Anatomy of Islamic venture capital: Typology of Bahraini/Indonesian Islamic venture capital. In *Dilemmas and challenges in Islamic Finance: Looking at equity and microfinance*. Taylor and Francis. https://doi.org/10.1201/9781315105673

Syed Azman, S. M. M., & Engku Ali, E. R. A. (2019). *Islamic social finance and the imperative for social impact measurement*. ISTAC.

The World Bank. (2013). *Crowdfunding's potential for the developing world. Finance and Private Sector Development Department*. The World Bank.

The World Bank. (2020, October). Leveraging Islamic FINTECH to improve financial conclusion. *Inclusive growth & sustainable finance, hub in Malaysia*.

Thiele, F. K. (2017). Family businesses and non-family equity: Literature review and avenues for future research. *Management Review Quarterly, 67*(1), 31–63. https://doi.org/10.1007/s11301-017-0123-5

Todorof, M. (2019). FinTech on the Dark Web: the rise of cryptos. *ERA Forum, 20*(1). https://doi.org/10.1007/s12027-019-00556-y

Wang, X., Sadiq, R., Khan, T. M., & Wang, R. (2021). Industry 4.0 and intellectual capital in the age of FinTech. *Technological Forecasting and Social Change, 166*. https://doi.org/10.1016/j.techfore.2021.120598

Wulan, M., Khairunnisa, H., & Bahri, E. S. (2018). Internal audit role in digital Zakat finance: Case study at a Zakat Institution in Indonesia. In *International conference of Zakat*. Zakat Institution in Indonesia.

Yahaya, M. H., & Ahmad, K. (2019). Factors affecting the acceptance of financial technology among asnaf for the distribution of zakat in Selangor-A Study Using UTAUT. *Journal of Islamic Finance, 8*, 35–46.

Zavolokina, L., Dolata, M., & Schwabe, G. (2016). FinTech: What's in a name? In *2016 international conference on information systems, ICIS 2016*. https://www.scopus.com/inward/record.uri?eid=2-s2.0-85011313931&partnerID=40&md5=151a0787ac5465c74ac6853ad3cf9027

Fintech, Pandemic, and the Islamic Financial System: Innovative Financial Services and Its *Shariah* Compliance

M. Kabir Hassan, Mustafa Raza Rabbani, Ammar Jreisat, and Muhammad Mostofa Hossain

1 Introduction

Financial technology also termed as Fintech has emerged as the most disruptive technology since the global financial meltdown of 2008 (Le et al., 2021; Zhang-Zhang et al., 2020). It is the most disruptive technology as it has changed the way financial forms are used to operate (Abu Daqar et al., 2020; Aliyu et al., 2017). Fintech firms started to

---

M. K. Hassan
Department of Economics and Finance, University of New Orleans, New Orleans, LA, USA
e-mail: mhassan@uno.edu

M. R. Rabbani (✉) · A. Jreisat
Department of Economics and Finance, College of Business Administration, University of Bahrain, Zallaq, Bahrain
e-mail: mrabbani@uob.edu.bh

A. Jreisat
e-mail: abarham@uob.edu.bh

© The Author(s), under exclusive license to Springer Nature Switzerland AG 2022
M. K. Hassan et al. (eds.), *FinTech in Islamic Financial Institutions*, https://doi.org/10.1007/978-3-031-14941-2_12

emerge post-financial crisis and forced the traditional financial institutions to forge partnership with them and co-develop value-based financial services for customers (Coetzee, 2019). Fintech blends finance with technology to provide the seamless financial services in the most innovative way at the least possible cost (Rabbani et al., 2020). Hassan et al. (2020) define Fintech as the improved way of offering financial services to the modern-day customers using information technology at the backdrop (Khan et al., 2022). Several factors contributed toward the rise of Fintech, including the rising demand for modern technology-driven services and an increase in the degree of technology awareness among millennials (Anagnostopoulos, 2018). The COVID-19 pandemic has disrupted the normal way of life having strong social, economic, and financial consequences (Conlon et al., 2020). Financial worlds are trying to find ways to combat the aftershocks created by the pandemic and Fintech is expected to critical role in reaching out to the people with its innovative financial services (Corbet et al., 2020; Wójcik, 2021).

Islamic finance also known as the *shariah*-compliant finance has been born out of the ethical, social, and moral doctrines of Islam, aimed at removing the injustice, inequality, and economic exploitation (Hassan, 2014; Hassan et al., 2018). It is the way to manage the finance within an organization or an individual within the moral principles of Islam, which covers all facets of human life like saving, borrowing, investment, buying, and selling. Islamic finance is based on the principles that prohibit interest payment or receipt (prohibition of *Riba*/usury), and removal of exploitative practice that favors lenders at the expense of the borrower (Hassan & Hippler, 2014; Hassan & Soumaré, 2015). It follows the *Shariah* law which is considered as the religious law forming part of the Islamic tradition. The sharia law is derived from the holy *Qur'an* and *Sunnah* of the Prophet Muhammad (*pbuh*). Besides many other principles forming part of the Islamic finance, the following principles forms the core of Islamic financial system.

M. M. Hossain
Department of Fiqh and Usul, Wilayah Persekutuan Kuala Lumpur, Jalan Profesor Diraja Ungku Aziz, Kuala Lumpur, Malaysia
e-mail: shahinccc1@gmail.com

1. *Riba* (interest) is prohibited under Islamic finance, which means the use of money for the purpose of making money is prohibited.
2. Financial contracts with excessive risk (*gharar*), gambling (*maysir*) are also prohibited in Islamic finance.
3. All the Islamic financial contracts must aim to benefit the larger sections of the society besides generating profit for the owners. Islamic finance aims to remove the evils of the society like unequal distribution of wealth through the Islamic social finance instruments such as, *Zakat, Sadaqa, Qardh-Al-Hasan*, etc., and bringing social justice in terms of providing social security and protection of the weak, poor, and vulnerable against the rich and strong.
4. The aims are to bridge the gulf between the rich and the poor which the conventional system has failed to do so.
5. The investment must be asset-backed. It means that all the investments in Islamic finance must have the backing of a real asset. Derivative instruments like option and forward contracts are prohibited in Islamic finance.
6. Islamic finance makes strong provisions against the earning of wealth by the unethical and unlawful (*haram*) means. For example, earning wealth by selling of alcohol, etc., is prohibited.

Fintech is a welcome addition to the Islamic financial landscape as it is considered as a tool to help in achieving the Islamic finance objective of financial inclusion and serve the unmet financial needs of the poor and vulnerable sections of the society which are ignored by the conventional finance players and traditional financial services do not have that reach. Thus, Fintech is a tool to achieve the objective of financial inclusion.

Islamic Fintech is defined as the sharia-compliant version of the financial technology which prohibits the earnings from the debt, interest-based instruments, and prohibited investments such as alcohol, tobacco, gambling, etc. Islamic Fintech has been on the rise recently as it is projected that it will reach up to $128 Billion by 2025 at 21% compound annual growth rate (CAGR) and compared to the 15% CAGR for the conventional Fintech in the same period. Islamic Fintech has the potential to make Islamic finance more competitive by offering Islamic social finance services in combination with the technology to help in the fight against the adversities of the COVID-19.

There are few studies highlighting the importance of Islamic Fintech enabled financial services against the negative impact created by the pandemic (Atif et al., 2021; Hassan et al., 2020; Mohammad et al., 2020; Rabbani et al., 2021a, 2021b; Rabbani, 2022). In their study on the role of Fintech in combating the aftershocks of the pandemic Rabbani et al. (2021a, 2021b), explore the possibilities of Islamic Fintech in combating the economic reverberations created by the pandemic. The authors concluded that the basic ethical tenets of Islamic finance in combination with the technology can work wonders and help in creating a more resilient and sustainable financial system post-pandemic. Hassan et al. (2020), explored the challenges of the Islamic Finance post-pandemic and the role that Islamic Fintech must play in overcoming those challenges. The authors concluded that the Fintech-based Islamic social finance is the way to go post-pandemic. Mohammad et al. (2020), proposed an integrated *Zakat* and *Qardh-Al-Hasan*-based Islamic Fintech model to fight against the adversities of the pandemic. In another study Rabbani (2022), analyzed the impact of pandemic on the supply chain financing and proposed that Islamic countries must trust Islamic Fintech and Islamic social finance tools can play a critical role in supplying the critical supply chain financing to the pandemic affected small industries and corporates and sole proprietors. These studies fail to provide a practical workable solution that can help in the fight against the adversities of the pandemic.

The study is expected to the existing strand of literature in the following ways. First, it is the first study providing the practical and workable integrated Islamic Fintech model to help in fight against the adversities of the pandemic. Second, it will open an avenue for the future researchers and practitioners to explore more possibilities of Islamic Fintech in helping poor, vulnerable, and affected. Third, it will help the regulators and policymakers in identifying the potentials of Islamic Fintech and devise favorable economic policies accordingly. Finally, it will add the existing strand of literature on Fintech, pandemic, and Islamic financial system (Atif et al., 2021; Hassan et al., 2020, 2021; Khan et al., 2021a, 2021b; Mohammad et al., 2020; Rabbani et al., 2021a, 2021b; Rabbani, 2022).

The remaining paper proceeds as follows. In the next section, we provide a discussion on the economic impact of pandemic and the role of Islamic finance. Section three explores the role of Islamic Fintech in Financial inclusion. Section four provides the proposed integrated Islamic Fintech model. Finally in section five we conclude and provide the further scope of the study.

2 The Role of FinTech in Islamic Finance

Kotilaine Jarmo The Chief Economic Development Officer of the Economic Development Board of Bahrain (EDB) sums up: what applies to conventional banking in technology is also used in Islamic banking. He stated the following: Use financial technology to enhance the quality of banking experience with clients. Experience speed and accuracy are impacted. Technology makes things more customer friendly. We are going towards a situation where business and economic development must depend more on productivity than ever before, thus better administration, more innovation as well as new distribution channels, and new capital are needed (Mulyani et al., 2020; Sabandar, 2019). However, how can we find out which FinTech app needs Shariah sensitivity? This is answered by Prof. Akram Laldin, Managing Director of ISRA.

The Shariah concept governing commercial transactions (Muamalat) points out this view: Unless there is a clear prohibition in the text, any transaction is legal. Innovative business strategies and new financial methods are allowed by the acceptable principle. According to Muamalat, all inventions are legal and encouraged. FinTech innovations should only be prohibited under these circumstances if robust evidence exists that they contradict (are contrary to) Shariah principles. The FinTech industry is undergoing the same type of development as Islamic finance (Sarea et al., 2021).

Although FinTech was not widely recognized in the industry of Islamic Finance till 2015, The accomplishments of 2016 and 2017 are noteworthy. An attempt by FinTech start-ups at the beginning of 2016 proved to be more intentional (Hamdani et al., 2019). Among those deserving of mention are the globe's associated characteristics (Saba et al., 2019).

I. **DIB Branchless Banking**: The MoU to develop a branch-less DIBP banking platform was established between the Islamic Bank of Pakistan and Zing Digital Commerce on February 8, 2018. This endeavor has the possibility to pave the way for the digitization and unbanked population of Islamic financial services. DIBP is working with Zing Digital Trade which previously worked in a similar program with Shanghai F-Road. This is a crucial step to achieve the objective of DIBP, which is to provide substantial economic services at every customer's door from scratch with simplicity and dependability (Al-Dmour et al., 2020; Jagtiani & John, 2018).

II. **Meezan UPaisa**: It was founded in 2016 as the first Islamic digital banking service because of a strategic partnership between Ufone and Meezan Bank. It allowed users from all over Pakistan to send and receive money, pay service fees, and upgrade their mobile phones without visiting physical locations (Bhagat & Roderick, 2020; Romanova & Kudinska, 2016).

III. **Electronic Commodity Murabaha**: First electronic Murabaha transaction took place between Pakistan Mercantile Exchange Ltd (PMEX) and Meezan Bank Ltd. Their purpose was to increase the markets for Islamic funding. In establishing this Shariah-compliant trading platform, PMEX got Shariah technical support from Meezan Bank (Alam et al., 2019).

IV. **Investment Account Platform (IAP)**: On February 17, 2016, with a capital initial of RM 150 million, Malaysia is the first to set up the Islamic banking system's multi-bank. Its objective was to create a unified market for funding companies. Also, it was the first Internet-based bank aims to mix Islamic banks' ability to route money to viable businesses with technological efficiency (Glas, 2019; Procházka, 2018).

V. **Islamic Fintech Alliance (IFT Alliance)**: On April 1, 2016, eight Islamic Crowdfunding Platforms in Kuala Lumpur (Malaysia) operators from all over the world were established by Islamic Fintech Alliance. The aim of this partnership is to increase FinTech's growth among IFIs with the expectation that it will have a major beneficial worldwide impact (Ashta & Biot-Paquerot, 2018; Blakstad & Allen, 2018).

VI. **The First Global Islamic FinTech Hub**: This FinTech Centre's purpose is to enhance the business climate in GCC, in Bahrain. There is also a virtual network connecting several firms in the proposal, managers, and international hackathons to promote growth for Fintech in all expanding locations (DinarStandard, 2021)

As a result of FINTECH effecting the Islamic finance, assorted services provided by the Islamic institutions such as.

3 Fintech and Bitcoin

In the recent past, the popularity of cryptocurrencies, particularly Bitcoin, has increased customers are excited, but monetary authorities throughout the world are stepping carefully. The crucial topic now is whether Bitcoin is Shariah-compliant and may be utilized in Islamic financing. As Meera (2018) pointed out, Bitcoin that does not have real assets is not Shariah-compliant. Bitcoin is not real cash or real money. Because of its lack of inherent value and lack of control, Bitcoin has the potential to be misused. Furthermore, *maysir and gharar* may violate *Maqasid al-Shariah* by contributing to social inequity (Meera, 2018).

Fintech and Blockchain (BC)

BC is being used frequently by Islamic financial institutions. According to Nor et al. (2022), in Waqf organizations, the use of BC technology can boost innovation and efficiency. Elasrag (2019) analyzes the issues and limits associated with implementing BC in Islamic banking. He emphasized four main issues: technological scalability, network confidence (skill), innovation (business), and current legislation (Elasrag, 2019).

4 Fintech-Based Islamic Financial Services

COVID-19 has already done the severe damage to the core sectors of the economy. Due to the ethical nature of financial services at the disposal of the Islamic finance industry, it has the ingredient to fight such shocks as seen during the financial crisis (Atif et al., 2021, 2022; Dharani et al., 2022; Hassan et al., 2021). Since the nature of damage done by the pandemic is quite distinct from the global financial crisis of 2008 and it needs to be seen how Islamic finance reacts to the damage caused by the pandemic. Fintech provides that missing impetus to the Islamic finance industry to combine its financial services with the technology and reach out to the affected and vulnerable during and post-pandemic to minimize the damage (Hassan et al., 2020; Khan et al., 2020; Rabbani et al., 2022b). As depicted in Fig. 1, we provide an overview of the Fintech-based Islamic innovative financial services to fight the adversities of the pandemic.

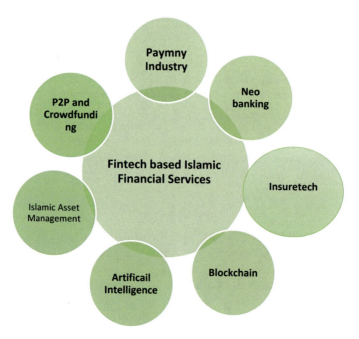

Fig. 1 Fintech-based Islamic Financial Services (*Source* Author's own compilation)

Payments Industry

Payment has always been goods of utility nature and the number of products, mostly transactional and tactical. Indeed, payment is often considered the final step in a transaction with little or no opportunity to provide extra value or services (Hassan et al., 2020; Rabbani et al., 2022a, 2022b, 2022c). At present, the payment business is constantly changing, with numerous major economic, technological, and demographic drivers underlying this sector along the whole value chain. The sector has been progressively fragmented by rapidly developing technologies across the value chain. New entrants in the shape of Fintech companies and large digital companies (Facebook, PayPal Amazon), non-bank payment systems have generated massive disruptions and obsoleted standard mediation in important areas of banking and spending (DinarStandard, 2020).

The payment's goal is to deliver key strategic solutions by 2020, as well as to transfer value in support of large-scale operations in a variety of sectors, including investment, commerce, retail, public, and marketing. According to the PwC Market Resources Centre, the volume of non-cash transactions will increase by 69% between 2013 and 2020, with a transaction value of US$1,000,000 per minute. 2016 (Pricewaterhouse-Coopers). It may and will enhance its acceptance and delivery of financial services in cloud, open source, large-scale and analytical data, on-demand developers, social networks and open application, distribution, etc. Such technologies have the potential to replace antiquated payment procedures and systems in a wide range of industries, including international transfers. Furthermore, the usage of contactless trade payments via NFC, Bluetooth, and QR codes is promoting traditional payment methods (DinarStandard, 2020).

P2P Lending and Crowdfunding

P2P loans are defined as the practice of lending money using online businesses that link lenders with lenders. P2p credit, also known as debt and market lending or MPL, is abbreviated as P2P. Lending Club, which was founded in San Francisco in 2006, is the world's largest P2P platform in terms of permitted loan volume and income. P2P lending typically lends to industrialists and to SMEs who were unable to acquire credit from regulated banking institutions (Hassan et al., 2022). In 2020, marketplace lending is expected to achieve $290 billion, expanding at a rate of 51% per annum, according to Morgan Stanley. However, in a more positive scenario, this industry is expected in 2020 to surpass US$490 billion (Hassan et al., 2021; Rabbani et al., 2021a, 2021b).

The terminology Crowdfunding means the process of raising cash for a worthy reason and company through soliciting contributions from many individuals or organizations. When a creative and fresh concept with the ability to make income and create employment needs financial backing to develop a certainty, crowdfunding is used. It takes place primarily on crowdfunding platforms (CFPs) which are online and connect fundraisers with funders to support a specific campaign by a sizable number of people. These CFPs give cash and capital to a portion of the population that would not otherwise be able to obtain it through traditional channels (Bagheri et al., 2019; Bi et al., 2019).

Neo-Banking

The emergence of this kind is seen as a fundamental shift in the banking industry (Mohamad & Saravanamuttu, 2015). These neo-banks are also known as challenger banks and app-only start-up banks. Neo-banking is more than merely Internet distribution. It has an integrated view and tries to engage customers on all digital channels and to provide the services they desire via their channels of choice. Instead of digital integration into the heart of neo-banks, they do not have a distinct digital team for digital project. In contrast to traditional banks, neo-banks provide more clarity and cost-effectiveness in the provision of banking goods and services.

There are now about fifty-seven new banks in several nations, most of them in the UK, including Atom, Monzo, Tandem, and Metro. These banks have been funded by several investors for millions of dollars. Tandem has raised US$77 million, Starled has raised US$70 million, Nuclear 268 million, and Monzo has raised US$46 million (Walker, 2017). They attract customers in real time by giving the technologically advanced generation of this digital era with a cheaper and superior offer. These challenged banks are a potential way of reaching customers through novel business strategies and digital platforms (Mustafa Raza Rabbani, 2020).

Asset Under Management

There are already substantial levels of distortions caused by banking creation that have already begun to change the structure of payments and procedures in lending. According to the worldwide Fintech study of PwC, half (53%) of participants in asset management expected that this business will also be disrupted by Fintech businesses (52%) (Salampasis & Mention, 2018). Blockchain can be significantly improved in terms of consumer profiling. Customer profile data stored in Blockchain permits the sharing of data points, preference data, net worth, account data and, when suitable, social network profiles, and secure retention of all data blocks (reading, writing, editing) by a person as required. A regionalized header technology also enables the dispersion, disintermediation of authorities, of the trusted value transfer and execution: the network becomes an intermediate. Thus, master books kept in clearers and banks, for instance, are replaced with distributed books without middlemen (Ahlers et al., 2016; Makina, 2019).

InsurTech

It is an area of financial innovation addressing contemporary insurance industry possibilities, prospects, and difficulties. Seventy-four percent of respondents viewed financial innovations as a danger to their sector in a 2016 PwC poll. The result is the application of good technologies such as big data analysis and blockchain, the development of a shared economy and the opportunity to improve operations (Rabbani et al., 2022a, 2022b, 2022c).

5 BLOCKCHAIN

Distributed ledger technology is another name for Blockchain technology. Blockchain is a publicly accessible corporate transaction ledger. A Blockchain network serves as an intermediary for the exchange of property and information in a decentralized system. The two major technology components are peer-to-peer (or shared data storage) and public-key cryptography (Crosby et al., 2016; Halamka et al., 2017). According to Accenture research, Blockchain is one of the most talked topics in the present financial services business. 90% of bank executives are interested in Blockchain, and their organizations are now researching the use of Blockchain in the payments industry (Morkunas et al., 2019).

Cloud Computing

Cloud Computing provides online computer power, database management systems, equipment, and additional IT sources under the pay-as-you-go price structure for cloud service offerings. Instead of owning their own computing equipment or data centers, organizations may rent anything from software to storage from a cloud service provider (CSP). One advantage of adopting Cloud Computing services is that businesses may avoid starting expenses and difficulties by just paying for what they need to construct and maintain their IT infrastructure as needed (Khan et al., 2020, 2021a, 2021b).

Big Data Analysis

According to the International Data Corporation (IDC), Big Data indicates that the smart economy creates a continuous stream of data that is monitored and analyzed. The flow is aided by social interactions, simulations, transportable equipment, equipment, R&D, and physical infrastructure (Buck et al., 2014). According to IDC, the big services and data business would develop at a CAGR of 23% by 2019. Furthermore, yearly spending in 2019 is expected to reach $46.6 billion USD (Khan & Rabbani, 2020a, 2020b, 2020c; Sun et al., 2020). Data is growing at an exponential rate, with over 16 trillion GB of usable data anticipated to be created by 2020. (Khan & Rabbani, 2020a).

Robo-Advisors (RA)

RA are a digital platform that offers financial planning and investing services automated and powered by algorithms. This service can only be monitored by minimal or no people. RA collects information about the financial situation and future ambitions of a client. You must conduct a survey or answer a few online questions to do so. They then use the information you supplied to make recommendations. By providing services directly to clients, the emergence of modern robot consultants drastically changed the story (Khan & Rabbani, 2020a, 2020b, 2020c).

Artificial Intelligence

Dartmouth Institution in New Hampshire's Allen Newell, Nathaniel Rochester, John McCarthy, and Herbert Simon assumed in 1956 that every aspect of intelligence and learning could be described in principle in such a way that a computer could be created. The "Modern AI" dads were asked to attend the summer school. The day is commemorated as the start of AI, when numerous research groups across the world began to work on artificial systems that could match, imitate, or perhaps surpass human mental and physical capabilities (Khan & Rabbani, 2020a, 2020b, 2020c; Khan & Rabbani, 2021; Khan et al., 2021b; Rabbani et al., 2021a, 2021b). In the 1960s, the US Defense Department got interested in such work and started teaching computers to repeat basic human thinking. In the 1970s, for example, the DARPA carried out street mapping projects and smart virtual assistants in 2003. The DARPA was also responsible for the implementation of programs. AI is a branch of computer science in which intelligent machines that operate and behave like humans may be built. AI allows computers to learn from their experiences, adapt themselves to new inputs, and carry out tasks like humanity. Computers can be trained to do tasks utilizing current technologies for processing huge data quantities and detecting data patterns. This has led to Artificial Intelligence (AI) being a hot subject, many of them arguing how it helps the highly controlled financial services company. AI can assist banks in their anti-money laundering and counter-terrorism funding efforts by replacing time-consuming manual operations (Rabbani et al., 2021a, 2021b).

6 Conclusion

The study investigated the economic impact of the COVID-19 pandemic, its impact on the Islamic financial system, and its potential role of Islamic Fintech in overcoming the economic disruptions created by the pandemic. The study also provides the unique solution to the finance world to embrace Islamic finance in combination with Fintech to fight the evils of the pandemic. Islamic financial services such as Zakat in combination with Artificial Intelligence and Blockchain can prove to be a blessing in disguise.

The study provided an overview of financial technology (Fintech) as a financial innovation and its application in Islamic Finance industry. Fintech has emerged as the most exciting innovation of the twenty-first century, and it has disrupted life in the financial services industry like never. The study also defined the concept of Fintech and in context to the sharia provision of the Islamic Finance and provided an overview of the Fintech industry and its potential to transform the Islamic Finance industry. The findings of the study reveal that Islamic finance industry is the way to go in future and Fintech has provided the missing impetus to the Islamic finance industry to compete with its conventional counterpart on equal grounds in providing innovative solutions. Islamic financial services such as *Zakat, Qardh-Al-Hasan, Awqaf, Islamic Microfinance, Sadaqa*, etc., in combination with the Artificial Intelligence, Blockchain, and other innovative solutions can prove to be a wonder for the industry and community at large. The findings of the study are expected to help the Islamic financial institutions, governments, regulators, and policymakers efficient use of Fintech in solving the problems created by the pandemic. The study is also expected to contribute to creating a more sustainable and resilient alternative to the conventional financial system.

REFERENCES

Abu Daqar, M. A. M., Arqawi, S., & Karsh, S. A. (2020). Fintech in the eyes of Millennials and Generation Z (the financial behavior and Fintech perception). *Banks and Bank Systems*, 15(3), 20–28. https://doi.org/10.21511/bbs.15(3).2020.03

Ahlers, O., Hack, A., Kellermanns, F., & Wright, M. (2016). Opening the black box: Power in buyout negotiations and the moderating role of private equity specialization. *Journal of Small Business Management*, 54(4), 1171–1192. https://doi.org/10.1111/jsbm.12235

Alam, N., Gupta, L., & Zameni, A. (2019). *Fintech and Islamic finance: Digitalization, development and disruption*. Digitalization, Development and Disruption. Springer International Publishing. https://doi.org/10.1007/978-3-030-24666-2

Al-Dmour, H., Asfour, F., Al-Dmour, R., & Al-Dmour, A. (2020). The effect of marketing knowledge management on bank performance through fintech innovations: A survey study of jordanian commercial banks. *Interdisciplinary Journal of Information, Knowledge, and Management*, 15, 203–225. https://doi.org/10.28945/4619

Aliyu, S., Hassan, M. K., Mohd Yusof, R., & Naiimi, N. (2017). Islamic banking sustainability: A review of literature and directions for future research. *Emerging Markets Finance and Trade*. https://doi.org/10.1080/1540496X.2016.1262761

Anagnostopoulos, I. (2018). Fintech and regtech: Impact on regulators and banks. *Journal of Economics and Business*, 100, 7–25. https://doi.org/10.1016/j.jeconbus.2018.07.003

Ashta, A., & Biot-Paquerot, G. (2018). FinTech evolution: Strategic value management issues in a fast changing industry. *Strategic Change*, 27(4), 301–311. https://doi.org/10.1002/jsc.2203

Atif, M., Hassan, M. K., Rabbani, M. R., & Khan, S. (2021). Islamic FinTech: The digital transformation bringing sustainability to Islamic finance. In *COVID-19 and Islamic Social Finance* (pp. 94–106). Routledge.

Atif, M., Rabbani, M. R., Bawazir, H., Hawaldar, I, T., Chebab, D., Karim, S., & Alabbas, A. (2022). Oil price changes and stock returns: Fresh evidence from oil exporting and oil importing countries. *Cogent Economics & Finance*, 10(1), 2018163.

Bagheri, A., Chitsazan, H., & Ebrahimi, A. (2019). Crowdfunding motivations: A focus on donors' perspectives. *Technological Forecasting and Social Change*, *146*, 218–232. https://doi.org/10.1016/j.techfore.2019.05.002

Bhagat, A., & Roderick, L. (2020). Banking on refugees: Racialized expropriation in the fintech era. *Environment and Planning A*, *52*(8), 1498–1515. https://doi.org/10.1177/0308518X20904070

Bi, G., Geng, B., & Liu, L. (2019). On the fixed and flexible funding mechanisms in reward-based crowdfunding. *European Journal of Operational Research*, *279*(1), 168–183. https://doi.org/10.1016/j.ejor.2019.05.019

Blakstad, S., & Allen, R. (2018). FinTech revolution: Universal inclusion in the new financial ecosystem. In *FinTech Revolution: Universal Inclusion in the New Financial Ecosystem*. Springer International Publishing. https://doi.org/10.1007/978-3-319-76014-8

Buck, C., Horbel, C., Kessler, T., & Christian, C. (2014). Mobile consumer apps: Big data brother is watching you. *Marketing Review St. Gallen*, *31*(1), 26–35.

Coetzee, J. (2019). Risk aversion and the adoption of Fintech by South African banks. *African Journal of Business and Economic Research*, *14*(4), 133–153. https://doi.org/10.31920/1750-4562/2019/14n4a6

Conlon, T., Corbet, S., & McGee, R. J. (2020). Are cryptocurrencies a safe haven for equity markets? An international perspective from the COVID-19 pandemic. *Research in International Business and Finance*, *54*. https://doi.org/10.1016/j.ribaf.2020.101248

Corbet, S., Larkin, C., & Lucey, B. (2020). The contagion effects of the COVID-19 pandemic: Evidence from gold and cryptocurrencies. *Finance Research Letters*, *35*. https://doi.org/10.1016/j.frl.2020.101554

Crosby, M., Nachiappan, P. P., & Sanjeev Verma, V. K. (2016). Blockchain technology: Beyond bitcoin. *Applied Innovation*, *71*(2), 6–10.

Dharani, M., Hassan, M. K., Rabbani, M. R., & Huq, T. (2022). Does the Covid-19 pandemic affect faith-based investments? Evidence from global sectoral indices. *Research in International Business and Finance*, *59*, 101537.

DinarStandard. (2020). State of the Global Islamic Economy Report 2020/21. In *Dubai International Financial Centre*. https://haladinar.io/hdn/doc/report2018.pdf

DinarStandard. (2021). Islamic Fintech Report 2018: Current Landscape & Path Forward. In *Dubai Islamic Economy Development Centre*. https://www.dinarstandard.com/wp-content/uploads/2018/12/Islamic-Fintech-Report-2018.pdf

Elasrag, H. (2019). Blockchains for Islamic finance: Obstacles & Challenges. *Munich Personal RePEc Archive*.

Glas, T. N. (2019). Investments in cryptocurrencies: Handle with care! *Journal of Alternative Investments*, 22(1), 96–113. https://doi.org/10.3905/jai.2019.22.1.096

Halamka, J. D. Lippman, A., & Ekblaw, A. (2017). The potential for blockchain to transform electronic health records. *Harvard Business Review*, 3(3), 2–5.

Hamdani, N. A., Herlianti, A. O., & Amin, A. S. (2019). Society 5.0: Feasibilities and challenges of the implementation of fintech in small and medium industries. In A. A.G., N. A.B.D., W. I., D. A.A., & A. C.U. (Eds.), *4th Annual Applied Science and Engineering Conference, AASEC 2019* (Vol. 1402, Issue 7). Institute of Physics Publishing. https://doi.org/10.1088/1742-6596/1402/7/077053

Hassan, M. K. (2014). Editor's notes. *International Journal of Islamic and Middle Eastern Finance and Management*. https://doi.org/10.1108/imefm-04-2014-0034

Hassan, M. K., & Hippler, W. J. (2014). Entrepreneurship and Islam: An overview. *Econ Journal Watch*. https://doi.org/10.2139/ssrn.3263110

Hassan, M. K., Paltrinieri, A., Dreassi, A., Miani, S., & Sclip, A. (2018). The determinants of co-movement dynamics between sukuk and conventional bonds. *Quarterly Review of Economics and Finance*. https://doi.org/10.1016/j.qref.2017.09.003

Hassan, M. K., Rabbani, M. R., & Ali, M. A. (2020). Challenges for the Islamic Finance and banking in post COVID era and the role of Fintech. *Journal of Economic Cooperation and Development*, 43(3), 93–116.

Hassan, M. K., Rabbani, M. R., & Abdullah, Y. (2021). Socioeconomic Impact of COVID-19 in MENA region and the Role of Islamic Finance. *International Journal of Islamic Economics and Finance (IJIEF)*, 4(1), 51–78.

Hassan, M. K., Rabbani, M. R., Brodmann, J., Bashar, A., & Grewal, H. (2022). Bibliometric and Scientometric analysis on CSR practices in the banking sector. *Review of Financial Economics*.

Jagtiani, J., & John, K. (2018). Fintech: The impact on consumers and regulatory responses. *Journal of Economics and Business*, 100, 1–6. https://doi.org/10.1016/j.jeconbus.2018.11.002

Kabir Hassan, M., & Soumaré, I. (2015). Guarantees and profit-sharing contracts in project financing. *Journal of Business Ethics*. https://doi.org/10.1007/s10551-014-2201-0

Khan, S., & Rabbani, M. R. (2020a). Artificial Intelligence and NLP based Chatbot as Islamic Banking and Finance Expert. *2020a International Conference on Computational Linguistics and Natural Language Processing (CLNLP 2020a), Seoul, South Korea on July*, 20–22.

Khan, S., & Rabbani, M. R. (2020b). Chatbot as Islamic Finance Expert (CaIFE) When Finance Meets Artificial Intelligence. *Proceedings of the 2020b 4th International Symposium on Computer Science and Intelligent Control*, 1–5.

Khan, S., & Rabbani, M. R. (2020c). In depth analysis of blockchain, cryptocurrency and sharia compliance. *International Journal of Business Innovation and Research, 1*(1), 1. https://doi.org/10.1504/ijbir.2020.10033066

Khan, S., Rabbani, R. M., Thalassinos, I. E., & Atif, M. (2020). Corona virus pandemic paving ways to next generation of learning and teaching: Futuristic cloud based educational model. *Available at SSRN 3669832.*

Khan, S., & Rabbani, M. R. (2021). Artificial Intelligence and NLP based Chatbot as Islamic Banking and Finance Expert. *International Journal of Information Retrieval Research (IJIRR), 11*(3), 65–77.

Khan, S., Al-Dmour, A., Bali, V., Rabbani, M. R., & Thirunavukkarasu, K. (2021a). Cloud computing based futuristic educational model for virtual learning. *Journal of Statistics and Management Systems, 24*(2), 357–385.

Khan, S., Hassan, M. K., & Rabbani, M. R. (2021b). An Artificial Intelligence-based Islamic FinTech model on Qardh-Al-Hasan for COVID 19 affected SMEs. In *Islamic Perspective for Sustainable Financial System.*

Khan, M. S., Rabbani, M. R., Hawaldar, I. T., & Bashar, A. (2022). Determinants of Behavioral intentions to use Islamic financial technology: An empirical assessment. *Risks, 10*(6), 114.

Le, T. N.-L., Abakah, E. J. A., & Tiwari, A. K. (2021). Time and frequency domain connectedness and spill-over among fintech, green bonds and cryptocurrencies in the age of the fourth industrial revolution. *Technological Forecasting and Social Change, 162.* https://doi.org/10.1016/j.techfore.2020.120382

Makina, D. (2019). The potential of FinTech in enabling financial inclusion. In *Extending Financial Inclusion in Africa* (pp. 299–318). Elsevier. https://doi.org/10.1016/B978-0-12-814164-9.00014-1

Meera, A. K. M. (2018). Cryptocurrencies from Islamic Perspectives: The case of bitcoin. *Buletin Ekonomi Moneter Dan Perbankan, 20*(4), 443–460. https://doi.org/10.21098/bemp.v20i4.902

Mohamad, M., & Saravanamuttu, J. (2015). Islamic banking and finance: Sacred alignment, strategic alliances. *Pacific Affairs, 88*(2), 193–213. https://doi.org/10.5509/2015882193

Mohammad, H., Khan, S., Mustafa, R. R., & Yannis, E. T. (2020). An artificial intelligence and NLP based Islamic FinTech model combining Zakat and Qardh-Al-Hasan for countering the adverse impact of COVID 19 on SMEs and individuals. *International Journal of Economics and Business Administration, VIII*(2), 351–364. https://doi.org/10.35808/ijeba/466

Morkunas, V. J., Paschen, J., & Boon, E. (2019). How blockchain technologies impact your business model. *Business Horizons, 62*(3), 295–306. https://doi.org/10.1016/j.bushor.2019.01.009

Mulyani, S. R., Kadarisman, S., & Paramarta, V. (2020). Opportunities and threats of development of financial technologies (Fintech) against competitiveness of banks (at national conventional commercial banks). *Journal of Advanced Research in Dynamical and Control Systems*, 12(3), 97–110. https://doi.org/10.5373/JARDCS/V12I3/20201171

Nor, F. M., Johari, F., Haron, H., Shafii, Z., Shahwan, S., Misbah, H., ... & Yusoff, M. M. (2022). Conceptualisation and validating benefidonors model in waqf. *The Journal of Muamalat and Islamic Finance Research*, 106–119.

Procházka, D. (2018). Accounting for bitcoin and other cryptocurrencies under IFRS: A comparison and assessment of competing models. *International Journal of Digital Accounting Research*, 18, 161–188. https://doi.org/10.4192/1577-8517-v18_7

Rabbani, M. R. (2020). The competitive structure and strategic positioning of commercial banks in Saudi Arabia. *International Journal on Emerging Technologies*, 11(3), 43–46.

Rabbani, M. R. (2022). COVID-19 and its impact on supply chain financing and the role of Islamic Fintech: Evidence from GCC countries. *International Journal of Agile Systems and Management (IJASM)*. In press.

Rabbani, M. R., Khan, S., & Thalassinos, E. I. (2020). FinTech, blockchain and Islamic finance: An extensive literature review. *International Journal of Economics and Business Administration*, 8(2), 65–86. https://doi.org/10.35808/ijeba/444

Rabbani, M. R., Bashar, A., Nawaz, N., Karim, S., Ali, M. A. M., Khan, A., Rahiman, H., & Alam, S. (2021a). Exploring the role of Islamic Fintech in combating the after-shocks of COVID-19: The open social innovation of the Islamic financial system. *Journal of Open Innovation: Technology, Market, and Complexity*, 7, 136.

Rabbani, M. R., Khan, S., Hassan, M. K., & Ali, M. (2021b). 7 Artificial intelligence and Natural language processing (NLP) based FinTech model of Zakat for poverty alleviation and sustainable development for Muslims in India. *ICOVID-19 and Islamic Social Finance: 104*.

Rabbani, M. R., Kayani, U., Bawazir, H. S., & Hawaldar, I. T. (2022a). A commentary on emerging markets banking sector spillovers: Covid-19 vs GFC pattern analysis. *Heliyon*, 8(3), e09074.

Rabbani, M. R., Khan, S., & Atif, M. (2022b). Machine Learning based P2P Lending Islamic FinTech Model for Small and Medium Enterprises (SMEs) in Bahrain. *International Journal of Business Innovation and Research*, In press.

Rabbani, M. R., Sarea, A., Khan, S., & Abdullah, Y. (2022c). Ethical concerns in Artificial Intelligence (AI): The role of regtech and Islamic finance. *Artificial Intelligence for Sustainable Finance and Sustainable Technology* (p. Forthcoming).

Romanova, I., & Kudinska, M. (2016). Banking and fintech: A challenge or opportunity? *Contemporary Studies in Economic and Financial Analysis* (Vol. 98, pp. 21–35). Emerald Group Publishing Ltd. https://doi.org/10.1108/S1569-375920160000098002

Sabandar, S. Y. (2019). Financial technology: Smes answer the opportunities and challenges of industrial revolution 4.0. *Journal of Advanced Research in Dynamical and Control Systems, 11*(8), 2337–2348. https://www.scopus.com/inward/record.uri?eid=2-s2.0-85076039916&partnerID=40&md5=7d741305713cc845a91a4939ba5a94cb

Salampasis, D., & Mention, A.-L. (2018). FinTech: Harnessing innovation for financial inclusion. *Handbook of Blockchain, Digital Finance, and Inclusion* (Vol. 2, pp. 451–461). Elsevier Inc. https://doi.org/10.1016/B978-0-12-812282-2.00018-8

Sarea, A., Rabbani, M. R., Alam, M. S., & Atif, M. (2021). 8 Artificial intelligence (AI) applications in Islamic finance and banking sector. *Artificial Intelligence and Islamic Finance: Practical Applications for Financial Risk Management* (pp. 108–121). Routledge.

Sun, H., Rabbani, M. R., Sial, M. S., Yu, S., Filipe, J. A., & Cherian, J. (2020). Identifying big data's opportunities, challenges, and implications in finance. *Mathematics, 8*(10). https://doi.org/10.3390/math8101738

Walker, G. (2017). Financial technology law—A new beginning and a new future. *International Lawyer, 50*(1), 137–215. https://www.scopus.com/inward/record.uri?eid=2-s2.0-85032010410&partnerID=40&md5=565002e4221f98bfcec60318ceb13ca1

Wójcik, D. (2021). Financial geography II: The impacts of FinTech—Financial sector and centres, regulation and stability, inclusion and governance. *Progress in Human Geography, 45*(4), 878–889. https://doi.org/10.1177/0309132520959825

Zhang-Zhang, Y., Rohlfer, S., & Rajasekera, J. (2020). An eco-systematic view of cross-sector fintech: The case of Alibaba and Tencent. *Sustainability (Switzerland), 12*(21), 1–25. https://doi.org/10.3390/su12218907

An Islamic Finance Perspective of Crowdfunding and Peer-To-Peer (P2P) Lending

*M. Kabir Hassan, Mustafa Raza Rabbani,
Shahnawaz Khan, and Mahmood Asad Moh'd Ali*

1 Introduction

Financial Technology (commonly known as Fintech) is the technology which is used to provide traditional financial services through innovative technology. The upcoming or novel technologies which help in automating and improving the use and delivery of financial services can be utilized to describe financial technology (Abdullah & Rabbani, 2021; Bashar et al., 2021). The last decade has witnessed a number of Fintech solutions, the major innovations have been based on Blockchain such as Bitcoin, Ethereum cryptocurrencies, etc. (Khan & Rabbani, 2022). Other

---

M. K. Hassan
Department of Economics and Finance, University of New, Orleans, New Orleans, LA, USA
e-mail: mhassan@uno.edu

M. R. Rabbani (✉)
Department of Economics and Finance, College of Business Administration, University of Bahrain, Zallaq, Bahrain
e-mail: mrabbani@uob.edu.bh

© The Author(s), under exclusive license to Springer Nature Switzerland AG 2022
M. K. Hassan et al. (eds.), *FinTech in Islamic Financial Institutions*,
https://doi.org/10.1007/978-3-031-14941-2_13

examples include crowdfunding platforms, mobile payments apps, stock-trading apps, robo-advising and budgeting apps, etc. There have been many Fintech innovations for business-to-business as well as business-to-client. These innovations in Fintech have been done by startups and existing tech giants and financial institutions. Financial Technologies have always been working in the back offices of the financial institutions and banks and were rarely the focus of investors and venture capitalists. In recent past, it has taken the centerstage and the investments in Fintech have increased to 20% (Hassan et al., 2020a). Fintech has become the day-to-day thing and nowadays Fintech-based solutions are being used by everyone (Khan et al., 2022; Rabbani et al., 2022).

Fintech has been playing a key role in reshaping the financial and banking landscape (Rabbani, 2022). The emergence of Fintech has been a cause of concern for the banks and other traditional institutions as customers are finding it more attractive to use new and innovative financial services offered by the Fintech companies (Hasan et al., 2020). They are also concerned about the unequal playing field because Fintech companies are not coming under the same rigorous legal framework. Many banks have already accepted Fintech companies as partners than competitors. Fintech companies have taken this innovation to another level. These Fintech companies have made it possible to provide financial services with more efficient and that too at the reduced cost (Bashar et al., 2021; Hassan et al., 2020b).

As this innovative and unique source of fund-raising is only at the initial shaper and started to take a shape. The present chapter explores the sharia compliance of the crowdfunding and P2P lending. It will help the investors decide in terms of designing the campaign in accordance with the provision of the sharia. It is also expected to help the policymak

---

S. Khan
Faculty of Engineering, Design, and Information & Communications Technology, Bahrain Polytechnic, Isa Town, Bahrain
e-mail: shahnawaz.rs.cse@itbhu.ac.in

M. A. M. Ali
Department of Management and Marketing, College of Business Administration,
University of Bahrain, Zallaq, Bahrain
e-mail: mamali1@uob.edu.bh

ers and sharia governance to make startup-friendly law to further boost the growth of sharia-compliant crowdfunding and P2P lending. It will help the regulators to develop a crowdfunding model relevant to their needs and compliant with their ideals.

The remaining chapter is organized as follows. In the next section we provide an overview of the crowdfunding and P2P lending. Section three discusses the Challenges in Existing Islamic Crowdfunding and P2P lending platforms. Finally, in section four we provide the conclusion and further scope of the study.

2 Crowdfunding and Peer-To-Peer Lending: An Overview

Crowdfunding and P2P lending are the two of those innovations emerging from the financial innovation by Fintech. Banks are increasing the credit limit of the borrowers who have used P2P lending especially those customers with the lower credit worthiness earlier. Customers are also using cheaper P2P lending to finance their expensive bank loan (Xiang et al., 2018). There is still lack of awareness among the people about the peer-to-peer lending and crowdfunding as alternative medium of financing instrument, however people are aware about the developments going on in the Fintech world and they take this development in a positive direction (Rusdin et al., 2017; Tajudin et al., 2020). After years of high interest rates and difficulty in obtaining them, borrowers are looking for the loans with lower interest rates, ease of obtaining and faster processing of loans. It all started after the global financial crisis when lost confidence in the traditional financial system and started looking for the alternative medium of finance and Crowdfunding and Peer-to-Peer lending has provided a lease of life for such firms (Scholz, 2015; Wu et al., 2015).

A Fintech initiative, P2P lending and crowdfunding have provided options to the lenders as well as borrowers. It is easy, faster, cheaper and affordable (Rodríguez et al., 2018). Crowdfunding has become the first-choice source of finance for the startups ad experiencing very high growth (Zhang & Chen, 2019). On the other hand, Peer-to-Peer lending is competing with the banks for their market share by matching borrowers with the lenders without the cost of maintaining branches (Arshad et al., 2020). Crowdfunding and Peer-to-Peer lending are offering critical support to the startups and MSMEs, still there is a lack of awareness among the borrowers about these innovative platforms. Fintech companies need to create more awareness among the people about these new options available to them. With no support from government, individual and institutions, equity crowdfunding along with the P2P lending will continue to grow in the foreseeable future (Benna, 2018; Yan et al., 2018).

Crowdfunding

Crowdsourcing and Crowdfunding are the two words which emerged recently. Crowdsourcing was coined by Mr. Jeff Howe in 2006. Mr. Howe defined the crowdsourcing as the practice of sourcing ideas, services and content from the large pool of people, mainly online or through social media (Younkin & Kashkooli, 2016). A famous example of crowdsourcing is the Wikipedia. The content in Wikipedia is a result of various contributors from around the world. Crowdfunding also emerged in 2006 itself and it was coined by Michael Sullivan. According to Mr. Michael Sullivan, *"Crowdfunding is an innovative way to get financial contributions from the people, mainly from online community for a specific venture or project."* Both these terms consider 'crowd' as the online community from whom something needed may be obtained (Bœuf et al., 2014). Crowdfunding is a work based on the ability to pool money from the people who have common interests and are ready to give small contributions for a common goal. The term has gained momentum in this age of internet (Honisch & Ottenbacher, 2017). It is not only the new and innovative way to connect people and investors but to convince them to give money for a venture of common interest. It is mainly internet based method of finance by taking a small amount of money from ordinary people (Valančienė & Jegelevičiūtė, 2014). There are four types of crowdfunding available based on the type of financing available. The four types of Crowdfunding includes equity crowdfunding, debt crowdfunding, reward-based and donations-based crowdfunding. Various types of crowdfunding are described in Table 1.

Table 1 Types of crowdfunding with description

Name	Description
Equity-based crowdfunding	The investors invest a significant amount of capital in the project in return for the ownership of the company. This is very popular method of crowdfunding for raising money for risky and innovative enterprises (Giudici, 2015)
Debt-based crowdfunding	The investors lend money to the enterprise just like a traditional loan without any stake in the ownership of the company (Suryono et al., 2019)
Reward-based crowdfunding	It involves individuals contributing a small amount of money to projects in return for rewards like watch, TV, etc. The size of reward depends on the amount of money invested (Jiang et al., 2020)
Donation-based crowdfunding	It is a form of crowdfunding where a small amount of money is raised for a personal or social cause (Sannajust et al., 2014)

Peer-To-Peer (P2P) Lending

Peer-to-Peer lending also abbreviated as P2P lending is the latest trend in the online lending. P2P lending also known as 'social lending' or 'crowd lending' is relatively a new term, that came into existence in 2005 (Suryono et al., 2019). It is an alternative to the traditional loan provided by the banks and other financial institutions where a P2P lending platform works as a matchmaker that matches borrowers with a lender. Online P2P lending claims to be beneficial for both borrowers as well as lenders. It reduces transaction costs by eliminating intermediaries. P2P lending enables lenders to directly contact the borrowers and vice versa to obtain/give loans by eliminating the intermediaries (Lehner, 2016). There is a lot of similarity between crowdfunding as P2P lending as both these platforms provide funds to the borrowers via online medium by eliminating the intermediaries. Also, both these platforms are versatile as money can be arranged for entrepreneurial ventures, commercial projects, creating concepts and social and political projects. But, these two methods are not the same (Ali et al., 2020; Khan & Rabbani, 2021). There are many differences between the two, as mentioned in Table 2:

Table 2 Difference between crowdfunding and P2P lending

Points	Crowdfunding	P2P lending
Equity/Loan	Crowdfunding gives investors the ownership right in the project. By investing in the project through crowdfunding, investors get ownership rights and have the right to participate in the management affairs of the project	P2P lending is more of debt-based financing. It is an alternative to the loan provided by the banks and financial institutions. Money provided by the lender is returned by the borrower together with interest. The lender does not get any ownership right in the deal
Scope	The scope of the crowdfunding is for a single project. The money can be used for a startup or for an expansion of a specific project	The scope of P2P lending is broader in nature. The money provided can be used for the multiple projects. Investors know the risk profile of the borrower but reason for borrowing is not known
Rate of return	Since Crowdfunding is equity investment. The rate of return on crowdfunding is unknown. The rate of return depends on the profit earned by the company	The rate of return is fixed. The borrower must pay the agreed rate of interest even in case of loss
Risk	This is a high-risk investment. The investor might lose the capital if the project fails. The investor does not get anything if the project fails to earn profit	The risk is low, as it is more secured investment. The rate of profit is fixed plus cumulative. If profit is not paid year it is accumulated in the next year
Duration of investment	It is an equity investment as investor holds shares of the company. It can be forever or till the time investors sells his stake to someone else	It is for a limited period, usually for 5 years. As the amount of loan is repaid to the lender the relationship ends
Flexibility	It is more rigid as the fund raised cannot be used for the purpose other than the reason mentioned	It is more flexible financing method. P2P offers more accessible and flexible way of financing for established businesses

(continued)

Table 2 (continued)

Points	Crowdfunding	P2P lending
Sharia compliance	It is closer to sharia principles. The investors take risk and the rate of return is not pre-fixed	It violates the basic ethos and principles of sharia as investors receive fixed rate of return and there is no risk for the investor

3 Challenges in Existing Islamic Crowdfunding and P2P Lending Platforms

All technological advancements and innovations are permissible in Islam as long as it does not violate the basic ethos and principle of sharia (Atif et al., 2021; Rabbani et al., 2021a, 2021b). The same concept applies to the financial technologies as well, for example, one of the most popular Fintech innovation, which is cryptocurrencies, can be accepted if it follows the Sharia law (Khan & Rabbani, 2021). However, there are different opinions of the scholars on cryptocurrencies as well, some scholars consider it as halal and others classify it as haram. There have been seen a large growth in Islamic Fintech in terms of revenues and customers. Malaysia, followed by London and Indonesia, has the maximum number of firms based on Islamic Fintech (Firmansyah & Anwar, 2019). As the number of Islamic Fintech firms increase, so the need of regulating these firms also increase. If the regulations are a little relaxed, then it might result in neglecting the privacy and protection of the customer's data and if the regulations are very strict then it might hinder the proper functioning of the firms. The rules and regulations should maintain the balance of the interests of both parties. Therefore, one of the major challenges is regulation of the Islamic Fintech.

Most of the governments around the world do not have suitable regulations for Islamic Fintech based firms or in general Fintech firms (Firmansyah & Anwar, 2019). For a Fintech firm to be sharia-compliant, it should agree with Sharia law such as the firm should not be involved in impermissible/haram business, firm should share the loss and profits, should not charge interest if it is lending money or if the bills are delayed, etc. (Muneeza, 2020). Most of the crowdfunding firm falls into this category and are in agreement with the Sharia law and some loan-based crowdfunding firms need to adapt Sharia law (Aghdam et al., 2020; Berns et al., 2020; Rusdin et al., 2017). Blockchain-based crowdfunding solution can be a game changer in this field as it can mitigate some of the risks faced by the stakeholders in crowdfunding such as their contribution would be returned if the targets are not achieved. Using Blockchain technology, smart contracts can be issued to provide a guarantee that if the targets are not met contributors' contribution would be returned (Zhou & Ye, 2019). However, using Blockchain technology has its own challenges such as lack of internet access (more than 50%), more than one billion people lack digital literacy (Martínez-Climent et al., 2020), Blockchain technology is in its early stage and Blockchain requires financial industry to adjust their infrastructure to use it (Karim et al., 2022; Khan & Rabbani, 2020).

Online Peer-to-Peer Lending (P2P) platforms have seen a large growth in the last decade as the innovations in financial technologies have increased. The success of P2P platform is influenced by both internal and external stakeholders and lenders' performance. The interaction with the external stakeholders is a crucial factor in success of the P2P lending websites. However, internal factors such as the organizational design and business model are also vital factors for the success of P2P platforms (Dorfleitner & Hornuf, 2019). Information asymmetry is also a significant challenge in P2P lending. Information asymmetry refers to the differences in information among different stakeholders. Big data has been suggested a possible solution for reducing information asymmetry (Beheshti et al., 2018; Ignatyuk et al., 2020; Sun et al., 2020). Researches also suggest that the trustworthiness of the borrowers is also an important factor to run a successful fund-raising campaign on P2P platforms (Huang et al., 2020). The confidence about borrower (borrower's score) is a crucial factor and identifying it, is a major challenge for P2P lending platforms. P2P lending platforms collect data from third parties, so the credibility of the data is also an issue. Different techniques have been employed to evaluate the credit score of the borrowers such as Profit Scoring (Serrano, 2018), LightGBM and XGboost algorithms (Dushnitsky & Fitza, 2018; Hervé & Schwienbacher, 2018), Score Matrix (Mollick, 2014), Decision Support, Decision Tree, Random Forest, Bayesian Hyper-Parameter Optimization, Hybrid Random Walk Approach, Classification Method, AdaBoost Algorithm, Feature Selection, Prediction performance Loan with Data Mining and other Machine

Learning Algorithms (Barrales-Molina et al., 2020; Chan et al., 2020; Ebelebe, 2019; Leone & Schiavone, 2019; Sahaym et al., 2019; Scholz, 2015).

P2P lending platforms bring the lenders and borrowers together, any kind of rumors (positive or negative) about the borrowers will affect the decision of the lenders, rumors can trigger the herding behavior (Zhao et al., 2020) (Xiang et al., 2018). A research study shows that the gender of the investors can also be a decisive factor as female borrowers receive more funding than the male borrowers (Zheng et al., 2017). Regulation and policy related to Fintech are not clear in majority of the countries. Any novel financial technological model must face this challenge. Same applies to the P2P lending platforms as well. Complying with regulations and policies has been a big challenge in proper functioning of the P2P lending platforms (Davis et al., 2017) (Chan et al., 2020) and in some cases it leads to scams as well (Kim et al., 2017). If the regulations and governmental policies approve Islamic Fintech, Islamic Finance-based P2P lending platform can be a viable modal. Instead of guaranteed or predetermined profit, a risk-sharing model can overcome most of the challenges of P2P lending platforms (Mohammad et al., 2020; Rabbani, 2020; Rabbani et al., 2021a, 2021b).

4 Conclusion and Future Work

This study discusses and analyzes the disruption innovation Crowdfunding and Peer-to-Peer lending methods of finance with respect to Islamic Finance. Sharia principle-based Fintech models for Crowdfunding and Peer-to-Peer lending platforms can resolve most of the existing problems and challenges of these platforms. This study discusses in detail how Crowdfunding and Peer-to-Peer lending platform function and how Crowdfunding and Peer-to-Peer lending models are different from each other and how they can be a game changer for the startups and small and medium enterprises (SMEs). The study also examines and identifies the challenge faced by crowdfunding and Peer-to-Peer lending platforms. It further reports that Crowdfunding and Peer-to Peer-lending could be the future of Islamic Fintech, especially for the high-risk startups and small and medium enterprises (SMEs), however, it needs to be further investigated, researched and developed by the academia, regulating bodies, researchers and other stakeholders. The researchers are already working in this direction and plenty of work has already been done (Biancone & Secinaro, 2016; Biancone et al., 2019; Wahjono et al., 2015a, 2015b). At the end, it is concluded that between crowdfunding and P2P lending, former is closer to the sharia principles, as it works on the principle of risk sharing and equity participation (Rosavina et al., 2019; Tamara & Kasri, 2020). On the other hand, Islamic Finance-based P2P lending platform can be a viable modal of financing if instead of guaranteed or predetermined profit, a risk-sharing model can overcome most of the challenges of P2P lending platforms.

REFERENCES

Abdullah, Y., & Rabbani, M. R. (2021). COVID-19 and GCC Islamic Market Indices. In *2021 International Conference on Sustainable Islamic Business and Finance (SIBF)*.

Aghdam, M. S., Alamtabriz, A., Qazvini, A. S., & Zandhessami, H. (2020). A system dynamics approach to designing a crowdfunding model in technological entrepreneurship ecosystem with a focus on technology incubator centers. *Journal of Optimization in Industrial Engineering, 13*(1), 113–122.

Ali, M. A. M., Bashar, A., Abdullah, Y., & Rabbani, M. R. (2020). Transforming business decision making with internet of things (IoT) and machine learning (ML). In *IEEE explore, DASA'20*.

Arshad, N., Ramírez-Pasillas, M., & Hollebeek, L. D. (2020). Sustainable Crowdfunding for Subsistence Entrepreneurship. *Contributions to Management Science*, 49–62.

Atif, M., Hassan, M. K., Rabbani, M. R., & Khan, S. (2021). Islamic FinTech: The digital transformation bringing sustainability in Islamic finance. In *COVID-19 and Islamic Social Finance* (In press).

Barrales-Molina, V., Riquelme-Medina, M., & Llorens-Montes, F. J. (2020). When do start-ups patent their inventions? Evidence from a broad approach. *Entrepreneurship Research Journal*.

Bashar, A., Rabbani, M. R., Khan, S., & Ali, M. A. M. (2021). Data driven finance: A bibliometric review and scientific mapping. In *2021 International Conference on Data Analytics for Business and Industry (ICDABI)* (pp. 161–166).

Beheshti, A., Schiliro, F., Ghodratnama, S., Amouzgar, F., Benatallah, B., Yang, J., Sheng, Q. Z., Casati, F., & Motahari-Nezhad, H. R. (2018). IProcess: enabling IoT platforms in data-driven knowledge-intensive processes enabling IoT platforms in data-driven knowledge-intensive processes. *LNBIP, 329*, 108–126.

Benna, A. (2018). Collaborative consumption as a tool for agricultural expansion in developing countries: Enriching farmers by delivering value to consumers. In *Crowdfunding and Sustainable Urban Development in Emerging Economies* (pp. 39–59). Durham University, United Kingdom: IGI Global.

Berns, J. P., Figueroa-Armijos, M., da Motta Veiga, S. P., & Dunne, T. C. (2020). Dynamics of lending-based prosocial crowdfunding: Using a social responsibility lens. *Journal of Business Ethics, 161*(1), 169–185.

Biancone, P. P., & Secinaro, S. (2016). The equity crowdfunding Italy: A model Sharia compliant. *European Journal of Islamic Finance*, (5).

Biancone, P. P., Secinaro, S., & Kamal, M. (2019). Crowdfunding and Fintech: Business model Sharia compliant. *European Journal of Islamic Finance*, (12).

Bœuf, B., Darveau, J., & Legoux, R. (2014). Financing creativity: Crowdfunding as a new approach for theatre projects. *International Journal of Arts Management, 16*(3), 33–48.

Chan, C. S. R., Park, H. D., Huang, J. Y., & Parhankangas, A. (2020). Less is more? Evidence for a curvilinear relationship between readability and screening evaluations across pitch competition and crowdfunding contexts. *Journal of Business Venturing Insights, 14*.

Davis, B. C., Hmieleski, K. M., Webb, J. W., & Coombs, J. E. (2017). Funders' positive affective reactions to entrepreneurs' crowdfunding pitches: The influence of perceived product creativity and entrepreneurial passion. *Journal of Business Venturing, 32*(1), 90–106.

Dorfleitner, G., & Hornuf, L. (2019). *FinTech and data privacy in Germany: An empirical analysis with policy recommendations*. Springer International Publishing.

Dushnitsky, G., & Fitza, M. A. (2018). Are we missing the platforms for the crowd? Comparing investment drivers across multiple crowdfunding platforms. *Journal of Business Venturing Insights, 10*.

Ebelebe, U. B. (2019). Reinventing nollywood: the impact of online funding and distribution on Nigerian cinema. *Convergence, 25*(3), 466–478.

Firmansyah, E. A., & Mokhamad, A. (2019). Islamic Financial Technology (Fintech): Its Challenges and Prospect, *216*(Assdg 2018), 52–58.

Giudici, G. (2015). Equity crowdfunding of an entrepreneurial activity. In *University Evolution, Entrepreneurial Activity and Regional Competitiveness* (Vol. 32). Politecnico di Milano - School of Management, Milan, Italy: Springer International Publishing.

Hasan, R., Hassan, M. K., & Aliyu, S. (2020). Fintech and Islamic finance: Literature review and research agenda. *International Journal of Islamic Economics and Finance (IJIEF), 1*(2), 75–94.

Hassan, M. K., Rabbani, M. R., & Ali, M. A. (2020a). Challenges for the Islamic finance and banking in post COVID era and the role of Fintech. *Journal of Economic Cooperation and Development, 43*(3).

Hassan, M. K., Rabbani, M. R., & Ali, M. A. (2020b). Challenges for the Islamic finance and banking in post COVID era and the role of Fintech. *Journal of Economic Cooperation and Development, 43*(3), 93–116.
Hervé, F., & Schwienbacher, A. (2018). Crowdfunding and innovation. *Journal of Economic Surveys, 32*(5), 1514–1530.
Honisch, E., & Ottenbacher, M. (2017). Crowdfunding in restaurants: Setting the stage. *Journal of Culinary Science and Technology, 15*(3), 223–238.
Huang, J., Sena, V., Li, J., & Ozdemir, S. (2020). Message framing in P2P lending relationships. *Journal of Business Research.*
Ignatyuk, A., Liubkina, O., Murovana, T., & Magomedova, A. (2020). FinTech as an innovation challenge: From big data to sustainable development. In *2020 International Conference on Sustainable Futures: Environmental, Technological, Social and Economic Matters, ICSF 2020* (Vol. 166), edited by S. S., C. S., Sakhno S., S. A., O. V., S. V., V. T., N. P., B. O., and D. H. Taras Shevchenko National University of Kyiv, Faculty of Economics, 90-A Vasylkivska Str.02090, Ukraine: EDP Sciences.
Jiang, H., Wang, Z., Yang, L., Shen, J., & Hahn, J. (2020). How rewarding are your rewards? A value-based view of crowdfunding rewards and crowdfunding performance. *Entrepreneurship: Theory and Practice.*
Karim, S., Rabbani, M. R., & Bawazir, H. (2022). Applications of blockchain technology in the finance and banking industry beyond digital currencies. In *Blockchain Technology and Computational Excellence for Society 5.0* (pp. 216–238). IGI Global.
Khan, S., & Rabbani, M. R. (2020, November). Chatbot as Islamic Finance Expert (CaIFE) When Finance Meets Artificial Intelligence. In Proceedings of the 2020 4th International Symposium on Computer Science and Intelligent Control (pp. 1–5).
Khan, S., & Rabbani, M. R. (2021). Artificial intelligence and NLP-based chatbot for islamic banking and finance. *International Journal of Information Retrieval Research (IJIRR), 11*(3), 65–77.
Khan, S., & Rabbani, M. R. (2022). In-depth analysis of blockchain, cryptocurrency and sharia compliance. *International Journal of Business Innovation and Research, 29*(1), 1–15.
Khan, M. S., Rabbani, M. R., Hawaldar, I. T., & Bashar, A. (2022). Determinants of behavioral intentions to use islamic financial technology: An empirical assessment. *Risks, 10*(6), 114.
Kim, T., Por, M. H., & Yang, S. B. (2017). Winning the crowd in online fundraising platforms: The roles of founder and project features. *Electronic Commerce Research and Applications, 25*, 86–94.
Lehner, O. M. (2016). Crowdfunding social ventures: A model and research agenda. In *Routledge Handbook of Social and Sustainable Finance* (pp. 139–160). Taylor and Francis.

Leone, D., & Schiavone, F. (2019). Innovation and knowledge sharing in crowdfunding: How social dynamics affect project success. *Technology Analysis and Strategic Management, 31*(7), 803–816.

Martínez-Climent, C., Mastrangelo, L., & Ribeiro-Soriano, D. (2020). The knowledge spillover effect of crowdfunding. *Knowledge Management Research and Practice.*

Mohammad, S., Khan, M., & Yannis. (2020). An artificial intelligence and NLP based Islamic FinTech model combining Zakat and Qardh-Al-Hasan for countering the adverse impact of COVID 19 on SMEs and individuals. *International Journal of Economics and Business Administration,* VIII(Issue 2), 351–364.

Mollick, E. (2014). The dynamics of crowdfunding: An exploratory study. *Journal of Business Venturing, 29*(1), 1–16.

Muneeza, A. (2020). Short-term sharīʿah-compliant islamic liquidity management instruments to sustain Islamic banking: The case of Maldives. *Journal of Islamic Accounting and Business Research, 11*(2), 428–439.

Rabbani, M. R. (2020). The competitive structure and strategic positioning of commercial banks in Saudi Arabia. *International Journal on Emerging Technologies, 11*(3), 43–46.

Rabbani, M. R., Bashar, A., Nawaz, N., Karim, S., Ali, M. A. M., Khan, A., Rahiman, H., & Alam, S. (2021a). Exploring the role of Islamic Fintech in combating the after-shocks of COVID-19: The open social innovation of the Islamic financial system. *Journal of Open Innovation: Technology, Market, and Complexity, 7,* 136.

Rabbani, M. R., Hassan, M. K., Khan, S., & Ali, M. A. (2021b). Artificial Intelligence and NLP Based Fintech model on Zakat for poverty alleviation and sustainable development for Muslims in India. In *Islamic Perspective for Sustainable Financial System.*

Rabbani, M. R. (2022). Fintech innovations, scope, challenges, and implications in Islamic finance: A systematic analysis. *International Journal of Computing and Digital Systems, 11*(1), 1–28.

Rabbani, M. R., Kayani, U., Bawazir, H. S., & Hawaldar, I. T. (2022). A commentary on emerging markets banking sector spillovers: covid-19 vs GFC pattern analysis. *Heliyon, 8*(3), e09074.

Rodríguez, P. M., Martínez, V. J. S., & Muñoz, A. E. P. (2018). The crowdfunding phenomenon in an emerging context: The case of Colombia. In *31st International Business Information Management Association Conference: Innovation Management and Education Excellence through Vision 2020, IBIMA 2018* (pp. 4366–4375), edited by S. K.S. Universidad del Norte, Barranquilla, Colombia: International Business Information Management Association, IBIMA.

Rosavina, M., Rahadi, R. A., Kitri, M. L., Nuraeni, S., & Mayangsari, L. (2019). P2P lending adoption by SMEs in Indonesia. *Qualitative Research in Financial Markets*.

Rusdin, M. F., Ghazali, M., & Razak, S. A. (2017). Online crowdfunding as academic grants: A systematic literature review. *Journal of Telecommunication, Electronic and Computer Engineering*, 9(3–4 Special Issue), 187–193.

Sahaym, A., (Avi) Datta, A., & Brooks, S. (2019). Crowdfunding success through social media: Going beyond entrepreneurial orientation in the context of small and medium-sized enterprises. *Journal of Business Research*.

Sannajust, A., Roux, F., & Chaibi, A. (2014). Crowdfunding in France: A new revolution? *Journal of Applied Business Research*, 30(6), 1909–1918.

Scholz, N. (2015). *The Relevance of Crowdfunding: The Impact on the Innovation Process of Small Entrepreneurial Firms*. Manchester, United Kingdom: Springer Science+Business Media.

Serrano, W. (2018). Fintech model: The random neural network with genetic algorithm. In *22nd International Conference on Knowledge-Based and Intelligent Information and Engineering Systems, KES 2018* (Vol. 126, pp. 537–546), edited by T. C., H. Y., H. R. J., J. L. C., & J. L. C. Intelligent Systems and Networks Group, Imperial College London, London, United Kingdom: Elsevier B.V.

Sun, H., Rabbani, M. R., Sial, M. S., Yu, S., Filipe, J. A., & Cherian, J. (2020). Identifying big data's opportunities, challenges, and implications in finance. *Mathematics*, 8(10).

Suryono, R. R., Purwandari, B., & Budi, I. (2019). Peer to Peer (P2P) lending problems and potential solutions: A systematic literature review. In *5th Information Systems International Conference, ISICO 2019* (Vol. 161, pp. 204–214) edited by Y. A. Faculty of Computer Science, Universitas Indonesia, Depok, 16424, Indonesia: Elsevier B.V.

Tajudin, M., Omar, R., Smedlund, A., & Aziz, R. P. (2020). Financing with heart and intelligence: Augmenting intimacy and sustainability through Islamic Fintech. *International Journal of Advanced Science and Technology*, 29(9 Special Issue), 1638–1664.

Tamara, P., & Kasri, R. A. (2020). The impact of Sharia Peer-to-Peer lending financing on the business performance of Islamic micro enterprises: Case study of PT. Ammana Fintek Syariah. In *Research on Firm Financial Performance and Consumer Behavior*.

Valančienė, L., & Jegelevičiūtė, S. (2014). Crowdfunding for creating value: Stakeholder approach. *Procedia—Social and Behavioral Sciences*.

Wahjono, S. I., Marina, A., & Widayat. (2015a). Islamic crowdfunding : Alternative. *1st World Islamic Social Science Congress*.

Wahjono, S. I., Marina, A., & Widayat. (2015b). Islamic crowdfunding : Alternative funding solution. *1st World Islamic Social Science Congress*.

Wu, S., Wang, B., & Li, Y. (2015). How to attract the crowd in crowdfunding? *International Journal of Entrepreneurship and Small Business, 24*(3), 322–334.

Xiang, D., Zhang, Y., & Worthington, A. C. (2018). Determinants of the use of Fintech finance among Chinese small and medium-sized enterprises. In *1st Annual International Symposium on Innovation and Entrepreneurship of the IEEE Technology and Engineering Management Society, TEMS-ISIE 2018*. China Institute for Micro Small and Medium-sized Enterprises, School of Business Administration, Qilu University of Technology, Shandong Academy of Sciences, China: Institute of Electrical and Electronics Engineers Inc.

Yan, Z., Wang, K., Tsai, S. B., & Zhou, L. (2018). An empirical study on internet startup financing from a green financial perspective. *Sustainability (Switzerland), 10*(8).

Younkin, P., & Kashkooli, K. (2016). What problems does crowdfunding solve? *California Management Review, 58*(2), 20–43.

Zhang, H., & Chen, W. (2019). Crowdfunding technological innovations: Interaction between consumer benefits and rewards. *Technovation, 84–85*, 11–20.

Zhao, Y., Xie, X., & Yang, L. (2020). Female entrepreneurs and equity crowdfunding: The consequential roles of lead investors and venture stages. *International Entrepreneurship and Management Journal*.

Zheng, H., Xu, B., Wang, T., & Chen, D. (2017). Project implementation success in reward-based crowdfunding: An empirical study. *International Journal of Electronic Commerce, 21*(3), 424–448.

Zhou, H., & Ye, S. (2019). Legitimacy, worthiness, and social network: An empirical study of the key factors influencing crowdfunding outcomes for nonprofit projects. *Voluntas: International Journal of Voluntary and Nonprofit Organizations, 30*(4), 849–864.

Islamic Finance and Cryptocurrency: A Systematic Review

Mustafa Raza Rabbani, M. Kabir Hassan, Fahmi Ali Hudaefi, and Zakir Hossen Shaikh

1 Introduction

Cryptocurrency is a new phenomenon getting huge attention from the academic and industry practitioners. It uses a new technology which has huge potential to serve as the long-term financial assets. It can be

---

M. R. Rabbani (✉)
Department of Economics and Finance, College of Business Administration, University of Bahrain, Zallaq, Bahrain
e-mail: mrabbani@uob.edu.bh

M. K. Hassan
Department of Economics and Finance, University of New Orleans, New Orleans, LA, USA
e-mail: mhassan@uno.edu

F. A. Hudaefi
Institute Agama Islam Darussalam (IAID) Ciamis, Indonesia and BAZNAS Center of Strategic Studies, Jakarta, Indonesia
e-mail: alihudzaifi@gmail.com

Z. H. Shaikh
Faculty, Commercial Studies Division, Ministry of Education, Bahrain Training Institute, Isa Town, Bahrain
e-mail: zakir.shaikh@bti.moe.bh

© The Author(s), under exclusive license to Springer Nature Switzerland AG 2022
M. K. Hassan et al. (eds.), *FinTech in Islamic Financial Institutions*, https://doi.org/10.1007/978-3-031-14941-2_14

defined as "the digital currency where the transactions are verified by the decentralized ledger system and using the technology called cryptography without any central authority" (Akyildirim et al., 2019; Galanov et al., 2018). In other words, it can be defined as "the digital currency designed to serve as the medium of exchange using computer network without any interference from the central authority" (Khan et al., 2022).

Shariah scholars are divided over the legality of cryptocurrency as per the Islamic finance point of view but the general consensus is that it is haram and it is not advisable for a Muslim to invest in cryptocurrencies such as Bitcoin, Ethereum, Litecoin, etc. (Khan & Rabbani, 2021). From the very core of the Islamic finance, Islamic finance aims to create a financial system free from all kinds of interest/*Riba*, high speculation/uncertainty, *Gharar*, *Maisir* and protect the right of the investors from all kinds of unfair trade practices and fraud (Abdullah & Rabbani, 2021; Rabbani et al., 2022). Cryptocurrency was developed to facilitate peer-to-peer transaction that works independently without any interference of the central banks. Cryptocurrency such as the Bitcoin is popular among the young millennials (Alam et al., 2019). At its core, cryptocurrency is a financial asset or a protocol that facilitates the transfer of funds between two unrelated persons or organizations over the internet ensuring that the transaction has been completed and value has been transferred from one party to the other. The transactions are automatically recorded in a public ledger and verified through a technology called cryptography by a network of highly secured decentralized computers. The computers securing the transactions are decentralized, which enables these to operate without the intervention from traditional financial intermediaries, leading to direct solutions for the users (Ghosh et al., 2020). Cryptocurrency is a form of digital asset, which is gaining momentum as a medium exchange (Haffke et al., 2020). It uses Blockchain in its backdrop that offer higher levels of security (Rabbani, 2021).

The concept of cryptocurrency came into the limelight in the year 2008 when Satoshi Nakamoto published a white paper and subsequently paved the way for the creation of the first cryptocurrency called Bitcoin in 2009 (Phillip et al., 2018). Since then, it has emerged as one of the most exciting and popular financial innovations in the finance world (Harvey & Branco-Illodo, 2020). Despite the fact that it is extremely volatile and amounts to high risk in the transactions, it has been popular among the investors (Mazambani & Mutambara, 2020). The popularity of Cryptocurrencies can be attributed to the development and innovations and mass adoption of information technology (Saleh et al., 2020a, 2020b). The transitions based on the Blockchain-based technologies are extremely safe and confidential. The rise and popularity of cryptocurrencies are also received attention from anti-social elements, such as drug dealers, extortionist and terrorists (Kethineni & Cao, 2020). These anti-social elements use it for doing illegal activities such as tax evasion, extortion, money laundering, ransom, etc. (Rabbani et al., 2021c). It poses a challenge to the law enforcement agencies and government bodies to identify the intention behind these transactions as criminals hide behind the popularity, privacy and anonymity of the cryptocurrency (Barone & Masciandaro, 2019). The complexity and volatility of the cryptocurrencies are yet to be exposed as they pose a great threat to the investors. The new evidence suggests that Cryptocurrency like Bitcoin possesses greater susceptibility to high price volatility (Muedini, 2018).

In simple terms, once a transaction is done, a message is sent to the network requesting that the amount has been deducted from the buyer's digital wallet and added to the seller's wallet. The request remains on the network for a while till the miners complete to process the blocks of transactions and an update is made on the Blockchain (Asif, 2018; Nuraliati & Azwari, 2019). Once the Blockchain is updated the transaction becomes irreversible. This process might take time between 10 seconds to 10 minutes depending on the type of cryptocurrency in question (Hassan et al., 2020; Rabbani et al., 2020a).

The unprecedented positive return on cryptocurrency has also attracted the Muslim investors to invest in it and include Cryptocurrency in their portfolio of assets (Abdul et al., 2019). There are many Muslim investors who have already invested in different cryptocurrencies and became part of this dynamic market (Rabbani et al., 2020b). The obvious factors related to the cryptocurrency such as, the volatility in return, no regulating authority, no real form, only digital without intrinsic not redeemable to another currency, high speculation and so on. Now the question to be asked is, whether it is as per the sharia and does Islamic finance recognize it?

The present chapter attempts to answer this question and examine the compatibility of cryptocurrency such as Bitcoin with the context of Islamic law. It presents an extensive review of the concept of money in Islamic finance and the requirement of a currency to be called as money as per sharia. Extensive review of the existing available sharia-compliant cryptocurrencies. Challenges in developing and implementing the sharia version of cryptocurrencies. The findings of the study will help to understand the current climate of the cryptocurrencies, their sharia compliance and its use in the modern finance world.

The study applied a systematic review of the reports, opinions of sharia scholars based on various published research papers, online search engines and commentaries related to the Islamic finance and sharia compliance.

The remaining part of the chapter is structured as follows; First part introduces the topic, and second part presents an overview of literature and methodology used for the study. Third section highlights the characteristics of money as per Islamic finance principles and requirements of Cryptocurrency to be called as money. In the fourth section we review the existing sharia-compliant cryptocurrencies available in the Islamic finance market. In Sect. 5, we conclude and provide the scope for future researchers to research in this area.

2 AN OVERVIEW OF THE LITERATURE ON CRYPTOCURRENCY AND SHARIA COMPLIANCE

There is only a handful of literature available on Cryptocurrency and its Sharia compliance. The available literature also lacks substance as it does not provide valid arguments and discussion on the Shariah relevance of the instruments. An overview of some of the related studies is provided in Table 1:

The most comprehensive study on sharia compliance of cryptocurrency came from (Khan & Rabbani, 2021), they provided a comprehensive review of Cryptocurrency and its sharia compliance. In the paper they argued that Cryptocurrency is the need of the hour for Muslim Ummah and if it is allowed it can benefit the community at large. The sharia scholars should find some ways and allow it with certain restrictions. It was concluded that the existing Cryptocurrencies like Bitcoin, Ethereum, etc., are not in consistent with the sharia principles. However, researchers strongly believe that the underlying technology Blockchain is a revolutionary technology and there is scope to overcome the arguments from the opponents and develop a Cryptocurrency which is as per sharia principles by using the Blockchain technology. Another important study came from (Aliyu et al., 2020), where they reviewed some of the existing sharia-compliant cryptocurrencies available in the Islamic finance market. In the paper they concluded that the sharia compliance of the cryptocurrencies will motivate and encourage the prospective Muslim investors and it will

Table 1 An overview of the literature on Cryptocurrency and sharia compliance

Paper Info	Purpose	Methodology	Results	Weakness
(Meera, 2018)	The paper discusses and analyzes the cryptocurrency from the perspective of sharia	Theoretical and discussion paper	• There is no evidence that Bitcoin violates the norms of sharia • If volatility of the Cryptocurrencies gets in comparison to the major fiat currencies, it must be allowed by the sharia	The paper is limited to theoretical discussion only with no practical substance
(Siswantoro et al., 2020)	The paper applied the data of 23 Cryptocurrencies and related information to draw the conclusion	Mixed method of empirical research, data study and descriptive literature	• Cryptocurrency is hugely volatile and does not qualify to be called money • It can be allowed as a medium of exchange of digital currency but shall not be called money	Only 17 Cryptocurrencies were taken for the empirical study

(continued)

Table 1 (continued)

Paper Info	Purpose	Methodology	Results	Weakness
(Aliyu et al., 2020)	To review the existing sharia-compliant cryptocurrencies and check whether it exactly comply with the norms of sharia	Theoretical and discussion-based paper	• Accepting and recognizing the Cryptocurrency in the Islamic finance will go a long way in enhancing the Islamic finance business globally • All claimed sharia-complied cryptocurrencies are not fully complied with the sharia	There is no mechanism to test the sharia compliance of a cryptocurrency
(Widyatama et al., 2019)	To propose a sharia-based cryptocurrency for the benefits of the Ummah	Theoretical concept-based research	• The cryptocurrency can be used in *Muamlat* and sell-based transactions as long as it does not have an element of *Riba*, and it is made voluntary	Discussion paper

Paper Info	Purpose	Methodology	Results	Weakness
(Abubakar et al., 2019)	To check the implication of the development of the Blockchain and Cryptocurrency market for the Islamic financial system	Theoretical and conceptual approach	• The development in the cryptocurrency market will bring many benefits to the Islamic financial system • It will help in developing a unified decentralized financial system and Islamic financial system must be proactive about the ongoing development in the Crypto market	The paper does not provide the valid argument or does not provide the model, rather it vaguely reviews the existing literature only
(Oziev & Yandiev, 2018a, 2018b)	The paper discusses the Cryptocurrency from the sharia perspective	Review of existing literature	• Cryptocurrencies are volatile as compared to paper money • Cryptocurrency must be allowed but with strict restrictions	No empirical evidence

(continued)

Table 1 (continued)

Paper Info	Purpose	Methodology	Results	Weakness
(Lahmiri & Bekiros, 2019)	The paper examines the breakdown of the structure of green and sharia-compliant and green cryptocurrencies	Multi-step resolution with empirical evidence	• The return of sharia-compliant and green cryptocurrencies presents anti-persistent dynamics • The volume and volatility present higher persistence in comparison to conventional cryptocurrencies	
(Aloui et al., 2020)	The paper examines the difference between conventional and gold-backed Islamic cryptocurrencies	Empirical study by using a multivariate GARCH model	• Sharia-compliant cryptocurrencies have a positive relationship with the gold prices as compared to its counterpart • Sharia compliant cryptocurrencies are not sensitive to the macroeconomic factors	

Paper Info	Purpose	Methodology	Results	Weakness
(Mensi et al., 2020)	The paper investigates the dynamic conditional correlation between the major cryptocurrency markets	Multivariate generalized family models	• There is a significant positive dynamic correlation between these markets • It is suggested that investors should hold more LiteCoin (LTC) than Bitcoin (BTC)	
(Lim & Masih, 2017)	The paper empirically examines the diversification benefits of Bitcoin along the Islamic capital market	Empirical study by using multivariate GARCH model	• No correlation found between returns of Islamic stocks and Bitcoin. Rather they are negatively correlated	The paper focuses only on the equity market. An important element of capital, i.e., SUKUK market is ignored
(Rehman et al., 2020)	The paper examines the spillover between the Islamic equity market and Bitcoin	It uses VaR, CoVaR and ΔCoVaR to empirically test the variable	• Islamic equity markets provide effective hedge benefits along with Bitcoin • There is a presence of risk spillover between Islamic equity market and Bitcoin	The paper focuses only on the equity market. An important element of capital, i.e., SUKUK market is ignored

(continued)

Table 1 (continued)

Paper Info	Purpose	Methodology	Results	Weakness
(Lahmiri & Bekiros, 2019)	The paper forecast the price of three key digital currencies from different markets	Use of deep learning to forecast the price of three key digital currencies namely, Bitcoin, Ripple and Digital cash	• The time series of all the sample digital currencies indicate factual dynamics and self-similarity • The predictability of Long-short term memory neural networks (LSTM) is higher than the general regression architecture	The paper is mainly focusing on European markets rather than the Islamic equity or SUKUK market
(Uddin et al., 2020)	The paper investigates whether Bitcoin constitutes a hedging instrument with portfolio diversification among different asset classes including Islamic asset class	Empirical study with multivariate generalized autoregressive conditional correlation	• The findings indicate that Bitcoin returns are sustainable and can be classified as a sustainable asset class and its return does not crush down to zero in the long run • It offers portfolio diversification with almost all the equity indices	

Paper Info	Purpose	Methodology	Results	Weakness
(Khan et al., 2020)	The paper introduces a SUKUK tokenization based on Blockchain technology	Theoretical and conceptual work	• The paper highlights the new and innovative trends in the SUKUK market • Case study was done on the SUKUK tokenization with smart contracts and Blockchain technology	Other types of SUKUK are ignored in the paper as it only focused on Murabaha SUKUK

help in widening the Islamic finance market. There have been many cryptocurrencies issues in the market recently to address the sharia compliance criticism. However, still the sharia scholars are divided over the sharia-compliant of these cryptocurrencies. There is a need for unanimity and consensus among the sharia scholars in calling a Cryptocurrency as Islamic or non-Islamic. It creates confusion and distrust among the Muslim investors which do not augers good for the future of Islamic finance industry. Sun et al. (2020) and Widyatama et al. (2019), in their paper on sharia compliance of Cryptocurrency, they considered Cryptocurrency as a disruptive innovation and concluded that it should be allowed with certain limitations if it does contain usury (*Riba*). It should be allowed on a voluntary basis for a legitimate trade transaction.

Another important study came from (Abubakar et al., 2019), where compared and contrasted the Cryptocurrency tide and Islamic fiancé developments. They highlighted the advantages of Cryptocurrency over the fiat currency. They concluded that it possesses three advantages, first, it will create a unified global financial system through proper standardization with its decentralization. Second, it will keep a check on the central banks' ability to play on the supply of money through traditional money. Third, they are of the opinion that financial risk is common across the currencies, and it's not limited to only cryptocurrency. The volatility of the currency is more about the underlying nature of the transaction and not about the currency. They suggested to contextualizing the Bitcoin-based Islamic banking transaction in a complete Bitcoin financial system. They suggested to setting up an international task force in coordination with the International Research Academy of Islamic Finance (ISRA), Islamic Financial Services Board (IFSB) and Islamic Research Training Institute (IRTI) to monitor and regulate the issue of technical notes, standards and sharia guidelines. The task force shall also ensure the sharia positions for Islamic banks and financial institutions that are interested in dealing with cryptocurrencies.

In another study on Islamic approach to purifications of transaction with cryptocurrency (Saleh et al., 2020a, 2020b), they have done a qualitative study by conducting an interview of the investors to examine the negative perception of Cryptocurrency from the Islamic point of view. They concluded that the Use of Cryptocurrency is as legitimate as any other payment methods, they also claim that it has been supported by the *hadith*. They finally concluded that Cryptocurrency is to be accepted as the sharia-compliant mode of payment as good as fiat money and values must be measured and quantified in Cryptocurrency terms. By studying the requirements of Cryptocurrency for money from Islamic finance point of view, (Siswantoro et al., 2020) concluded that Cryptocurrency is extremely volatile and it does not qualify to be called as money and also it is limited and there are chances that it can be used for speculation which is not allowed as per sharia. They went on further to conclude that Muslims will not use Cryptocurrency as money, and it will hinder the development of Cryptocurrency in the Muslim countries. In another study on sharia compliance of Cryptocurrency (Oziev & Yandiev, 2018a, 2018b) conducted a qualitative and descriptive analysis and concluded that it shall be allowed as a medium of exchange but subject to the strict regulation and restriction. They argued that there is no evidence that Bitcoin and other traditional Cryptocurrencies contradicts sharia. The argument that it is very volatile, and prices reach up to 60 thousand USD (United States Dollar) does not mean that it is illegal from a sharia point of view. Considering the huge demand and popularity of the Cryptocurrency among the Muslim Youths, the authors recommended for creation and development of an Islamic Cryptocurrency under supervision of Islamic Development Bank (ISDB). Sharia-Compliant Cryptocurrency must be developed by taking into consideration all the concerns related to sharia compliance and must be acceptable to the parties concerned. In this way, ISDB will play a significant role in the growth of the Global Islamic finance industry. (Meera, 2018) concluded that keeping the surge in price of Bitcoin in 2008, it looks like it is a bubble and bubble can burst anytime and cause a great discomfort to the investors, hence investment in Cryptocurrencies like Bitcoin is indeed a gamble and gamble (*Maisir*) is strictly prohibited in Islam. They further concluded that, the massive popularity of the Bitcoin and other Cryptocurrencies indicate that the traditional fiat money is folding up and the international finance market is looking for an alternate option and Bitcoin has provided that stable option. Finally, it is concluded that the money with no reference material will lose its value sooner than later and can result in utter collapse and can cause losses for the investors, Bitcoin is the great example for that.

From the above Review of Literature, it can be concluded that the sharia scholars are divided over the legality of Cryptocurrency as per the sharia. This is a great matter of investigation and examination and to come to a consensus where there is Ijma among the Sharia scholars on whether to accept or reject this disruptive innovation. The present study is an attempt in this direction to put forward the different views from different sections of the scholars and draw conclusions from them.

3 Discussion and Findings

It is a matter of debate and discussion whether Cryptocurrency complies with the strict rules and regulations to be qualified as money and to be allowed as a medium of exchange.

Cryptocurrency has been analyzed from the sharia point of view by many scholars, the most notable works include, (Aliyu et al., 2020; Khan & Rabbani, 2021; Muedini, 2018; Siswantoro et al., 2020). Most of the studies focused on the requirements of a cryptocurrency to be classified as sharia-compliant and suitability of Cryptocurrency in the structure of Islamic banking and finance. While examining the dynamism and mechanism of Cryptocurrency toward Islamic finance (Abdul et al., 2019), state that there must be at least two factors present in the Cryptocurrency to be classified as the sharia-compliant. The two factors include backing from the real assets and legal authorization. This claim is also supported by the scholars such as, (Aliyu et al., 2020; Khan & Rabbani, 2021; Oziev & Yandiev, 2018a, 2018b; Rabbani et al., 2021d; Saleh et al., 2020a, 2020b; Siswantoro et al., 2020). We divide our discussion into two parts. First, we take the arguments from scholars who believe that Cryptocurrency must be declared *halal* and then we take the opinions of the scholars who oppose these arguments.

Arguments Against Cryptocurrency

Islam considers money as a medium of exchange and using it for the trading for earning profits and losses, violates the basic principle of Islamic economics (Oziev & Yandiev, 2018a, 2018b; Siswantoro et al., 2020). Shariah law prohibits money to be traded rather it must be used as a medium of exchange (Khan & Rabbani, 2021). The real challenge among the scholars and practitioners has been in understanding the background, the concepts, because any person talking about the Cryptocurrency or Blockchain must have a clear understanding of how it operates, a judgment can only be passed if prior understanding of a concept has embedded in a person. It is a complete innovation, and you cannot find something like this in history (Hassan et al., 2021; Rabbani et al., 2021a, 2021b). The cryptocurrency investments do not serve the real economy as it does not generate any production, do not promote real growth of the economy and do not boost services (Abdul et al., 2019; Adam, 2017). Cryptocurrency has an element of *Gharar* and that makes it high-risk investment and it does not have any central authority regulating it that makes it susceptible like a bubble that can burst anytime and it is to be declared as haram (Meera, 2018; Oziev & Yandiev, 2018a, 2018b). The following arguments are given by the scholars to declare Cryptocurrency as haram commodity.

Excessive Uncertainty

There is a high degree of risk, uncertainty and fraud lance in Cryptocurrency trading and that makes it vulnerable for the small investors and traders (Alam et al., 2019; Ruslianor Maika et al., 2019; Siswantoro et al., 2020). Take for instance, as depicted in Fig. 1, it is so volatile that it's like a roller coaster ride for the investors. In the last one year itself, the most popular Cryptocurrency, Bitcoin has reached up to 24,433 from 10,260 as of 23/12/2020 from the same day last year (source: https://www.coindesk.com/price/bitcoin). There is no deep or systematic control over the issuance of these digital currencies and it is extremely sensitive to the market rumors and market conditions and it is also not linked to any established marketplace or economy (Ahmed et al., 2020; Gurdgiev & O'Loughlin, 2020). The instability and volatility in return and associated risk factor makes it against the basic principles of sharia and it is not to be allowed for trading (Abu Bakar et al., 2017).

Not Backed by the Real Assets

One of the key factors in Islamic finance is that all the transactions are backed by the real assets, and it is known as the asset-backed financing. The conventional banks and financial institutions can deal in money and papers only but in case of Islamic finance, money is not considered as subject matter of trade rather it is treated as the medium of exchange, i.e., it has no intrinsic utility. (Kabir Hassan & Aldayel, 1998; Maroney et al., 2019; Özkan et al., 2016). Each unit of money in Islamic finance is equal to 100% of the other denomination of money. Therefore, there is no scope for generating any profit if an exchange transaction is done for having intrinsic utility is sold or currencies are exchanged (Rabbani, 2022; Rabbani et al., 2021c). The profit earned from the transaction of dealing in money (of the same currency) is considered as interest (*Riba*) and that is declared as *haram* (Hassan et al., 2020; Mohammad et al., 2020). Cryptocurrency is digital money, there is no physical coin or bill, it's all online, besides the fact that it is widely being used for exchange transactions, it is used as a commodity which is against the principles of sharia (Khan & Rabbani, 2021).

Fig. 1 Bitcoin return in last one year (*Source* https://www.coindesk.com/price/bitcoin)

No Regulating Bodies
There are many Islamic scholars who argue that Cryptocurrency must be allowed based on *Maslaha*. Cryptocurrency is neither a fiat money nor a real money and it is also not backed by the real assets, and absence of intrinsic value and zero supervision by the regulating agency makes it vulnerable to being misused by the anti-social elements (Khan & Rabbani, 2021; Meera, 2018; Oziev & Yandiev, 2018a, 2018b).

Safety and Security of the Investors
Cryptocurrency uses cloud computing-based Blockchain technology, which is secure and temper proof, because Blockchain uses innovative and sophisticated math algorithm rules which are difficult for the attackers to break and manipulate (Ali et al., 2020; Atif et al., 2021). It is basically a decentralized and distributed ledger technology which records the movement of digital assets (Khan, 2020; Rabbani et al., 2021d; Saba et al., 2019). It's not that Blockchain technology cannot be hacked, or it does not possess any risk. It possesses the same risk as in the case of any other risk with the current business process like value transfer risk because Blockchain enables value transfer without any intermediary (Mohammad et al., 2020; Rabbani et al., 2020b). The year 2020 has

been the year of highest cryptocurrency theft as between January and May 2020, 1.36 Billion has been stolen in Crypto crimes (Anush et al., 2020).

Misuse by the Anti-social Elements
Most of the Cryptocurrencies transaction done are cross-border and there is a great chance that it is being used for terrorism funding (Carroll & Windle, 2018; Choo, 2015). The rise and popularity of cryptocurrencies are also attributed to its popularity among the criminals such as drug dealers, extortionist and terrorists (Kethineni & Cao, 2020). Islam is the religion of compassion and it has no place for the anti-social elements like money laundering, tax theft or terrorism and any transaction linked to these elements are strictly declared haram as per *Qur'an* and *Sunnah* (Chamberlain et al., 2020; Rivlin, 2008).

At the end of this section, it can be concluded that Cryptocurrency is a disruptive financial innovation and can be sharia-compliant if structured correctly. An investor should invest in Cryptocurrencies if the currencies have passed the sharia screening test which will determine if the core business activity is sharia-compliant. Therefore, there is a need to have a global Islamic task force to determine the sharia compliance of the particular cryptocurrency (Abubakar et al., 2019).

Arguments in Favor of Cryptocurrency

There are sharia scholars who favor Cryptocurrency and strongly argue that it must be allowed as per sharia and there is nothing wrong to be called against the sharia (Widyatama et al., 2019). Cryptocurrency is born because of financial innovation and any innovation is welcome in Islam if it does not violate the basic principles of sharia. It uses Blockchain technology and there is nothing non-Islamic about the Blockchain technology (Conlon et al., 2020; Lawal, 2019). The following arguments are provided by the scholars to be called it as sharia-compliant.

It's not Just Current and there is More to it

> Scholars such as (Hammad, 2018; Zubaidi & Abdullah, 2017) argue that Cryptocurrency is not just a currency it has more into it. It can serve as a transfer of value from one party to another by saving time and cost.

Volatility of currency shall not be the reason to declare it as haram because fiat currency is also volatile in value and keeps on changing. Both Fiat and cryptocurrency share the same nature as far as volatility is concerned.

Blockchain Technology
Cryptocurrency uses a technology called Blockchain and it is a very broad technology. Cryptocurrency is just a part of it, it can be used for multiple purposes such as, creating a permanent transparent ledger system for recording like land deals are any other transaction (Ali et al., 2020; Rabbani, 2020). This technology is fast and secure and speeds up the transaction for the benefit of its users. Blockchain-based technology can be used for the payment and collection of Zakat to bring more transparency in transaction (Mohammad et al., 2020; Rabbani et al., 2021c).

Uncertainty and Gharar
Uncertainty and *Gharar* is cited as the major reason behind declaring Cryptocurrency as haram by the sharia scholars. The scholars such as, (Lawal, 2019) and (Zubaidi & Abdullah, 2017), argue that there is a need to understand the difference between *Gharar* and risk. The risk factor is there even in fiat currency, and it cannot be declared haram based on risk factor.

Can Help in Fight Against Money Laundering
Spending through the Cryptocurrency can bring accountability. For instance, the donor of Zakat can ensure that the Zakat amount given by him has reached the right person, in this way money laundering can be prevented (Hassan et al., 2021; Khan et al., 2021).

There are many scholars supporting the above arguments in favor of Cryptocurrency to be declared as per the sharia-compliant (Lawal, 2019; Saleh et al., 2020a, 2020b). Table 2 presents the comparison of views of the scholars on compliance and non-compliance of Cryptocurrency as per sharia.

Table 2 Analysis of sharia compliance of Cryptocurrency

Cryptocurrency is sharia-compliant		Cryptocurrency is not sharia-compliant	
Paper Info	*Argument*	*Paper Info*	*Argument*
(Abubakar et al., 2019)	The stakeholders in Islamic finance must not be passive but be proactive in accepting financial innovation and should develop standards and guidelines to take part in migration to this future currency	(Oziev & Yandiev, 2018a, 2018b)	Cryptocurrency is not allowed in its current form but considering the huge demand interest of the internet users and investors, there is a need to develop a specialized Islamic Cryptocurrency under the guidelines of Islamic Development Bank (IDB)
(Hammad, 2018)	Cryptocurrency like Bitcoin is not haram on their own, its permissibility as per sharia depends on what we are doing with that currency. Bitcoin is just a tool and with that tool both a *Halal* and *Haram* work can be done. It is like cash and cash can also be used for buying an illegal drug or illegal purpose	(Siswantoro et al., 2020)	The cryptocurrency is banned in countries like China and Russia due to high risk and volatility. It is more volatile than the equity index such as S&P. Islam is a religion which does not encourage such risky investment and it shall not be allowed

(continued)

Table 2 (continued)

Cryptocurrency is sharia-compliant		Cryptocurrency is not sharia-compliant	
Paper Info	Argument	Paper Info	Argument
(Widyatama et al., 2019)	It can be used by the Muslims in *Mua'mlaat* if it does not amount to *Riba*	(Shariah Review Bureau, 2018)	The *sharia* screening is to be done for the Cryptocurrency or coin. Without proper sharia screening it can be allowed
(Saleh et al., 2020a, 2020b)	The use of Cryptocurrency for payment is as legitimate as any other currency. Cryptocurrencies must be accepted like a fiat currency for transactions purposes as its value can be measured and quantified	(Aliyu et al., 2020)	The *Shariah* compliance of Cryptocurrency will encourage the investors to invest in this form of currency. It is not Islamic in its existing form
(Lawal, 2019)	Cryptocurrency is an economic innovation, and it does pass the sharia test to be regarded as Islamic. It is recommended to prepare guiding principles to ensure full disclosure of transaction related to Cryptocurrency	(Abdul et al., 2019; Virgana et al., 2019)	The Cryptocurrency in its current form promotes, greed, *riba*, corruption and uneven prosperity which is against the basic principles of Islam. There is a need for sharia-based cryptocurrency for the goodness of Muslims and the world

Cryptocurrency is sharia-compliant		Cryptocurrency is not sharia-compliant	
Paper Info	Argument	Paper Info	Argument
(Zubaidi & Abdullah, 2017)	Cryptocurrencies are like the money stored in the bank account and it will help in better understanding, use and application of Blockchain for the betterment of the Muslims. It will help the Muslim countries in enforcing the basic principle of Islam finance, i.e., fairness and social justice	(Khan & Rabbani, 2021)	Blockchain: the underlying technology to create Cryptocurrency is very much in accordance with *sharia*. The existing Cryptocurrencies, like Bitcoin, Litecoin, Ethereum, etc., are not sharia-compliant. There is a need to develop a sharia-compliant cryptocurrency

4 Conclusion

The debates whether Cryptocurrency is haram, or halal will go longer, and it is not expected to be resolved soon. The sharia scholars are divided over this issue, and they have their arguments in favor or against it. After the extensive review of available literature and analysis of opinions of the scholars, we conclude that trading in Cryptocurrencies such as Bitcoin, Ripple and Ethereum is not halal, and it must be declared haram. We strongly believe that trading in these cryptocurrencies is not having value and neither economic growth give it any value and its return has any origin. It is highly volatile and chances of fluctuation in the prices are very high (*Gharar*), there are great chances that it might be used for the unfair trade practices such as terrorism, gambling, tax evasion, money laundering, etc. (Muedini & Ph, 2018). Any legitimate Islamic government has still not adopted it by considering it to be regarded as legitimate. Most of the characteristics of Cryptocurrency fall in the haram category as per sharia. However, considering the huge popularity and demand from the Muslim youth and investors there is a need to develop and fully sharia-compliant Cryptocurrency by removing these obstacles to provide them with an alternative investment avenue which is safe, sustainable and follows the ethos and principles of sharia.

References

Abdul, M., Chowdhury, M., Bin, D., & Razak, A. (2019). Dynamism and mechanism of digital currency (cryptocurrency) towards Islamic finance. *European Journal of Islamic Finance*, (14), 1–9. https://doi.org/10.13135/2421-2172/3736

Abdullah, Y., & Rabbani, M. R. (2021). COVID-19 and GCC Islamic market Indices. *2021 International Conference on Sustainable Islamic Business and Finance (SIBF)*.

Abu Bakar, N., Rosbi, S., & Uzaki, K. (2017). Cryptocurrency framework diagnostics from Islamic finance perspective: A new insight of bitcoin system transaction. *International Journal of Management Science and Business Administration*. https://doi.org/10.18775/ijmsba.1849-5664-5419.2014.41.1003

Abubakar, M., Hassan, M. K., & Haruna, M. A. (2019). Cryptocurrency tide and islamic finance development: Any issue? *International Finance Review*. https://doi.org/10.1108/S1569-376720190000020019

Adam, F. (2017). Bitcoin:Shariah Compliant? *Amanah Finance Consultancy Ltd*. www.afinance.org

Ahmed, S., Grobys, K., & Sapkota, N. (2020). Profitability of technical trading rules among cryptocurrencies with privacy function. *Finance Research Letters*, 35. https://doi.org/10.1016/j.frl.2020.101495

Akyildirim, E., Corbet, S., Katsiampa, P., Kellard, N., & Sensoy, A. (2019). The development of Bitcoin futures: Exploring the interactions between cryptocurrency derivatives. *Finance Research Letters.* https://doi.org/10.1016/j.frl.2019.07.007

Alam, N., Gupta, L., & Zameni, A. (2019). *Fintech and Islamic finance: Digitalization, development and disruption.* Fintech and Islamic Finance: Digitalization, Development and Disruption. Springer International Publishing. https://doi.org/10.1007/978-3-030-24666-2

Ali, M. M., Bashar, A., Rabbani, M. R., & Abdullah, Y. (2020). Transforming business decision making with internet of things (IoT) and machine learning (ML). *2020 International Conference on Decision Aid Sciences and Application (DASA), Sakheer, Bahrain, 2020* (pp. 674–679). https://doi.org/10.1109/DASA51403.2020.9317174

Aliyu, A., Abu Bakar, K., Matsuda, G., Darwish, T., Abdullah, A. H., Ismail, A. S., Raja Mohd Radzi, R. Z., Yusof, A. F., Mohamad, M. M., Idris, M. Y., Ismail, Z., Yaacob, A. C., & Herman, H. (2020). Review of some existing shariah-compliant cryptocurrency. *Journal of Contemporary Islamic Studies*, 6(1), 23–44. https://doi.org/10.24191/jcis.v6i1.2

Aloui, C., Hamida, H. B., & Yarovaya, L. (2020). Are Islamic gold-backed cryptocurrencies different? *Finance Research Letters.* https://doi.org/10.1016/j.frl.2020.101615

Anush, B., Inna, G., Tatyana, S., Aleksey, D., & Tetyana, B. (2020). Comparative and informative characteristic of the legal regulation of the blockchain and cryptocurrency: State and prospects. *Test Engineering and Management.*

Asif, S. (2018). The halal and haram aspects of cryptocurrencies in Islam. *Journal of Islamic Banking & Finance.*

Atif, M., Hassan, M. K., Rabbani, M. R., & Khan, S. (2021). Islamic FinTech: The digital transformation bringing sustainability to Islamic finance. In *COVID-19 and Islamic Social Finance* (pp. 91–103). Routledge.

Barone, R., & Masciandaro, D. (2019). Cryptocurrency or usury? Crime and alternative money laundering techniques. *European Journal of Law and Economics, 47*(2), 233–254. https://doi.org/10.1007/s10657-019-09609-6

Carroll, P., & Windle, J. (2018). Cyber as an enabler of terrorism financing, now and in the future. *Journal of Policing, Intelligence and Counter Terrorism, 13*(3), 285–300. https://doi.org/10.1080/18335330.2018.1506149

Chamberlain, T., Hidayat, S., & Khokhar, A. R. (2020). Credit risk in Islamic banking: Evidence from the GCC. *Journal of Islamic Accounting and Business Research, 11*(5), 1055–1081. https://doi.org/10.1108/JIABR-09-2017-0133

Choo, K. K. R. (2015). Cryptocurrency and virtual currency: Corruption and money laundering/terrorism financing risks? In *Handbook of Digital Currency: Bitcoin, Innovation, Financial Instruments, and Big Data* (pp. 283–307). https://doi.org/10.1016/B978-0-12-802117-0.00015-1

Conlon, T., Corbet, S., & McGee, R. J. (2020). Are cryptocurrencies a safe haven for equity markets? An international perspective from the COVID-19 pandemic. *Research in International Business and Finance, 54*. https://doi.org/10.1016/j.ribaf.2020.101248

Galanov, V. A., Perepelitsa, D. G., Galanova, A. V, Chelukhina, N. F., & Asyeva, E. A. (2018). The concept and models of the cryptocurrency market. *International Journal of Engineering and Technology (UAE), 7*(3.14 Special Issue 14), 311–315. https://www.scopus.com/inward/record.uri?eid=2-s2.0-85071487178&partnerID=40&md5=8d98fd64713abfd07b1906f2cada077a

Ghosh, A., Gupta, S., Dua, A., & Kumar, N. (2020). Security of Cryptocurrencies in blockchain technology: State-of-art, challenges and future prospects. *Journal of Network and Computer Applications, 163*. https://doi.org/10.1016/j.jnca.2020.102635

Gurdgiev, C., & O'Loughlin, D. (2020). Herding and anchoring in cryptocurrency markets: Investor reaction to fear and uncertainty. *Journal of Behavioral and Experimental Finance, 25*. https://doi.org/10.1016/j.jbef.2020.100271

Haffke, L., Fromberger, M., & Zimmermann, P. (2020). Cryptocurrencies and anti-money laundering: The shortcomings of the fifth AML directive (EU) and how to address them. *Journal of Banking Regulation, 21*(2), 125–138. https://doi.org/10.1057/s41261-019-00101-4

Hammad, F. (2018). Is bitcoin mining halal? Investigating the sharia compliance of bitcoin mining. *2018 International Conference on Innovation and Intelligence for Informatics, Computing, and Technologies, 3ICT 2018.* https://doi.org/10.1109/3ICT.2018.8855738

Harvey, J., & Branco-Illodo, I. (2020). Why cryptocurrencies want privacy: A review of political motivations and branding expressed in "privacy coin" whitepapers. *Journal of Political Marketing, 19*(1–2), 107–136. https://doi.org/10.1080/15377857.2019.1652223

Hassan, M. K., Rabbani, M. R., & Ali, M. A. (2020). Challenges for the Islamic Finance and banking in post COVID era and the role of Fintech. *Journal of Economic Cooperation and Development, 43*(3), 93–116.

Hassan, M. K., Rabbani, M. R., & Abdullah, Y. (2021). Socioeconomic Impact of COVID-19 in MENA region and the Role of Islamic Finance. *International Journal of Islamic Economics and Finance (IJIEF), 4*(1), 51–78.

Kabir Hassan, M., & Aldayel, A. Q. (1998). Stability of money demand under interest-free versus interest-based banking system. *Humanomics*. https://doi.org/10.1108/eb018821

Kethineni, S., & Cao, Y. (2020). The rise in popularity of cryptocurrency and associated criminal activity. *International Criminal Justice Review, 30*(3), 325–344. https://doi.org/10.1177/1057567719827051

Khan, N. (2020). AI Applications in the Islamic Finance Industry. October 2019.

Khan, N., Kchouri, B., Yatoo, N. A., Kräussl, Z., Patel, A., & State, R. (2020). Tokenization of sukuk: Ethereum case study. *Global Finance Journal.* https://doi.org/10.1016/j.gfj.2020.100539

Khan, S., & Rabbani, M. R. (2021). In depth analysis of blockchain, cryptocurrency and sharia compliance. *International Journal of Business Innovation and Research.* https://doi.org/10.1504/ijbir.2020.10033066

Khan, S., Hassan, M. K., & Rabbani, M. R. (2021). An artificial intelligence-based Islamic FinTech model on Qardh-Al-Hasan for COVID 19 affected SMEs. *Islamic Perspective for Sustainable Financial System.*

Khan, M. S., Rabbani, M. R., Hawaldar, I. T., & Bashar, A. (2022). Determinants of behavioral intentions to use Islamic financial technology: An empirical assessment. *Risks, 10*(6), 114.

Lahmiri, S., & Bekiros, S. (2019). Cryptocurrency forecasting with deep learning chaotic neural networks. *Chaos, Solitons and Fractals, 118,* 35–40. https://doi.org/10.1016/j.chaos.2018.11.014

Lawal, I. M. (2019). The suitability of cryptocurrency in the structure of Islamic banking and finance. *Jurnal Perspektif Pembiayaan Dan Pembangunan Daerah, 6*(6), 639–648. https://doi.org/10.22437/ppd.v6i6.6603

Lim, S. J., & Masih, M. (2017). Exploring portfolio diversification opportunities in Islamic capital markets through bitcoin: Evidence from MGARCH-DCC and Wavelet approaches.

Maroney, N., Wang, W., & Kabir Hassan, M. (2019). Incorporating active adjustment into a financing based model of capital structure. *Journal of International Money and Finance.* https://doi.org/10.1016/j.jimonfin.2018.09.011

Mazambani, L., & Mutambara, E. (2020). Predicting FinTech innovation adoption in South Africa: The case of cryptocurrency. *African Journal of Economic and Management Studies, 11*(1), 30–50. https://doi.org/10.1108/AJEMS-04-2019-0152

Meera, A. K. M. (2018). Cryptocurrencies from Islamic perspectives: The case of bitcoin. *Buletin Ekonomi Moneter Dan Perbankan, 20*(4), 443–460. https://doi.org/10.21098/bemp.v20i4.902

Mensi, W., Al-Yahyaee, K. H., Al-Jarrah, I. M. W., Vo, X. V., & Kang, S. H. (2020). Dynamic volatility transmission and portfolio management across major cryptocurrencies: Evidence from hourly data. *North American Journal of Economics and Finance, 54.* https://doi.org/10.1016/j.najef.2020.101285

Mohammad, H. S., Khan, S., Rabbani, M. R., Mustafa, & Yannis, E. T. (2020). An artificial intelligence and NLP based Islamic FinTech model combining

Zakat and Qardh-Al-Hasan for countering the adverse impact of COVID 19 on SMEs and individuals. *International Journal of Economics and Business Administration*, *VIII*(Issue 2), 351–364. https://doi.org/10.35808/ijeba/466

Muedini, F. (2018). The compatibility of cryptocurrencies and Islamic finance. *European Journal of Islamic Finance*, (10), 1–11. https://doi.org/10.13135/2421-2172/2569

Nuraliati, A., & Azwari, P. C. (2019). Akuntansi untuk cryptocurrency. *I-Finance: A Research Journal on Islamic Finance*. https://doi.org/10.19109/ifinance.v4i2.2885

Oziev, G., & Yandiev, M. (2018a). Cryptocurrency from a shari'ah perspective. *Al-Shajarah*, *23*(2), 315–338. https://www.scopus.com/inward/record.uri?eid=2-s2.0-85059697564&partnerID=40&md5=0ae3d746ef33578ed255cdea62f4e24e

Oziev, G., & Yandiev, M. (2018b). Cryptocurrency from a shari'ah perspective. *Al-Shajarah*, *23*(2), 315–338. https://doi.org/10.2139/ssrn.3101981

Özkan, B., Kabir Hassan, M., & Hepşen, A. (2016). Returns predictability in emerging housing markets. *Journal of Economic Cooperation and Development*.

Phillip, A., Chan, J., & Peiris, S. (2018). A new look at Cryptocurrencies. *Economics Letters*, *163*, 6–9. https://doi.org/10.1016/j.econlet.2017.11.020

Rabbani, M. R. (2020). The competitive structure and strategic positioning of commercial banks in Saudi Arabia. *International Journal on Emerging Technologies*, *11*(3), 43–46.

Rabbani, M. R. (2021). COVID-19 and its impact on supply chain financing and the role of Islamic Fintech: Evidence from GCC countries. *International Journal of Agile Systems and Management*. In press.

Rabbani, M. R., Abdullah, Y., Bashar, A., Khan, S., & Ali, M. A. M. (2020a). Embracing of Fintech in Islamic finance in the post COVID era. *2020 International Conference on Decision Aid Sciences and Application (DASA), Sakheer, Bahrain, 2020* (pp. 1230–1234). https://doi.org/10.1109/DASA51403.2020.9317196

Rabbani, M. R., Khan, S., & Thalassinos, E. I. (2020b). FinTech, blockchain and Islamic finance: An extensive literature review. *International Journal of Economics and Business Administration*, *8*(2), 65–86. https://doi.org/10.35808/ijeba/444

Rabbani, M. R., Khan, S., Hassan, M. K., & Ali, M. (2021a). 7 Artificial intelligence and Natural language processing (NLP) based FinTech model of Zakat for poverty alleviation and sustainable development for Muslims in India. In *ICOVID-19 and Islamic Social Finance*, 104.

Rabbani, M. R., Jreisat, A., AlAbbas, A., Bashar, A., & Ali, M. A. M. (2021b). Whether cryptocurrency is a threat or a revolution? An ESG perspective. *2021b International Conference on Sustainable Islamic Business and Finance (SIBF).*

Rabbani, M. R., Bashar, A., Nawaz, N., Karim, S., Ali, M. A. M., Khan, A., Rahiman, H., & Alam, S. (2021c). Exploring the role of Islamic Fintech in combating the after-shocks of COVID-19: The open social innovation of the Islamic financial system. *Journal of Open Innovation: Technology, Market, and Complexity, 7,* 136.

Rabbani, M. R., Sarea, A., Khan, S., & Abdullah, Y. (2021d, September). Ethical concerns in artificial intelligence (AI): The role of RegTech and Islamic finance. In *The International Conference On Global Economic Revolutions* (pp. 381–390). Springer, Cham.

Rabbani, M. R. (2022). Fintech innovations, scope, challenges, and implications in Islamic Finance: A systematic analysis. *International Journal of Computing and Digital Systems, 11*(1), 1–28.

Rabbani, M. R., Kayani, U., Bawazir, H. S., & Hawaldar, I. T. (2022). A commentary on emerging markets banking sector spillovers: Covid-19 vs GFC pattern analysis. *Heliyon, 8*(3), e09074.

Rehman, M. U., Asghar, N., & Kang, S. H. (2020). Do Islamic indices provide diversification to bitcoin? A time-varying copulas and value at risk application. *Pacific Basin Finance Journal.* https://doi.org/10.1016/j.pacfin.2020.101326

Rivlin, P. (2008). The development of Islamic banking. *Orient, 49*(3), 4–11. https://www.scopus.com/inward/record.uri?eid=2-s2.0-77952605495&partnerID=40&md5=be3ddeba4854736d329d81a35e1c5890

Ruslianor Maika, M., Fidiana, F., & Kautsar, I. (2019). Model dinar and dirham digital currency for Islamic commercial transaction. *Test Engineering and Management, 81*(11–12), 1333–1343. https://www.scopus.com/inward/record.uri?eid=2-s2.0-85077251704&partnerID=40&md5=7b05262286f386f2c64b12e41c2778cc

Saba, I., Kouser, R., & Chaudhry, I. S. (2019). Fintech and Islamic Finance-challenges and Opportunities. *Review of Economics and Development Studies, 5*(4), 581–590. https://doi.org/10.26710/reads.v5i4.887

Saleh, A.-H. A. I., Ibrahim, A. A., Noordin, M. F., & Mohd Mohadis, H. (2020a). Islamic approach toward purification of transaction with cryptocurrency. *Journal of Theoretical and Applied Information Technology, 98*(6), 1050–1067. https://www.scopus.com/inward/record.uri?eid=2-s2.0-85083805038&partnerID=40&md5=44ad6f96d03e03867010064a3a7e89df

Saleh, A. J., Alazzam, F. A. F., Aldrou, K. K. A. R., & Zavalna, Z. (2020b). Legal aspects of the management of cryptocurrency assets in the national security system. *Journal of Security and Sustainability Issues, 10*(1), 235–247. https://doi.org/10.9770/jssi.2020.10.1(17)

Shariah Review Bureau. (2018). *The Shariah Factor in Cryptocurrencies and Tokens. April*, 1–16. http://shariyah.com/wp-content/uploads/2018/08/Crypto-Currencies-with-changes-1.pdf

Siswantoro, D., Handika, R., & Mita, A. F. (2020). The requirements of cryptocurrency for money, an Islamic view. *Heliyon*, 6(1). https://doi.org/10.1016/j.heliyon.2020.e03235

Sun, H., Rabbani, M. R., Naveed, A., Sial, M. S., Guping, C., Zia-ud-din, M., & Fu, Q. (2020). CSR, co-creation and green consumer loyalty: Are green banking initiatives important? A moderated mediation approach from an emerging economy. *Sustainability (Switzerland), 12*(24), 10688.

Uddin, M. A., Ali, M. H., & Masih, M. (2020). Bitcoin—A hype or digital gold? Global evidence. *Australian Economic Papers*. https://doi.org/10.1111/1467-8454.12178

Virgana, R. A. E., Saudi, M. H. M., & Sinaga, O. (2019). Conceptual research: Sharia-based cryptocurrency. *Journal of Advanced Research in Dynamical and Control Systems, 11*(3 Special Issue), 138–143. https://www.scopus.com/inward/record.uri?eid=2-s2.0-85069701139&partnerID=40&md5=1c96c715afbcb1ad7913c87a48b57b59

Widyatama, U., Haizam, M., Saudi, M., & Widyatama, U. (2019). *Conceptual Research : Sharia-based Cryptocurrency. August*.

Zubaidi, I. B., & Abdullah, A. (2017). Developing a digital currency from an Islamic perspective: Case of blockchain technology. *International Business Research*. https://doi.org/10.5539/ibr.v10n11p79

Islamic Fintech, Blockchain and Crowdfunding: Current Landscape and Path Forward

M. Kabir Hassan, Mustafa Raza Rabbani, Mamunur Rashid, and Irwan Trinugroho

1 Introduction

Financial technology is the portmanteau of the terms: "finance" and "technology". It is often termed as Fintech, which symbolizes to any business function which uses technology to simplify business activity, to deliver efficiency and a superior customer experience (Dimbean-Creta, 2018). It has created unparalleled impact in delivery of financial services during last decade (Abi-Lahoud et al., 2018). Fintech has become a recent trend among the new disruptive technologies as an insertion for the high-tech in the financial services industry (Wonglimpiyarat, 2019).

M. K. Hassan
Department of Economics and Finance, University of New Orleans, New Orleans, LA 70148, USA
e-mail: mhassan@uno.edu

M. R. Rabbani (✉)
Department of Economics and Finance, College of Business Administration, University of Bahrain, Zallaq, Kingdom of Bahrain
e-mail: mrabbani@uob.edu.bh

© The Author(s), under exclusive license to Springer Nature Switzerland AG 2022
M. K. Hassan et al. (eds.), *FinTech in Islamic Financial Institutions*, https://doi.org/10.1007/978-3-031-14941-2_15

The presence of Fintech has considerable impact on the working of financial institutions both conventional and Islamic (Jagtiani & John, 2018). Fintech as a term emerged way back in 1972 by *Abraham Leo Bettinger*, but it began to flourish only in the 1990s internet based and ecommerce business models emerged. The much needed push for the growth and acceptance of Fintech was provided by the global financial crisis of 2008, when people lost confidence in the traditional banking and financial services as security and transparency became more important than ever people started looking for the alternative model of financial services (Rabbani, 2020). The shift in mindset pavend way for the innovation in the financial services industry and advent technology such as cloud computing made it possible to invent new tech-based financial services which are more customized and standardized (Mackenzie, 2015). With an interminable expectation from the regulators and customers, Fintech companies design new products that deliver sustainable benefits (Atif et al., 2021a).

Apart from the fact that the Fintech-based financial services are cheaper, the reach of these innovations is very diverse (Khan et al., 2022; Rabbani, 2021; Rabbani et al., 2022a, 2022b). It is so diverse that it builds direct customer relationship by crowdfunding and P2P lending (Sun et al., 2020a, 2020b), it brings social change with the Artificial intelligence and Blockchain-based digital microfinance and digital lending platforms, online insurance policies (InsureTech), including data handling, data protection, *robo* advising for the asset management and customized portfolio management, complete digital currency in the form of Cryptocurrencies (Lee & Shin, 2018; Puschmann, 2017). Fintech has disrupted almost all walks of life including social cultural and financial sphere (Romanova & Kudinska, 2016).

M. Rashid
Christ Church Business School, Canterbury Christ Church University, Kent, UK
e-mail: mamunur.rashid@canterbury.ac.uk

I. Trinugroho
Faculty of Economics and Business, Center for Fintech and Banking, Universitas Sebelas Maret, Surakarta, Indonesia
e-mail: irwan.trinugroho@gmail.com

The Blockchain technology has created disruption in many fields including finance (Bogusz et al., 2020). It uses a combination of tools called as public key identifiers, cryptography and distributed ledger technology to maintain a record of transaction that once created cannot be inverted (Du et al., 2020). Blockchain is the uses distributed ledger instead of centralized databased that can record any number of records and information and these records are distributed, published and stored in many locations (Eyal, 2017; Lee Kuo Chuen & Deng, 2017; Rabbani, 2020). Blockchain is the underlying technology behind the most disruptive financial innovation of twenty-first century i.e. Cryptocurrency/Bitcoin (Zhang et al., 2020). It has the characteristics of decentralization, anonymity, security, privacy, non-tampering and stability inbuilt in it (Bogusz et al., 2020). Blockchain can be used to record, store and process the financial information through the effective integration of financial resources (Ozili, 2019). Blockchain is an underlying technology, the goal of which is to integrate several other technologies such as Big data (Sun et al. 2020a, 2020b), Artificial intelligence (AI) (Atif et al., 2021b), cloud computing and Internet of things (IoT) (Ali et al., 2020) to finance no matter what kind of economic or finance related information is to be integrated (Owen et al., 2019; Ozili, 2019; Reepu, 2019; Varma, 2019; Yaksick, 2019). Blockchain technology improves the overall operational efficiency, transparency and services quality of the financial system (Zhang et al., 2020). It can be observed from Fig. 1 that, Blockchain technology has very wide application in Islamic finance and banking. It can be used for smart contracts for Islamic financial services like Musharaka, Mudaraba and Sukuk (Li et al., 2019; Zhang & Lee, 2019), Supply chain; Blockchain can enable more accurate and end to end tracking in supply chain to facilitate Islamic finance transactions (Du et al., 2020), digital asset trading; Blockchain can simplify the online tracing of the Islamic finance assets like Sukuk, commodities, etc. (Gomber et al., 2017), Sharia compliant payment systems; Blockchain can ease the sharia compliant digital payment system with end to end sharia and halal process (Paston & Harris, 2019), big data-based decision-making; Blockchain enables decision-making based on facts rather than on intuition. Islamic finance encourages evidence-based financial decision-making (Mnif et al., 2020).

Crowdfunding is one of the disruptive financial innovations of twenty-first century in entrepreneurial finance that allows an easy and quick access of capital from a large pool of investors to the relatively new

Fig. 1 Blockchain application in Islamic finance (*Source* Adapted from Hassan et al. [2020a, 2020b])

project owners through the use of technology (Bi et al., 2019; Jovanović et al., 2019; Ryu et al., 2020). It is defined as the process of raising small amount of money from a large pool of people through the use of internet (Colombo & Shafi, 2019; Shen et al., 2020). Crowdfunding reinstates the power of internet and social networks in raising funds and managing business activities (Zhao et al., 2020). It provides several benefits to both project owner and investors including: it is fast and easy with no upfront fee, it gives media attention and free marketing of the products and services to the project owner (Hassan et al., 2021a, 2021b), social networking websites provide free advice and feedback to the project owners and help in enhancing the idea and finally, it's easy for those who cannot access the traditional financial institutions due to excessive documentation and other requirements (Colombo & Shafi, 2019; Lins et al., 2018; Quero et al., 2017; Ryu et al., 2020). Like all other Fintech innovation, Crowdfunding is also sharia compliant unless or until proved otherwise (Hasan et al., 2020). In fact, Crowdfunding has the same participatory method (PLS method) and risk sharing, which is the basic cornerstone of the Islamic finance (Tajudin et al., 2020). Currently, there are many variants of Crowdfunding platforms available in the market, of which equity crowdfunding satisfies the principles of sharia as it is based on the PLS method and risk sharing (Baber, 2020; Saiti et al., 2018).

Remaining paper proceeds as follows; In the next section we review the relevant literature in three parts, related to Islamic Fintech in general, Blockchain and Crowdfunding. Section three comprises Islamic Fintech, Blockchain & crowdfunding—a roadmap. In section four we provide the discussion part and finally, in section five, we provide conclusion, recommendation and future scope of the study.

The present study is expected to not only contribute to the existing strand of available literature in massive ways but also it is believed to work as the guiding light to the Islamic financial institutions and Islamic banks in Fintech adoption. One of the most prominent features of this paper is that we provide a clear roadmap for the Islamic financial institutions to utilize these disruptive technologies. The study will help the governments and regulators in creating a healthy and sustainable Islamic Fintech ecosystem. It will help the future researchers to identify the right track and provide the scientific research for the academia and industry. Besides this, the present study will identify the risk and repercussions resulting from the execution of Islamic Fintech by the IFIs in the digitization process.

2 Review of Literature

The available literature on Islamic Fintech, Blockchain & Crowdfunding was reviewed to get the current stock of the situation in the discipline and based on that the future path will be proposed. The whole review is divided into three parts, part one reviews available literature on Fintech in general followed by the review on Blockchain and Crowdfunding.

Fintech

Fintech is defined differently by authors. The originator of the world *Abraham Leo Bettinger* himself defines, Fintech as "*Fintech is a contraction which combines banks experience and expertise with the information technology*" (Kalra, 2019). Rabbani et al. (2020) defines Fintech as "*Fintech is the fusion of Information Technology and Finance for better financial services and at affordable cost and seamless user experience*". The author of the paper defines Fintech as "*software and other modern technologies used in delivering the more automated and improved financial services for the hassle-free customer experience at an affordable cost*".

Technology evolves very fast and Fintech has evolved even faster with many technological advancements in the past (Jun & Yeo, 2016; Zavolokina et al., 2016). The financial institutions have to be on its toes to embrace these disruptions to gain competitive advantage and avoid losing market share (Jan & Marimuthu, 2016; Joju et al., 2017). Though Islamic financial institutions have already embraced this innovation and trying to compete its conventional counterpart, the transformation has relatively been slow (Baber, 2019). There is need to a create more robust and sustainable Islamic Fintech ecosystem to provide immediate benefit to the IFIs. Fintech can be used as a tool to resolve the long due problems of Islamic finance and hinders it from realizing its true potential. Fintech could help the Islamic finance industry in how they interact with their customers, how they present their products and services and how they process and market their products and services (Darmansyah et al., 2020).

Apart from the fact that the Fintech-based financial services are cheaper and improved, the reach of these technological innovations is very diverse (Pizzi et al., 2020). It is so diverse that it builds direct customer relationship with crowdfunding and P2P lending, it is bringing social change with the Artificial intelligence and Blockchain-based digital microfinance and digital lending platforms, online insurance policies (InsureTech), including data handling, data protection, *robo* advising for the asset management and customized portfolio management, complete digital currency in the form of Cryptocurrencies (Lee & Shin, 2018; Puschmann, 2017). Fintech has disrupted almost all walks of life including social cultural and financial (Romanova & Kudinska, 2016).

Islamic Fintech

Islam embraces all the innovations and technological advancement as long as it does not violate the basic ethos and principles of sharia (Hassan & Hippler, 2014; Hassan & Lewis, 2007). Fintech is one such innovation which is not against the basic principles of Islam or Islamic finance (Rabbani, 2020). It is in the basic nature of Islamic finance to bring transparency and efficiency in the economic transactions and Fintech-based financial services are in consistent with this nature of Islamic finance (Hasan et al., 2020). Fintech in general and Islamic Fintech is no different, the main point of departure is sharia compliance (Sharia—Islamic law based on the Holy Qur'an and teachings of Prophet Muhammad [pbuh]). Islamic Fintech is designed to comply the principles laid down by the sharia and it focuses on delivering the innovative and tech-based financial services and products that are in consistent with the legislation, codes and rules laid down by the sharia (Alam et al., 2019). *Islamic Fintech is defined as the "digital delivery of Islamic financial services that comply with the sharia through the innovative solutions"* (Atif et al., 2021a).

Islamic Fintech solutions are going to lead the new wave of growth in the Islamic finance industry post COVID-19 and during the third decade of twenty-first century (Hassan et al., 2020). Islamic Fintech provides tremendous opportunities to the Islamic Financial Institutions (IFIs) as Islamic banking institutions are taking up the Fintech-based financial services to reach out the customers with the improved and attractive financial services at a relatively lower cost (Syed et al., 2020). According to an estimate from (IFSB, 2020), over 1400 Islamic financial institutions are operating in over 80 countries and are raring to innovate and provide the innovative solution to its customers. The forecasts of Islamic Fintech looks tantalizing. During the last few years the number of Islamic Fintech has increased steadily from 116 in 2017 to 166 in 2019 and 142 till June 2020 (IFSB, 2020). As depicted in Fig. 2, United Kingdom (UK) has the greatest number of Islamic Fintech firms in the world totaling

24, followed by the Malaysia with 19, United Arab Emirates (UAE) 15, Indonesia 13, Saudi Arabia and United States of America (USA) 9 each. It's interesting to note that US and UK have 33 combined number of firms with a little percentage of Islamic finance market share. Islamic Fintech based startups are leading the race as it is the new solution to the problem of providing new, innovative and digital Islamic finance solutions to the customers.

Number of Fintech Startups by Core technology: Fig. 3 depicts the number of Islamic Fintech firms by core technology based on the Dinar standard analysis. It is observed that majority of the startups are based on Crowdfunding and P2P lending. It is the new trend to opening the market for the new investors, individual as well as institutional investors. It has gained growing interest among the micro and small-scale enterprises due to the ease in procurement of fund (Ali et al., 2018; Berns et al., 2020). After the massive popularity of the Cryptocurrency, the Blockchain-based startups are finding the way into the Islamic Fintech landscape with 14 startups identified. The list here includes the active companies engaged in the customer interaction, providing front office services and recognized through the external credible source (DinarStandard, 2021).

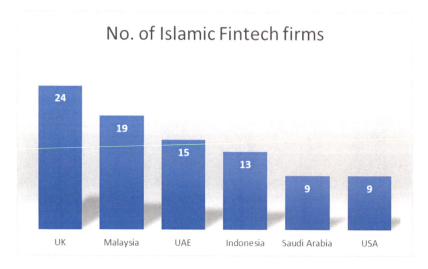

Fig. 2 No of Fintech Firms in selected OIC countries (*Source* IFN Islamic Fintech)

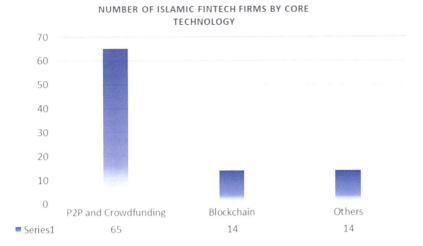

Fig. 3 Number of Fintech startups by core technology (*Source* DinarStandard [2018])

Blockchain

There are many theories related to the integration of Blockchain technology with the finance and economics. The first theory is proposed by Babbitt and Mahoney (2001), that talks about the convergence of all the financial data, information and assets to the computer and information technology using Blockchain. Ultimately, it will be all digitized world with complete digitation of resources from goods and services to manufacturing, sales, supply chain and even marketing activities. Second theory is studies by Ahram et al. (2017) and Chen et al. (2017), where they studied the free currency and concluded that the currency shall not be the state's property as it must be free from the state ownership and should be completely decentralized. The Blockchain technology provides the opportunity for all kinds of digital currencies to be freely exchanged, transferred and also it provides trading platform for the digital currencies (Fisch et al., 2020). The theory proposed by Marcel et al. (1976) on information asymmetry on corporate governance examines the trust problem between the parties using the Blockchain technology. They stated that Blockchain can provide the digital reward through the optimum apportionment of resources for mining to create a distributed system for universal sharing.

The Blockchain technology has to be trusted to increase its efficiency and trust (Di Pietro et al., 2018; Jin et al., 2018).

Figure 4 depicts the data structure in Blockchain technology. It can be observed that it is a back linked list of blocks of transactions, which is ordered as previous block, time stamp, random data and the target hash. The lower part of the figure consists of the information data and Blockchain body. Each block can be identified as hash (L and R hash). A hash function is necessary for Blockchain management as it is a function that converts input of functions into an encrypted output of fixed length (Feng et al., 2019). A Blockchain data structure is made up of many sub-structures. The keys can be mapped to the buckets by its hash value. A hash table is required when one needs to store many related information, for example, when an Islamic bank stores data related to a customer's account, purchases, contact details, purchase and sales details, etc. The customer ID can be created by hashing the customer's name and more information can be added, deleted to edited by finding the buckets.

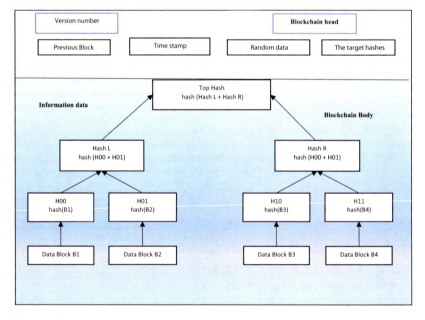

Fig. 4 Blockchain data structure

We describe the overall structure of Blockchain economy and Islamic finance in Fig. 4. The overall structure is described in four layers. Each layer has its own unique characteristics as it is designed as per the sharia principles. The first layer is explained through the Cloud computing, distributed ledger, metadata data storage, data file storage and big data. The data layer consists of the digital signature, hash, Merkel tree and transactions. The second layer is regarding the sharia compliance. In this layer the rules and regulations regarding the unique features of Islamic finance are mentioned. Islamic finance works on the rules of sharia, which is quite distinct from conventional finance. Sharia compliance refers to the obedience to the sharia, every single transaction going through the Blockchain technology must abide by the sharia law. Therefore, the Fintech-based systems are required to work in conformity with the sharia law and must not include any prohibited elements such as *Gharar, Maisir, Riba* and other *haram* elements. The application layer of Blockchain consists of the Islamic financial instruments like SUKUK, TAKAFUL, third-party payment and sharia compliant digital currency like Islamic Cryptocurrencies. The network layer is also known as the hardware layer of the Blockchain as in this layer it is described by the P2P network topology, the point where clients can access and communicate to each other (Fig. 5).

Crowdfunding

Discussion

If we look at the concentration of assets in global Islamic finance world, it is concentrated in Middle east, Asia and MENA region. According the IFSB report, Asia, GCC and MENA region contributes to around 96% of the global Islamic finance assets (IFSB, 2020). This is where the opportunity arises for the Islamic Fintech to tap this untapped market. In Asia alone, two of the largest country with Muslim population, Pakistan and Indonesia have only 15% and 5.8% of the total Islamic banking assets, respectively, whereas these countries have Muslim population percentage of 96% and 87%, respectively. There is opportunity for the Islamic Fintech to grow in these two largest Muslim countries, because Pakistan is one of the world's most country in terms of financial inclusion as it has only 14% population as financially included (State of Financial Inclusion of Women in Pakistan, 2018), on the other hand Indonesia has around 76.1% population as financially included (Nuryakin et al., 2017). Therefore, innovative financial solution led by the Fintech can help in gaining more market share by adopting the right strategy of financial inclusion.

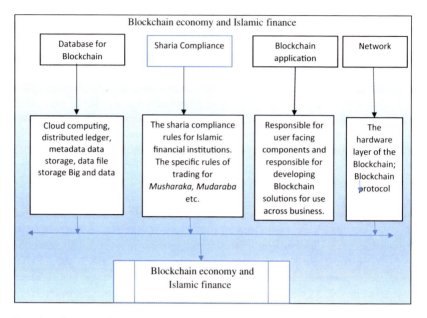

Fig. 5 The overall structure of Blockchain economy and Islamic Finance (*Source*)

Muslim represent 1 in every 4 people in the world and more than 50% of them offers a great opportunity and potential market for the Islamic finance. The potential size is significant as most of the Muslim population is young and tech savvy and that offers a huge opportunity for the investors to convert this into revenue from this huge market by providing financial services to these unbanked populations.

Mobile phone has made a significant contribution toward financial inclusion in developing countries due to the high mobile phone penetration rate in the last decade or so (Zins & Weill, 2016). Mobile payments have been a key factor in Fintech world and it is being regarded as the next big thing within the Fintech space (Iman, 2018). It has become so popular for the payment that now people do not need to carry the traditional wallet for making even small payments. The popularity of mobile payments and high penetration of mobile phones has paved way for capturing the underbanked population in countries like Pakistan and other densely Muslim populated countries (Liu et al., 2020). It can be observed that smart phone penetration is comparatively low in Muslim majority countries. Top 10 countries all have smart phone penetration of more than 60% as compared to the selected the countries from the Organization of Islamic Cooperation countries (OIC), where highest penetration is in Indonesia with 66%. It is observed that the ratio of smart phone penetration in comparison to financial inclusion is exceedingly high and that provides opportunity for the Islamic Fintech to emerge as the tool and act as a bridge to bring financial inclusion. Most of the countries with high mobile phone penetration provides opportunity to the Islamic Fintech to provide access to the valuable financial services like mobile payment, digital banking, crowdfunding, Islamic microfinancing, etc. (Fig. 6, Table 1).

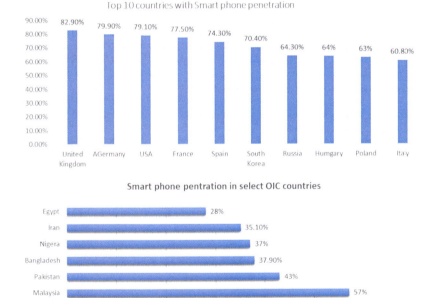

Fig. 6 Smart phone penetration in top 10 countries in the world vs. select OIC countries (September 2018) (*Source* O'Dea [2020])

Table 1 Current landscape of Islamic Fintech and future technologies

Technology	Description	Islamic Fintech provider
Artificial intelligence	Artificial Intelligence (AI) is the set of technologies such as Natural Language Processing (NLP) and machine learning, which enables a computer program to execute task automatically (Khan et al., 2021). It is the perfect blend of machine learning in software application. Sharia compliant *robo* advisors by the Islamic banks can advise the customers in account opening, asset management, any query related to the sharia compliance of the financial services (Khan & Rabbani, 2020, 2021a, 2021b)	The example includes The Islamic bank Chatbot launched by ABU DHABI Islamic Bank (ADIB), it is with artificial intelligence and can handle queries in Arabic as well as English language. Another example includes, AI-based Chatbot launched by the Kuwait Finance House. Various Islamic financial institutions are using AI in its interface for automatic accounting opening, face recognition, etc
Quantum computing	Quantum computing is another Fintech-based disruptive technology which has the potential to be the next generation financial technology. It applies principles from Quantum theory and it is super computers which can perform infinite number of hypothesis testing sequentially (Orús et al., 2018)	The fourth industrial revolution is expected to see the implementation of several emerging technologies like quantum computing in Islamic finance and banking. The industry 4.0 could see the rise of quantum computing besides, Internet of Things (IoT), 3D printing and Nano-technology (Ali et al., 2020)
Big data analytics	Big data is the use of "Big data analytics" to analyze, extract and process the complex and large volume of data that is otherwise difficult to process with the traditional data processing methods (Liu et al., 2018; Serrano, 2019)	The examples of big data application by Islamic Financial Institutions (IFIs) include tracking the customer spending patterns, track customers based on their search history on Google, Facebook, Instagram and other social media, personalized and customized products based on individual pattern

(continued)

Table 1 (continued)

Technology	Description	Islamic Fintech provider
Crowdfunding/P2P lending	Crowdfunding/P2P lending is also called as the social lending. It is the process of lending small amount of money from large pool of investors mainly through the internet (Rabbani et al., 2021). It is the sharia compliant way of funding a project by relatively modest investment from small investors and used for the startups and early stage funding mainly through the internet (Saiti et al., 2018)	Islamic crowdfunding/P2P lending has emerged as the biggest emerging sector in Islamic Fintech. It has 64% customer engagement in the year 2019 as compared to the second of around 40% for the Blockchain/Cryptocurrency (IFSB, 2020). Equity method of Islamic Crowdfunding are quite popular and it complies with the requirements of sharia (Baber, 2020)
Open banking	Open banking is a financial service as the part of growing financial technology. It is a banking practice that provides third party access to the customer's data, records, financial information and other transaction related information through the use of open Application Programming interface (APIs). It is the secure way to give third party access to the customer's data (Brodsky & Oakes, 2017; Mansfield-Devine, 2016)	Khaleeji Commercial Bank from Kingdom of Bahrain has recently announced its "Khaleeji 360", platform where they will provide customers with the open banking services to its customers. The platform is developed with the "Tarabut Gateway", which is a leading Fintech services provider in MENA region. By opening data and collection more information through open banking, the banks can bring more transparency and efficiency in its operation (Open Banking Implementation Entity, 2019)
Blockchain	Blockchain is the decentralized, distributed ledger technology used to record the movement of an electronic asset (Lu, 2018; Saad & Mohaisen, 2018). In other words, it is the distributed ledger used to record the data digitally and keep records digitally in a business network (Tredinnick, 2019). It is the technology at the heart of the most disruptive innovation of twenty-first century i.e. Cryptocurrency/Bitcoin (Tewari, 2019)	The most prominent application of Blockchain is the Cryptocurrency and this hype has also impressed the Islamic finance investors as many sharia compliant Cryptocurrencies have already been launched. OneGram, a gold backed sharia compliant Cryptocurrency where each coin is backed by at least one gram of gold X8 Cryptocurrency; It is the only sharia compliant Cryptocurrency which operates on the ethereum platform (Khan & Rabbani, 2020)

(continued)

Table 1 (continued)

Technology	Description	Islamic Fintech provider
Regtech	Regtech is another financial technology that uses cloud computing to technology to help business comply the rules and regulations efficiently and by spending very little. Islamic Regtech is aimed to provide supportive services in complying the complex requirements of the sharia (Turki et al., 2020)	In 2017, Central bank of Bahrain launched the "regulatory sandbox" in order to supervise the Regtech companies. "*Capnovum*" is an Islamic Regtech services provider, that helps those IFIs who struggle to keep up with the changing sharia regulations. It has the combination of AI and automation to seamlessly guide on sharia compliance matters
Cyber security	Cyber security or network security is the protection of computer network, data, software and hardware from theft, damage or harm. In other words, it is the practice of defending one's computer, mobile, server, network, and data from unwanted attack (Bendovschi, 2015)	Islamic banks such as Al-Baraka bank and Bahrain Islamic bank uses machine learning and AI-powered cyber analytics to protect them from cyber threat. IFIs are keeping up with the pace of the market to increase the operational efficiency and to reduce the risk
Mobile payments	Mobile payment is the payment of money to the service provider through mobile devices like tablets or cellphone. Mobile payment is the top most Fintech adoption in the Islamic Fintech segment (Atif et al., 2021a)	Almost every IFI has adopted mobile payment for the convenience of its users. Mobile Applications like Benefit pay, B-wallet, Viva cash and Apple pay are quite popular among the Islamic bank customers

3 Future Islamic Fintech-Based Financial Services

Islamic Fintech must cater to both voluntary and involuntary unbaked population in Muslim countries to provide them access to the financial services. There are many reasons for the financial exclusion of Muslims population in OIC countries, the reasons are both religious and non-religious. The people who avoid having access to the financial services due to religious reason can be provided with the interest free banking based on risk sharing (Demirguc-Kunt et al., 2014; Zulkhibri, 2016). This will encourage asset-backed financing and sustainable Islamic fintech and it will help the individuals and SMEs to increase their wealth by partnership mode of transaction (World Bank, 2020). Another way to bring these underprivileged and vulnerable into the mainstream financial system is to distribute Islamic charitable contributions like *Sadaqa, Zakat* and *Awqaf* through the Islamic Fintech (Khan et al., 2021; Rabbani et al., 2021). Some of the future Islamic Fintech-based financial services are depicted in Fig. 6 and described as follows.

Islamic Microfinance: Islamic Microfinance has the potential to emerge as the single, most prominent finance tool to alleviate poverty from the Muslim world (Dhumale & Sapcanin, 1998; Rahman, 2010). Islamic Microfinance refers to the short-term sharia compliant financing with a tenure of less than a year. Islamic Microfinancing is used mainly for the individuals and SMEs who do not have access to the formal financial institutions due to high documentation formalities. Islamic microfinance is a lease of life for those young potential entrepreneurs with a little or no prior business experience and no financial backup and want to start a micro or small business (Hassan et al., 2013; Md Saad, 2012). Religion is the primary reason behind going for the Islamic Microfinancing in the OIC countries (World Bank, 2020). Islamic Microfinancing can be combined with the different Islamic financial services such as Zakat (Hassan et al., 2012; Muhd Adnan et al., 2020), *Qardh-Al-Hasan* (Hassan, 2014; Wulandari, 2019), *Awqaf* (Haneef et al., 2014; Zauro et al., 2020), *Murabaha* (Fianto et al., 2018), *Musharaka* (Islam & Ahmad, 2020; Saad & Razak, 2013), *Ijarah* (Mansori et al., 2015) and *Takaful* (Khairunnisa et al., 2019). There are many Islamic financial services that can be combined with the Fintech and customized as Fintech-based microfinancing (Macchiavello, 2017; Shaikh, 2020).

Muslim population in the Islamic countries constitutes one-fourth of the global population and 50% of the poor population of the world lives in these countries (Reazul Islam et al., 2020). These poor do not have access to the formal financial system as even the Islamic commercial banks usually provide loans and finance to high worth corporates loans or to the high- and middle-income individuals as consumer finance (Rabbani, 2020). Even the SMEs have very little share in total financing of the Islamic commercial banks (El-Komi & Croson, 2013). Thus the poor population is forced to either go to the local money lenders or look for the Microfinancing option and Islamic Microfinance serves as an alternative to these poor and deprived Muslim population (Widiarto & Emrouznejad, 2015). Fintech-based Microfinancing model for *Murabaha, Mudaraba, Ijarah* and *Musharaka* can provide an opportunity to improve efficiency through digitization of financing process and it can bring small industries, poor individuals, startups and vulnerable into the mainstream finance. Islamic Microfinance is still underutilized as a financing option and it has huge potential in countries like Pakistan, Bangladesh, Nigeria, Indonesia and Malaysia, large Muslim population resides. Fintech-based Islamic Microfinance can help in large outreach and reduction in the administration and maintenance cost (Salman Ahmed Shaikh, 2020). Further, Artificial intelligence-based Islamic Fintech model can be used for client screening, documentation and suggestion purposes to find the most suitable client to reach objective of financial inclusion and socio-economic stability (Khan et al., 2021; Rabbani et al., 2021).

Zakat: *Zakat* is one of the five pillars of Islam, referring to the obligation that every Muslim has to donate a certain portion of its wealth for the benevolent purpose (Abdullah et al., 2012; Asmalia & Kasri, 2019; Hamid & Hamid, 2020; Kadir et al., 2019; Mattson, 2003). It is the fundamental part of being a Muslim and acts as the purification of one's wealth for the sake of Allah almighty (Tanvir Mahmud et al., 2014). Zakat is one of the most important tools in the Islamic social finance (Alam Choudhury & Syafri Harahap, 2008; Salleh, 2015). Integrating Zakat with Fintech can result in poverty alleviation and financial inclusion (Khan et al., 2019; Salleh, 2015). Fintech-based Zakat collection and distribution system can bring speed, transparency, accessibility, security and operational efficiency in Islamic social finance (Khan et al., 2021; Rabbani et al., 2021). The use of Fintech-based Zakat during the COVID-19 pandemic has provided benefits to the millions of Muslim populations across the globe. In Pakistan alone "Ehsaas Emergency cash relief program" by the government of Pakistan, the Fintech was a huge success and resulted into massive financial inclusion as Mobile money transfer reached 6.8 million families in less than a week (Islamic Development Bank Group, 2020) (Fig. 7).

Blockchain wave has already made inroads in the world of Islamic finance. Islamic financial institutions have embraced this disruptive technology in the early stage itself to offer efficiency in their operation and bring quality in its financial services (Alidin et al., 2019; Mohamed & Ali, 2018). Islamic financial institutions can not only apply Blockchain to reduce transaction cost and bring operational efficiency but also create new, innovative and trendy financial services to gain more market share and gain revenue streams (Atif et al., 2021a, 2021b; Hassan et al., 2020a, 2020b). There are various applications of Blockchain in Islamic finance including, Blockchain-based smart contracts (Fatema et al., 2018), *Zakat*

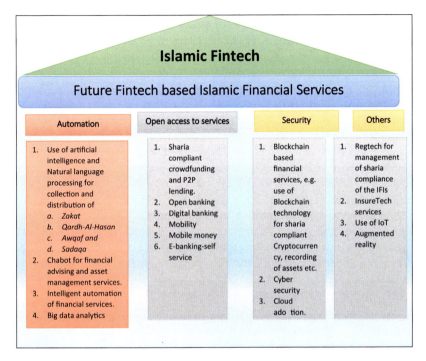

Fig. 7 Future Fintech-based Islamic financial services (*Source* Author's own compilation)

collection and distribution (Khan & Rabbani, 2021a, 2021b; Mohammad et al., 2020; Rabbani et al., 2021), distribution of *Qardh-Al-Hasan* by Islamic banks (Khan et al., 2021), Chatbot for financial planning and advising (Khan & Rabbani, 2022, 2021a, 2021b), etc. Islamic financial services can be linked with Blockchain to provide the financial assistance to reach the COVID-19-affected individuals and SMEs, it can help in easy identification of actual beneficiary and keeping a record of help provided to the affected and vulnerable (Hassan et al., 2021a, 2021b; Rabbani, 2020). Blockchain-based financial services can help in achieving the objective of financial inclusion which is one of the key objectives of Islamic social finance (Gabor & Brooks, 2017; Saraswati et al., 2020).

Figures 8 and 9 portray the impact of Blockchain technology on delivery of Islamic financial services. Figure 8 shows the Islamic trade finance services without the use of Blockchain technology. It can be observed that trade finance services which are practiced currently without Fintech are mainly manual and consumes a lot of time, money and physical efforts. For example, if an importer orders goods from a foreign country he has to apply for the letter of credit from the importer's Islamic bank and provide it to the exporter's Islamic bank. After obtaining the letter of credit from the importer's Islamic bank, the exporter's bank authorizes the exporter to ship the goods to the importer and all these processes are time consuming and stressful, whereas Fig. 8 represents the Blockchain-based future trade finance, where everything is done through the click of a mouse. As explained earlier, Blockchain is a distributed ledger technology where it has the ability to create a digital ledger of the transactions that can be distributed among the users of the transaction with the help of cryptography. It allows the tracking and recording of transactions without the central authority like the banks. All these processes are performed with the help of automatically executable smart contract.

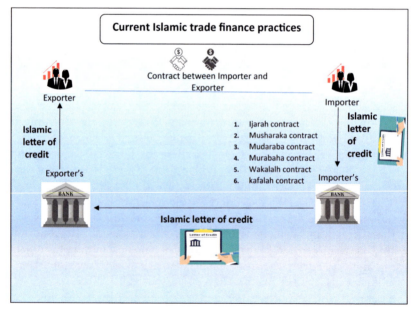

Fig. 8 Current Islamic trade finance practices (*Source* Author's own architect)

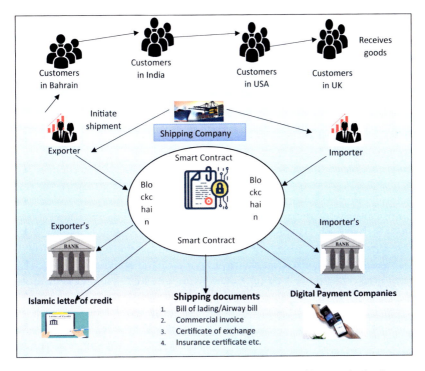

Fig. 9 Future Blockchain-based Islamic trade finances (*Source* Author's own architect)

4 Conclusion

While the world addresses the economic consequences caused by the ongoing COVID-19 pandemic, digital financial services have found acceptance to another level and Fintech-based service providers are booming with the growing demand and market penetration. The fourth industrial revolution has already fostered growth through innovative technologies, automation, disintermediation and decentralization in the global finance marketplace. Over 15,000 Fintech startups have already disrupted every section of finance. The industry 4.0-driven technologies such as Cloud computing, Blockchain, Crowdfunding, InsureTech Regtech, etc. are exponentially enhancing the existing financial services, business models and customer engagements. These Fintech-based innovations are more focused on the process automation to speed up the product innovation process and to enable the new business models to bring greater operational efficiency. The Fintech evolution is yet to reach its peak but it is certainly growing at a rapid pace and COVID-19 has only accelerated its pace (Rabbani, 2020).

Islamic finance was a silver lining from the global financial crisis of 2008 and established itself as the greatest challenger to the conventional financial system (Ashraf et al., 2018; Hippler III et al., 2019). The present study concludes that COVID-19 will further enhance the credentials of Islamic financial system as the robust and sustainable financial system. Islamic Fintech is gaining acceptance and it is becoming more relevant in combination with the technologies like Crowdfunding and Blockchain. On one hand the Islamic Fintech-based crowdfunding is expected to solve the long due problem of fund acquisition for the startups and small and medium enterprises, on the other hand Sharia compliant Blockchain technology is helping it to reach new frontiers, new markets with more transparency, better efficiency and increased security.

The study further concludes that the future of Islamic Fintech in combination with the Crowdfunding and Blockchain technology looks promising. Islamic Fintech has so much to offer, and it can reach to its full potential with the alliance of Fintech startups and existing Islamic financial institutions. The Islamic Financial institutions that are already working in association with the Fintech startups are in better shape to innovate, experiment and take its services offering to another level of efficiency and profitability. The paper is expected to contribute positively to understanding of Islamic Fintech and application of Fintech-based innovations in the Islamic finance industry. We have made an honest attempt to provide necessary direction to government institutions and policy makers for preparation and implementations of regulatory measures for the betterment of Islamic finance industry. The findings of the present study are expected to shed new lights in this growing area of research.

References

Abdullah, L. H., Ahmad, W. M. W., Rahman, N. N. A., Ali, A. K., Nor, M. R. M., Khalil, S. A., & Al-Nahari, A. A. A. Q. (2012). Juristic discourse on the delay in payment and distribution of Zakat. *Middle East Journal of Scientific*

Research, 12(2), 176–181. https://doi.org/10.5829/idosi.mejsr.2012.12.2.1682

Abi-Lahoud, E., Raoul, P.-E., & Muckley, C. (2018). Linking data to understand the fintech ecosystem. In *Posters and demos track of the 13th international conference on semantic systems SEMANTiCS, SEMPDS 2017* (Vol. 2044). CEUR-WS. https://www.scopus.com/inward/record.uri?eid=2-s2.0-85045884009&partnerID=40&md5=9a446b6f301c1b5f839dec27df6e0765

Ahram, T., Sargolzaei, A., Sargolzaei, S., Daniels, J., & Amaba, B. (2017). Blockchain technology innovations. In *2017 IEEE technology and engineering management society conference, TEMSCON 2017*. https://doi.org/10.1109/TEMSCON.2017.7998367

Alam Choudhury, M., & Syafri Harahap, S. (2008). Interrelationship between Zakat, Islamic bank and the economy: A theoretical exploration. *Managerial Finance*. https://doi.org/10.1108/03074350810890967

Alam, N., Gupta, L., & Zameni, A. (2019). Fintech and Islamic finance: Digitalization, development and disruption. *Springer*. https://doi.org/10.1007/978-3-030-24666-2

Ali, M. A. M., Bashar, A., Abdullah, Y., & Rabbani, M. R. (2020a). Transforming business decision making with internet of things (IoT) and machine learning (ML). In *IEEE Explore, DASA'20*. IEEE.

Ali, M. M., Bashar, A., Rabbani, M. R., & Abdullah, Y. (2020b). Transforming business decision making with internet of things (IoT) and machine learning (ML). In *2020b international conference on decision aid sciences and application (DASA)*, Sakheer, Bahrain, (pp. 674–679). https://doi.org/10.1109/DASA51403.2020b

Ali, W., Muthaly, S., & Dada, M. (2018). Adoption of Shariah compliant peer-to-business financing platforms by SMES: A conceptual strategic framework for fintechs in Bahrain. *International Journal of Innovative Technology and Exploring Engineering*, 8(2 Special Issue 2), 407–412. https://www.scopus.com/inward/record.uri?eid=2-s2.0-85064182993&partnerID=40&md5=88499f335e16a460fe79e631d17880cb

Alidin, A. A., Ali-Wosabi, A. A. A., & Yusoff, Z. (2019). Overview of blockchain implementation on Islamic finance: Saadiqin experience. In *2018 cyber resilience conference, CRC 2018*. Institute of Electrical and Electronics Engineers Inc. https://doi.org/10.1109/CR.2018.8626822

Ashraf, A., Lane, W., & Hassan, M. K. (2018). Monetary policy responses to the 2008 financial crisis: Quantitative easing evidence in the United Kingdom. *Journal of Economic Cooperation and Development*. https://doi.org/10.2139/ssrn.2944499

Asmalia, S., & Kasri, R. A. (2019). Analyzing the intention to pay Zakat among Indonesian muslims based on the theory of planned behavior. In *Challenges of the global economy: Some Indonesian issues* (pp. 183–203). Nova Science

Publishers, Inc. https://www.scopus.com/inward/record.uri?eid=2-s2.0-850 89055067&partnerID=40&md5=c657e17534cced6637c3eceff8825431

Atif, M., Hassan, M. K., Rabbani, M. R., & Khan, S. (2021a). Islamic FinTech: The digital transformation bringing sustainability in Islamic finance. In *COVID-19 and Islamic social finance* (pp. 91–103). Routledge.

Atif, M., Hassan, M. K., Rabbani, M. R., & Khan, S. (2021b). Islamic FinTech: The digital transformation bringing sustainability to Islamic finance. In *COVID-19 and Islamic social finance* (pp. 94–106). Routledge.

Babbitt, T. G., & Mahoney, J. T. (2001). Understanding the digital economy: Data tools, and research. *Academy of Management Review*. https://doi.org/10.5465/amr.2001.4845862

Baber, H. (2019). Relevance of e-SERVQUAL for determining the quality of FinTech services. *International Journal of Electronic Finance, 9*(4), 257–267. https://doi.org/10.1504/IJEF.2019.104070

Baber, H. (2020). FinTech, Crowdfunding and customer retention in Islamic banks. *Vision, 24*(3), 260–268. https://doi.org/10.1177/0972262919869765

Bendovschi, A. (2015). Cyber-attacks: Trends, patterns and security countermeasures. *Procedia Economics and Finance*. https://doi.org/10.1016/s2212-5671(15)01077-1

Berns, J. P., Figueroa-Armijos, M., da Motta Veiga, S. P., & Dunne, T. C. (2020). Dynamics of lending-based prosocial crowdfunding: Using a social responsibility lens. *Journal of Business Ethics, 161*(1), 169–185. https://doi.org/10.1007/s10551-018-3932-0

Bi, G., Geng, B., & Liu, L. (2019). On the fixed and flexible funding mechanisms in reward-based crowdfunding. *European Journal of Operational Research, 279*(1), 168–183. https://doi.org/10.1016/j.ejor.2019.05.019

Bogusz, C. I., Laurell, C., Sandström, C., & Sandström, C. (2020). Tracking the digital evolution of entrepreneurial finance: The interplay between crowdfunding, blockchain technologies, cryptocurrencies, and initial coin offerings. *IEEE Transactions on Engineering Management, 67*(4), 1099–1108. https://doi.org/10.1109/TEM.2020.2984032

Brodsky, L., & Oakes, L. (2017). Data sharing and open banking. McKinsey on Payments.

Chen, P. W., Jiang, B. S., & Wang, C. H. (2017). Blockchain-based payment collection supervision system using pervasive Bitcoin digital wallet. *In International Conference on Wireless and Mobile Computing, Networking and Communications*. https://doi.org/10.1109/WiMOB.2017.8115844

Colombo, M. G., & Shafi, K. (2019). Receiving external equity following successfully crowdfunded technological projects: An informational mechanism. *Small Business Economics*. https://doi.org/10.1007/s11187-019-00259-1

Darmansyah, F. B. A., Hendratmi, A., & Aziz, P. F. (2020). Factors determining behavioral intentions to use Islamic financial technology: Three competing models. *Journal of Islamic Marketing.* https://doi.org/10.1108/JIMA-12-2019-0252

Demirguc-Kunt, A., Klapper, L., & Randall, D. (2014). Islamic finance and financial inclusion: Measuring use of and demand for formal financial services among muslim adults. *Review of Middle East Economics and Finance.* https://doi.org/10.1515/rmeef-2013-0062

Dhumale, R., & Sapcanin, A. (1998). *An application of Islamic Banking principles to microfinance.* Study by the Regional Bureau for Arab States, United Nations Development Programme, in Cooperation With the Middle East and North Africa Region.

Di Pietro, F., Prencipe, A., & Majchrzak, A. (2018). Crowd equity investors: An underutilized asset for open innovation in startups. *California Management Review, 60*(2), 43–70. https://doi.org/10.1177/0008125617738260

Dimbean-Creta, O. (2018). Fintech in corporations: Transforming the finance function. *Quality—Access to Success, 19*(S3), 21–28.

DinarStandard. (2018). *Islamic Fintech report 2018: Current landscape & path forward.* Dubai Islamic Economy Development Centre.

DinarStandard. (2021). *Islamic Fintech report 2018: Current landscape and path forward.* Dubai Islamic Economy Development Centre. https://www.dinarstandard.com/wp-content/uploads/2018/12/Islamic-Fintech-Report-2018.pdf

Du, M., Chen, Q., Xiao, J., Yang, H., & Ma, X. (2020). Supply Chain finance innovation using blockchain. *IEEE Transactions on Engineering Management, 67*(4), 1045–1058. https://doi.org/10.1109/TEM.2020.2971858

El-Komi, M., & Croson, R. (2013). Experiments in Islamic microfinance. *Journal of Economic Behavior and Organization.* https://doi.org/10.1016/j.jebo.2012.08.009

Eyal, I. (2017). Blockchain technology: Transforming libertarian cryptocurrency dreams to finance and banking realities. *Computer, 50*(9), 38–49. https://doi.org/10.1109/MC.2017.3571042

Fatema, M., Islam, M. A., & Bakar, R. (2018). Halal purchase intention- a study on Islamic banks of Bangladesh. *Journal of Social Sciences Research, 4*(12), 402–412. https://doi.org/10.32861/jssr.412.402.412

Feng, Q., He, D., Zeadally, S., Khan, M. K., & Kumar, N. (2019). A survey on privacy protection in blockchain system. *Journal of Network and Computer Applications, 126,* 45–58. https://doi.org/10.1016/j.jnca.2018.10.020

Fianto, B. A., Gan, C., Hu, B., & Roudaki, J. (2018). Equity financing and debt-based financing: Evidence from Islamic microfinance institutions in Indonesia. *Pacific Basin Finance Journal.* https://doi.org/10.1016/j.pacfin.2017.09.010

Fisch, C., Meoli, M., & Vismara, S. (2020). Does blockchain technology democratize entrepreneurial finance? An empirical comparison of ICOs, venture capital, and REITs. *Economics of Innovation and New Technology.* https://doi.org/10.1080/10438599.2020.1843991

Gabor, D., & Brooks, S. (2017). The digital revolution in financial inclusion: International development in the fintech era. *New Political Economy, 22*(4), 423–436. https://doi.org/10.1080/13563467.2017.1259298

Gomber, P., Koch, J.-A., & Siering, M. (2017). Digital Finance and FinTech: Current research and future research directions. *Journal of Business Economics, 87*(5), 537–580. https://doi.org/10.1007/s11573-017-0852-x

Hamid, S. A., & Hamid, M. L. (2020). Zakat and the empowerment of the hardcore poor in the 21st century. *Journal of Critical Reviews, 7*(5), 136–139. https://doi.org/10.31838/jcr.07.05.22

Haneef, M. A., Muhammad, A. D., Pramanik, A. H., & Mohammed, M. O. (2014). Integrated waqf based Islamic microfinance model (IWIMM) for poverty alleviation in OIC member countries. *Middle-East Journal of Scientific Research, 19*(2), 286–298. https://doi.org/10.5829/idosi.mejsr.2014.19.2.12565

Hasan, R., Hassan, M. K., & Aliyu, S. (2020b). Fintech and Islamic finance: Literature review and research agenda. *International Journal of Islamic Economics and Finance (IJIEF), 1*(2), 75–94. https://doi.org/10.18196/ijief.2122

Hassan, A. (2014). The challenge in poverty alleviation: Role of Islamic microfinance and social capital. *Humanomics, 30*(1), 76–90. https://doi.org/10.1108/H-10-2013-0068

Hassan, M. K., & Hippler, W. J. (2014). Entrepreneurship and Islam: An overview. *Econ Journal Watch.* https://doi.org/10.2139/ssrn.3263110

Hassan, M. K., & Lewis, M. K. (2007). Islamic finance: A system at the crossroads? *Thunderbird International Business Review.* https://doi.org/10.1002/tie.20137

Hassan, M. K., Rabbani, M. R., & Abdullah, Y. (2021a). Socioeconomic impact of COVID-19 in MENA region and the Role of Islamic finance. *International Journal of Islamic Economics and Finance (IJIEF), 4*(1), 51–78.

Hassan, M. K., Rabbani, M. R., & Ali, M. A. (2020a). Challenges for the Islamic Finance and banking in post COVID era and the role of Fintech. *Journal of Economic Cooperation and Development, 41*(3), 93–116.

Hassan, M. K., Rabbani, M. R., Khan, S., & Ali, M. A. M. (2021b). *An Islamic finance perspective of crowdfunding and peer to peer lending* (In press).

Hassan, N. M., Nor, A. H. B. M., & Rom, N. A. M. (2012). Institutional collaboration in enhancing zakat distribution for production ASNAF: Reaping the benefits or diminishing the institutions' roles.

5, 2501–2514. https://www.scopus.com/inward/record.uri?eid=2-s2.0-848 96387277&partnerID=40&md5=0290a92d6dc74e1fd974236aea39517b

Hassan, S., Rahman, R. A., Bakar, N. A., Mohd, R., & Muhammad, A. D. (2013). Designing islamic microfinance products for Islamic banks in Malaysia. *Middle East Journal of Scientific Research*. https://doi.org/10.5829/idosi.mejsr.2013.17.03.12160

Hippler, W. J., III., Hossain, S., & Hassan, M. K. (2019). Financial crisis spillover from Wall Street to Main Street: Further evidence. *Empirical Economics, 56*(6), 1893–1938. https://doi.org/10.1007/s00181-018-1513-9

IFSB. (2020). *Stability report 2020*. Islamic Financial Services Board.

Iman, N. (2018). Is mobile payment still relevant in the Fintech era? *Electronic Commerce Research and Applications*. https://doi.org/10.1016/j.elerap.2018.05.009

Islam, R., & Ahmad, R. (2020). Applicability of Mudarabah and Musharakah as Islamic micro-equity finance to underprivileged women in Malaysia. *European Journal of Development Research, 32*(1), 176–197. https://doi.org/10.1057/s41287-019-00225-3

Islam, R., Ahmad, R., Ghailan, K., & Hoque, K. E. (2020). An Islamic microfinance approach to scaling up the economic life of vulnerable people with HIV/AIDS in the Muslim society. *Journal of Religion and Health*. https://doi.org/10.1007/s10943-019-00832-8

Islamic Development Bank Group. (2020). *The Covid-19 crisis and Islamic finance* (Issue, September). https://irti.org/product/the-covid-19-crisis-and-islamic-finance/

Jagtiani, J., & John, K. (2018). Fintech: The impact on consumers and regulatory responses. *Journal of Economics and Business, 100*, 1–6. https://doi.org/10.1016/j.jeconbus.2018.11.002

Jan, A., & Marimuthu, M. (2016). Bankruptcy profile of foreign versus domestic Islamic Banks of Malaysia: A post crisis period analysis. *International Journal of Economics and Financial Issues, 6*(1), 332–347. https://www.scopus.com/inward/record.uri?eid=2-s2.0-84979842240&partnerID=40&md5=078eb13e325cb7d9e04795c8dbf20a38

Jin, S.-J., Hwang, I. T., & Kang, S. M. (2018). Improving sustainability through a dual audit system. *Sustainability (Switzerland), 10*(1). https://doi.org/10.3390/su10010137

Joju, J., Vasantha, S., & Manoj, P. K. (2017). Financial technology and service quality in banks: Some empirical evidence from the old private sector banks based in Kerala, India. *International Journal of Applied Business and Economic Research, 15*(16), 447–457. https://www.scopus.com/inward/record.uri?eid=2-s2.0-85028348312&partnerID=40&md5=e644e2ab6a26593cd73a61087962c390

Jovanović, T., Brem, A., & Voigt, K.-I. (2019). Who invests why? An analysis of investment decisions in B2B or B2C equity crowdfunding projects. *International Journal of Entrepreneurship and Small Business, 37*(1), 71–86. https://doi.org/10.1504/IJESB.2019.099886

Jun, J., & Yeo, E. (2016). Entry of FinTech firms and competition in the retail payments market. *Asia-Pacific Journal of Financial Studies, 45*(2), 159–184. https://doi.org/10.1111/ajfs.12126

Kadir, M. R. A., Tarmidi-Tokhid, M. B., & Abdullah, A. A. (2019). Business Zakat conditions and their relationships with accounting principles: An exploratory study. *International Journal of Innovation, Creativity and Change, 8*(4), 355–366. https://www.scopus.com/inward/record.uri?eid=2-s2.0-85075981183&partnerID=40&md5=0f8ca55a8536a11bd05434e2c5260e1d

Kalra, D. (2019). Overriding FINTECH. In *Proceeding of 2019 international conference on digitization: Landscaping artificial intelligence, ICD 2019*. https://doi.org/10.1109/ICD47981.2019.9105915

Khairunnisa, S., Muzayanah, I. F. U., & Kasri, R. A. (2019). Impact of Islamic microfinance on quality of life: Maqasid Al-Shariah approach. In *Challenges of the global economy: Some Indonesian issues* (pp. 205–227). Nova Science Publishers, Inc. https://www.scopus.com/inward/record.uri?eid=2-s2.0-85089058485&partnerID=40&md5=24fafb9a52417027c7f1b054082b7cd7

Khan, S., Hassan, M. K., Rabbani, M. R., & Atif, M. (2021). An artificial intelligence-based Islamic FinTech model on Qardh-Al-Hasan for COVID 19 affected SMEs. In *Islamic perspective for sustainable financial system* (pp. 234–249).

Khan, S., & Rabbani, M. R. (2020). Chatbot as Islamic finance expert (CaIFE) when finance meets artificial intelligence. In *Proceedings of the 2020b 4th international symposium on computer science and intelligent control* (pp. 1–5).

Khan, S., & Rabbani, M. R. (2021a). Artificial intelligence and NLP based Chatbot as Islamic banking and finance expert. *International Journal of Information Retrieval Research (IJIRR), 11*(3), 65–77.

Khan, S., & Rabbani, M. R. (2021b). In depth analysis of blockchain, cryptocurrency and Sharia compliance. *International Journal of Business Innovation and Research* (In press). https://doi.org/10.1504/ijbir.2020.10033066

Khan, S., & Rabbani, M. R. (2022). In-depth analysis of blockchain, cryptocurrency and sharia compliance. *International Journal of Business Innovation and Research, 29* (1), 1–15.

Khan, M. S., Rabbani, M. R., Hawaldar, I. T., & Bashar, A. (2022). Determinants of behavioral intentions to use Islamic financial technology: An empirical assessment. *Risks* (in press).

Khan, S., Sheikh, A. E., Abu Bakar, M., & Abidullah. (2019). Zakat: financial inclusion nexus: Empirical evidence from Pakistan. *International Journal of Innovation, Creativity and Change*.

Lee, I., & Shin, Y. J. (2018). Fintech: Ecosystem, business models, investment decisions, and challenges. *Business Horizons*. https://doi.org/10.1016/j.bushor.2017.09.003

Lee Kuo Chuen, D., & Deng, R. (2017). *Handbook of blockchain, Digital finance, and inclusion, Volume 1: Cryptocurrency, FinTech, InsurTech, and regulation*. Elsevier Inc. https://doi.org/10.1016/C2015-0-04334-9

Li, X., Su, C., Xiong, Y., Huang, W., & Wang, W. (2019). Formal verification of BNB smart contract. In *Proceedings—5th international conference on big data computing and communications, BIGCOM 2019* (pp. 74–78). https://doi.org/10.1109/BIGCOM.2019.00021

Lins, E., Fietkiewicz, K. J., & Lutz, E. (2018). Effects of impression management tactics on crowdfunding success. *International Journal of Entrepreneurial Venturing*, *10*(5), 534–557. https://doi.org/10.1504/IJEV.2018.094607

Liu, J., Li, X., & Wang, S. (2020). What have we learnt from 10 years of fintech research? A scientometric analysis. *Technological Forecasting and Social Change*. https://doi.org/10.1016/j.techfore.2020.120022

Liu, Y., Peng, J., & Yu, Z. (2018). Big data platform architecture under the background of financial technology—in the insurance industry as an example example. In *2018 international conference on big data engineering and technology, BDET 2018* (pp. 31–35). https://doi.org/10.1145/3297730.3297743

Lu, W. (2018). Blockchain technology and its applications in FinTech. In *2nd international conference on intelligent, secure and dependable systems in distributed and cloud environments, ISDDC 2018*: Vol. 11317 LNCS (pp. 118–124). Springer. https://doi.org/10.1007/978-3-030-03712-3_10

Macchiavello, E. (2017). Microfinance and financial inclusion: The challenge of regulating alternative forms of finance. *Taylor and Francis*. https://doi.org/10.4324/9781315623962

Mackenzie, A. (2015). The Fintech revolution. *London Business School Review*, *26*(3), 50–53. https://doi.org/10.1111/2057-1615.12059

Mansfield-Devine, S. (2016). Open banking: Opportunity and danger. *Computer Fraud and Security*. https://doi.org/10.1016/S1361-3723(16)30080-X

Mansori, S., Kim, C. S., & Safari, M. (2015). A Shariah perspective review on Islamic microfinance. *Asian Social Science*. https://doi.org/10.5539/ass.v11n9p273

Marcel, B., Ortan, T., & Otgon, C. (1976). Information asymmetry theory in corporate governance systems. *Economic Science Series*.

Mattson, I. (2003). Status-based definitions of need in early Islamic zakat and maintenance laws. In *Poverty and charity in Middle Eastern contexts* (pp. 31–51). State University of New York Press. https://www.scopus.com/inward/record.uri?eid=2-s2.0-80054482654&partnerID=40&md5=3c9357426d4531cf4ef9109e95abed1c

Md Saad, N. (2012). Microfinance and prospect for Islamic microfinance products: The case of Amanah Ikhtiar Malaysia. *Advances in Asian Social Science, 1*(1), 27–33.

Mnif, E., Jarboui, A., Hassan, M. K., & Mouakhar, K. (2020). Big data tools for Islamic financial analysis. *Intelligent Systems in Accounting, Finance and Management.* https://doi.org/10.1002/isaf.1463

Mohamed, H., & Ali, H. (2018). Blockchain, Fintech, and Islamic finance: Building the future in the new Islamic digital economy. *De Gruyter.* https://doi.org/10.1515/9781547400966

Mohammad, H. S., Khan, S., Mustafa, R. R., & Yannis, E. T. (2020). An artificial intelligence and NLP based Islamic FinTech model combining Zakat and Qardh-Al-Hasan for countering the adverse impact of COVID 19 on SMEs and individuals. *International Journal of Economics and Business Administration, VIII*(issue 2), 351–364. https://doi.org/10.35808/ijeba/466

Muhd Adnan, N. I., Mohd Kashim, M. I. A., Endut, W. A., Ismail, S., Abd. Khafidz, H., Furqani, H., Ab Rahman, Z., Mohd Noor, A. Y., & Zakaria, M. B. (2020). Zakat distribution through micro financing: Hukm (Islamic ruling) and form of AQAD (contract). *Journal of Critical Reviews, 7*(5), 1032–1038. https://doi.org/10.31838/jcr.07.05.208

Nuryakin, C., Sastiono, P., Maizar, F. A., Amin, P., Yunita, L., Puspita, N., Afrizal, M., & Tjen, C. (2017). *Financial inclusion through digital financial services and branchless banking: Inclusiveness, challenges and opportunities* (LPEM-FEBUI Working Paper). LPEM-FEBUI.

Open Banking Implementation Entity. (2019). *Open banking, preparing for lift off.* The Open Data Institute.

Orús, R., Mugel, S., & Lizaso, E. (2018). Quantum computing for finance: Overview and prospects. *Reviews in Physics, 4,* 100028.

Owen, R., Macan Bhaird, C., Hussain, J., & Botelho, T. (2019). Blockchain and other innovations in entrepreneurial finance: Implications for future policy. *Strategic Change, 28*(1), 5–8. https://doi.org/10.1002/jsc.2250

Ozili, P. K. (2019). Blockchain finance: Questions regulators ask. In *International finance review* (Vol. 20, pp. 123–129). Emerald Group Publishing Ltd. https://doi.org/10.1108/S1569-376720190000020014

Paston, A., & Harris, M. (2019). Fintech 2.0: Software as the future of payments distribution. *Journal of Payments Strategy and Systems, 13*(3), 226–236. https://www.scopus.com/inward/record.uri?eid=2-s2.0-85073923557&partnerID=40&md5=04f1e857d7741505d3e755e95d8d7efa

Pizzi, S., Corbo, L., & Caputo, A. (2020). Fintech and SMEs sustainable business models: Reflections and considerations for a circular economy. *Journal of Cleaner Production.* https://doi.org/10.1016/j.jclepro.2020.125217
Puschmann, T. (2017). Fintech. *Business and Information Systems Engineering.* https://doi.org/10.1007/s12599-017-0464-6
Quero, M. J., Ventura, R., & Kelleher, C. (2017). Value-in-context in crowdfunding ecosystems: How context frames value co-creation. *Service Business, 11*(2), 405–425. https://doi.org/10.1007/s11628-016-0314-5
Rabbani, M. R. (2020). The competitive structure and strategic positioning of commercial banks in Saudi Arabia. *International Journal on Emerging Technologies, 11*(3), 43–46.
Rabbani, M. R. (2021). COVID-19 and its impact on supply chain financing and the role of Islamic Fintech: Evidence from GCC countries. *International Journal of Agile Systems and Management* (In press).
Rabbani, M. R., Abdullah, Y., Bashar, A., Khan, S., & Ali, M. A. M. (2020a). Embracing of Fintech in Islamic Finance in the post COVID era. In *2020a international conference on decision aid sciences and application (DASA),* Sakheer, Bahrain, 2020a (pp. 1230–1234). https://doi.org/10.1109/DASA51403.2020a.9317196.
Rabbani, M. R., Khan, S., & Thalassinos, E. I. (2020b). FinTech, blockchain and Islamic finance: An extensive literature review. *International Journal of Economics and Business Administration, 8*(2), 65–86. https://doi.org/10.35808/ijeba/444
Rabbani, M. R., Khan, S., & Atif, M. (2022a). Machine learning based P2P lending Islamic FinTech model for small and medium enterprises (SMEs) in Bahrain. *International Journal of Business Innovation and Research* (In press).
Rabbani, M. R., Kayani, U., Bawazir, H. S., & Hawaldar, I. T. (2022b). A commentary on emerging markets banking sector spillovers: Covid-19 vs GFC pattern analysis. *Heliyon, 8*(3), e09074.
Rabbani, M. R., Khan, S., Hassan, M. K., & Ali, M. (2021). Artificial intelligence and natural language processing (NLP) based FinTech model of Zakat for poverty alleviation and sustainable development for Muslims in India. In *ICOVID-19 and Islamic social finance* (pp. 104–114). Routledge.
Rahman, A. R. (2010). Islamic microfinance: An ethical alternative to poverty alleviation. *Humanomics.* https://doi.org/10.1108/08288661011090884
Reepu. (2019). Blockchain: Social innovation in finance and accounting. *International Journal of Management, 10*(1), 14–18. https://doi.org/10.34218/IJM.10.1.2019/003
Romanova, I., & Kudinska, M. (2016). Banking and fintech: A challenge or opportunity? *Contemporary Studies in Economic and Financial Analysis.* https://doi.org/10.1108/S1569-375920160000098002

Ryu, S., Park, J., Kim, K., & Kim, Y.-G. (2020). Reward versus altruistic motivations in reward-based crowdfunding. *International Journal of Electronic Commerce, 24*(2), 159–183. https://doi.org/10.1080/10864415.2020.1715531

Saad, M., & Mohaisen, A. (2018). Towards characterizing blockchain-based cryptocurrencies for highly-accurate predictions. In *2018 IEEE conference on computer communications workshops, INFOCOM 2018* (pp. 704–709). https://doi.org/10.1109/INFCOMW.2018.8406859

Saad, N. M., & Razak, D. A. (2013). Towards an application of Musharakah Mutanaqisah principle in Islamic microfinance. *International Journal of Business and Society, 14*(2), 221.

Saiti, B., Musito, M. H., & Yucel, E. (2018). Islamic crowdfunding: Fundamentals, developments and challenges. *Islamic Quarterly, 62*(3), 469–485. https://www.scopus.com/inward/record.uri?eid=2-s2.0-85062840918&partnerID=40&md5=c90f190a304de6e7479ea5f3171b4af7

Salleh, P. M. A. M. H. A. (2015). Integrating financial inclusion and saving motives into institutional zakat practices: A case study on Brunei. *International Journal of Islamic and Middle Eastern Finance and Management.* https://doi.org/10.1108/IMEFM-12-2013-0126

Saraswati, B. D., Maski, G., Kaluge, D., & Sakti, R. K. (2020). The effect of financial inclusion and financial technology on effectiveness of the Indonesian monetary policy. *Business: Theory and Practice, 21*(1), 230–243. https://doi.org/10.3846/BTP.2020.10396

Serrano, J. L. G. (2019). Big data and Fintech tools to prevent and relieve consumer overindebtedness: A proposal. *Revista Chilena De Derecho y Tecnología, 8*(2), 5–32. https://doi.org/10.5354/0719-2584.2019.54051

Shaikh, S. A. (2020). Using Fintech in scaling up Islamic microfinance. *Journal of Islamic Accounting and Business Research.* https://doi.org/10.1108/JIABR-10-2019-0198

Shen, T., Ma, J., Zhang, B., Huang, W., & Fan, F. (2020). "I invest by following lead investors!" The role of lead investors in fundraising performance of equity crowdfunding. *Frontiers in Psychology, 11.* https://doi.org/10.3389/fpsyg.2020.00632

SO'Dea. (2020). *Smartphone users worldwide 2020.* Statista.

State of Financial Inclusion of Women in Pakistan. (2018). *State of financial inclusion of women in Pakistan.* https://doi.org/10.1596/31323

Sun, H., Rabbani, M. R., Sial, M. S., Yu, S., Filipe, J. A., & Cherian, J. (2020a). Identifying big data's opportunities, challenges, and implications in finance. *Mathematics, 8*(10). https://doi.org/10.3390/math8101738

Sun, H., Rabbani, M. R., Naveed, A., Sial, M. S., Guping, C., Zia-ud-din, M., & Fu, Q. (2020b). CSR, Co-creation and green consumer loyalty: Are green banking initiatives important? A Moderated mediation approach from an emerging economy. *Sustainability (switzerland)*, *12*(24), 10688.

Syed, M. H., Khan, S., Rabbani, M. R., & Thalassinos, Y. E. (2020). An artificial intelligence and NLP based Islamic FinTech model combining zakat and Qardh-Al-Hasan for countering the adverse impact of COVID 19 on SMEs and individuals. *International Journal of Economics and Business Administration*, *8*(2), 351–364. https://doi.org/10.35808/IJEBA/466

Tajudin, M., Omar, R., Smedlund, A., & Aziz, R. P. (2020). Financing with heart and intelligence: augmenting intimacy and sustainability through islamic fintech. *International Journal of Advanced Science and Technology*, *29*(9 Special Issue), 1638–1664. https://www.scopus.com/inward/record.uri?eid=2-s2.0-85084368157&partnerID=40&md5=c195213f22e8b1fa570194ac7037a627

Tanvir Mahmud, K., Kabir Hassan, M., Ferdous Alam, M., Sohag, K., & Rafiq, F. (2014). Opinion of the zakat recipients on their food security: A case study on Bangladesh. *International Journal of Islamic and Middle Eastern Finance and Management*. https://doi.org/10.1108/IMEFM-08-2012-0079

Tewari, H. (2019). Blockchain research beyond cryptocurrencies. *IEEE Communications Standards Magazine*, *3*(4), 21–25. https://doi.org/10.1109/MCOMSTD.001.1900026

Tredinnick, L. (2019). Cryptocurrencies and the blockchain. *Business Information Review*, *36*(1), 39–44. https://doi.org/10.1177/0266382119836314

Turki, M., Hamdan, A., Cummings, R. T., Sarea, A., Karolak, M., & Anasweh, M. (2020). The regulatory technology "RegTech" and money laundering prevention in Islamic and conventional banking industry. *Heliyon*. https://doi.org/10.1016/j.heliyon.2020.e04949

Varma, J. R. (2019). Blockchain in Finance. *Vikalpa*, *44*(1), 1–11. https://doi.org/10.1177/0256090919839897

Widiarto, I., & Emrouznejad, A. (2015). Social and financial efficiency of Islamic microfinance institutions: A Data Envelopment Analysis application. *Socio-Economic Planning Sciences*. https://doi.org/10.1016/j.seps.2014.12.001

Wonglimpiyarat, J. (2019). Analysis of FinTech in the banking industry. *International Journal of Business Innovation and Research*, *19*(1), 125–138. https://doi.org/10.1504/IJBIR.2019.099752

World Bank. (2020a). *Malaysia Islamic finance and financial inclusion*. CFA Institute Magazine.

World Bank. (2020b). *Leveraging Islamic Fintech to improve financial inclusion*. https://doi.org/10.1596/34520

Wulandari, P. (2019). Enhancing the role of Baitul Maal in giving Qardhul Hassan financing to the poor at the bottom of the economic pyramid: Case study of Baitul Maal wa Tamwil in Indonesia. *Journal of Islamic Accounting and Business Research, 10*(3), 382–391. https://doi.org/10.1108/JIABR-01-2017-0005

Yaksick, R. (2019). Overcoming supply chain finance challenges via blockchain technology. In *International Finance Review* (Vol. 20, pp. 87–100). Emerald Group Publishing Ltd. https://doi.org/10.1108/S1569-376720 190000020012

Zauro, N. A., Saad, R. A. J., Ahmi, A., & Mohd Hussin, M. Y. (2020). Integration of Waqf towards enhancing financial inclusion and socio-economic justice in Nigeria. *International Journal of Ethics and Systems.* https://doi.org/10. 1108/IJOES-04-2020-0054

Zavolokina, L., Dolata, M., & Schwabe, G. (2016). The FinTech phenomenon: Antecedents of financial innovation perceived by the popular press. *Financial Innovation, 2*(1). https://doi.org/10.1186/s40854-016-0036-7

Zhang, L., Xie, Y., Zheng, Y., Xue, W., Zheng, X., & Xu, X. (2020). The challenges and countermeasures of blockchain in finance and economics. *Systems Research and Behavioral Science, 37*(4), 691–698. https://doi.org/10.1002/sres.2710

Zhang, S., & Lee, J.-H. (2019). Poster: Smart contract-based miner registration and block validation. In *AsiaCCS 2019: Proceedings of the 2019 ACM Asia conference on computer and communications security* (pp. 691–693). https://doi.org/10.1145/3321705.3331010

Zhao, Y., Xie, X., & Yang, L. (2020). Female entrepreneurs and equity crowdfunding: The consequential roles of lead investors and venture stages. *International Entrepreneurship and Management Journal.* https://doi.org/10.1007/s11365-020-00659-w

Zins, A., & Weill, L. (2016). The determinants of financial inclusion in Africa. *Review of Development Finance.* https://doi.org/10.1016/j.rdf.2016.05.001

Zulkhibri, M. (2016). Financial inclusion, financial inclusion policy and Islamic finance. *Macroeconomics and Finance in Emerging Market Economies.* https://doi.org/10.1080/17520843.2016.1173716

COVID-19 Challenges and the Role of Islamic Fintech

Sitara Karim, Mustafa Raza Rabbani, Mamunur Rashid, and Zaheer Anwer

1 Introduction

With the rapid upsurge of COVID-19, global businesses have experienced the worst economic downfall Initiated from Wuhan, China, the virus has casted an enduring impact on the overall economic and financial system of the world where an emergency state declared in March 2020 seized all operations of the world. It is important to note that COVID-19 has not only impacted a few business sectors similar to the global financial crisis which significantly influenced the financial industry, but the aftermath of coronavirus has spread worldwide impacting all of the business sectors in

---

S. Karim
Nottingham University Business School, University of Nottingham Malaysia Campus, Semenyih, Malaysia

M. R. Rabbani (✉)
Department Economics and Finance, College of Business Administration, University of Bahrain, Zallaq, Bahrain
e-mail: mrabbani@uob.edu.bh

M. Rashid
Christ Church Business School, Canterbury Christ Church University, Canterbury, Kent, UK

© The Author(s), under exclusive license to Springer Nature Switzerland AG 2022
M. K. Hassan et al. (eds.), *FinTech in Islamic Financial Institutions*, https://doi.org/10.1007/978-3-031-14941-2_16

a devastating way. Since the financial industry plays a key role in overall growth of any country, collapse of the overall economic system is marked as one of the most serious plagues which have attacked the globe.

Discussing the greater impact of COVID-19 on industry by industry it can be stated that the world is currently facing an on-going crisis of production, consumption, and supply chain. This crisis is led by the controlled mobility of individuals, maintaining social distancing parameters, and travelling within a state in a limited capacity has created a huge consumption gap where needy people are in search of their helpers whereas givers are in search of takers. The consumption crisis has bereaved the families and children of Yemen, Syria, Palestine, and other parts of the world. The ongoing havoc of the coronavirus pandemic is responsible for uneven distribution of resources and created differences in the consumption patterns of individuals. The other most affected area is disrupted supply chain mechanisms where no physical movement of vehicles and logistics cells has significantly impacted their growth. Since supply chains are well-organized and connected with each other to provide ease of access to the resources and to deliver them to their destined places, COVID-19 has embarked on a major threat to the sustainability of the supply chains. However, as a means to an end, companies and several supply chain partners are working on the re-engineering process of supply chains to deliver the semi-finished products to their destinations and offering significant changes in the whole mechanism. Thus, through this re-engineered process, companies are trying to solve the problems of food shortages, minimum supplies, and less varieties provided during and post-COVID period (Arunachalam & Crentsil, 2020).

Another most impacted industry is micro, small, and medium enterprises with low-income people striving to find sufficient wages for their labor work. With the worldwide emergency, the COVID-19 pandemic has significantly impacted the livelihood of small businesses and particularly those people who earn on a daily wages system. In these circumstances,

---

e-mail: mamunur.rashid@canterbury.ac.uk

Z. Anwer
Dr. Hasan Murad School of Management, University of Management and Technology, Lahore, Pakistan
e-mail: zmanwar@gmail.com

Islamic finance has provided efficient solutions to combat the aftermaths of the coronavirus pandemic through its emergency assistance mechanism where needy people are provided with voluntary *Sadaqat, Zakat, and Qardh-al-Hasan* to help them in their time of need (Hassan et al., 2020; Rabbani et al., 2021a, 2021b). Correspondingly, where most of the business sectors got affected by the havocs of outbreak of COVID-19, the financial sector also experienced severe challenges where regulators, policymakers, and higher authorities have put their attention toward lower interest rates, development of solidarity groups, and establishing self-help groups to assist the society in the time of economic intensity. In this way, the role of Islamic finance and Islamic fintech is substantial to overcome these challenges in a meaningful and effective way. The Islamic finance, ideologically and methodologically different from traditional finance, has provided innovative solutions that helped several entities in both short and long run.

Particularly the role of Islamic fintech in overcoming these challenges is significant where branchless banking, smart contracts, digitization of processes, maintaining individual identities, blockchain technology, the use of artificial intelligence in Islamic banking and Islamic fintech (Sarea et al., 2021), Big Data, and several other technologies have helped the Islamic banking system to speed up the overall banking experience specifically during and post-COVID-19 (Khan and Rabbani 2020a, 2020b, 2020c). This study aims to highlight these specific technologies compatible with the Islamic banking system and comply with the Islamic Sharia.

The rest of the study is arranged in the following manner. Section 2 presents the evolution of fintech and its significance for Islamic banking through the use of blockchain technology and artificial intelligence. Section 3 discusses the usefulness of Islamic fintech in overcoming the COVID-19 shocks. Section 4 concludes the study along with future research recommendations.

2 The Rise of Fintech and Its Significance for Islamic Banking Through the Use of Blockchain Technology and Artificial Intelligence

Evolution of FinTech

Ever since the use of smartphones and handheld devices, the transactions have become quite easier for the customers using the banking services (Dinarstandard, 2020). A survey on internet users reported that nine out of ten customers use the mobile banking applications on their smartphones as they provide the user-friendly experience to them (Rabbani et al., 2021c). The use of simple internet technology with mobile applications has made it easier to access their accounts on a regular basis. In 1967, the Barclay's Bank innovation of Automatic Teller Machines (ATMs) marked the first step toward FinTech and financial innovation. With this technology, the eras of fintech evolution commenced which are parallel to the industrial revolution phases (Ali et al., 2020, Rahim et al., 2018).

Consistent with the industrial revolution phases, the FinTech evolution is also divided into four stages where the initial phase contains FinTech 1.0 solutions and Trans-Atlantic communication cables were mainly used for information transmission from one point to another. Mainframe computers also belonged to the first stage of FinTech 1.0. The second stage is FinTech 2.0 where internet and internet of things (IoT) were the main technologies introduced to provide effective solutions to the information transmission. The third stage includes FinTech 3.0 where data transfer and data operated technologies were introduced. This stage mainly introduced online apps, mobile-friendly tools, different technology-backed transaction mechanisms, and use of the technologies of 3G. The fourth and current stage of FinTech is the transition stage where most of the business operations are turning to the use of artificial intelligence, machine learning, deep learning, blockchain technology, Big Data, and several other technologies to facilitate the customers with the real-time experience of providing service in their hands.

Evolution of Islamic FinTech

The application of FinTech is mainly observed in conventional banks and its application is limited in Islamic banking system due to compliance with the Islamic law (Hassan et al., 2020). Many Sharia advisors and Islamic scholars have forbidden the FinTech applications in bitcoin and several other cryptocurrencies as their compliance with the Sharia is questionable (Hassan et al., 2020). COVID-19 pandemic has brought the disruption and forced the world to shut itself behind the doors and experience the magic of technology like video conferencing using Microsoft Teams, ZOOM, Zoho, Skype (Hilburg et al., 2020), online learning and teaching using Microsoft teams, Blackboard, ZOOM, Google classroom (Khan et al., 2020b, 2022) and use of artificial intelligence and other technologies in medical field from getting real-time COVID-19 data to combating the shocks of the pandemic (Sun et al., 2020a, 2020b). Researchers such as Hilburg et al. (2020) argue that the pandemic has exacerbated the use of technology, whereas the researchers such as Aguilera-Hermida (2020) and Whitelaw et al. (2020) are of the opinion that COVID-19 has due the pandemic acceptance and adoption of technology has gone higher and it has elevated the need to use and to adopt the technology. Finance industry was already experiencing the massive digital transformation in the form of financial technology (FinTech) (Alam et al., 2021; Rabbani et al., 2021a) and the pandemic has given the additional boost and acceptance to the already growing FinTech industry to provide the digital financial services to the customers at its doorstep (Hassan et al., 2020). Technology such as artificial intelligence will have an increased role to play in recovery post COVID-19 as the next generation belongs to the technology (Rabbani et al., 2021c).

Islamic finance industry has emerged as the most robust and resilient finance industry post the global financial crisis of 2008 (Ahmed, 2009, 2010; Asmild et al., 2019). It has witnessed the stern test of the financial crisis and emerged as the winner with its social and ethical financial services (Belanès et al., 2015; Trad et al., 2017). Financial experts, researchers, and academicians all across the globe are looking at the Islamic finance industry with much hope and aspiration to bail them out of the financial distress caused by the pandemic (Hassan et al., 2020, 2021). The emergence of technology will add a positive boost to the industry and success in tackling the adversities of the pandemic will depend on the use of the technology (Mohammad et al., 2020). The growth of Islamic finance industry post COVID-19 will greatly depend on its ability to master technology such as FinTech, blockchain, and artificial intelligence (Rabbani, 2021).

Discussing the role of Islamic FinTech in Islamic banking, it is argued that Islam embraces all types of innovations if they do not violate the basic principles and ethos of Shari'a (Hassan et al., 2020). Particularly, Islamic financial industry adopts and adapts to the use of technological inventions abiding by the rules and regulations of Islamic Shari'a. For this reason, it is permissible to adopt the financial innovations in terms of technology unless they do not harm the basic principles of Islam. Islamic Fintech in Islamic banking promotes Islamic financial industry that delivers the Islamic finance products using different technologies and meets the needs of Islamic Finance customers to achieve financial inclusion, to reduce income inequality, and to bring social justice to the community (Karim et al., 2020a, 2020b, 2020c). Thus, Islamic FinTech in Islamic financial system plays a significant role in delivering Islamic products at a quicker pace. And, based on Islamic Shari'a (Hasan et al., 2020) it is not prohibited to include technological innovations unless they do not break the Shari'a limits.

Artificial Intelligence

The exposure of Islamic financial industry to the different uncertain challenges, as indicated by the COVID-19 pandemic, necessitates the adoption of artificial intelligence in different business processes to ensure growth and sustainability (Karim, 2021a, 2021b). The acceptance of Islamic financial sector toward AI and changing patterns of FinTech warrants that adopting AI and implementing different technologies is the need of the hour. Islamic financial industry basically consists of financial activities rooted on the principles of Shari'a (Islamic law) that is not a single entity but involves Islamic Financial Institutions (IFIs) where principles of Islamic finance are sourced from the Holy Qur'an (Tabash & Dhankar, 2018). It shows that Islamic Financial Institutions are not only banks, but they also cover other types of financial intermediaries following the principles of Shari'a and abide by the Islamic code of conduct for doing business. It also ensures a complete moral system with unique characteristics for carrying out the business operations following the ethical values provided by Islam. Relating it to the adoption of AI and financial technology, Rahim et al. (2018) indicated that digital banking 4.0,

FinTech, and artificial intelligence have tracked significant applications since 2017 which ensures that adequate information is needed to align the interests of Islamic Finance with the adoption of AI.

The rising challenges of COVID-19 have embarked the Islamic financial industry to adapt to the different technologies to ensure sustained growth and economic strength. Referring back to the global financial crisis of 2007 and 2008, the financial industry is one of the significant industries which bear economic shocks in the form of volatile interest rates, moral hazard problems, and lack of trust among stakeholders (Karim et al., 2020a, 2020b, 2020c). Increasing global threats, sudden lockdowns, uncertain circumstances, rapid closure of all running processes, and widespread of novel coronavirus around the world created an alarming situation for whole businesses, production units, supply chains, and financial markets. Financial sector, having a significant role in the financial markets, is also not spared from the challenging circumstances that appeared due to COVID-19 spread across the globe. Banks are considered as the main drivers of economic growth and they are directly related to the money supply and demand within an economic state (Hassan et al., 2022). Global financial crisis of 2007 and 2008, similar to the recent crisis of COVID-19, created a state of bewilderment among the financial partners that raised the questions of their deposits and investments in the financial sector which led to various types of risks such as financial risk, insolvency risk, bankruptcy risk, liquidity risk, etc. In this perplexed state of affairs, the role of regulatory authorities is enhanced manifolds where they have to maintain a balance between the risks and ensure the creditworthiness of the banking sector in a way that customers' investments and deposits are less prone to uncertain circumstances. Islamic financial sector, one of the pillars of the financial markets across the globe, is also not spared from the aftermath of the pandemic. Conspicuously, while there is conventional or Islamic finance, the role of AI is substantiated manifold when such uncertain risk environments are propelled. The role of regulatory authorities in combating the aftershocks of these drastic crises is also substantiated.

In this stream, Islamic financial industry, being in its infancy, needs to adopt artificial intelligence mechanisms to better ensure customer's user-friendly experience and attain technological advancements. In current circumstances, customers are more sophisticated and concerned about their investments and they prefer to make financial transactions where there is less human involvement (Karim et al., 2019; Rahim et al., 2018).

For this reason, technological innovations have broader scope to improve the customer experiences and to provide efficiency to the overall financial system. Artificial intelligence is considered as the most popular way to improve the efficiency of the financial system through smart contracts which is a computer program that prepares and records a list of all the customers whether they are senders or receivers (suppliers and buyers). This program has its application in other areas for instance, banking system, takaful (insurance), and management-related programs. Like any other technological innovation, AI has its application in the Islamic Financial Sector and its products. It is argued by Mijwel (2015) that adoption of AI in Islamic financial system can create machine learning tools and deep neural networks that bring a new unique experience to the whole financial industry.

Prior literature also highlights that AI will have a huge influence on the future growth and prospects of Islamic Financial industry with the relevant adoption of different technologies to provide efficiency to the whole banking mechanism. It is argued that Islamic Financial industry, having significant implications for Muslims and religious ethnicity, cannot deny the importance of adoption of AI into its processes and operations. Given these arguments, it can be said that artificial intelligence has covered the major proportion of businesses while minimizing the human workload and increasing the efficiency and output of processes and Islamic financial industry, having significant contribution to the economy, must also adopt to the changing circumstances and embracing the technological innovations particularly post-COVID-19 period.

Overall, it is revealed that Islamic FinTech needs to be promoted significantly during and post-COVID-19 and several technologies such as blockchain and artificial intelligence can be implemented in the Islamic financial industry. Given these stances, it is described that Islamic banks can adopt multiple FinTech solutions for providing better solutions to customers in the recovery era of COVID-19, but it must be understood by the regulators, bankers and managers that these innovations do not violate the principles of Islamic law.

3 Usefulness of Islamic FinTech in Overcoming the COVID-19 Shocks

The Islamic fintech offers significant tools to combat the devastating effects of COVID-19. The differentiation in the categories of Islamic social finance is of basically voluntary and compulsory acts. Voluntary acts include the charitable deeds, *Sadaqah, and Waqf* whereas compulsory acts include Zakat. Table 1 illustrates the orientation of both voluntary and compulsory deeds with various perspectives. First, parameters on which *Zakat, Sadaqah,* and Waqf are assessed have been mentioned. Five parameters are wealth sharing mechanisms, occurrence of donations, beneficiaries or recipients of donations, type of contribution and overall social impact of both voluntary and compulsory acts as explained in Table 1.

The relevance of these voluntary and compulsory donations in the COVID-19 outbreak is very much essential where both types of donations provide basis for monetary assistance for the needy people. In an uncertain environment where many families, businesses and working conditions were unsuitable for individuals, such kinds of donations are helpful for the bereaved individuals to fulfill their needs.

The other significant technology backed tools to assist Islamic finance are categorized into five types. Table 2 provides the list of FinTech solutions and their probable role toward social inclusion.

It is highlighted that the first category consists of artificial intelligence and data analytics which are used for the assessment of creditworthiness in spite of limited credit capacities in emerging economies. The second category is about mobile enabled tools such as online banking and P2P lending for facilitating open banking systems. The third category is related to distributed ledger which is one of the significant applications of blockchain where each party is assured of speedy transactions with no or minimum cost and reducing risk for both parties. Fourth category is cloud computing to facilitate FinTech innovations in Islamic finance for enabling an automatic response from a third-party server that will initiate the process of transactions automatically. The final category is cybersecurity where it is necessary to manage the risks related to the internet and cybercrimes.

Given the situation of COVID-19 pandemic, where most of the offices shifted from built-in offices to cloud based working conditions, the use of these technologies is creating a threshold for the Islamic financial institutions and Islamic banking system to assist their customers and clients with technology efficient products and services. Since strict requirements of social distancing were imposed by the World Health Organization on the onset of COVID-19, it is noteworthy that implementing various

Table 1 Voluntary and compulsory acts of Islamic social finance

Parameters	Compulsory Zakat	Voluntary Waqf	Sadaqah
Wealth sharing mechanism	Zakat is compulsory obligation on the Muslims with excess money and holdings beyond certain thresholds/limits for a particular period of time	Voluntarily donating a certain amount to a trust or a charitable society for fulfilling social obligations	Voluntarily giving some amount of money for seeking the pleasure of ALLAH Almighty and helping others
Occurrence of donations	Defined on an annual basis with specified limit based on numerical figures	Donations are not subject to time or a specific amount. They can be made at any time maintaining a specific perpetuity	Donations for this category are not bound by specific time and amount and there is no need to retain a principal amount
Beneficiaries/recipients	As specified in Al-Quran, Zakat must be given to eight categories such as: poor, needy, slave, revert, debtor, Mujahid, traveler, and collectors of Zakat	It can be donated to some institutions, relatives, needy, widows, and orphans. For example, it can be donated to a mosque, to a relative, or for other charitable causes who do not have sufficient resources to meet their ends	It can be given to anyone to fulfill their needs unless it does not involve any abandoned acts
Type of contribution	Usually in terms of cash but the amount must be given according to pre-specified proportion	These are basically assets which have long lasting advantages	It can be anything which is beneficial to the receiver of the Sadaqah
The overall social impact	Extreme poverty can be reduced if proper framework is developed for distributing Zakat among the societies	Usually, it provides an opportunity to set some amount as a limit to distribute to the society in terms of assets distribution	It is the blend of both Zakat and Waqf to help the needy people

Source World Bank Group (2020)

Table 2 Islamic Fintech and social inclusion elements

FinTech innovations	Social inclusion elements
Artificial intelligence and data analytics	It is used for assessment of creditworthiness of the customers by analyzing different patterns such as online activities, social media usage, call records, and location availability. This information is processed through artificial intelligence to convert it into algorithms for maintaining a record for a specific customer
Mobile payments, P2P finance, and open banking system	Mobile payments have enabled several customers to initiate transactions and send money online to other beneficiaries. P2P financing is also relevant to mobile payments. In this way, an open banking system facilitates user-friendly experience to provide access to the financial information of a customer and is enabled through apps-systems of banks. Its basic purpose is to facilitate ease of accessibility of the financial system from remote areas too
Distributed ledgers	It is an application of blockchain technology which receives, processes, and converts the received information into information blocks to improve the experience of users with high-speed transactions and minimum transaction costs. Distributed ledger also assures authenticity of both parties and on time delivery of funds
Cloud	Particularly for Islamic finance, this technology provides useful solutions for saving the information managed by cloud-software. For start-up companies and small firms, such a type of technology is useful for managing information into a single platform
Cybersecurity	With the increased use of technology, it is necessary to manage risks related to information transmission. The information theft, cybercrimes, identity theft, information leakage, hacking agencies, etc., all raise serious concerns for the cybersecurity of customers as well as financial institutions

Source World Bank Group (2020)

technologies in the daily business operation will assist the Islamic financial system to reap sustainable projects with long lasting impact on the economy.

Studies also reveal that COVID-19 has brought unprecedented challenges to the overall economy of the world were maintaining social distancing SOPs to save lives of millions was the core purpose behind the closure of all business operations. But labor earning on daily wages suffered the most in the developing nations where providing sufficient sustenance to their families seemed impossible due to closure of all business operations. With these uncertainties, Islamic fintech solutions provide sufficient support for individuals, businesses, and needy persons to maintain their sustenance even if the economic conditions are harsh. In this way, the purpose of serving the community and attaining the pleasure of ALLAH Almighty goes equally well. Therefore, Islamic financial system is completely providing support to less privileged individuals while ensuring even circulation of money in the society.

4 Conclusion and Recommendations

This study presented the role of Islamic fintech and Islamic finance as a response to COVID-19 pandemic. The qualitative nature of study provided significant insights on the evolution of FinTech, emergence of Islamic fintech, different fintech solutions facilitating Islamic financial industry, voluntary and compulsory acts of donations, and the modes of social inclusion through various Islamic fintech innovations. It is observed that the recovery period of COVID-19 pandemic has embarked several opportunities for micro, small, and medium enterprises. For an emergency state of affairs where worldwide lockdowns were announced in the mid of March 2020, the abrupt response of Islamic finance is in terms of Zakat, Awqaf, and Sadaqah for the needy people. Moreover, as the market conditions started stabilizing, the recovery process also soothes by providing funds to several entrepreneurs who want to start their businesses with lower investments. The long-term recovery process needs establishment of medium enterprises with their outreach toward significant industries. The Islamic fintech innovations for such uncertain circumstances have provided support to several employees and customers where employees can work from their homes using the latest technological advancements and customers can experience mobile banking and open banking systems through their hand-held devices. In this way, Islamic fintech and Islamic finance have generated significant opportunities for underprivileged individuals in providing a hand to them in their time of need.

The study has generated several policy and regulatory recommendations where regulators need to fully incorporate the technological innovations in their banking systems to enjoy speedy transactions systems. Meanwhile, it is also noted that these innovations must be within the limits of Islamic Sharia and do not violate their stipulated regulations as they will directly impact on the smooth system of Islamic financial system. Needless to say, Islamic fintech has provided sufficient solutions in the recovery phase of the coronavirus period where it strengthened the mutual relationships of brotherhood, ensured urgent assistance in the emergency situation and created several opportunities for entrepreneurs. The study recommends initiating awareness programs for the employees and customers to inform them about different facets of using technological innovations. Moreover, starting training and development programs will also bring substantial knowledge for the banking personnel to understand and learn the timely solution of Islamic fintech. In this way, COVID-19 has created a greater mess around the globe and as a response to its devastation Islamic fintech has provided workable and pragmatic solutions to implement them in the Islamic financial system.

REFERENCES

Aguilera-Hermida, A. P. (2020). College students' use and acceptance of emergency online learning due to Covid-19. *International Journal of Educational Research Open, 1*, 100011.

Ahmed, H. (2009). Financial crisis, risks and lessons for Islamic finance. *ISRA International Journal of Islamic Finance.*

Ahmed, A. (2010). Global financial crisis: An Islamic finance perspective. *International Journal of Islamic and Middle Eastern Finance and Management.* https://doi.org/10.1108/17538391011093252

Alam, M., Rabbani, M. R., Tausif, M. R., & Abey, J. (2021). Banks' performance and economic growth in India: A panel cointegration analysis. *Economies, 9*(1), 38.

Ali, M. A. M., Bashar, A., Rabbani, M. R., & Abdullah, Y. (2020). Transforming business decision making with internet of things (IoT) and Machine Learning (ML). *2020 International Conference on Decision Aid Sciences and Application (DASA)* (pp. 674–679). https://doi.org/10.1109/DASA51403.2020.9317174

Arunachalam, R. S., & Crentsil, G. L. (2020, June). Financial Inclusion in the Era of COVID-19. In *An Online Participative Conference For Central Bankers, Ministries of Finance, Financial Sector Development & Financial Inclusion Professionals, Commercial & Microfinance Bankers, NBFIs, DFIs, MFIs, Consultants, FINTECH & RegTech Companies, Investors, Ins.*

Asmild, M., Kronborg, D., Mahbub, T., & Matthews, K. (2019). The efficiency patterns of Islamic banks during the global financial crisis: The case of Bangladesh. *Quarterly Review of Economics and Finance, 74*, 67–74. https://doi.org/10.1016/j.qref.2018.04.004

Belanès, A., Ftiti, Z., & Regaïeg, R. (2015). What can we learn about Islamic banks efficiency under the subprime crisis? Evidence from GCC Region. *Pacific-Basin Finance Journal, 33*, 81–92.

DinarStandard. (2020). State of the global Islamic economy report 2020/2021. In *Dubai International Financial Centre.* https://haladinar.io/hdn/doc/report2018.pdf

Hassan, M. K., Rabbani, M. R., & Ali, M. A. (2020). Challenges for the Islamic finance and banking in post COVID era and the role of Fintech. *Journal of Economic Cooperation and Development, 43*(3), 93–116.

Hassan, M. K., Rabbani, M. R., & Abdullah, Y. (2021). Socioeconomic impact of COVID-19 in MENA region and the role of Islamic finance. *International Journal of Islamic Economics and Finance (IJIEF), 4*(1), 51–78.

Hassan, M. K., Rabbani, M. R., Brodmann, J., Bashar, A., & Grewal, H. (2022). Bibliometric and scientometric analysis on CSR practices in the banking sector. *Review of Financial Economics.*

Hilburg, R., Patel, N., Ambruso, S., Biewald, M. A., & Farouk, S. S. (2020). Medical education during the COVID-19 pandemic: Learning from a distance. *Advances in Chronic Kidney Disease.*

Karim, S., Manab, N. A., & Ismail, R. B. (2019). Legitimising the role of corporate boards and corporate social responsibility on the performance of Malaysian listed companies. *Indian Journal of Corporate Governance, 12*(2), 125–141.

Karim, S., Manab, N. A., & Ismail, R. B. (2020a). Assessing the governance mechanisms, corporate social responsibility and performance: The moderating effect of board independence. *Global Business Review.* https://doi.org/10.1177/0972150920917773

Karim, S., Manab, N. A., & Ismail, R. B. (2020b). The interaction effect of independent boards on CG-CSR and performance nexus. *Asian Academy of Management Journal, 25*(1), 61–84.

Karim, S., Manab, N. A., & Ismail, R. B. (2020c). The dynamic impact of board composition on CSR practices and their mutual effect on organizational returns. *Journal of Asia Business Studies, 14*(4), 463–479.

Karim, S. (2021a). An investigation into the remuneration-CSR nexus and if it can be affected by board gender diversity. *Corporate Governance: The International Journal of Business in Society.* https://doi.org/10.1108/CG-08-2020-0320

Karim, S. (2021b). Do women on corporate boardrooms influence the remuneration patterns and socially responsible practices? Malaysian evidence. *Equality Diversity, and Inclusion: An International Journal.* https://doi.org/10.1108/EDI-07-2020-0213

Karim, S., Rabbani, M. R.; Khan, M. A. (2021). Determining the key factors of corporate leverage in Malaysian service sector firms using dynamic modeling. *Journal of Economic Cooperation and Development.* In press.

Khan, S., & Rabbani, M. R. (2020a). Artificial intelligence and NLP based Chatbot as Islamic banking and finance expert. *2020 International Conference on Computational Linguistics and Natural Language Processing (CLNLP 2020), Seoul, South Korea on July,* 20–22.

Khan, S., & Rabbani, M. R. (2020b). Chatbot as Islamic Finance Expert (CaIFE): When finance meets Artificial Intelligence. In Proceedings *2020 International Conference on Computational Linguistics and Natural Language Processing (CLNLP 2020), Seoul, South Korea* (pp. 1–5).

Khan, S., & Rabbani, M. R. (2020c). In depth analysis of blockchain, cryptocurrency and sharia compliance. *International Journal of Business Innovation and Research, 1*(1), 1. https://doi.org/10.1504/ijbir.2020.10033066

Khan, M. S., Rabbani, M. R., Hawaldar, I. T., & Bashar, A. (2022). Determinants of behavioral intentions to use Islamic financial technology: An empirical assessment. *Risks, 10*(6), 114.

Mijwel, M. M. (2015). History of artificial intelligence. *Journal for Computer Science and Mathematics,* 1–6.

Mohammad, H. S., Khan, S., Rabbani, M. R., & Yannis, E. T. (2020). An artificial intelligence and NLP based Islamic FinTech model combining Zakat and Qardh-Al-Hasan for countering the adverse impact of COVID 19 on SMEs and individuals. *International Journal of Economics and Business Administration, VIII*(Issue 2), 351–364. https://doi.org/10.35808/ijeba/466

Rabbani, M. R., Khan, S., & Atif, M. (2021a). Machine learning based P2P lending Islamic FinTech model for small and medium enterprises (SMEs) in Bahrain. *International Journal of Business Innovation and Research.* In press.

Rabbani, M. R., Bashar, A., Nawaz, N., Karim, S., Ali, M. A. M., Rahiman, H. U., & Alam, M. S. (2021b). Exploring the role of Islamic Fintech in combating the aftershocks of COVID-19: The open social innovation of the Islamic financial system. *Journal of Open Innovation: Technology, Market & Complexity, 7,* 136. https://doi.org/10.3390/joitmc7020136

Rabbani, M. R., Ali, M. A. M., Rahiman, H. U., Atif, M., Zulfikar, Z., & Naseem, Y. (2021c). Response of Islamic financial service to the COVID-19 pandemic: The open social innovation of the financial system. *Journal of Open Innovation: Technology, Market, and Complexity, 7*(1), 85. https://doi.org/10.3390/joitmc7010085

Rabbani, M. R., Kayani, U., Bawazir, H. S., & Hawaldar, I. T. (2022). A commentary on emerging markets banking sector spillovers: Covid-19 vs GFC pattern analysis. *Heliyon, 8*(3), e09074.

Rahim, S. R., Mohamad, Z. Z., Abu Bakar, J., Mohsin, F. H., & Md Isa, N. (2018). Artificial intelligence, smart contract, and Islamic finance. *Asian Social Science, 14*(2), 145.

Sarea, A., Rabbani, M. R., Alam, M. S., & Atif, M. (2021). 8 Artificial intelligence (AI) applications in Islamic finance and banking sector. *Artificial Intelligence and Islamic Finance: Practical Applications for Financial Risk Management*, 108.

Sun, H., Rabbani, M. R., Sial, M. S., Yu, S., Filipe, J. A., & Cherian, J. (2020a). Identifying big data's opportunities, challenges, and implications in finance. *Mathematics, 8*(10). https://doi.org/10.3390/math8101738

Sun, H., Rabbani, M. R., Ahmad, N., Sial, M. S., Cheng, G., Zia-Ud-Din, M., & Fu, Q. (2020b). CSR, co-creation and green consumer loyalty: Are green banking initiatives important? A moderated mediation approach from an emerging economy. *Sustainability, 12*(24), 10688.

Tabash, M. I., & Dhankar, R. S. (2018). The relevance of Islamic finance principles in economic growth. *International Journal of Emerging Research in Management and Technology, 3*(2), 49–54.

The World Bank. (2020). Leveraging Islamic FINTECH to Improve Financial Conclusion. *Inclusive Growth & Sustainable Finance, Hub in Malaysia*. October 2020.

Trad, N., Trabelsi, M. A., & Goux, J. F. (2017). Risk and profitability of Islamic banks: A religious deception or an alternative solution? *European Research on Management and Business Economics, 23*(1), 40-45.

Whitelaw, S., Mamas, M. A., Topol, E., & Van Spall, H. G. C. (2020). Applications of digital technology in COVID-19 pandemic planning and response. *The Lancet Digital Health*.

Index

A
Analytical techniques, 76
Artificial Intelligence (AI), 3, 4, 8, 14, 16, 19–21, 30, 50, 55, 57, 66, 68, 73, 75, 78–80, 83, 91, 114, 117, 118, 120, 122, 123, 132–134, 142, 145, 146, 161, 162, 177, 179, 194, 227, 229, 235, 254, 255, 308, 309, 312, 320, 322, 324, 343–349
Asset management, 90, 209, 252, 308, 313, 320

B
Big data analysis, 118, 254
Big data analytics, 90, 118, 133, 186, 227, 320
Blockchain, 4, 11–14, 16, 17, 19, 38, 57, 66–69, 75, 76, 83, 91, 95, 102, 117, 118, 122, 132–134, 142, 145, 146, 162, 166, 177, 179, 181, 182, 185, 194–196, 210, 228–230, 235, 252, 253, 255, 263, 270, 280–282, 285, 289, 292, 294–296, 299, 308–312, 314–317, 321, 324–328, 343, 344, 346, 348, 349

C
Cloud computing, 77, 118, 186, 194, 233, 253, 294, 308, 309, 317, 322, 327, 349
Crowdfunding, 4, 13, 18, 30, 34, 35, 40, 42, 67, 82, 95, 102, 113, 116–118, 120, 122, 132, 143, 162, 179, 180, 184, 185, 194, 205–207, 213, 226, 230–233, 248, 251, 264–272, 308, 309, 311, 312, 314, 319, 321, 327, 328
Cyber security, 17, 40, 118, 123, 178, 228, 322, 349

D
Debt based crowdfunding, 267
Donation based crowdfunding, 267

© The Editor(s) (if applicable) and The Author(s), under exclusive license to Springer Nature Switzerland AG 2022
M. K. Hassan et al. (eds.), *FinTech in Islamic Financial Institutions*, https://doi.org/10.1007/978-3-031-14941-2

E
Emerging technologies, 68, 72, 73, 83, 180, 320
Equity based crowdfunding, 267
Evolution of FinTech, 343, 352
Evolution of Islamic FinTech, 345

F
Financial Accessibility, 94
Financial inclusion, 5, 18, 19, 55, 57, 115, 122, 132, 133, 177, 178, 183, 207, 214, 223–225, 229, 231–233, 235, 245, 246, 317–319, 324, 325, 346
Financial Knowhow, 94
Financial technology, 2, 29, 30, 39, 66, 69, 74, 83, 89, 100, 117, 118, 120, 134, 157, 161, 163–165, 169, 177–179, 186, 193, 204, 212, 213, 223, 225, 229, 235, 243, 245, 247, 255, 263, 307, 320–322, 345, 346

G
Gharar, 9, 179, 207, 245, 249, 280, 292, 296, 300, 317

I
Industry, 2–4, 8, 11, 14, 16, 30–32, 40, 53, 66–68, 70, 72, 74, 75, 79, 81, 83, 91, 99, 100, 115–118, 120–123, 131–133, 135, 158, 159, 161–163, 167, 169, 170, 176–183, 186, 193–196, 201, 211, 225, 229, 230, 235, 247, 249, 251–253, 255, 270, 279, 290, 291, 307, 308, 311–313, 320, 327, 328, 341, 342, 345–348, 352

InsureTech, 4, 13, 14, 132, 308, 313, 327
Internet of Things (IoT), 74, 75, 79, 117, 118, 132, 194, 309, 320, 344
Islamic Fintech, 4–6, 14–19, 21, 50, 55, 57, 66–68, 83, 114–116, 118–124, 135, 163–165, 168–170, 176–181, 183, 185–187, 196, 201–203, 211–215, 229, 231, 234, 245, 246, 255, 269, 271, 311–314, 317, 319, 321–324, 328, 343, 346, 348, 351–353

L
Legal Sandbox, 82

M
Maqasid al-Shariah, 50, 54, 249
Mobile payment, 11, 12, 30, 33, 34, 38, 40, 42, 113, 117, 121, 227, 264, 318, 319, 322

N
Neo-banking, 252

O
Open banking, 70, 74, 78, 204, 205, 228, 321, 349, 352

P
P2P Finance, 227, 229
Peer to peer lending, 265, 270, 271

Q
Quantum computing, 8, 91, 132, 227, 320

R

Regulation technology (Regtech), 4, 20, 30, 42, 95, 132, 162, 179, 228, 322, 327

Regulatory sandbox, 42, 73, 82

Robo-advisors (RA), 132, 209, 210, 254

S

Smart Sukuk, 14, 210

T

Traditional banks, 6–8, 34, 41, 102, 115, 122, 124, 181, 185, 203–206, 208, 227, 252, 308

U

Unicorns, 200

Z

Zakat, 16, 18, 50, 55–58, 122, 161, 181, 182, 184, 185, 230, 232, 245, 246, 255, 296, 323, 324, 343, 349, 352

Printed in the United States
by Baker & Taylor Publisher Services